FRANCE OBSERVED
IN THE SEVENTEENTH CENTURY
BY BRITISH TRAVELLERS

Also by John Lough

Locke's Travels in France (ed.)
An Introduction to Seventeenth Century France
Paris Theatre Audiences in the Seventeenth and Eighteenth
    Centuries.
Writer and Public in France from the Middle Ages to the
    Present Day
Seventeenth Century French Drama: the Background

FRANCE
OBSERVED
IN THE
SEVENTEENTH
CENTURY
BY
BRITISH TRAVELLERS

JOHN LOUGH

ORIEL PRESS
STOCKSFIELD

BOSTON · MELBOURNE · HENLEY · LONDON

France Observed in the Seventeenth
Century by British Travellers

© *1985, John Lough*

First published in 1984
by Oriel Press Limited
Stocksfield, Northumberland,
England, NE43 7NA.
9 Park Street, Boston,
Mass. 02108, U.S.A. and
6th Floor, 464 St. Kilda Road,
Melbourne, Victoria 3004, Australia.

Set in Times and
printed by Knight & Forster, Leeds.

Trade enquiries to
Routledge & Kegan Paul PLC
Broadway House, Newtown Road,
Henley-on-Thames, Oxon, RG9 1EN.

ISBN 0 85362 218 3

CONTENTS

FRANCE, 1610~1715

Present-day frontier
Territories annexed 1610-1715

FLANDERS

ARTOIS

Strasbourg

Rouen

LORRAINE

ALSACE

PARIS

Rennes

Dijon

Nantes

FRANCHE
COMTÉ

La Rochelle

Lyons

SAVOY

Bordeaux

NICE

Avignon

Toulouse

Montpellier

Marseilles

ROUSSILLON

PREFACE

It is now some thirty years since I edited Locke's journals and other papers for the years which he spent in France at the height of the reign of Louis XIV. This task inevitably involved some considerable acquaintance with accounts of seventeenth-century France left behind by other British travellers, and over the years I have continued to add to my list of works of this kind. It is no easy task to make contact with all these sources. Bibliographies of travel literature are only of limited use; valuable assistance can be gained from consulting the British Library catalogue under *France* and such works as F.W. Stoye's *English Travellers Abroad 1604-1667* and Esmond de Beer's edition of Evelyn's *Diary*. Even so, additions to the list on which this work is based and which make it fuller than any so far available have often come from chance discoveries in unexpected places. Who would have guessed that the letters of Bishop Berkeley or Jethro Tull's *Horse-Hoeing Husbandry* would throw light on the France of Louis XIV?

Unpublished travellers' accounts are scattered around the libraries of this country; texts published at the time or shortly after are seldom to be found except in old-established libraries, while more recent publications are dispersed in a wide variety of books and periodicals. It would seem therefore that an interesting and useful book could be produced by extracting from these varied accounts, published and unpublished, long and short, what is of interest today to the student of seventeenth-century France and by bringing this material together under suitable headings in a single volume. An essential part of the task would be to provide the resulting work with a detailed index; this would make it useful as a work of reference by enabling the reader to discover whether or not these travellers had anything of interest to say on a given topic.

All the travellers' accounts which appeared in print between 1600 and 1715 have been drawn upon as well as most of those, long and short, which first appeared in print after that date. Quite a number of hitherto unpublished manuscripts have also been made use of, though here completeness would be a vain ideal; there are no doubt other manuscript accounts in private as well as public libraries. Even though not all the accounts studied have been drawn upon (in order to furnish as complete a list as possible, those which have not been used are listed in the appendix), well over fifty works, long and short, published and unpublished, have been brought under contribution.

Though a considerable number of the travellers' accounts had to be sought for elsewhere, fortunately a high proportion of those which appeared in book form at the time are available in the Durham University Library. The production of this volume involved visits to a variety of libraries between Newcastle upon Tyne and Paris, but the main part of the work has been carried out with the resources of the nearest university library. Other local assistance, also gratefully acknowledged, has come from the Department of English; Mr David Crane has devoted a great deal of time to checking my transcription of passages from unpublished manuscripts and, with assistance from Professor T.W. Craik, has also solved many of the problems which scribbled notes inevitably present. I am also greatly indebted to Professor P.J. Yarrow of the University of Newcastle upon Tyne and Dr. J.M. Black of the University of Durham who read the typescript and effected a number of improvements in it.

Durham   J.L.

A NOTE ON FRENCH MONEY IN THE SEVENTEENTH CENTURY

The basic unit of money was the *livre* or *franc* for which our travellers sometimes used the symbol '£' although the *livre* was worth considerably less than the pound sterling. Exchange rates varied considerably during this period, but Locke, for instance, received in the period 1675-9 approximately 13 *livres* for each pound he changed.

The *livre* was divided into *sous* and *deniers*: 1 *livre* = 20 *sous*. 1 sou =12 *deniers*.

It is difficult to state briefly what was the value of various coins in this period as the government frequently manipulated the coinage: 3 *livres* = 1 *écu* (or '*crown*'); 1 *louis* = 10-12 *livres* at various times in the century (it was very roughly equivalent to £1). There was also the *pistole*, a Spanish or Italian coin which circulated in France and which the travellers sometimes call simply a 'pistol'; it was generally taken to be worth 10 *livres*.

SOURCES AND ABBREVIATIONS

Sir Thomas Abdy, *A Journal Annotated of my Travells in France.* (Bodleian Library, Rawlinson MS. 1285, pp. 69-99.)

Sir Thomas Abdy, *Journal*

A breife description of my Travells taken by my selfe anno domini 1648 (Bodleian Library, Rawlinson MS. D 120).

A breife description

A New Journey to France, with an exact description of the sea coast from London to Calais and of the roads from thence to Orleans, and back again to Dieppe, etc., London, 1715.

A New Journey

Popery and Tyranny: or, the Present State of France: in relation to its Government, Trade, Manners of the People, and Nature of the Countrey As it was sent in a Letter from an English Gentleman abroad, to his Friend in England, London, 1679.

Popery and Tyranny

George Berkeley, *Works,* ed A.A. Luce and T.E. Jessop, London, 1948-57, 9 vols.

George Berkeley, *Works*

Charles Bertie, *Diary of a Journey in France, 1660-1662* (Historical Manuscripts Commission, Vol 79), London, 1942, pp 275-372.

Charles Bertie, *Diary*

[William Bromley,] *Remarks in the grande tour of France and Italy. Lately performed by a Person of Quality,* London, 1692.

Bromley, *Remarks*

Edward Browne, *A Journal of a Visit to Paris in the year 1664,* ed. G. Keynes, London, 1923

Edward Browne, *Journal*

— , Sir Thomas Browne, *Works,* ed. S. Wilkin, London, 1836, 4 vols, Vol I, pp. 57-72, 98-114.

Works

Thomas Browne, Ibid., pp. 17-22.

Thomas Browne, *Works*

Gilbert Burnet, *Some letters containing an account of what seemed most remarkable in Switzerland, Italy, etc.,* Rotterdam, 1686.

Burnet, *Letters*

— , *History of his own time*, London, 1724-34, 2 vols.   *History*

John Buxton, *Diary* (Historical Manuscripts Commission, *Reports*, Vol 55, Pt. II, London, 1903, pp 273-81). (This is followed by 3 letters by the same and by another by his cousin, John Herne, pp. 281-4).   Buxton, *Diary*

Sir George Carew, *A Relation of the State of France* in Thomas Birch, *An Historical view of the Negotiations between the Courts of England, France, and Brussels, from the year 1592 to 1617*, London, 1749.   Sir George Carew, *Relation*

[John Clenche], *A Tour in France & Italy, made by an English Gentleman, 1675*, London, 1676.   Clenche, *Tour*

Thomas Coryate, *Crudities Hastily gobled up in five Moneths travells in France, Savoy, Italy, Rhetia . . ., Helvetia . . ., some parts of high Germany, and the Netherlands*, London, 1611.   Coryate, *Crudities*

Sir George Courthop, *Memoirs 1616-1689*, ed. S.C. Lomas, London, 1907 (Camden Miscellany, vol. IX, pp. 95-157).   Sir George Courthop, *Memoirs*

John Covel, *Autograph Journals of Dr. John Covel during his travels in Asia Minor, Greece, Switzerland, Italy and France* (British Library Add. MS. 22914).   Covel, *Journal*

[Sir Robert Dallington], *A Method for Travell. Shewed by taking the view of France as it stoode in the yeare of our Lord, 1598*, London, n.d. (1604?).   Dallington, *Method for Travell*

John Downes, *Journal* (British Library, Sloane MS. 179A, ff.1-48).   John Downes, *Journal*

John Evelyn, *Diary*, ed. E.S. de Beer, London, 1955, 6 vols.   Evelyn, *Diary*

— , *The State of France as it stood in the IXth Year of this present Monarch, Louis XIIII*, London, 1652.   *State of France*

Ann, Lady Fanshawe, *Memoirs* in *The Memoirs of Anne, Lady Halkett, and Ann, Lady Fanshawe*, ed. J. Loftis, London, 1979.   Lady Fanshawe, *Memoirs*

Richard Ferrier, *The Journal of Major Richard*   Ferrier, *Journal*
Ferrier M.P., while travelling in France in the year
1687 (Camden Miscellany, New Series 53, Vol.
IX, London, 1895, pp. 15-48).

Sir John Finch, *Journal* (Historical Manuscripts   Finch, *Journal*
Commission, *Report on the Manuscripts of Allen*
George Finch Esq., vol. I, London, 1913, pp.
59–73).

— , *Letter of 19 April 1652 (Calendar of State*   Letter
Papers, Domestic, Commonwealth 1651-4, vol.
IV, pp. 205-9).

Edward, Lord Herbert of Cherbury, *Life*, ed. J.M.   Herbert, *Life*
Shuttleworth, London, 1976.

Peter Heylyn, *A full relation of two journeys: the*   Heylyn, *Relation*
one into the Main-Land of France; the other into
some of the adjacent Islands, London, 1656.

James Howell, *Epistolae Ho-Ellianae, Familiar*   Howell, *Epistolae*
Letters, domestic and forren, . . . upon emergent
occasions, London, 1645 (2nd edition, 1650).

— , *Instructions for Forreine Travell*, ed.   *Instructions*
E.Arber, London, 1869 (first published 1642).

White Kennet, *Un Voyage à Calais, Guines,* ed. C.   Kennet, *Voyage*
Landrin, Paris, 1893. (The text, in English, is
transcribed from British Library, Lansdowne MS.
937, ff. 21v-25r).

Thomas Killigrew, letter of 7 December 1635   Thomas Killigrew, *Letter*
from Orleans (copies in British Library, Add. MS.
27402, ff.70-2 – incomplete; Bodleian Library,
Ashmolean MS. 800, art. iii, ff. 21-7; Pepys
Lbrary, PL 2099 (3). The second is reproduced in
the *European Magazine*, Feb. 1803, Vol. XLIII,
pp. 102-6).

Richard Lassels, *Diary of the Journey of Lady*   Lassels, *Diary*
Catherine Whetenall British Library, Add. MS.
4217).

— , *The Voyage of Italy, or a Complete Journey*   *Voyage*
through Italy, Paris, 1670.

Sir John Lauder, Lord Fountainhall, *Journals with*   Lauder, *Journals*
his Observations on Public Affairs and other
Memoranda, 1665-1676, ed. D.Crawford, Edinburgh, 1900.

John Maitland, 1st Duke of Lauderdale, Letter of   Lauderdale, *Letter*
12 March 1659 in Richard Baxter, *The Certainty
of the World of Spirits*, London, 1691, pp. 82-92.

Early Science in Oxford, ed. R.T. Gunther,   Lhwyd, *Letters*
Vol.XIV. *Life and Letters of Edward Lhwyd, Sec-
ond Keeper of Musaeum Ashmoleanum*, Oxford,
1945, pp. 439-45.

Martin Lister, *A Journey to Paris in the Year 1698*,   Lister, *Journey*
London, 1698.

Lister MSS., Bodleian Library.   *MSS.*

William Lithgow, *A Most Delectable and true dis-*   Lithgow, *Peregrination*
*course of an admired and painefull peregrination
from Scotland to the most famous Kingdomes in
Europe, Asia and Africke, etc.*, London, 1632,
(first published in 1614).

John Locke, *Travels in France 1675-1679, as*   Locke, *Travels*
*related in his Journals, Correspondence and other
papers*, ed. J.Lough, Cambridge, 1953.

Robert Montagu, 3rd Earl of Manchester, *Diary*   Robert Montagu, *Diary*
(Bodleian Library, Rawlinson MS. D.76).

Francis Mortoft, His Book, being his travels   Mortoft, *Book*
through France and Italy, 1658-1659, ed. M. Letts
(Hakluyt Society, 2nd series, no. lvii, 1925).

Fynes Moryson, *An Itinerary, containing his ten*   Moryson, *Itinerary*
*yeares travell through the twelve dominions of
Germany Bohmerland, Sweitzerland, Netherland,
Denmarke, Poland, Italy, Turkey, France, England, Scotland and Ireland*, London, 1617.

Peter Mundy, *Travels in Europe and Asia 1608-*   Mundy, *Travels*
1667, ed. R.C. Temple (Hakluyt Society, 2nd
series, no. xvii, 1907).

John Northleigh, *Topographical descriptions, with*   Northleigh, *Observations*
*historico-political and medico-physical observa-
tions made in two ... voyages through ...
Europe*, London, 1702.

[Sir Thomas Overbury] *Observations in his*   Overbury, *Observations*
*Travailes upon the State of the XVII. Provinces as
they stood Anno Dom. 1609. The Treatie of Peace
being then on foote*, n.p., 1626 (also contains,
pp.12-28, *Observations on the State of France,
1609, under Henry the Fourth*).

Letters of Sir Philip Perceval and his tutor, John Gailhard, 1676-9 (Historical Manuscripts Commission, *Reports*, Vol. 63, Part II, London, 1909, pp.51-81).   Perceval, *Letters*

John Pridgeon, *Diary of Lord Willoughby's Travels in France, 1647-1649.* (Historical Manuscripts Commission, *Reports*, Vol.66, London, 1907, pp.418-24.   Pridgeon, *Diary*

John Ray, *Observations topographical, moral and physiological made in a Journey through part of the Low Countries, Germany, Italy and France with a Catalogue of Plants not native of England found spontaneously growing in those parts, and their virtues,* London, 1673.   Ray, *Observations*

Sir John Reresby, *Memoirs and Travels,* ed. A. Ivatt, London, 1904.   Reresby, *Memoirs and Travels*

— , *Memoirs,* ed. A. Browning, Glasgow, 1936.   *Memoirs*

Joseph Shaw, *Letters to a Nobleman from a gentleman travelling thro' Holland, Flanders, and France, with a Description of Ghent, Lisle, &c. and of the Courts of Versailles and St. Germains,* London, 1709.   Joseph Shaw, *Letters to a Nobleman*

Sir Philip Skippon, *An Account of a Journey through part of the Low Countries, Germany, Italy and France in company with the celebrated Mr. Ray (*in *A Collection of Voyages and Travels,* London, 1732, Vol. VI).   Skippon, *An Account*

Richard Symonds, *Travel Notes* (British Library, Harleian MS. 943) (extracts from these are printed in Appendix G of the *Travels* of Peter Mundy, q.v.)   Symonds, *Travel Notes*

— , *Description de Ville de Paris. Paris according to the method of Malingre.* (British Library, Harleian MS. 1278).   *Description*

Jethro Tull, *The New Horse - houghing Husbandry: or, an Essay on the Principles of Tillage and Vegetation,* London, 1731.   Jethro Tull, *The New Horse-Houghing Husbandry*

— , *Horse-Hoing Husbandry: or an Essay on the Principles of Tillage and Vegetation, wherein is shown a method of introducing a sort of Vineyard-Culture into the Corn-Fields,* London, 1733.   *Horse-Hoing Husbandry*

Memoirs of the Verney Family during the Seventeenth Century, ed. F.P. and M.M. Verney, 3rd edition, London, 1925, 2 vols. Vol I, pp.309-482.

Sir Ralph Verney, *Memoirs*

Ellis Veryard, *An account of diverse Choice Remarks ... Taken in a Journey through the Low Countries, France, Italy and part of Spain, with the Isles of Sicily and Malta, as also a Voyage to the Levant,* London, 1701.

Veryard, *An Account*

Thomas Wentworth, *Diary* (Wentworth Woodhouse Papers, Sheffield Central Library, Str. P.30).

Thomas Wentworth. *Diary*

— , Three letters from France (ibid., Str.P.21-24).

Letters

Sir Christopher Wren, Letter of 1665 in C. Wren, *Parentalia, or Memoirs of the Family of the Wrens,* London, 1750.

Sir Chrstopher Wren, *Parentalia*

INTRODUCTION

In the following pages what is understood by 'seventeenth century' is the period between the end of the Wars of Religion in the 1590s and the death of Louis XIV in 1715. The printed books, diaries, letters and other writings which describe travels in France in these years are inevitably a very mixed lot, ranging from a substantial volume such as Heylyn's *A Full Relation* or that furnished by Locke's journals for the period 1675-9 to short jottings of the kind provided by Peter Mundy in his headlong dash from the frontier with Savoy to Paris and on to Calais or by White Kennet's fortnight's trip to the Calais region. Some accounts of life in France were based on several years' residence there whereas others consist merely of scrappy notes written down while crossing the country on the way to or from Italy.

What is meant by 'France' also needs to be made clear as today the country is somewhat larger than it was during the reign of Henry IV or even, despite the territories annexed by France in this long period, during that of Louis XIV. For the purposes of this book 'France' is defined as the country as it stood at the end of the seventeenth century. As things turn out, this poses no serious problems. The Alsace-Lorraine region was scarcely frequented at all by our travellers, so that the fact that Lorraine did not become part of France until 1766 is of no significance. The only difficulty arises with two regions, Savoy and Nice, which were not acquired until 1860; a considerable number of our travellers made their way to or from Italy through one or the other of these regions; both have been excluded from this work on the grounds that they were not yet part of France.

The travellers' accounts which have come down to us are not evenly distributed over the whole period. There is a fair amount of comment on the France of Henry IV and the young Louis XIII and surprisingly little on the years in which Richelieu was the virtual master of the country. The long reign of Louis XIV from 1643 to the 1680s is well covered, particularly for the years of the *Roi Soleil's* triumphs, but there is rather a dearth of comment on the last twenty-five years during most of which England and France were at war. Two substantial travellers' accounts, those of Northleigh and Veryard, which appeared at the beginning of the eighteenth century, describe journeys made in the 1680s.

Inevitably the aspects of life in France on which the travellers chose to comment were not always those which interest us most three centuries later. There is a superfluity of information about certain topics and very little or sometimes nothing at all on those of much greater importance. One could well have spared some of the mocking passages in which most of our travellers describe the display of relics in Catholic churches for other details about what they saw and heard during their stay in France. If this volume has little or no nothing to say on some important topics, this must be laid at the door of the travellers and not the compiler.

What travellers in France in our period chose to write down about their impressions of life there was sometimes disappointingly little. Despite the long stays which Lord Herbert of Cherbury made in France at different periods his *Life* contains relatively little of interest from our point of view while the *Private Memoirs* of Sir Kenelm Digby which break off in 1629 offer nothing at all. Of the two great English philosophers of the age John Locke left for posterity a record of his long stay in France in the 1670s in the shape of journals, notebooks and a few letters; Thomas Hobbes who made several visits to France and spent there the whole of the 1640s appears to have left no record of his impressions of life there.

On the other hand almost all the varied writings at our disposal can be counted on to produce at least one observation which can be put alongside those furnished by other travellers who make a much larger contribution to our understanding of life in France in the seventeenth century.

It seemed right to reproduce the spelling, punctuation and use of capitals of those works which were published by the authors themselves, though the printer's lavish use of italics has not been followed. Where modern editions of manuscripts reproduce the spelling of the original, their text has been followed; unpublished manuscripts transcribed by the compiler also follow the spelling of the original though contractions have been expanded, capitals provided for the opening words of sentences, and a modest amount of punctuation added. On the other hand where editors of texts of which no manuscript is available for inspection have modernized the spelling, this has had to be followed even if the result must appear somewhat inconsistent.

FRANCE OBSERVED
IN THE SEVENTEENTH CENTURY
BY BRITISH TRAVELLERS

MAP SHOWING THE PLACES VISITED

Dunkirk
Calais
St. Omer
Boulogne
Lille

Dieppe
Abbeville
Amiens
Péronne

Le Havre
Rouen • Beauvais
Caen
R. Seine
PARIS

St. Malo
Brest

Chartres
Fontainebleau
Sens
Rennes
Le Mans
Orléans
Auxerre
La Flèche
Gien
Angers
Blois
Cosne
Nantes
Tours
Saumur
Bourges • Nevers
Loudun
Chalon
R. Saône
Poitiers
Mâcon
Moulins

Ile de Ré
La Rochelle
Roanne
Tarare
Ile d'Oléron
Rochefort
Lyons

Angoulême
Grande
Chartreuse
Grenoble
Blaye
R. Rhône
Valence

Bordeaux

R. Garonne
Agen
Avignon
Montauban
Nîmes
Arles
Aix
Antibes
Toulouse
Canal
Montpellier
Béziers
Castelnaudary
du Midi
Sète
Marseilles
Hyères
Carcassonne
Narbonne
Toulon

I THE TRAVELLERS AND HOW THEY TRAVELLED

Although this book is mainly concerned with the light which the record of their visits throws on life in seventeenth-century France, we need to know something about the travellers themselves. They are best dealt with on a chronological basis even if this can only be done approximately as several of them made stays at widely separated periods. For convenience we may begin with the travellers who visited France during the reign of Henry IV and then deal with those who were there during the early part of the reign of Louis XIII. After the curious shortage of information for the second part of his reign, the period of Richelieu, we can deal successively with those who visited the country during Mazarin's period of power, at the high point of the reign of Louis XIV from the 1660s to the 1680s, and finally in the years of decline down to 1715.

The first of our many travellers was Fynes Moryson (1566–1617?), a fellow of Peterhouse, Cambridge, who made two long journeys in the 1590s. The second of these took him as far afield as Tripoli, Jerusalem and Constantinople; during his first journey he went as far as Italy, but his contact with France was very slight as on his return he passed rapidly through eastern France and on to Dieppe in May 1595. This was when the country was still in an unsettled state in the last stages of the Wars of Religion. His observations on France, though very vivid, occupy only a tiny place in his *Itinerary*. A much fuller account of the country is provided by Sir Richard Dallington (1561–1637) in *A Method for Travell, shewed by taking the view of France, as it stoode in the yeare of our Lord, 1598*. After a pirated edition of this work had appeared in 1604, the author republished it with a preface bitterly attacking the morals of publishers and offering some introductory remarks on the subject of travel. A schoolmaster and for a time Gentleman of the Privy Chamber to Prince Henry and Prince Charles, he ended his career as Master of the Charterhouse. This work is not an account of Dallington's travels in France, but a general study of conditions there, occasionally enlivened with references to his own experiences.

The state of France towards the end of the reign of Henry IV when some recovery had taken place from the disasters of the Wars of

Religion is described in three different works. In his *Crudities*
Thomas Coryate (1577?–1617) gives an account of a five months'
tour of France, Savoy, Italy, Switzerland, Germany and the
Netherlands. Although he spent only just over three weeks in France
in May and June 1608, he describes in considerable detail his journey
from Calais to Paris and then on through Lyons into Savoy. In
contrast, *Observations on the State of France 1609, under Henry the
Fourth*, which is generally attributed to Sir Thomas Overbury
(1581–1613) who died of poisoning while a prisoner in the Tower of
London, does not offer an account of any travels made there by the
author; it is merely a brief but incisive essay on conditions in that
year. A rather longer work of the same date is the *Relation of the State
of France* addressed to James I by Sir George Carew (?–1612) on his
return from his embassy in Paris which lasted from the end of 1605 to
July 1609.

The diary of Thomas Wentworth, the first Earl of Strafford
(1593–1641), furnishes the first example of a source on which we
shall have other occasions to draw — the record of a journey to
France, sometimes also to other parts of the Continent, especially
Italy, kept by a youth who was sent abroad accompanied by a tutor
and servants. Early in the reign of Louis XIII, in December 1611
shortly after his marriage, Thomas Wentworth was sent over to
France. After some weeks in Paris he moved on to Orleans where he
spent five months; the rest of the year 1612 was devoted to a long tour
of the provinces, first down the Loire Valley, then on to La Rochelle.
From there he travelled to Bordeaux and then to Montpellier via
Toulouse, Montauban and Narbonne. From there he moved on to
Marseilles and Lyons from where he made an excursion to Geneva.
On 2 January 1613 he wrote to his father from Orleans where his
diary ends to say that in a week's time he intended to leave for Paris
where he would spend three or four weeks and then have two months
in the Low Countries before he came back to England by the end of
April. His diary is by far the most interesting of those that remain
unpublished.[1]

Lord Herbert of Cherbury (1583–1648) was in France for a
considerable period, in 1608–9, a stay very briefly described in his
Life. He also made a brief excursion from Savoy as far as Lyons in
1616, but his longest stays in France began only in the following year
when he was appointed ambassador to the court of Louis XIII, a post
which he held until 1624 though with a long break in the years
1621–2 after he had quarrelled with the king's favourite, the Duc de
Luynes. He also paid a relatively brief visit to Paris at a much later
date, in 1647. Considering his long contact with France, his *Life* is

rather disappointing from our point of view.

Two well-known globe-trotters of the time, William Lithgow (1582–1645?) and Peter Mundy (1596?–1667), relate briefly how they passed through France at pretty high speed during the early part of the reign of Louis XIII, but the little they have to say about the country is much less interesting than what can be gleaned from the letters of the Welshman, James Howell (1594?–1666), who ended his days as historiographer royal to Charles II. He describes in his letters three visits to France in the period 1619–23, followed by others in 1635 and 1641; he is one of the rare travellers to mention the existence of Richelieu during the latter's lifetime.[2] A good deal of valuable information on conditions in France in 1625 is contained in the account of a five-week visit there made by the historian and theologian, Peter Heylyn (1600–1662). A protégé of Laud, he later became a chaplain to Charles I and a canon of Westminster, suffering for his support of the royalist cause during the Civil War. His account of his visit to France was published only in 1656 after a pirated version had appeared.

Our travellers' accounts give very little coverage to the period when Richelieu was the virtual ruler of France. It is true that four travellers besides Howell have left some record of their presence there in the 1630s, but only one furnishes a diary. Sir Thomas Abdy (1612–1686) spent over a year in France from June 1633 before going on to Italy; starting from Blois, he did a tour of France following very much the same route as Thomas Wentworth; the greater part of his diary is kept in his best French, starting with: 'Je suis parti de Blois 29 Avrill 1634 pour commencer l'entreprise du voyage de la France'. Two other travellers of the same period furnish most interesting accounts of the exorcism of the possessed nuns of Loudun, but only in one single letter, that of the playwright, Thomas Killigrew (1611–1683) and merely in part of a letter of John Maitland, the first Duke of Lauderdale (1616–1682). Even the memoirs of Sir George Courthop (1616–1685) provide hardly anything of interest except for his firsthand account of the strange happenings in this Loudun convent.

In contrast we are offered a good deal of information about the state of affairs in France during the regency of Anne of Austria and the early part of the reign of Louis XIV down to the death of Mazarin in 1661. The famous diary of John Evelyn (1620–1706) covers the stays which he made in France in 1643–4 on his way to Italy and in 1646–7 on his return as well as his long exile between 1649 and 1652. In addition he produced a substantial essay on the state of France which he published in 1652 on his return to England.

A little may be gleaned from the letters of Sir Ralph Verney (1613–1696) who, torn between his Anglicanism and his support of the Parliamentary cause, decided to leave England with his wife and family early in 1644 and spent the next nine years abroad. For six of these he lived in Blois; he then made a round tour of France before moving on into Italy.

For the years 1647–9 we have the diary of a certain John Pridgeon who accompanied the young Lord Willoughby (1630?–1701) on his travels over a good area of Northern France. An anonymous diarist, presumably a member of St. John's College, Oxford, was abroad from June 1648 to November 1649; after a considerable stay at Tours (unlike Blois 'a place voide of Inglish') he travelled through Nantes, La Rochelle, Bordeaux, Montpellier and Marseilles to Cannes where he sailed for Italy, returning through Geneva and Lyons to Paris and Calais. There is more meat in the journal kept by the young Robert Montagu, Lord Mandeville, later the third Earl of Manchester (1634–1683) although he was only fifteen when in May 1649, as the son of a Parliamentary general, he was taken by frigate to Dieppe to begin his grand tour. He was to remain in France until June 1651, having Saumur as his main base, but making all sorts of excursions both in the neighbourhood and as far afield as La Rochelle and Saintes. He was twice in Paris, the second time on his way to Lyons, Geneva and Italy. To the same period belongs the notebook kept by Richard Symonds (1617–c.1691), a man from the opposing side; after serving in the royal bodyguard, in January 1649 he thought it advisable to go abroad. His travels took him across France to the frontier with Savoy. He arrived in Paris to find the city involved in a civil war on which he has some interesting comments to make. He also produced an illustrated description of Paris from which much of value can be gleaned, particularly about the university and its different colleges.

The memoirs of Ann, Lady Fanshawe (1625–1680), add some picturesque touches to accounts of this period. They describe how she and her husband, while returning in 1650 from San Sebastian, were shipwrecked on the coast near Nantes and how in 1659 she made a perilous escape from England with a passport secured under a false name in order to rejoin her husband in Paris. Sir John Finch (1626–1682), a physician who was later to become ambassador in Constantinople, and his friend, Thomas Baines, spent some six months in France in 1651–2 on their way to study medicine in Italy; Finch's journal is chiefly of interest for its glimpses of the disordered state of the provinces during the civil war of the Fronde. During the Protectorate Sir John Reresby (1634–1689) spent several years abroad. He was in France for some two and a half years between 1654 and 1656 and also spent a few months there on his return journey in 1658; he came back again in October 1659 and stayed for another ten months. In 1658 an unidentified Francis Mortoft spent nearly three months touring in France on his way to Italy.

The first thirty years or so of the personal reign of Louis XIV are those for which travellers' accounts of France offer most material. Charles Bertie (1634–1711) was in France in March 1661 at the time of the death of Mazarin and the assumption of power by the young king; he had landed at Dieppe in 1660 and, after spending some time in Paris, made his way to the Loire Valley. After making a long stay at Angers, in May 1662 he set out on the usual tour of the French provinces, taking in La Rochelle, Bordeaux, Toulouse, Montpellier and Marseilles, finally leaving France for Geneva from Lyons in September. If the author of the *Religio Medici* left only five pages of jottings to describe a journey from Venice to Bordeaux earlier in the century, his sons, Thomas (1647–1667) and Edward, (1642–1708), offer some material for the early part of the personal reign. Before joining the Navy, the younger brother wrote an account of a journey from Bordeaux to Paris via La Rochelle and Nantes. We have not only some letters of Edward Browne for the period of six months which he spent in France in 1664–5 on his way to and from Italy, but also quite a detailed journal covering his stay in Paris on his way south. This journal is interesting for various reasons, but particularly for what it tells us about the teaching available to a medical student in the capital.

The visit to Paris described by Martin Lister (1638?–1712) in *A Journey to Paris in the year 1698* was by no means his first stay in France; in it he speaks of 'the great benefit of the French Air I had experienced 3 times before'.[3] We know nothing of a visit he made there in 1681 except that in July of that year he and his party were given a passport for their journey.[4] His longest stay in France was undoubtedly made in the period 1663–6 when as a young man he spent a good deal of time in Montpellier; unfortunately our information about these years is decidedly scrappy.[5] His presence in Montpellier in 1665 is referred to not only by Edward Browne, but also by the famous naturalist, John Ray (1627–1705), and his companion, Philip Skippon (1641–1691), a young Cambridge graduate who was later to become an M.P. Ray and Skippon spent only a few days in France in 1663 on their way to the Spanish Netherlands, but when they returned from Italy in July 1665, they remained there until April of the following year. Like Lister, they were compelled to cut short their stay when Louis XIV ordered all

Englishmen to leave the country after his half-hearted declaration of war on England to aid the Dutch. Ray's *Travels* are mainly of botanical interest, but Skippon's account of their stay in France contains observations on a great variety of topics. Skippon mentions the presence in Montpellier of John Downes (1627–1694), a graduate of the University of Leyden who became physician to St. Bartholomew's and Christ's Hospitals. He arrived in France in May 1664 and travelled to Paris (there are several references to his presence there in Edward Browne's journal). We can follow in his diary his progress down the Loire Valley as far as Nantes and then it breaks off, offering only numerous notes in French and Latin and a few references to Montpellier and the surrounding region. The exact dates of the visit to Paris of a more illustrious personage, Sir Christopher Wren, are not known as almost all our information about it comes from a single letter of his. He seems to have reached Paris in July 1665 and to have been back in England by the following spring.

To this same period of the reign belongs the *Journals* of the Scotsman, John Lauder (1646–1722) who was later to become a judge and to receive the title of Lord Fountainhall. He was a somewhat callow youth when he arrived in France in 1665; as a law student he spent most of his fifteen months in France in towns where there were Law faculties, first in Orleans and then for a much longer period in Poitiers. His *Journals* thus offer a good deal of information about life in the provinces. To the same decade belongs *The Voyage of Italy* by the Catholic divine, Richard Lassels (1603?–1668), which appeared posthumously in Paris in 1670. In it he describes the route to Italy through Paris and Marseilles and on to Genoa by sea and offers in passing a few interesting remarks about France. In 1649–50 he had accompanied Lady Catherine Whetenall and her husband on a journey from the Spanish Netherlands via Calais, Paris and Lyons to Italy; at her request Lassells kept a diary of the journey from which some details of interest about France may be extracted.

For the 1670s, a decade which saw the military triumphs of Louis XIV, we also have quite a number of travellers' accounts. There is the rather sneering work of a certain John Clenche — *A Tour in France and Italy, made by an English Gentleman, 1675* — which appeared anonymously in 1676. This is not a travel diary; it contains no indication of how long the author spent on his quite extensive travels in France, but merely furnishes notes on the towns and regions which he visited. A number of interesting points can be gleaned from the letters sent back from France by Sir Philip Perceval (1656–1680) and his tutor in the period between 1676 and 1679 before and after an

Italian tour. John Covel (1638–1722), later to become master of Christ's College, Cambridge, returned home through France after serving as chaplain to the Levant Company in Constantinople. The manuscript journal of his travels contains a number of pages on his journey from Geneva through Paris to Calais. Though twice mentioned in Locke's *Journals* (they met in Paris), he does not return the compliment by mentioning the then unknown philosopher.

Unquestionably the most detailed account of France at the high point of the reign of Louis XIV left behind by a British traveller is to be found in Locke's *Journals* for the years 1675–9; these can be supplemented by certain notebooks and other papers covering these years. There are, it is true, occasions when one could have wished that he had been less reticent in describing what he saw and heard during these three and a half years. Even so, he does offer a great deal of information about all sorts of aspects of French life, both in Paris and the provinces. What exactly he was doing in France for this long period is, like many aspects of his career, somewhat mysterious. He appears to have hastened to the South of France, to Montpellier, at the end of 1675 to seek a cure for his ill-health in this warmer climate and to have intended to make a relatively short stay there. After spending two winters in the South he returned to Paris to take charge of the son of a wealthy London merchant, returning there not by the Rhone valley by which he had come, but by way of Bordeaux and Poitiers. His stay in the capital was to last for over a year, after which he set out with his pupil on a second tour of France, travelling this time in the opposite direction, via the Loire valley and La Rochelle back to Montpellier and from there up the Rhone valley to Lyons. Bad weather having prevented them from going on into Italy, they returned to Paris where they spent another five months before coming back to England in May 1679.

With some hesitation one includes the anonymous pamphlet, *Popery and Tyranny: or the Present State of France In relation to its Government, Trade, Manners of the People, and Nature of the Country*, on the grounds that it is allegedly 'a Letter from an English Gentleman abroad, to his friend in England'. It was published in 1679 and is dated 'Paris May 12th'. Although the first word of the title and the opening sentence of the letter obviously endeavour to exploit the panic caused by the Popish Plot, there is little in it about popery but a great deal about the arbitrary power wielded by Louis XIV.

The period of the 1680s is also well covered. There is a lively account of a journey from Montpellier to Chambéry in 1681 in a portion of a diary kept by a young gentleman from Norfolk named John Buxton who appears to have been in France for the sake of his health. White Kennet (1660–1728) who had just taken his degree at Oxford and was in due course to become first dean, then bishop of Peterborough, spent just over a fortnight in France in 1682. Considering that he was there such a short time and that he never got further beyond Calais than St. Omer, the notes on his journey offer a great deal of value to a modern reader. There is obviously more of substance in the writings of the Scotsman, Gilbert Burnet (1643–1715), who was to play an important part in the accession of William III and was rewarded by being made bishop of Salisbury. While abroad, he published in Holland in 1686 letters which he addressed to Robert Boyle describing his travels which included two journeys through France. Later, in his posthumous *History of His Own Time*, he gives an account of these and two earlier journeys, made in 1664 and 1683; on the second of these he was received by Louis XIV at Versailles. In 1687 Richard Ferrier (1663–1720), who was later to sit in several Parliaments as the Tory member for Great Yarmouth, made a four-month tour of France which took him as far south as Lyons.

In addition three works which were published after 1690 all describe visits to France made in the 1680s. William Bromley (1664?–1732), who was later to be Speaker of the House of Commons and for a short period a Secretary of State, published anonymously in 1692 his *Remarks in the grande tour of France and Italy*. This describes in some detail his outward journey through France and more briefly his return. Though it is difficult to date these two journeys precisely, the first took place after the inauguration of the statue of Louis XIV in the Place des Victoires (March 1686), and in describing his visit to Nîmes he speaks of it being 'before the late Persecution eminent for the great Resort of the Protestants'.[6] His return journey must have taken place before his election as an M.P. in 1689; he was one of the 92 members who declined to recognize William III.

In 1701 Ellis Veryard who had matriculated at Cambridge in 1676 and who was probably the Vergard who matriculated in Leyden two years later, published an account of his travels which had taken him as far as the Levant. His general observations on the state of France were obviously written at a later date, but his journey through Péronne, Paris, Poitiers, Toulouse, Montpellier, Toulon and Lyons into Italy seems to belong to the early 1680s; the account of his travels begins with sections on Holland and the Spanish Netherlands which he crossed on his way to France. He arrived in Holland on 6 April 1682.[7]

John Northleigh (1657–1705), at one time a fellow of King's

College, Cambridge, who for many years practised as a physician in Exeter, published in 1702 the first (and last) volume of his travels on the Continent. Like Veryard, he concluded his account of France with some general observations which are undoubtedly of a later date, but the two journeys in France which he describes must have taken place considerably earlier. This is shown by his reference to the Pont Royal in Paris which collapsed in 1684; the foundation stone of the new bridge was laid in October 1685. 'There was a handsome new one building while I was first in Paris . . . ', writes Northleigh, 'and finish'd at my last being there'. As regards his second visit he states that Bossuet's *Histoire des variations des Églises protestantes* which was published in 1688 appeared 'while I was at Paris' and he speaks of being present at the funeral service for the 'late Queen of Spain, Daughter of our Henrietta, who was born in Exeter, and was afterwards Duchesse of Orleans';[8] this took place on 30 April 1689. From this we may deduce that his first visit to France was in 1685–6 and the second in 1688–9.

Understandably, given first the Nine Years War and then the War of the Spanish Succession, there are relatively few travellers' accounts for the last twenty-five years of the reign. There is, of course, the substantial volume of Martin Lister's *A Journey to Paris in the year 1698* which appeared in print before that year was out. Though it is crammed with detailed observations on a great many aspects of life which he made during his six months in the capital, it naturally has very little to say about the provinces although he knew them well from earlier visits. Another account of travels in France which falls in this interval between the Treaty of Ryswick and the outbreak of the next war is the apparently anonymous *Letters to a Nobleman from a Gentleman travelling through Holland, Flanders and France* which did not appear until 1709; the dedication to the third Earl of Shaftesbury is signed by the legal writer, Joseph Shaw (1671–1733). The last two letters describe a journey from the Spanish Netherlands to Paris and offer some general reflections on the French character and institutions. Before the outbreak of the War of the Spanish Succession in May 1702 Edward Lhwyd (1660?–1709), the second keeper of the Ashmolean Museum in Oxford, made a trip to Brittany. Two letters of his tell the sad story of how he and his companion were arrested as spies and spent eighteen days in prison in Brest before they secured their release.

In those far-off days travel in a land with which one's own country was at war was not absolutely ruled out. In the first version of his famous work — *The New Horse-Houghing Husbandry*, published in 1731 — Jethro Tull (1674–1741) makes two references to the vineyards of the South of France; in the fuller version, published in 1733 under the title *Horse-Hoing Husbandry*, he informs the reader: 'I formerly lived some years in Languedoc'. There are also references in the same work to agriculture in other parts of France. According to the *Dictionary of National Biography*, Tull was compelled for health reasons to travel in France and Italy in the years 1711–14. 'Vineyards', the index states, 'owe their great Products to the Hoe-Tillage; and from them the Author first took his Scheme'.

The war with France had been over for six months when the philosopher George Berkeley (1685–1753), the future bishop of Cloyne, arrived in Paris on his way to Italy as chaplain to an ambassador extraordinary, the third Earl of Peterborough; he returned through France in the following year. His letters during this period contain some interesting references to the poor condition of the country at the end of the war. The last work to be drawn upon is the anonymous *A New Journey to France*, published in 1715. It describes a stay of some four months in the previous year, spent first in Paris and then in Orleans where the author claims to have spent seven years as a student. The book opens with a very John Bull sentence: 'Having spent formerly some time in France when it was in a most flourishing Condition, and being of late informed of the present Miseries of that Country, I had the curiosity of making a trip over to be Eye-witness of the low Ebb it is reduc'd to by the Valour of British Arms'. It is a curious work; it contains, for instance, a lurid story of seeing an actor arrested on the stage of the Comédie Française during a performance of Molière's *Le Malade imaginaire* and of how this man and a nun were later executed for their hideous crimes;[9] reference to the registers of this theatre shows that this play was not performed there during the time the author was in Paris. Yet, like all other travellers' accounts, long and short, this work does offer its quota of observations of interest to a modern reader.

To assess the value of the travellers' observations on life in France one needs to know how well equipped they were linguistically to communicate orally with the French people they met and to read all manner of documents which they might encounter. If nowadays French is the first modern language taught in most British schools, it had no place in the curriculum in the seventeenth century and while today British tourists can get by on a smattering of half-forgotten French words and phrases, or on no French at all, this is partly because English/American is the first modern language to be taught in the majority of French schools. In the seventeenth century the modern languages known amongst the educated minority of the population of France were Italian and Spanish. A knowledge of English was long to remain a very unusual accomplishment.

There was, however, available at that time in Latin an international language which most of our travellers and the Frenchmen with an equivalent education whom they encountered had beaten into them in their youth. Throughout our period one traveller after another makes it plain that recourse was frequently had to Latin in encounters with such Frenchmen as were also capable of conversing in that language. On his way south from Calais in 1608 Coryate fell in with a young cleric: 'He was *Ordinis Praemonstratensis*, a young man of the age of two and twenty years, and a prety Latinist'. At Amiens he met his first pilgrim who, in contrast, was 'a very simple fellow, who spake so bad Latin that a country Scholler in England should be whipped for speaking the like'. Later in Lyons, he tells us, he met another pilgrim, adding: 'I had a long discourse with him in latin'. There he even met a Turk who, he declares, 'spake sixe or seven languages besides the Latin, which he spake very well . . . I had a long discourse with him in Latin of many things'.[10]

Attempts to make conversation with strangers in Latin were not always a success. Heylyn, for instance, complains of the ignorance of some members of the Catholic clergy: 'When I had lost myself in the streets of Paris, and wanted French to enquire homeward, I used to apply myself to some of these reverend habit. But *O seclum insipiens & infacetum!* you might as easily have wrung water out of the flint, as a word of Latine out of their mouths'. He maintains that this ignorance was to be found among even more exalted clerical personages, quoting the example of his encounter with a canon at Orleans: 'Perceiving me to speak to him in a strange tongue, for it was Latine, he very readily asked me this question, *Num potestis loqui Gallia?* which when I had denyed, at last he broke out into another interrogatory, *viz. Quam diu fuistis in Gallice?* To conclude, having read over my Letter, with two or three deadly pangs, and six times rubbing of his temples, he dismissed me with this cordiall, and truly it was very comfortable to my humour, *Ego negotias vestras curabo*'.[11] A similar disappointment could be met with in dealings with a Protestant pastor. White Kennet records in his account of his visit to France shortly before the Revocation of the Edict of Nantes: 'Ambitious of having some conference with Monseiur Troulier, but when I accosted him, his only answer was in the French tonge that he had been absent from his place of education, Geneva, for 15 years & by a disuse had wholly forgott the familiar talking of Latine'.[12] Such encounters could be somewhat frustrating, as Locke found at the beginning of his stay in France when he visited the famous Servières museum in Lyons: he explains that he could not get any further information about certain of the exhibits, 'he haveing not Latin nor I French'.[13] When Edward Lhwyd and his companion were arrested as spies and imprisoned in Brest, they drew up a petition in Latin, requesting to be interrogated, only to be told that so highly placed an official as the *Intendant de la Marine* 'was not conversant in that language'.[14]

However, in the travellers' accounts we continue right through the period to find echoes of conversations in Latin with French people whom they encountered. Thus William Bromley tells how at Lyons a Jesuit father asked him 'whether I had read my Countrey-man Lassel's *Voyages* which, he said, he had often (to use his own expression) *cum plurimâ, imo cum summaâ voluptate*'.[15] A knowledge of Latin was, of course, essential if one was to follow the disputations and many of the lectures in French universities at this period. Edward Browne, while a student in Paris, recorded in his journal a visit to the Collège Montaigu: 'I heard a dispute in logick in Collegio Montis acuti', and he was far from pleased at first with the medical lectures of Guy Patin for linguistic reasons: 'I was much disappointed in my expectation of understanding all hee said by reason hee used the French tongue so much'.[16] Veryard noted that the French predilection for their native tongue meant that they 'not only publish the greatest part of their Books therein, but even in explicating their Dictates in the Schools use as much French as Latin, tho' they are very expert in both'.[17] The Scottish law student, John Lauder, noted one practical difficulty arising in Franco-British exchanges in Latin: 'The accent the French gives the Latin is so different from ours that sometymes we would not have understood some of them (for the most part I understood them weil enought), nor some of them us'.[18] Naturally he was convinced that the French pronunciation was wrong. He also noted another difference which he must have encountered in attending lectures that were dictated — that the French used different Latin terms for punctuation marks.

Though Latin could be useful in certain circumstances, a reasonable knowledge of French must have been just as necessary then as it is today for any real understanding of what the travellers experienced during their stay in France. Most of them, it must be said, arrived in the country with little or no knowledge of French, and unless they stayed some length of time cannot have greatly increased their command of the language. Heylyn who spent only five weeks in France confesses that at the end of his stay he and his companions 'had learned only so much of the French, as a little child after a years practise hath of his mother tongue'.[19] and in 1698 even Lister who as a young man had spent a long period in France was very modest about his knowledge of the language when it came to understanding either a tragedy or what was sung in opera or even a sermon, saying, for instance, of a preacher whom he heard in Paris: 'I am not so good a French-Man as to understand all he said'.[20] Veryard admits to being 'poorly skill'd in the French Tongue'.[21]

A number of our travellers took steps to remedy their linguistic deficiencies. On his arrival in Paris in 1643 Evelyn 'tooke a Master of the French Tongue', and during the month he spent in Tours, he tells us: 'Here I tooke a Master of the Language, and studyed the tongue very diligently'.[22] Then as now, removing oneself from contact with other English people was recognized as one aid to learning the language. Howell, for instance, writes during his stay in France in 1619–20: 'I am lodged here hard by the Bastile, because it is furthest off those places where the English resort; for I would go on to get a little Language as soon as I could', and on a later visit he could write: 'Now that I understand French indifferently well . . . '[23] One of Reresby's objects in making a long stay in Saumur was to 'improve myself in the language'; after spending the best part of a year there he moved on, he tells us, 'having got enough of the language to introduce me into the company of the people of the country'.[24]

Students like Edward Browne and John Lauder record in some detail their attempts to learn French. Though early in his stay in Paris the former had been put off by Guy Patin's use of French in his lectures, he was already making some effort to learn the language. A few days after his arrival he noted: 'I bought the Gazette for 5 Solz, which though I could not understand it all, I hammered out the meaning of a great part of it'. After less than a fortnight he wrote down a whole French sentence, though not very correctly: 'Je commence parle un peu François et j'esper que je parlerai mieux dan un Mois', and ten days later, describing the second service which he attended at the Protestant *temple* at Charenton, he noted: 'I begin to understand the Minister'.[25] By the time he left Paris after a stay of nearly four months and had made his way to Montpellier, he was able to tell his father that despite the great distance he had travelled, 'haveing somewhat of the language, I could entertain my self with the French, who are good companions in a journey'.[26]

John Lauder had been sent over to France, as his father put it, 'to study the french tongue and the Laws'. While he took French lessons, he also used his knowledge of Latin in some encounters. At Orleans, he visited the Jesuits' college where, he tells us, 'I discoursed with the praefectus Jesuitarum, who earnestly enquired of what religion I was, for a long tyme I would give him no other answer but that I was religione christianus'. During his stay there he made an excursion into the country in mixed company and had a long theological discussion with a *curé* after mass. 'We was in dispute above an hower and all in Latin; in the tyme gathered about us neir the half of the parish, gazing on me as a fool and mad man that durst undertake to controlle their curé, every word of whose mouth, tho they understood it no more nor the stone in the wall did, they took for ane oracle.' Despite the lessons he had received since his arrival at Orleans two months earlier, his French was still decidedly shaky as he goes on to recount: 'In our returning amongst the best merriments we had was my French, which moved us sewerall tymes to laughter; for I stood not on steeping stones to have assurance that it was right what I was to say, for if a man seek that, he sall never speak right, since he cannot get assurance at the wery first but must acquire it by use'.[27] No doubt during the year he later spent in Poitiers he acquired a greater command of French, though some of the French quotations in his journal cannot be said to have been very correctly transcribed.

After spending two months visiting Paris and a variety of provincial towns from Lyons to Caen, Ferrier and his companions arrived at Dieppe 'where', he tells us, '(being desirous to get something more than we had in the French languidge) we stayed a month, at the end of which time we went to board about 3 leagues in the Country for as much longer'.[28] Though considerably older than any of these men (he was forty-three when he began his long stay in France), Locke began to take French lessons as soon as he and his companion, George Walls, arrived in Montpellier. 'This day', he recorded in his journal, 'I got me a French Master who was to teach Mr Wall & me one hour per diem 5 days in the weak at 4 crowns per month'. Two sheets, endorsed by Locke: 'Mr. Pasty, Grammar Francois.76', have been preserved; these contain exercises in French grammar in the handwriting of both teacher and pupil. Characteristically both Pasty's explanations and Locke's notes are in Latin. Later Locke maintained to a French correspondent that if he should take it into his head to learn English, he ought to follow his method which was to read every day a chapter of the New Testament. 'En un mois', he adds, 'vous deviendrez maistre'.[29] No doubt Locke's knowledge of French in which he read widely became quite considerable during his three and a half years in France though he always transcribed passages in French very carelessly.

Though they made little contact with such regions as Brittany, Flanders and particularly Alsace in which non-Romance languages were spoken, our travellers show some awareness of the complex linguistic situation in the France of their day where, besides these languages, *patois* of French were spoken north of the Loire and a variety of Occitan dialects in the southern half of the country. Their ideas on the subject are not always very clear. Dallington, for instance, speaks of the different dialects of France 'where the Picard speaks one, the Norman another, the Britton his, the Gascoigne his, the Provençall and Savoyard theirs, the Inlanders theirs'.[30] Naturally enough the Welshmen are best informed about the Breton language, and Howell also has rather more precise notions than Dallington on the general linguistic situation:

> The French have three dialects, the Wallon (vulgarly called among themselves *Romand*,) the Provencall, (whereof the Gascon is a sub-dialect) and the speech of Languedoc: They of Bearne and Navarre speak a Language that hath affinity with the Bascuence or the Cantabrian tongue in Biscaie, and amongst the Pyrenean mountaines: The Armorican tongue, which they of Low Brittaine speake (for there is your *Bas-Breton*, and the *Breton-Brittonant* or *Breton Gallois*, who speaks French) is a dialect of the old Brittish as the word *Armorica* imports, which is a meere Welsh word, for if one observes the Radicall words in that Language they are the same that are now spoken in Wales, though they differ much in the composition of their sentences, as doth the Cornish.[31]

Though Edward Lhwyd's visit to Brittany had to be cut short, he has some interesting remarks to make on the state of the Breton language. In one letter he writes: 'I had been before in Cornwal during the space of three or four months; and coming hither found that the Armorican and Cornish differ'd less than the present English of the vulgar in the North from those of the West of England; but in respect of us the difference is greater. The Cornish is much more corruptly spoken than the Armorican, as being confin'd to half a score parishes towards the Land's End; whereas Armorican is the common language of a country almost as large as Wales'. To another correspondent he writes: 'Their Language is much the same with the Cornish; and both so near to the Dialect of South Wales: that in a months time at farthest a Welshman may understand their writings; but as to the speaking part their affinity creates some confusion. 'Tis spoken at least for a Hundred miles, and their Gentry and Merchants speak it in their Great Towns; but much more corruptly than ours in N.Wales'. If there is some exaggeration here, Lhywd does admit that the language was losing ground in competition with French when he observes that 'they seem to have been much more discourag'd by the Mounsieur's jeering them than those of sense and Education are among us'.[32]

c

Kennet was the only traveller to comment on the language spoken in Flanders; unfortunately he got it all wrong. On visiting St. Omer which had recently been wrested from the Spaniards, he writes: 'So great an alteration wrought in the language by its late Change of Master that whereas Flemish & Spanish were the only dialects 7 year agoe there is now scarce one word spoke or understood but French'.[33] Though Flemish was the original language spoken in this region, since the end of the sixteenth century, and even when it was part of the Spanish Netherlands, French had been the official language.

There are occasional references to the dialects of French spoken in the provinces of the northern half of the country. Thus Heylyn writes of the Norman dialect: 'It differeth from the Parisian, and more elegant French, almost as much as the English spoken in the North, doth from that of London or Oxford. Some of the old Norman words it still retaineth, but not many. It is much altered from what is was in the time of the Conqueror, few of the words in which our lawes were written being known to them'.[34] Though Lauder's observations on the relationship between the various dialects and French are quite wrong, he picked up at Poitiers an amusing anecdote on the subject:

> The present bischop of Poictiers[35] is a reasonable, learned man, they say. On a tyme a preist came to gett collation from him, the bischop, according to the custome, demanding of him if he know Latin, if he has learned his Rhetorick, read his philosophy, studied the scooll Divinity and the Canon Law, etc., the preist replied *quau copois*,[36] which in the dialect of bas Poictou (which differs from that they speak in Gascoigne, from that in Limosin, from that in Bretagne, though all 4 be but bastard French) signifies *une peu*. The bischop though it a very doulld[37] answer, and that he bit to be[37a] but a ignorant fellow. He begines to try him on some of them, but try him wheir he will he findes him better wersed then himselfe. Thus he dismissed him with a ample commendation; and severall preists, efter hearing of this, when he demanded if they had studied sick and sick things, they were sure to reply *cacopois*. He never examined them further, crying, go your wayes, go your wayes, they that answers *cacopois* are weill qualified.[38]

In his muddled way Lauder here touches upon an important point — that in provinces to the south of the Loire the mass of the population spoke dialects which formed part of a Romance language quite different from French and known variously as *langue d'oc* (to distinguish it from the *langue d'oïl* of the North), *Provençal* and *Occitan*. The author of *A New Journey*, who does not appear to have known anything but Northern France, does recognize in a confused way that the Gascons originally spoke a different language from

French: 'Their language is a Dialect of the Spanish, but very Corrupt, as also is what French they speak, both in the Words and Accent; for they commonly pronounce the (*b*) like a (*v*), and the (*v*) like a (*b*)'.[39] Those travellers who penetrated into the southern half of the kingdom make occasional references to the different language they encountered there. Locke, for instance, notes that the wine-growers at Gaillac, near Albi, famous for its white wines, 'marke all their wine casks with a coq burnt on, from Gal in pattoy being a cock'.[40] Though he spent a much shorter time than Locke in Montpellier, Skippon does contribute an interesting note on the language spoken there by ordinary people: 'The language of the vulgar is call'd *Patois*, very difficult for strangers and those born about Paris to understand, being a mixture of French, Spanish, and Italian, as may be observ'd by the following words and phrases therein: *Peccare! Ah Pau ra! Ques à quo. A Dieu Seas. Dieus vous le donne. Cavalisco. Pottone. Fullou. Fumée. Fringare. Scarabigliato. Cad. Began*'.[41]

This raises a curious point. Those of our travellers who spent some time in the southern half of France could communicate with members of the educated classes in such French as they had at their command since these people were usually bilingual. In their encounters with men who had had a training in Latin they could also use the international language of the period. Yet how they communicated with the mass of the population in these parts is a mystery. Locke's boundless curiosity led him to talk with all manner of people, including the peasants in the fields; yet only once does he confess that he was beaten by the language barrier. When he visited the famous Haut-Brion vineyard near Bordeaux, he noticed that some of the vines were high and staked and others close to the ground, adding 'The reason of this different way of culture I could not learne of the work men for want of understanding Gascoin'.[42] Yet in the following year, when in the same region, he records in great detail a conversation with a peasant woman about living conditions, and during his long stay in Montpellier he had conversations with a great variety of people who almost certainly spoke nothing but their Occitan dialect. This is all somewhat puzzling, but as none of our travellers who ventured into the southern part of the kingdom does anything to explain the mystery, it must remain unsolved.

Those of our travellers who describe their journeys in detail, mostly in the form of a diary, provide us with a great deal of information about the slow, expensive and often dangerous ways in which at that time people moved about over long distances.

While occasionally travellers from this country would enter France through the Spanish Netherlands via Péronne, the great majority came direct by sea and chose the shortest crossing, from Dover to Calais, returning in most cases by the same route. Other ports on the English side of the Channel were sometimes used (both Finch and Reresby sailed from Rye), while on the French side travellers could land at Dieppe or St. Malo or even Rouen. Heylyn and his companions returned from Boulogne to Dover, while Locke sailed from Gravesend to Calais, the ship calling in at Dover for water, and returned direct from Calais to London.

The most unusual arrival by sea was that effected by the Royalist, Sir Richard Fanshawe, and his wife who, coming from San Sebastian in 1650, were shipwrecked on the coast not far from Nantes. Their emotions on escaping from the sea are vividly described in Lady Fanshawe's memoirs:

> Thus, God be praised, we escaped this great danger and found ourselves near a little viladge, about 4 leagues from Nante. We hired there 6 asses upon which we rode, as many as could, by turnes, and the rest carried our goods. This journey took us up all the next day; for I should have told you that we stured not that night, because we sat up and made good cheere, for beds they had none, and we were so transported that we thought we had no need of any, but we had very good fires and Nance white wine, and butter and milk, and wallnuts and eggs, and some very bad cheese. And was this not enough with the escape of shiprack to be thought better than a feast? I am sure untill that houre I never knew such pleasure in eating, between which we a thousand times repeated what we had spoke when every word seemed our last. We praised God; I wept, your father then lifting up his hands admired so great a salvation. Then we often kissed each other, as if yet we feared death, sithed, and complained of the cruelty of the rebells that forced us to wander. Then we again comforted ourselves in the submitting to God's will for his laws and our country's, and remembered the lott and present suffering of our king. The much discourse and wearyness of our journey made us fall a sleep.[43]

Those travellers who crossed France on their way to and from Italy and who did not choose to go from Lyons through Savoy, but preferred to follow the Rhone valley, often made part of the journey by sea. Thus Lassels travelled on a galley from Marseilles to Genoa, and Bromley took a boat from Cannes to Nice, while on his return journey Burnet sailed direct from Civitavecchia to Marseilles.

In those days even the shortest sea crossing was generally a slow and sometimes a very unpleasant experience. Four or five hours seems to have been considered quite a reasonably fast crossing between Dover and Calais; Mundy speaks of reaching Dover after only three and a half hours thanks to 'a faire wynde'. A very much longer time could be spent on the water; Kennet, for instance, spent seventeen hours on the outward journey and sixteen on his return to Dover. He offers no explanation for such lengthy crossings, but Skippom is less laconic: 'About two in the afternoon we went aboard the packet boat; about eight in the evening we were becalm'd, and were forced to lie two leagues short of Calais till the morning, and then about five o'clock we arriv'd at Calais-shore, having sail'd eight leagues from Dover'.[44]

When the sea was rough, the crossing could be both unpleasant and dangerous as Evelyn found when he travelled over to France in August 1650;

> At 6 in the Evening we set saile, the wind not favorable. I was very sea-sick, coming to anker about one a Clock; about 5 in the morning we had a long-boate to carry us to land, though at good distance; this we willingly enter'd, because two Vessels were chasing us: but being now almost at the harbours mouth, through inadvertancy, there brake in upon us two such huge seas, as had almost sunke the boate, I being neere the middle up in Water: our steeres man, it seems, apprehensive of the danger was preparing to leape into the sea, and trust his swimming: but seeing the vessell emerge, put her into the peere, & so God be thanked we got wet to Calais, where I went immediately to bed, sufficiently discompos'd.[45]

Even when they had arrived on French territory, our travellers spent a good deal of their time on the water when they set out to explore the country. Given the slowness of travel by land, it is scarcely surprising to find them making the journey by boat between Bordeaux and Blaye on the estuary of the Gironde, but rivers were regularly used for all sorts of journeys, long and short. Quite a number could be made from Paris, for instance down the Seine to Rouen, though the meanderings of the river made this somewhat slow and laborious. In 1595 Fynes Moryson made this journey:

> They account fortie eight miles from Paris to Roane, whether I went by boat, and payed a French Crowne for my passage. The first day we passed eighteen miles to Poissy, a most faire and famous Nunnerie, and towards the evening wee passed by the Kings Pallace S.Germain. The next day we passed twentie leagues to Andale, and by the way passed by a bridge, dividing the County of France from the Dutchy of Normandy and did see the Palace Galeon,[45a] and a faire Monastery. Then we passed foure miles by water to Port S.Antoine, and one mile by land. Then wee hired another boat, in which we passed five leagues to Roane, and I payed for this passage three soulz.[46]

Over a hundred years later the author of *A New Journey* followed the same route though he started his journey at Poissy. The journey to Rouen took from one o'clock on the first afternoon to three on the second, and it must have been a pretty tedious business. At 2 a.m. they disembarked by a hamlet beyond Mantes from where they 'were forc'd to go a League by Land'. Taking another boat, they went past Vernon to another hamlet where they arrived at 6 a.m. and hired horses for the next part of the journey: 'The Seine makes so many meanders, that we crossed in Ferries at three several Places'. The last two leagues to Rouen were again travelled by water.[47]

Not all river journeys from Paris were as complicated as this. When Northleigh visited Fontainebleau, he went both ways by water, by what he calls 'a sort of Dutch drag-boat'. Describing the return journey, he writes: 'They run you this Course (as it may be call'd) with the Barge from Fontainbleau to Paris down the Sein, drawn by three or four Horses in a Boat, in about 10 or 12 Hours or less'.[48] Travellers going further afield would go up the Seine as far as Montereau and then follow the Yonne to Sens or Joigny. Edward Browne who had been ill during his stay in Paris writes to his father that, instead of going by coach to Lyons on the first stage of his journey south, 'I choose rather to creep up this river of Seine, and so strike over land to some towne upon the Sosne, from whence I may passe as far as I please downe that and the Rosne', and in his next letter, sent from Chalon-sur-Saône, he writes: 'In the water coach I came as far as Joigny, 4 dayes journey from Paris; passing through Melun, Montereau, Sens and Villeneuf'.[49]

Locke who had travelled to Chalon by land on his way to Lyons took the boat down the Saône. He enjoyed this experience ('The passage from Challon by water was very easy & convenient & the river very quiet'), although it involved spending a night ashore at Mâcon and it took two full days to get to Lyons.[50] From there many travellers went down the Rhone by boat as far south as Pont St.Esprit. Although Evelyn speaks of having 'bargain'd with a Waterman to transport us as far as Avignon upon the River', he explains that at Pont St.Esprit they 'went on shore, it being very dangerous to passe the bridg with a boate', and made the last part of the journey on horseback. After spending one night at Vienne, he tells us, 'the next Morning we Swam (for the river runs so exceedingly rapid, that we were onely steered) to a small Village call'd Tain'; from there they moved on to Valence where they spent a second night arriving at Pont St.Esprit on the third day. On his return journey from Italy Evelyn also found it convenient to travel down the Rhone from Geneva to Lyons: 'We tooke, or rather purchased a boate, for it could not be brought back againe, because of the streame of the Rhodanus running here about. Thus were we two days going to Lions'.[51] Another river journey — from Grenoble nearly to Orange — was made by Ray and Skippon: 'We took boat for Orange', Skippon writes, 'and went down the rivers Ysere, and the Rhone; twenty crowns was given for the boat, and the passengers pay'd proportionably to the length of their journey, some more, some less. Mr Ray and I paid four one half-quart d'escu apiece'. The journey which took two days, was not without its hazards: 'After we had left Grenoble three or four leagues, we durst not stir from the bank's side, a furious wind arising and stopping us for the space of an hour'.[52]

The great River Loire played an important part in the system of communications. For one thing it provided an alternative route from Lyons to Paris; travellers made their way by road to Roanne where they took a boat to Orleans. Peter Mundy who was travelling in an ambassador's train records that on arrival at Roanne 'there were two boates hired from hence to Orleance att Ten French Crownes per boate, one for my Lord and gentlemen and the other for the Attendants, in which wee departed'. On their arrival at Orleans he notes: 'The Boatemen that come downe from Rouana, as others that come downe the River, at their arrivall heere sell their boates, because they are not worth the labour to be carried backe against the streame, being but slightlie made'. It could be a slow journey as Mundy found: 'Wee were aground twenty or thirty tymes evey day'.[53] On this occasion it took six days. Evelyn seems to have had a much faster journey downstream on his return from Italy; though he tells us that at Roanne 'wee agreede with an old fisher, to row us as farr as Orleans', it seems as if the passengers (and he in particular) did most of the work. It was apparently an enjoyable journey; on the third day, he writes, 'we ariv'd at Orleans, taking our turn to row through all the former passages, & reckoning that my share amounted to litle lesse than 20 leagues; sometimes footing it through pleasant fields & medows, sometimes we shot at fouls & other birds, nothing came amisse, sometimes we play'd at Cards, while others sung, or were composing Verses; for we had the greate Poet Mr. Waller in our Companie, & some other ingenious Persons'.[54] Evelyn seems to have been lucky as later in the century Bromley records of this journey: 'At Roanne I took boat (the usual Conveyance) and went down the pleasant River Loire, where the Water was so low, I was six or seven days in getting to Orleans'.[55]

When they arrived at Orleans, most of our travellers took the road to Paris, though others continued on down the river. Many more arrived at Orleans from Paris and travelled down the Loire to such

places as Blois, Tours, Saumur, Angers and even as far as Nantes. Of
the numerous accounts of travelling down the Loire from Orleans the
sourest is that of Reresby who speaks of going by water to Blois 'in a
passage-boat, with some French men and women, who, by singing to
make the journey more pleasant (some of them having good voices)
made it less so; infecting the air at the same time with wafts of garlic (a
great food in that country, with bread) that it more nauseated the
smell than gratified the ear'.[56] At certain seasons this part of the river
could be dangerous; we are told that Lord Willoughby, while going in
November from Tours to Saumur, had 'a bad and dangerous passage
by reason of the ill-weather of continuall snow and high wind'.[57]
Locke and his pupil made a bad start when they set out from Orleans
at the end of July: 'From Orleans to Avery 8 leagues, for, the winde
being against us, we could not get to Bloys & therefor Mme de
Richmond who went in our boat, would stop here, being afraid of the
waves, & carried us to Mr. d'Avery's, a person of quality, where we
were well received & lodg'd'.[58] The rest of the journey down the river
as far as Ponts-de-Cé where they took horses for Angers was
uneventful. Ferrier who completed the whole journey from Roanne
to Nantes observed that the Loire's 'greatest fault' was 'its want of
water'.[59] Normally when going eastwards to Orleans or from there
south to Roanne, travellers went by road, but it was apparently
possible to travel upstream from Nantes to Orleans as the Fanshawes
did in 1650:

> We hired a boat to carry us up to Orleans, and we were towed
> up all the river of Loire so far. Every night we went a shoare to
> bed, and every morning carryed into the boat wine and fruit and
> bread, with sum flesh, which we dressed in the boat; for it had a
> hearth on which we burned charcoals. We like wise caught
> carpes, which were the fattest and the best I ever eat in my life.
> And of all my travells none was for travell's sake, as I may call it,
> so pleasant as this; for we saw the finest cityes, seats, woods,
> medows, pastures, vineyards, and champain, that ever I saw in
> my life, adorned with the most pleasant river of Loire.[60]

In South West France the Garonne formed a natural link between
Toulouse and Bordeaux. Edward Browne went this way, informing
his father that 'wee went to Bourdeaux by water, downe the most
pleasant river I ever yet saw'.[61] On his return from Montpellier to
Paris in 1677 Locke made use of part of the as yet uncompleted Canal
du Midi to travel from Castelnaudary to Toulouse: 'From
Castelnaudary to Montesquieu by the Canal 5 leagues ... From
Montesquieu to Tholose 5 leagues by the Canale. The price of
passage from Castelnaudari to Tholouse by the Canale 30s., you &

your portmantue, but it is a very incommodious passage if you have any carriage, for there is in this day's passage 17 Locks, & at each the goods are to be carried from one boat to an other, for at each locke the boat is changed'. From Toulouse to Bordeaux he travelled down the Garonne, a journey which took five days and had ill-effects for several weeks, as he explains: 'I was taken ill at Agen, feaverish & an extraordinary pain in my head, haveing between Tholose & that had a very cold & untoward passage by water, & a great pole haveing fell upon my head in the boat. Not knowing which to impute it to, but willing above all to secure my head as much as I could, if that had received any harm, I took a clyster in the afternoon, & the next morning, the pain in my head continueing with great violence, I bleeded, I believe, between 11 & 12 ozs. It proved afterwards a tertian ague'.[62]

When on *terra firma* some of our travellers went a certain distance on foot. Coryate offers no explanation as to why he walked all the way from Calais to Montreuil and then from Abbeville to Amiens, nor is he much more forthcoming when he tells us: 'I went . . . about sixe of the clocke from Tarare in my bootes, by reason of a certain accident, to a place about six miles therehence, where I tooke post horse'.[63] After describing how he and his companion travelled from Périgueux to Libourne, Veryard writes, again without any explanation: 'From hence we went two Leagues by Water to Chasteau-Braire, whence we had four Leagues more by Land to Bordeaux, which we travell'd on Foot'.[64] In contrast Howell does offer an excellent reason for walking all the way from Turin to Lyons: 'I was by some disaster brought to an extreme low ebb in money, so that I was forc'd to foot it along with some Pilgrims . . .'[65] In the unsettled state of the country in 1595 Fynes Moryson on his journey from Metz towards Paris was persuaded to sell his horse and to go on foot 'for they said, the bootie of a good Horse would surely cause mee to bee robbed by those, who might perhaps let mee passe quietly on foot, disguised in poore apparell; for they seeing mee well mounted, would surely set upon me, and twenty to one kill me aswel because they that rob in France do commonly kill them they rob, as because they would imagine mee to bee a souldier, either on the Kings, or on the Leagers side, and in that case, if I were on their owne side, would kill mee, for feare of being forced to restitution; and if I were on the adverse part, would thinke mee well killed as an enemie'.[66] Nonetheless on his way to Châlons-sur-Marne he was robbed, though he did get away with his life and even with some of his money which he had hidden. At the height of the Fronde Finch and Baines found that public transport was so disrupted that they had to make their way on foot, first from

Sens to Auxerre and then from there to Dijon since 'by reason of the souldiers no coach would venture'. On the way they were robbed by soldiers and were for a time in danger of their lives from civilian robbers. However, Finch concludes his account of this part of their journey: ' . . . and so blessed be God wee scaped massacre, and so on Good Friday, March the 29, marched to Dijon with two sergeants in the head of 300 foot though we went a mile before them'.[67]

When our travellers had recourse to such forms of land transport as a horse or a wheeled vehicle, they had to make use of highways which corresponded only very remotely with what we regard as roads. No doubt their expectations on arriving in France were not high, and although we encounter many complaints about the inns they frequented on their way, they have very little to say about the state of the roads. There is even some praise as in Evelyn's account of the road between Paris and Orleans though he has reservations: 'The Way from Paris to this City (as indeede most of the roades of France) is paved with a small square free-stone; so that the Country dos not much molest the Travelor with dirt and ill way as ours in England dos; onely 'tis somewhat hard to the poore horses feete which causes them to ride more temperately, seldome going out of the trot, or *grand pas*, as they call it'.[68] Some fifty years later Bromley also commented favourably on this particular road which he describes as 'a Paved Causey of broad stone, kept in good repair', and while on the journey from Calais to Paris he even maintains that one thing which proves to an Englishman that he is abroad is that 'the Roads are much better than ours'.[69]

A great many of our travellers' journeys 'were made on horseback. On much frequented routes they hired post-horses, paying according to the length of the different stages. Thus Locke on his journey back to England notes: 'From Clermont to Amiens 14 leagues post; we paid for 15'.[70] Alternatively between a great many towns, starting with Calais and Paris, horses would be provided by the so-called *messager* whose functions are admirably defined by Reresby in describing his journey from Rouen to the capital: 'I went by the messenger to Paris, who, according to the custom of that country, furnisheth passengers with meat, drink, lodging, carriage, and all other accommodation for so far as you contract to go with him, at a reasonable rate (though not very cleanly, yet a convenient way of travelling for strangers)'.[71] Locke is somewhat more critical of the system. In a letter describing his journey from Calais to Paris he observes sarcastically that the travellers accompanying the messenger 'usually obey all his commands willingly. Are they summond before day to rise? Course & stinkeing lodging makes them forward. Are durty, heavy boots to be put on? Want of slippers takes away all reluctancy. Is leane, ill dressed meat to be eat? A good stomach bids it well come. Are you to be dismounted & thrust into a rascally Inne, 4 or 5 in a chamber? Ten or eleven leagues on a dull, hobling jade will make you glad of it'.[72] This mode of travel was possible not only between Paris and Calais or Rouen, but also to Orleans and then on to Angoulême or Bordeaux or else to Lyons. Other journeys could be made in this fashion, for instance, between Lyons and Geneva, and inside France those recorded by Pridgeon — from Angers to Nantes, from St.Malo to Rennes, and from Rennes to Angers. In the South of France the term *voiturin*, from the Italian, was used for *messager*; Skippon even speaks of the *vitturine* with whom he and his party travelled from Nîmes to Avignon.[73] Locke notes the cost of the last stage of his journey south to Montpellier: 'We paid our Voiturin 12 crowns apeice for horse & provision from Lyons hither. We had liberty to goe out of the way or stay any where, but were to pay ourselves for our own & the horse meat where we stayed, which is usually 15s. dinner, 25s. supper, for all the company eat together, & 15s. for horsemeat a night'. With this one may compare the cost of his journey from Calais to Paris: 'I paid to the messenger for horse and diet between Calais and Paris 12 crowns, and 3 sous per lb. for bagage, except shoes and 6 lbs. which were allowed'.[74]

Very often, however, those who chose this method of travel made their own arrangements to hire horses, especially when they were making a circular tour or travelling by less frequented routes. Evelyn and his companions rode all the way on a tour which took them from Paris to Rouen, Dieppe, Le Havre, Caen and back to Paris,[75] as did Locke and his party on a trip from Montpellier into Provence.[76] On landing, Finch tells us, 'I hired a horse from Deape for 66 sols to Rouen where I came that night'.[77] After staying two days in Calais, Ferrier and his companions 'hired horses for Dunkirk', and although on their journey from Nantes to Dieppe, they appear to have travelled with the messenger as far as Rennes, his accounts contain entries 'for horsehire' for the rest of the journey through Caen to Dieppe.[78] For his journey from Saumur to Poitiers Lauder hired a horse, 'the fellow who aught the horse running at my foot'; once when he got separated from the man, he thought that since he had paid him most of the 17 livres which were to cover all his costs on the journey, 'he had sliped away with that that he might bear no more of my charges, being sure enough that he would get his horse back when I brought it to Poictiers'.[79] Pridgeon records how Lord Willoughby 'tooke horses *de louage*' for a trip from La Rochelle to Brouage and for the journey from La Rochelle to Poitiers and then on to Saumur,[80] while Skippon and Ray paid four crowns for two horses and a guide to go from Grenoble to the Grande Chartreuse, and later, 'giving 15 livres of France, hired three horses and a postilion' to take them from Avignon to the Pont du Gard and from there to Nîmes.[81] It was possible to hire horses for quite long journeys. On his arrival at Orleans with his pupil Locke records: 'Here we discharged our horses which brought us from Blay. For the 3 horses we paid 3£ per diem for hire & 3£ more per diem for their meat, & to our guide that rode one of them 10s. per diem for his hire & 10s. per diem for his meat, & the same rate of 7£ per diem for their returne, counting 8 days from Orleance to Blay'.

The horse was not the only animal used for the transport of persons. In Provence Locke saw 'young wenches rideing upon asses & belabouring them with their boots, soe that one might say they went faster then their asses or the young fellows that accompanied them'.[82] When shipwrecked near a village about four leagues from Nantes, Lady Fanshawe records: 'We hired there 6 asses upon which we rode, as many as could by turnes, and the rest carryed our goods. The journey took us up all the next day'.[83] It was also possible to ride post on asses. When he arrived at Sens in the middle of the Fronde, Finch relates: 'From hence it's usuall to take the commodity of the Bourrique or Post d'Asne to Auxerre, but there was none to be had so that I was forced to walk on foot from thence to Auxerre'.[84] 'Between Lyons & Vienne', Locke noted, 'we met people rideing post on Asses',[85] and on his slow journey down the Seine to Rouen the author of *A New Journey* relates how at one point 'we were forc'd to go a League by Land (it being Seven by Water) and hire Asses (there being no horses to be met with at that Place) to carry our Portmantuas, for which we paid Eightpence a-piece; some do ride on them, and it is called *la poste aux asnes*, or the *Ass post*'.[86]

On his journey south from Lyons Locke noted that mules were used for the transport of persons as well as goods: 'On the road we met severall drivers of mules, some where of we were told have 800 lb. weight upon them, and severall women rideing a stride, some with caps & feathers'.[87] Writing, it is true, at the beginning of the century, before a more luxurious means of transport became essential for members of the upper classes, Coryate observed in Paris 'great aboundance of mules, which are so highly esteemed amongst them, that the Judges and Counsellors doe usually ride on them with their foot clothes'.[88] Mules were used by Evelyn and his companions for their journey from Avignon to Marseilles and then on to Fréjus and Cannes.[89]

They were also used for another form of transport, the litter. John Buxton who was in poor health travelled by this means from Montpellier to Geneva from where he wrote: 'All this journey was performed in a litter, being much used in this country, or else I could not have done it'. At Grenoble he wrote in his diary: 'Here we took another litter, discharging him that came with us from Montpellier'. Even this form of transport was not without its dangers. When near Marseilles, he noted, 'in the afternoon, ascending a steep hill, one of the mules fell (but thanks be to God there was no hurt), we unloaded the mules and walked up the hill'.[90] Horses could also be used for the same purpose. During his long stay at Montpellier Locke suddenly jotted down the note: '5 livres a day the usuall rate of an horse litter'. Two years later he had occasion to ride in one with his pupil from Angers to Saumur: 'Hence we hired a litter for our selves, feareing the heat, & two horses for our servants, & there were with the litter 2 men on foot, al which at 1 Luisd or per diem till their returne home'.[91]

It was also possible to make use of wheeled vehicles for journeys long and short, though inevitably the travellers earlier in the century had fewer facilities of this kind than those who came later when transport of persons had considerably improved. It must be said that the variety of terms used by our travellers to describe the different vehicles they rode in is somewhat confusing. What, for instance, are we to understand by the 'long wagon' in which Fynes Morison travelled from Châlons to Paris in 1595 for the payment of two écus? Presumably, as this was before the age of stage coaches, it was some kind of carrier's waggon. In 1608, Coryate tells us, he travelled from Montreuil to Abbeville 'in a cart, according to the fashion of the country, which had three hoopes over it, that were covered with a sheet of course canvasse', though after walking from there to Amiens, he travelled the rest of the way to Paris 'in Coach'.[92] Over half a century later Edward Browne told his father: 'I passed in a carriole from Joigny to Auzerre',[93] this vehicle being defined in the 1694 edition of the *Dictionnaire de l'Académie française* as 'Petite charrette couverte qui est ordinairement suspendue'.

When Heylyn landed at Dieppe in 1625, he made his way to Rouen in an incredibly slow and uncomfortable vehicle which to his disgust was called a *chariot*, 'for so we must call it. An English man would have thought it a plain Cart'.[93a] Despite his heavy humour he does furnish a fairly precise description of the vehicle: 'At one end was fasten'd three carcasses of horses, or three bodies which had once been horses, and now were worn to dead images . . . The rain fell in us through our tilt, which for the many holes in it, one would have thought to have been a net. The durt brake plentifully upon us, through the rails of our Chariot: and the unequall and ill proportioned pase of it, startled almost every bone of us'. Spending a night at Tôtes, they arrived at Rouen after a further ten-hour journey; we are not told how many passengers the chariot could hold or whether it also carried goods. His journey from Rouen to Paris was made in what was clearly a stage coach, though he calls it a waggon: 'The French call it a Coach, but that matters not; so they would needs have the Cart to be a Chariot. These Waggons are the ordinary instruments of travell in those Counties ... This, in which we travelled, contained ten persons, as all of them commonly do'. He also calls the vehicle in which he travelled from Paris to Orleans and back again a waggon. He did not approve of the company on the return journey, declaring that 'in stead of the good and acceptable society of one of the French Nobles, some Gentlemen of Germany, and two Fryers of the Order of St.Austin' it consisted of 'four tradesmen of Paris, two *filles de joye*, and an old woman'. Yet even Heylyn uses the word 'coach' in describing the vehicle he travelled in from Paris to Amiens in returning to England.[94]

There seems to have been some uncertainty about terminology. If Heylyn speaks of a 'waggon', Lady Fanshawe tells us that on her escape from England in 1659, 'we hired a waggon coach for there is no other at Callais',[95] while according to Skippon in 1666 he, Lister and a third Englishman for their journey from Paris to Calais 'gave 18 livres a man, for our places in a coach waggon that will hold eight persons'. They had rejected the solution to their travel problems adopted by Ray and two other Englishmen of 'travelling by the *Chasse Marée*'.[96] This was the carrier who brought fish to Paris from the Channel ports at high speed (by the standards of the time); presumably he took passengers on the return journey, but one understands Skippon's reluctance to travel that way.

It is not until we come to the latest of all our accounts of travels in France, *A New Journey*, which deals with a visit made in 1714, that we find the expression 'stage coach' used. 'As my Business was only to see the Country', the author explains, 'I did not care to go in the Stage-coach, therefore I bought a Horse, or rather a scrubby Jade, at Calais for Thirty French Crowns'. On this animal of which he speaks so scornfully he made his way as far as Orleans where he spent about two months. 'Two days after my Arrival at Orleans', he writes, 'I sold my Horse for Twenty Five Crowns, being unwilling to be at the charge of keeping him, and I went to Paris in the Stage Coach'.[97]

Most of our travellers simply speak of a 'coach', though some of them use the French word, *diligence*, a vehicle which was supposed to be faster than an ordinary stage coach. Thus Locke writes of his departure from Paris for the South in December 1675: 'We took coach at Paris in the diligence for Lyons', a vehicle he tells us, with eight horses and two postilions. In practice Locke and his companion travelled in it only as far as Chalon-sur-Saône where they took a boat to Lyons. Although he found travelling down the Saône very pleasant, he did not enjoy the first part of the journey from Paris: 'Thus in 7 days we came from Paris to Lyons, 100 leagues, in a coach cald the diligence for which we paid 25 crowns. The passage to Challon in it was very troublesom, for we were most commonly cald up every morning between 2 & 3, staid about an hower at dinner & then on till an hower or 2 in night, & were some times inconveniently enough lodgd'.[98] A few years later Veryard writes without comment: 'Leaving Nantes we took places in the Coach, call'd *La Diligence*, which brought us to Rochelle in two Days and half'.[99] In contrast, Northleigh is decidedly sarcastic about the speed of these vehicles when, after describing his river trips between Paris and Fontainebleau, he adds: 'In the second Passage I made thro' this Country, their *Carosse de Diligence*, or flying Coach of Lyons, (that notwithstanding its voluble Name makes no more Speed than some of our ordinary Hackney Coaches) brought me thro' some of these Places, and thro' Fountainbleau'.[100]

Most of the journeys our travellers made by stage coach were on such obvious routes as those between Paris and Calais, Rouen, Orleans and Lyons, but cross-country journeys were also possible. Thus Edward Browne travelled by this means from Marseilles to Aix-en-Provence and from Montpellier to Toulouse, while, as we have just seen, Veryard could go from Nantes to La Rochelle. Stage coaches apparently ran between France and the Spanish Netherlands: Howell used this means of transport between Brussels and Paris in 1622, and some forty years later Lauder made the same journey in the opposite direction.

Apart from the physical dangers involved in these various means of transport our travellers faced further hazards, those from footpads as well as from marauding soldiers.[101] Many of them express the fear they felt at various points on their journeys that they and their companions might suddenly be attacked by robbers. Thus Coryate relates that when they came to the entrance to a large forest south of Montreuil, 'a French man that was in our company, spake to us to take our swords in our hands, because sometimes there are false knaves in many places of the Forrest that lurke under trees and shrubbes, and suddenly set upon travellers, and cut their throtes, except the true men are too strong for them'.[102] Half a century later Skippon noted on his journey from Fontainebleau to Paris: 'We rode about a league, and pass'd among rocks, where travellers are often robb'd',[103] and some twenty years later, on a journey from Rennes to Caen, Ferrier records: 'We were forced to goe through a very dangerous forest which though small there are a great many people loose their lives in it. There were not above a week or 8 days before our being there severall men taken out & condemned'.[104] Traveller after traveller records the ghastly sight of men left hanging from gallows or broken on the wheel[105] which they encountered along the roads of France. Yet this spectacle was not very effective as a deterrent. Evelyn records a narrow escape on the road from Étampes to Orleans:

> The next day we had excellent Way; but had like to come short home; for no sooner were we entred two or three leagues into the Forest of Orleans (which extends it selfe for many miles) after dinner; but the Company behind us, were set on by Rogues who shooting from the hedges and frequent Covert, slew fowre upon the spot, the rest flying: Amongst the slayne was a Captaine of Swisses of the Regiment of Picardy, a person much lamented: This disaster made such an Alarme in Orleans at our arrival; that the Prevost-Martial with his assistants going in pursuite, brought in two whom they had shot, and exposed them in the greate Market-place, to see if any would take cognizance of them. I have greate Cause to give God thankes for this Escape.[106]

Some of our travellers came closer still to real footpads. Lithgow relates a long story of how on his way from Cannes to Fréjus 'three French murderers set upon me in a theevish Wood twelve miles long; one of which had dogged me hither from Niece: Where having extremely given me a fearefull chase, for a long League, and not mending themselves, they gave me over'. He found an inn in the wood, but, he continues, 'after I had sup'd and going to bed, in came these aforesayd Villaines, accompanied by my Host; where, when seene, they straight accused me for my flight, and threatening me with stroakes, consulted my Death. Then I cryed to my Host for helpe, but hee stood dumbe, for he was their Companion'. Finally he persuaded them that he was a poor pilgrim who had no money, and they departed to eat and drink before leaving the inn at dawn. When he arrived at Fréjus, he adds, 'I learned that my Host was suspected to bee a Consort with these and many more Murderers; well afterwards I heard, hee was arraigned, hanged, and quartered, the house razed, and his wife put to death: and ever since the French King, keepeth a guard of Horse-men there to keepe that filthy and dangerous woode free from Murderers'.[107]

Apparently footpads could sometimes be less dangerous. Lassels relates with obvious admiration the resolute behaviour of Lady Catherine Whetenall when, on their entry into France from the Spanish Netherlands, they were accosted by footpads: 'But here her ladyship speaking to the rogues with an undaunted courage and scorning their threats to shoot us, made them fall much in their demands and instead of six pounds, which att first they asked, go away contented with somthing to drinke. Some Dutchmen comeing the same way a day or two after, were content to be robbed & stript by the same men'.[108]

The anonymous author of *A New Journey*, being well provided with firearms, was able to put up a successful resistance when travelling from Hesdin to Doullens half a century later. He and his two companions encountered 'a tall ill-looked Fellow with a Hunting Pole in his Hand, having a sharp Iron Point to it, like a half Pike, holding his Left-hand in his Coat pocket, with a pocket Pistol as we afterwards understood'. Seeing this man joined by three others, the writer provided his companions with pistols, and when they had to pass through a wood, he relates how 'we perceived these Four Foot-pads issuing out of the Wood, each having a Pole in one Hand, and a Pocket Pistol in the other. I charg'd them to keep off, that there was no Booty to be got by us: but still they approach'd, and the most forward fired his Pistol and wounded my Horse in the Thigh, at the same time the Scotchman fired and shot the Rogue in the Left Arm; whereupon he claping his Hand on the Wound, and crying *Sacre dieu, je suis mort*, they all made the best of their Way from us'.

According to the same writer French highwaymen were much more dangerous to travellers than English 'for they commonly first kill and then strip; because as they say, *Un chien mort n'abboye pas*, A dead Dog never Barks; thereby taking off the chief Evidence, which shews their Barbarity (notwithstanding all the renown's Civility of that Nation) in Comparison of our generous English Highway-men, who seldom or never kill, unless resistance is made, so that they may be in danger of their own Lives'.[109]

Despite the varied hardships and dangers met with on the roads, rivers and canals of seventeenth-century France, all our travellers survived to tell their tale.

D

II ECONOMIC AND SOCIAL CONDITIONS

(a) The Land and the Peasants

Coming from a small island with far fewer inhabitants and a harsher climate, many of our travellers were greatly struck with the size, population, fertility and wealth of France. On his return from his embassy in 1609 Sir George Carew wrote: 'The fertility of their territory considered, and that the country is everywhere stored with great and well peopled, yea, and well stored cities and towns, full of all sorts of artificers, and manufacturers; it may be accounted the greatest united and entire force of any realm or dominion at the present in Christendome'.[1] In speaking of the military might of France, Evelyn declared that 'another thing rendring this Kingdom very considerable for an Army, is their Prolifique multiplying; for Europe embraceth not a more populous nation, nor more abounding in Victuals, which is the belly of that cruel Beast, called War'.[2] Several decades later this impression of a fertile and densely populated country is also conveyed by Veryard: 'It's certainly the most populous Country of its extent in Europe, and no less fertile and abounding in Corn, Wine, Olives, Almonds and Figs, which, together with the Hemp, Flax, and Silk, have created a very considerable Commerce, greatly facilitated by diverse navigable Rivers, and Sea Ports commodiously seated for Traffick'.[3]

Despite the highly satirical tone of Heylyn's account of his travels, he waxes lyrical in his description of the magnificent harvests which he found on his arrival in Normandy:

> For, indeed, the Countrey of Normandie is enriched with a fat and liking soil . . . In my life I never saw Corn-fields more large and lovely, extended in an equal levell almost as far as eye can reach. The Wheat (for I saw little Barley) of a fair length in the stalke, and so heavy in the ear, that it even bended double. You would think the grain had a desire to kisse the earth its mother, or that it purposed by making it self away int~ the ground, to save the Plough-man his next years labour. Thick it groweth, and so perfectly void of weeds, that no garden can be imagined to be kept cleaner by Art, then these fields are by Nature.[4]

Those who penetrated into the southern half of the kingdom

inevitably fell for the exotic products of a Mediterranean climate. Bromley, it is true, does not altogether share the enthusiasm for Languedoc shown by some other writers. 'The Province of Languedoc', he declares 'is a poor, barren Country, mountainous, and full of Stones; yet in this steril Soil, covered in a manner wholly with Stones, good Corn is got; *Ingenii largitor est Venter*, is visible here; for they have many Vineyards; which, besides the Vines, are thick planted with Olive-Trees'.[5] Veryard gives a very different impression of this province when he describes how the tower of Narbonne cathedral offered him and his companion 'a pleasant prospect of a fruitful and most delicious Country, where human Industry has abundantly improv'd the natural Fertility and Beauty of the neighbouring Plains: which produce great abundance of excellent Wine, Lemmons, Oranges, Pomegranates, Almonds, and Olives'.[6] Bromley describes the part of Provence round Arles as 'generally rocky and barren', though he does add, 'Some of it is more fertil, affording great plenty of Olive, Almond, Fig and Walnut-Trees, besides their Vines'.[7] Once again Veryard is much more enthusiastic in his description of this province:

> Nothing could have been more pleasant and diverting than our Journey thro' Provence, where all our Senses were even cloy'd with an immense variety of the most agreeable and charming Objects. I fancied it to be one great Garden, where the Rival Products of Nature seem'd to contend for the Masterdom: the Fields and cultivated Hills are stor'd with Vines, Almonds, Olives, Figs, Oranges and Pomegranates: and the Wast Ground (if I may say so call it) is over-spread with Rosemary, Time, Marjoram, Lavender, Myrtil, and divers other odoriferous and medicinal Plants. In a word, it's the most fruitful and dilectable Province on this side of the Alpes, and justly stil'd the Paradise of France.[8]

Lister who was a young man had spent a long period in the South even urges Louis XIV as he grows older to abandon Versailles and to move his court to a warmer Mediterranean climate:

> The very Fields are most Excellent, and well furnisht Parterrs of Flowers, and are naturally Pottageries, or Kitchen Gardens. The Vineyards are very Orchards: and all the most tender Fruits with us are there Standards; as Figs and Grapes of all sorts, Apricocks, Peaches, Nectorins, Jujubs, &c. The delicious and large Cherries; and, whatever has been said to the contrary, Pipins and Pears there are in far greater perfection, than with us, or in any parts of France else, besides that happy Climate.

He recommends in particular the town of Pézenas 'seated in the bottom of a well Watered Valley, inclosed with perfumed Hills'.[9]

Yet from one end of this period to the other our travellers are practically unanimous in describing the lot of the average peasant as a most unhappy one. Writing, it is true, at the close of the Wars of Religion, Dallington declares: 'As for the poore Paisant, he fareth very hardly, and feedeth most upon bread and fruits', adding the not very consoling observation: 'but yet hee may comfort himselfe with this, that though his fare be nothing so good, as the ploughmans, and poore Artificers in England, yet it is much better then that of the *villano* in Italy'.[10] The reason why the French government is compelled to recruit so many mercenaries for the Army, declares Sir George Carew, is

> that they keep their yeomanry in such servitude, as neither dare they trust weapons in their hands, nor can they spare them from the tilling of their ground; nor yet are these capable of being good soldiers, being kept continually both out of heart, by the violent and proud commandment and insolence of their landlords, and from means of wealth to furnish themselves of necessaries requisite to be a soldier, or to make them bodies lusty and able; but their minds are base and dastardly, and their bodies wearish and shrimp-like.[10a]

At the same date Overbury writes in lurid terms of the lot of the peasants: 'For the people; All those that have any kinde of profession or Trade, live well: but for the meere Peasants that labour the ground, they are onely Spunges to the King, to the Church and the Nobilitie, having nothing to their owne, but to the use of them, and are scarce allowed (as Beasts) enough to keepe them able to doe service; for besides their Rent, they pay usually two thirds to the King'.[11]

Shortly after his arrival in France in 1619 James Howell sent his father from Rouen the usual lyrical account of the riches of France, only to stress how unequally the country's wealth was distributed:

> I am now upon the fair Continent of France, one of Natures choicest Master-peeces; one of Ceres chiefest Barns for Corn; one of Bacchus prime Wine-Cellars, and of Neptuns best Salt-Pits; a compleat self-sufficient Countrey, wher ther is rather a superfluity, then defect of any thing, either for necessity or pleasure, did *the policie of the Countrey correspond with Nature, in the equall distribution of the Wealth amongst the Inhabitants;* for I think there is not upon the Earth, a richer Countrey, and poorer people.[12]

A few years later Heylyn several times contrasts the lot of the peasant with that of the nobleman:

> Yet I cannot withall but affirme, that the Princes and Nobles

of France, do, for as much as concernth themselves, upon all advantages flie off from the Kings obedience: but all this while the poor Paisant is ruined: let the poor Tenant starve, or eat the bread of carefulnesse, it matters not, so they may have their pleasure, and be counted firm zelots of the common liberty. And certainly this is the issue of it, the former liveth the life of a slave to maintain his Lord in pride and lazinesse; the Lord liveth the life of a King to oppresse his Tenant by fines and exactions.

Writing in the troubled years of the reign of Louis XIII when the Crown was encountering much opposition from the princes of the blood and great nobles, Heylyn declares:

Thus live the French princes, thus the Nobles. Those sheep which God and the Lawes hath brought under them, they do not sheer but fleece; and which is worse than this, having themselves taken away the Wooll, they give up the naked carcasse to the King... Here the Lords and the King, though otherwise at oddes amongst themselves, will be sure to agree in this, the undoing and oppressing of the poor Paisant.[13]

In the pages which he devotes to the peasants Heylyn offers a remarkably black picture of their clothes, housing and meagre diet. Of men's clothing he writes:

For their Apparell it is well they can allow themselves Canvasse, or an outside of that nature. As for Cloth, it is above their purse equally, and their ambition: if they can aspire unto Fustian, they are as happy as their wishes, and he that is so arrayed, will not spare to aime at the best Place in the Parish, even unto that of the Church-warden. When they go to plough or to the Church, they have shoes and stockins; at other times they make bold with nature, and wear their skins. Hats they will not want, though their bellies pinch for it: and that you may be sure they have them, they will alwayes keep them on their heads: the most impudent custome of a beggerly fortune, that ever I met with.

The clothes of their womenfolk were even more wretched:

As for the women, they know in what degree nature hath created them, and therefore dare not be so fine as their Husbands: some of them never had above one pair of stockins in all their lives, which they wear every day, for indeed they are very durable. The goodnesse of their faces tell us, that they have no need of a band, therefore they use none. And as concerning Petticoats, so it is, that all of them have such a garment, but most of them so short, that you would imagine them to be cut off at the placket.

Such miserable clothes, when completely rotten with wear, 'are a new cut-out and fitted to the children'. The living conditions of peasants are depicted by Heylyn as equally miserable: 'Search into their houses, and you shall finde them very wretched, destitute as well of furniture as provision. No Butter salted up against Winter, no powdring tub, no Pullein in the Rick-barren, no flesh in the pot or at the spit, and which is worst, no money to buy them.

The peasants' diet, according to the same source, was extremely plain:

> The best provision they can shew you is a piece of Bacon wherewith they fatten their pottage; and now and then the inwards of Beasts killed for the Gentlemen. But of all miseries, this me thinketh is the greatest, that sowing so many acres of excellent wheat in an year, and gathering in such a plentifull Vintage as they do, they should not yet be so fortunate, as to eat white bread, or drink wine: for such infinite rents do they pay to their Lords, and such innumerable taxes to the King, that the profits arising out of those commodities, are only sufficient to pay their duties, and keep them from the extremities of cold and famine. The bread then which they eat, is of the coursest flowre, and so black, that it cannot admit the name of brown. And as for their drink, they have recourse to the next Fountain.

What made the peasant's lot even harder to bear, according to Heylyn, was the impossibility of escaping from 'this hell of bondage' owing to the exactions of the lord of the manor and the tax collector:

> If industry and a sparing hand hath raised any of these afflicted people so high, that he is but 40 s. or 5 l. richer then his neighbour, his Lord immediately enhaunceth his Rents, and enformeth the Kings task-masters of his riches, by which means he is within two or three years brought again to equall poverty with the rest. A strange course, and much different from that of England, where the Gentry take a delight in having their Tenants thrive under them, and hold it no crime in any that hold of them to be wealthy. On the other side, those of France can abide no body to gain or grow rich upon their farmes; and therefore thus upon occasions rack their poor tenants.[14]

One has to bear in mind that, although Heylyn visited only the relatively rich agricultural regions of Northern France, his contact with the peasants cannot have been very close since he spent just over two months in France, a good deal of the time in Paris. Consequently one cannot help feeling that the picture which he offers of the miseries of peasant life is rather too highly coloured.

Evelyn has very little to say about the peasantry, even in his essay on the state of France in 1652; but he does offer one vivid picture of what the peasants had to suffer in wartime from the depredations of armies, including their own. Returning from a short trip to England, he arrived in Calais in August 1650 at a time when a Spanish army was advancing from the frontier towards Paris and thus he encountered retreating French troops. 'Next morning', he writes, 'the regiment of Picardy consisting of about 1400 horse & foote, and among them a Captain whom I knew, being come to Towne; I tooke horses for myselfe & servant, and march'd under their Protection to Boulogne: 'Twas a miserable spectacle, to see how these tatter'd souldiers, pillag'd the poore People of their Sheepe, poultry, Corne, Catell & whatever came in their Way: but they had such ill pay, that they were ready themselves to sterve: 27: I din'd at Montreull & lay at Abb-Ville now past danger, and warning the poor people (infinitely inquisitive & thankfull) how the Souldiers treated their neighbours, & were marching towards them'.[15]

One can in fact glean little useful information about the peasant's lot in travellers' accounts produced in the middle of the century. Symonds who had done the same journey from Calais to Paris at the beginning of the previous year has only a few comments to offer such as that 'their Cottages stinke as bad as the inhabitants' and that 'Here the Country people pull off their hatts & goe out of the way with their waynes'. Later, on his journey from Roanne to Lyons, he noted in a village: 'The inhabitants barefooted of the common sort'.[16] Reresby who spent a much longer period in France has little of interest to offer, though he does observe that to have troops quartered on a district even in peace time could mean ruin to the inhabitants: 'But the officers, as well as soldiers, are so ill paid, that they wholly, in a manner, subsist by false musters, free quarter, and preying upon the country; so that an assignment of a country for winter quarters is considered as little less than the sale of it to the soldiery, to take their utmost advantage of, for that term'. However, his other remarks about the peasant's lot are merely wild generalizations, for instance, 'As to the peasants, they are certainly the most miserable, slavish people in the world'.[17]

Although Lauder's observations occasionally border on the puerile (he was only nineteen when he arrived in France), he has some interesting comments to offer on the condition of the peasants. It is true that he too produces some wild generalizations as when he speaks of 'the miserablenese and ignorantnese of the peasants of France above all other commonalty of the world; our beggars leading a better life than the most part of them do'. Yet he makes some more useful remarks about laws on hunting, though what he has to say applies not only to France since he seeks to explore 'the reasons that have moved the Princes to hem in so narrow bounds the rights of

Hunting'[18]; this does, however, involve a discussion of the hated *droit de chasse* which was such a burden on the peasants under the Ancien Régime. During his stay at Poitiers he also noted a clash between the peasants and the inhabitants of the town:

> About the end of Octobre the peasants brings in their fruits to Poictiers to sel, especially their Apples, and that in loadened chariots. The beggar wifes and stirrows[19] ware sure to be their, piking them furth in neiwfulles[20] on all sydes. I hav sein the peasents and them fall be ears thegither, the lads with great apples would have given him sick a slap on the face that the cowll[21] would have bein almost like to greet; yet with his rung[22] he would have given them a sicker neck herring[23] over the shoulders. I am sure that the halfe of them was stollen from many or they got them sold.[24]

More significant is his comment on farming leases in which as a budding lawyer he had an obvious interest:

> We are informed that a lardship of 5000 livres rent will sell in France for a 100,000 livres; and by consequence a place of 15,000 livres a year at 100,000 crounes; the prix being ay 20 years rents. It may wary in many places of France. Location-conduction[25] of lands, called their ferming, are very usuall in France; yea, the most part of Gentlemens houses rises with that, having bein first fermier or goodmen[26] (as we calle them) of the place.

There is no doubt some exaggeration in this last remark; yet it does show consciousness of the fact that, however poor a great many peasants may have been, there was also a small minority of prosperous tenant farmers who could gradually rise out of their class into the minor nobility.

One curious point made by Lauder in speaking of French as 'the Elegantest tongue' is his admiration for the way even the downtrodden peasants expressed themselves:

> We have bein whiles amazed to hear how copiously and richly the poor peasants in their meiting on another would expresse themselfes and compliment, their wery language bearing them to it; so that a man might have sein more civility in their expressions (as to their gesture its usually not wery seimly) then may be fund in the first compliments on a rencontre betuixt 2 Scots Gentlemen tolerably well breed.

Wooden shoes (*sabots*) which before the Revolution were often regarded in this country as a symbol of the poverty of the French peasantry are described quite objectively by Lauder who simply indicates both their advantages and disadvantages:

They have another use for wood in that country also which we know not: they make sabots of them, which the peasants serve themselves with instead of shoes; in some account they are better then shoes. They will not draw nor take in water as shoes whiles do, they being made of one intier lump of wood and that whiles meikle enough. Their disadvantage is this: non can run with them, they being loose and not fastened to our feet, yet some weill used them can also run in them. They buy them for wery little money.[27]

Other travellers were also struck by the use of wooden shoes. Coryate comments mainly on their cheapness when he states that at Nevers 'I saw many wooden shoes which are worne onely of the peasants of the countrey. I saw them worne in many other places also: they are usually sold for two Sowses which is two pence farthing'.[28] Lithgow appears to have been most impressed by the noise they made, since he warns the traveller not 'to lye neere the fore-streetes of a Towne; because of the disturbant clamours of the Peasant samboies or nayle-wooden shoes'.[29] When approaching Paris on his way from Lyons Covel notes laconically, 'Villanes in wooden shoes, yet look well and seem content'.[30] They are definitely associated with poverty by Skippon when he writes that 'the poor people about Montpelier wear wooden shoes in the winter-time, which they call *Sabou*'.[31] The point is made more forcefully by Northleigh: 'The wooden Shoes as hard as they are, fit easy enough, to those that never trod on leather; especially when they hear that in Germany some of their neighbouring Countreys, they have neither to wear'.[32] Locke, who sampled them on his way from Calais to Paris with the messenger, did not at all approve of them as he makes clear in writing to a friend: 'This smal tast of Sabots gave me a surfet of them and left such an aversion to them in my stomach that I shall never make choise of a country to passe my pilgrimage in, where they are in fashion.' He adds in the bantering tone which he sometimes adopts in his letters: ''Tis possible they may be very necessary to the aiery people of this country who, being able to run, skip & dance in these, would certainly mount into the aire & take most wonderful frisks, were there not such clogs at their heels; but I believe a dul, heavy Englishman might be as soon brought to dance & jig with a pair of stocks about his ankles, as to walke the streets in such brogues as these, though they were never soe curiously carved, as I have seen some of them'.[33]

It is to Locke that we must turn for a more detailed and above all a more balanced view of the lot of the peasants than that provided by the other travellers. In his three and a half years in France during which he twice toured a substantial part of the country, he made copious notes on the state of agriculture, even talking to peasants in the fields. It could not be said that he was favourably impressed by what he saw of their economic position and living standards. His views on Provence, when he ended his tour of it at Tarascon in April 1676, form a decided contrast with Veryard's lyrical passage on the richness of the province:

Here we passed the Rhosne again & left Provence, a country, however commended, wherein I had seen more barren ground then fruitful, & yet had passed the best part of it. The people too, if one may judg by their clothes & diet, had, like the country, 5 acres of poverty for one of riches, for I remember at Aix in a gardiner's house, where we found them eating, their Sunday dinner was noe thing but slices of congeald blood fried in oile which an English gent. was with me would needs tast, though to the turning his stomach.

Two years later while travelling on the other side of the country from Richelieu to La Meilleraye, he passed through a succession of small places 'which they called bourghs, but considering the poornesse & fewnesse of the houses in most of them, would in England but scarce amount to vilages. Their houses generally were but one story: and though such low buildings, which one can scarce see till one is amongst them, cost not much too keepe them up, yet, like groveling bodys without soules, they also sinke lower when they want inhabitants, of which sort of ruins we saw great numbers in all these bourgs, whereby one would guesse that the people of France doe not at present increase, at least in the country. But yet the country is all tilled & well cultivated'.

A most vivid passage, packed with precise detail, on the lot of the poorer peasants occurs in the entry in which Locke describes his visit to the Graves vineyards outside Bordeaux:

Talkeing in this country with a poore paisant's wife, she told us she had 3 children; that her husband got usually 7s. per diem, findeing himselfe, which was to maintein their family, 5 in number. She indeed got 3 or 3½s. per diem when she could get worke, which was but seldome. Other times she span hemp, which was for their clothes & yielded noe mony. Out of this 7s. per diem they 5 were to be mainteind, & house rent paid & their taile, & Sundays & holy days provided for.

For their house which, God wot, was a pore one roome & one story open to the tiles, without window, & a little vineyard which was as bad as noe thing (for though they made out of it 4 or 5 tiers of wine — 3 tiers make 2 hogheads — yet the labor & cost about the vineyard, makeing the wine & cask to put it in, being cast up, the profit of it was very litle) they paid 12 ecus per annum rent & for taile £4, for which, not long since, the collector had taken their frying pan & dishes, mony not being ready. Their ordinary food rie bread & water. Flesh is a thing seldome seasons their pots &, as she said, they make noe distinction between flesh & fasting days but when their mony reaches to a more costly meale, they buy the inwards of some beast in the market & then they feast themselves. And yet they say that in Xantonge & severall other parts of France the paisants are much more miserable than these, for these they count the flourishing paisants which live in Grave.[34]

No doubt one must not take these remarks too literally. They certainly could not apply to the lot of all peasants at the high point of the reign of Louis XIV, however true they might be of those inhabitants of the countryside who depended mainly or wholly for a living on their casual earnings as agricultural labourers.

Two other observations of Locke on the condition of the peasants are of interest. On his way from Saintes to Blaye he noted the dual purpose served by the new crop, maize: 'That which I observd particularly in it was plots of Maize in severall parts, which the country people call bled d'Espagne, &, as they told me, serves poore people for bred. That which makes them sow it, is not only the great increase, but the convenience also which the blade & green about the stalks yeilds them, it being good nourishment for their cattle.' Earlier, after leaving the Papal territory at Avignon, he observed that the land on the way to Tarascon was not as well cultivated as that in the Comtat Venaissin: 'Moderate taxes & a freedom from quarter', he concludes, 'gives the Pope's subjects, as it seems, more industry'.[35]

During his fortnight's trip to the Calais region Kennet, in speaking of the markets held at Ardres, noted one sign of poverty amongst the least favoured peasants: 'The only marketting of severall poor women no more than a bundle of wood which they bring on their backs 4 or 5 miles and sell for 4d'.[36] Bromley makes only one observation of interest on this topic and it is a very general one. Speaking of his journey from Calais through Paris to Lyons he writes: 'All along as I travelled hitherto, I could not but take notice of those great indications of Poverty that appeared in the Looks and Habits of the People, as well as their wretched Houses'.[37]

In his rapid summing up on the different social classes in France Northleigh too offers only a somewhat one-sided view of the peasant's lot: 'The Peasant is he that tills the Countrey and manures it too; for which, hard Fare, and small Wages, are all his Gains; a Belly full is all he aims at, and not Barns full; for Granaries he has none but what he carries about him'. His lot, he concludes, is a form of slavery from which there is no release: 'And if thro' several Reigns an uninterrupted War has so habituated them to hardship, if not Misery, that they do not feel it; whatever we may flatter ourselves the Government is the stronger by their weakness: When the sense of Liberty is worn out, and Prescription is to be pleaded for Slavery; what is there that a People won't suffer?' Their poverty, according to Northleigh, is what enables France to raise such large armies: 'No wonder their Armies are so numerous, when Men must ingloriously starve at home, or take honourable Pay to die abroad'.[38]

Veryard has little to say about the lot of the peasants except for those whom he encountered in the mountains on his way from the Grande Chartreuse into Savoy. 'The Natives of these Parts', he writes, 'are of a swarthy Complexion, miserably poor, and living for the most part on Milk, Butter and Cheese, which they have from a few Cows, Goats, and Sheep, they make a shift to feed amongst the Mountains; and for which they have little other Fodder in Winter, but the leaves and tender tops of Ash, which they cut off and dry in Summer, as we do our Hay. However, these poor People are as well satisfy'd and as light-hearted as if they enjoy'd all the Delights of an earthly Paradise'.

He has, however, some interesting remarks to make on the diet of the greater part of the population which he considers extremely frugal: 'The French are very sparing in their Diet; the poorer sort eat little but Bread, nay the greater part of the People use not much Flesh, feeding commonly on Sallet and Soupe'.[39] After seeing earlier on his journey from Calais evidence of the ravages caused by the incursions of armies in the recently ended War of the Spanish Succession, the author of *A New Journey* describes the poor fare which he and his companions were offered in a village halfway between Doullens and Amiens where they had dinner: 'We could get neither Flesh, Fish, or Wine, but were forc'd to be contented with sower brown Bread, nasty Butter, and a few Eggs, with musty stinking Beer, so miserable Poor the People are'.[40]

What made the lot of the mass of the population, especially the medium and poorer classes of peasants, harder to bear was their dependence on bread as the staple article of diet since its price was subject to violent fluctuations, produced by the recurring grain shortages. Our travellers seem to have managed to miss the worst periods of crisis such as that of 1693–4 with its devastating effects over a wide area of France. Locke did, however, note the wide seasonal fluctuations in wheat prices when he passed through Abbeville on his way home in May 1679: 'The best wheat sold to day in the market per boisseau 15s., almost double the price it was sold for at Christmas'. He also mentions the other side of the medal — the low agricultural prices which, except in periods of bad harvests, prevailed in most of France during the whole personal reign of Louis XIV. Three years earlier in Montpellier he made this laconic entry in his journal: 'The rents of Lands in France fallen above ½ in these few years by reason of the poverty of the people & want of mony'.[41]

The low standard of living of the great majority of the peasants was due in part to the population being beyond what the land could support, but also to primitive agricultural methods and the consequent low yields of crops. In the Calais region our travellers found a scene which was familiar to them — horses used for ploughing. 'Ploughs drove with 3 horses a breast while the same person holds & drives', Kennet noted,[42] while earlier Symonds observed: 'Here the Country people plough with 3 small horses that goe all abreast & wheele ploughs as in Kent and lay their land as in Kent'.[43] This was, of course, in the richer agricultural region of the North. As Locke travelled down the Rhone valley between Vienne and Pont St.Esprit he noted a very different spectacle — 'severall digging the ground & other where some a ploughing with a very litle, light plow with one handle, drawne by a pair of cows, steers or asses which the ploughman drives himself. The soyle is generally light & sandy, & they turne it up with their ploughs not above 2 or 3 inches deepe'. While in Montpellier he observed: 'They plough the earth here very shallow & usually with one mule', and then proceeded to give a detailed description of this primitive form of plough (the *araire*).[44]

Three decades later Jethro Tull was also in Languedoc and from seeing the way the peasants ploughed their vineyards without using dung he evolved his system for the cultivation of corn. 'From these', he writes, 'I took my Vineyard Scheme, observing that indifferent Land produces an annual Crop of Grapes and Wood without Dung'. His *Horse-hoing Husbandry* contains several references to agriculture in that part of France. 'The dung'd Vineyards in Languedoc, produce nauseous Wine', he declares, 'from whence there is a Proverb in that Country, That Poor People's Wine is best, because they carry no Dung to their Vineyards'. Virgil's plough, he writes in speaking of Italy, 'continues to this Day in those Countries', adding 'and in Languedoc'. Such a light plough, while suited to these regions, would not be of service in English conditions: 'This sort of Plow performs tolerably when Ground is fine, and makes a shift to break up light Land; and I could never find any other Land there; I am sure, none comparable to ours for strength: And it would be next to impossible, to break up such as we in England call Strong Land, with it'. He also has a good deal to say about the cultivation of lucerne in this and other regions of France.[45]

While spending three months in the country outside Montpellier in the summer of 1676, Locke remarked on the low yield of the grain crops: 'Their usuall increase of wheat is 4 for one, their greatest 7 or 8 for one'. He also made a long note on the way the peasants there threshed their corn:

> Their corn being cut, they carry it to some place in the fields and there put it together in little mows, and so, as fast as they can, thrash it in a round place about 30 or 40 steps diameter, made bare, or rather tread it out with mules and so winnow it on the place, and so keep it in granaryes all the year. Their way of winnowing or rather raying is with a great sieve hung up with one rope buckled to it with 3 straps of leather and supported with 3 sticks pyramidically erected. The sieve is a yard or more over and bottomed with a thick kind of parchment, cut with round and long holes to let the other seeds and earth through, for by this way of thrashing there is a great deal of dust and earth mixed with the corn. If during their threshing there happen any rain to make their threshing floor smoother & harder, they cover it with straw and so tread it over with mules, which they do in this manner. They hoodwink their mules and so, taking a halter of about 2 yards long, they fasten one end to a mule's head and the other end to an other like a long halter, which is likewise fastened to the other mule's head. To the mule thus haltered they tie about his neck the other mule haltered & blinded that so they go 2 abreast as in a cart. 8 being thus fitted and all their long halters fastened together, in the middle there stands a man who makes the mules trot about, and so, as he pleases, gently removes them from one side to the other of the thrashing floor. They tell me one pair of mules thrashes in a day 25 Septies of corn.

Earlier he had noted that when the corn was cut and made into little stacks in the fields, the peasants 'watch it night and day till it be thrashed there and so carried home'.[46]

It was not without reason that many of our travellers attribute a great part of the poverty of the peasants to an oppressive taxation system, since the main burden of direct taxation undoubtedly fell on them. At the very beginning of our period Dallington makes this clear when he speaks of the *taille*, the principal direct tax: 'These *tailles* are onely lyable upon the *Plat païs* (the County); all Cities are exempt, as also all Officers of the Kings house, all Counsellors, Lawyers, and Officers of Courtes of Parliament, all the Nobilitie, the *Gensdarmes*, the Officers of warre, the Graduates of Universities, &c'.[47] Sir

George Carew not only agrees that the peasants were the chief sufferers from the taxation system, but, far from supporting the notion that Henry IV was a popular king, he describes this section of the community as being 'so infinitely oppresst, as they have their mouths filled with imprecations and bitter complaints, exclaiming that their king seeketh not to be *Roy des François*, but *des Gueux*'.[48] Although in stressing the way in which the main burden of this tax fell on the peasants Heylyn seems merely to have copied Dallington, he does also make the point that whereas in this country the equivalent tax was 'granted by the people, and the sum of it certain', in France it was 'at the pleasure of the King, and in what manner he shall please to impose them'.[49]

He offers considerably more detail on the subject of the salt tax (*gabelle*) which he correctly described as not falling with equal weight on the different provinces, since some paid a very heavy tax, others a much lighter one, and some were totally exempt. His comments on this tax, particularly where it was most burdensome, are severe:

This Gabell, is, indeed, a Monopoly, and that one of the unjustest and unreasonablest in the World. For no man in the Kingdom (those Countries hereafter excepted) can eat any Salt, but he must buy of the King and at his price, which is most unconscionable; that being sold at Paris and elsewhere for five Livres, which in the exempted places is sold for one. Therefore that the Kings profits might not be diminished, there is diligent watch and ward, that no forain Salt be brought into the Land, upon pain of forfeiture and imprisonment. A search which is made so strictly, that we had much ado at Dieppe to be pardoned the searching of our trunks and port-mantles, and that not, but upon solemn protestation, that we had none of that commodity. This Salt is of brown colour, being only such as we in England call Bay-salt; and imposed on the Subjects by the Kings Officers with great rigour, for though they have some of their last provision in the house, or perchance would be contect (through poverty) to eat meat without it, yet will these cruell villaines enforce them to take such a quantity of them; or howsoever they will have of them so much money.[50]

Heylyn's account of other indirect taxes such as customs and excise duties (*traites* and *aides*) is not lacking in indignation, but is somewhat confused. The tax-farmers (*partisans* or *traitants*) who collected these taxes have their depredations described in scathing terms:

A Nation so abominably full of base and unmanly villaines in their severall charges, that the Publicans of Old-Rome, were milke and white broath to them. For so miserably do they abuse the poor Paisant, that if he hath in all the world but eight Sols, it shall go hard, but he will extort from him five of them . . . Their Taxings and Assessments are left arbitrary, and are exacted accordingly as these Publicans will give out of the Kings necessities; so that the Countryman hath no other remedy, then to give Cerberus a crust, as the saying is, to kisse his rod and hug his punishment.

The large fortunes to be made by *financiers* are duly stressed though Heylyn does mention that these ill-gotton gains were sometimes taken away:

By this means the Questors thrive abundantly, it being commonly said of them, *Hier bouvier auiourdhui chevalier*, to day a Swine-heard, tomorrow a Gentleman; and certainly they grow into great riches. Mr. Beaumarchais one of the Treasurers (Mr. De Vilroy, who slew the Marquesse d'Ancre, marryed his only Daughter) having raked unto himself, by the villanous abuse of his place, no lesse then 22 millions of Livres, as it was commonly reported. But he is not like to carry it to his grave, the King having seized upon a good part of it, and himself being condemned to the gallowes by the grand Chambre of Parliament, though as yet he cannot be apprehended and advanced to the Ladder. And this hath been the end of many of them, since the reign of this present King whom (it may be) for this cause, they call *Lewis the just*.[51]

The example given by Heylyn is perfectly correct so far as it goes. One of the *trésoriers de l'Épargne*, Vincent Bouhier de Beaumarchais, was sentenced to death by the Chambre de Justice, set up in 1624 to punish frauds on the Treasury; however, he was hanged only in effigy and later pardoned. Indeed through influence at court he even managed to avoid paying the heavy fine imposed on him.

In contrast Evelyn has relatively little to say on the subject of taxation, even in his *State of France*. It will be noticed that there he envies the French nobility its exemption from such taxes as the *taille*:

Nothwithstanding the Gentry and Nobility (for these tearms are coincident and convertible in France), Churchmen, and their dependants are exempt from these contributions; an immunity which they enjoy as a distinction, which ours of the same quality in England never so much as tasted off; so that (among us) if a person be not Rich, let him be never so well borne, the Peasant is as good a man every whit for any priviledg which the other enjoys above him; through which defect, as there remains little encouragement and reward for ancient vertue or future industry, so must it needs, in time, both utterly confound and degenerate the race of the most illustrious Families, which have hitherto remained.

He correctly notes the great discrepancies in the way in which the *gabelle* was levied when he speaks of people in some regions being compelled 'to buy a certain quantity of the King whether they wil or no; a rigour, some interpret extreamly approaching the very height of extortion: some particular places yet of the Kingdome (as towards the Frontiers and sea towns) are exempted, and have their salt quit of any impost at all'. He also correctly describes (and disapproves of) 'the *Droict d'Aubaine*, by which the goods of strangers dying in France most inhospitably escheat to the King, putting (in this respect) no difference between them and Bastards unnaturalized'.[52] Lauder also comments at some length on the *droit d'aubaine* whereby, as he puts it, on the death of foreigners who were not naturalized, 'dieng, the King is their heir'.[53] In 1650, not only did Sir Ralph Verney lose his wife; he also had to face severe financial loss. 'I have been shrewdly put to it in a way you little dreame off,' he wrote to a friend, 'for by the Lawes of France the king is the heire to all strangers & (the wife by custome being intituled to one halfe) a projecting favorite Begged & obteined this Droict d'Aubaine (that is, the succession of all my wife's estate in France, she dying heere without naturalized or French borne issue)'. However, there seems to have been at least the possibility of avoiding some of the loss, since, he continues, 'uppon a good friend's endeavour, there was a stopp put upon the graunt before the compleat expedition & sealing'. Meanwhile he was certainly taking what steps he could to reduce his losses: 'What Further charge this cunning Catchpole may bring uppon me, I cannot yet foresee, but I have taken what care I can to prevent his plots, & privately disposed the best of my goods, & sent my coach & horses about 40 miles off (to a French freind's house) where I shall (even uppon any Termes) endeavour to have them sould'.[54]

In the 1650s Reresby can offer only a very inadequate account of the system of direct and indirect taxation, ending with the sweeping statement: 'All these are paid by the third estate (the clergy and gentry being free), while the poor peasant is often forced to part with all he has, to the very bed he lies upon, to pay them'.[55] Nor with one notable exception do travellers during the personal reign of Louis XIV have much to say about the taxation system. Lauder notes the great variations in the price of salt between La Rochelle where it was produced and an inland town like Poitiers which was not one of those where the *gabelle* was heaviest: 'On the place wheir they make it its sold for a sous marky la livre which costs at Poictiers 20 sous'.[56] Skippon was struck by the contrast between the French people's complaints about the burden of taxation and their admiration for their young king. [57] The same point is made even more forcibly in

E

Popery and Tyranny: 'They are prouder of having their King take a Town, than of possessing any thing as their own, without being subject to the Griping hand of an Arbitary Publican'.[57a] A little later Veryard speaks merely of 'the People being generally so oppressed with Taxes, which encrease every Day, that their Estates are worth very little more than what they pay to the King; so that they are, as it were, Tenants to the Crown, and at such a rack Rent that they find great difficulty to get their own Bread' — a sweeping generalization if ever there was one.[58] Northleigh produces another wild statement: 'The King's raising of Money, and that of such vast Sums, is not so surprising, since in some few Years, not only the Revenue of the Country, but almost the Value of it, circulates through his Coffers; his Demesne is indeed most of the Kingdom, and Taxes and Impositions little the less'. It is true that elsewhere he offers some more precise comments on the taxation system, distinguishing between the direct taxes of the *taille*, *taillon* and *subsistance*: 'They have their *Taillon* that differs from their Tally, which was Establish'd for maintaining the Army, as the Subsistence has been raised for raising Soldiers since'. 'Their Taxes even in the time of Peace', he maintains, 'are not so well proportioned, and their Collection of them rigid in their Executions'. He has most to say about the *gabelle*, pointing out correctly that 'there are several places that are Frank, and can dispose of their Salt themselves; but those that are adjacent Houses, are obliged to take such a Quantity for their Families out of the King's Granaries'.[59] During his visit to Paris in 1698 Lister merely noted the great increase in excise duty on wine (the *aides*): 'The Tax upon Wines is now so great, that whereas before the War they drank them by Retail at 5d the Quart, they now sell them at 15d. the Quart and dearer, which has inhansed the Rates of all Commodities, and Workmens Wages'.[60]

By far the best informed and most detailed account of the taxation system, not only for the high point of the reign of Louis XIV, but for the whole century is provided by Locke. He went to endless trouble to collect material and always bore in mind that under the Ancien Régime there was nothing like a uniform system over the whole country. His first detailed account of the *taille* is to be found in a long entry in September 1676 when he was in Montpellier, in a province which had its own Estates and where the *taille* was *réelle*, i.e. levied on the amount of land, and not, as in most provinces which lacked estates, *personnelle*, i.e. levied on estimated income. Here it is the latter form of tax which he describes:

> The way of laying on the Taille is this. The King's Counsil judges how much is needed. That being agreed, they send to

every generality, v.g. Orleans, Commissioners to levy their quota. The Intendant of the place, with the Elus who are all officers appointed by the King, assess the several parishers within that generality and appoint collectors in each parish who assesse the rest of the parish. The assessment made, they bring it to the Elus who sign and soe ratifie it and give the collectors a commission to collect it, who are answerable for the money. If any one find him agreivd, he complains to the Elus, and if they right him not to his satisfaction, he must go to his Court of Aids at Paris. A Gent. pays nothing, i.e. he may keep in his hand as much land as he can manage with 2 ploughs. If he has any more, he must pay for it, but as well as they can, the burthen is shifted off on to the paisants, out of whose labour they wring as much as they can, and rot lights on the land.[61]

Some months later, when he reached Tours on his return journey to Paris, he expanded his notes on the subject, making clear the distinction between the *taille réelle* and the much more common *taille personnelle*, and emphasizing once again the hardship which the latter imposed on the peasant:

A bourgeois or trades man that lives in the town, if he have land in the country, if he keep it in his hand or set it to rent, which is the common way, that pays noe thing; but the paisant who rents it, if he be worth any thing, pays for what he has, but he makes no defalcation of his rent, for the manner of taxing in the country is this. The tax to be paid being laid upon the parish, the Collectors for that year assease every one of the inhabitants or house keepers of the parish, according to his proportion as they judg him worth, but consider not the land in the parish that belongs to any one liveing out of it. This makes them say that the taile in France is personal, but in Languedoc, sur le fonde, i.e. Land tax, which there always pays where it lyes. This is that which soe grinds the paisant in France. The collectors make their rates usually with great inequality. There lies an appeal for the overtaxed, but I finde not that the remedy is made much use of.[62]

Two days later, on his way to Orleans, he picked up various grumbles about the excessive burden of the *taille* — that in the region round Angoulême '100 escus pays at least 20 taile' and that 'in Normandie they often pay more for the taile then their land is worth to be lett', to which he adds, 'but this lights heaviest on the poor & lower sort of people, the richer sort befreinding & easeing one another. The collectors are answerable, wether they can get the mony or noe'.[63]

When he returned to Orleans a year later, he further amplified his notes on this tax, particularly as it concerned the collectors and the exemption enjoyed by many towns and cities:

> Where any one pays not, the Collector may seize his goods, all except his bed & the utensils of his calling. If any one be found non solvendo, his taxe is laid upon the rest of the parish. If the Collector pays not in the mony to a farthing by the day, he goes to prison. He has 1/40 for his pains. The inhabitants of free towns, as Paris, Orleans, etc. where of there are many in France, are not taliable, & sometimes the Land adjacent, as the land a league about Orleans, is free. The inhabitants of other townes, if they be not gentlemen or gens de lettres, are Taliable. The inhabitants of free towns that have land in the country perswade them selves, that they nor their land pay not, because 'tis the pore tenant that pays, but yet according to the increase of their taxes their rents decrease; & if their tenant leaves their land, they may keepe it in their hands for one yeare without paying anything, to have time to provide a new tenant; but if in that time they finde not one, they shall be obleiged to pay as much taile as their last tenant did.[64]

The exemption enjoyed by the inhabitants of these towns naturally attracted peasants to them, but, as Locke explains, there were penalties for leaving the land:

> A paisant that has land of his owne or otherwise, if he leaves his land & lets it to an other & goes & lives in a free towne he shall be obleiged to pay every year as much taile as he did the last year of his living in a tailiable place & this for 10 years togeather, his tenant paying neverthelesse as much taile also as he is assessed or judged able, but after ten years liveing in a free towne, a paisant becomes free of Taile unlessc he returne to his husbandry again. This makes all these people, as much as they can, send their children to live in free towns to make their persons free from taile.[65]

Moving to a town free from the *taille* could obviously be a solution only for at least moderately prosperous peasants; we remember the sad story, noted by Locke some two months later in the Graves region, of the poor peasant and his wife from whom 'not long since the collector had taken their frying pan & dishes, mony not being ready'.[66]

Even the system of direct taxation in force in Languedoc where the Estates levied a *taille réelle* was, Locke noted, far from being entirely equitable. Not only was the survey on which assessments were based over a hundred years old which meant, for instance, that the apothecary in whose house he took his meals admitted that he had paid less than half the tax he should if assessments were brought up to date; the two privileged orders also enjoyed various exemptions as in the rest of France. 'From these taxes are exempted all Noble land which is to pay a year's value to the King every 20 years, but as they order the matter, they pay not above 3/4 year's value. All ancient priviledged land of the Church is also exempt, but any that is given to the Church that hath been used to pay taxes, pays it after the donation'. Later he discovered that even with this last category of land exemption from the *taille* could be secured: 'Monks, when they get land by gift or purchase, if the Estates do not spare them, they usually get the King to ennoble them and so the burthen still increases on the rest'.[67]

Locke's journal also offers a number of interesting entries on the *gabelle*. He was quick to note the extraordinary variations in the price of salt as the tax fell very unevenly on the different provinces. As Montpellier was in a *pays de petite gabelle* (one in which the tax was lower than in many other places), the price of salt was moderate: 'Salt here is £18 per minot, at Paris 48£ per Minot'.[68] However, he had earlier noted that at Aigues-Mortes, only some twenty-five miles away, the same amount of salt (approximately a hundredweight) cost only 5 sous. Later, when he visited La Rochelle, he was informed that there salt 'is sold for 4 or 5s. the boyseau by the proprietors, but the marchant pays 44 or 45s., for out of every Boyssseau the King has 40s. duty for all that is exported, but the inland vent pays yet a much higher tax, for the boisseau that by the proprietor is sold here at 4s., noe further off then Saumur is sold for 40 lb'.[69]

The great disparities in the price of salt led to smuggling on a vast scale from those regions where it was cheap to those where it was heavily taxed. Despite an army of *gabeleurs* to keep watch and despite ferocious penalties to deter smugglers, the practice could never be stamped out. On one of his excursions from Montpellier Locke visited the salt pans at Peccais on the Mediterannean coast; he noted in his journal: 'The stealeing the duty of this commodity is of such consequence that, if a man should be taken with but an handfull of salt not bought & paid for at this rate of the Farmers, he would be sent to the Gallys.[70] An even more vivid entry occurs during his visit to Angers in a *pays de grande gabelle* where the tax was extremely high:

> Here a boisseau of Salt costs a Luis d'or & about 10 livres of it is sold for 10s. This makes them here very strict in examining all things that enter into towne, there being at each gate two officers of the Gabelle who serch all things where they suspect may be any salt. They have also in their hands iron bodkins about 2 foot long which have a little hollow in them neare the point, which they thrust into any packs where they suspect there

may be salt concealed, & if there be any, by that means discover it. The penalty for any one that brings in any salt that is not a Gabeller, pays 100 ecus or goes to the gallys. It is also as dangerous to buy any salt but of them. A boisseau of salt weighs about lib.24.

I saw a Gabeller at the gate serch a litle girle at her entrance, who seemd only to have gon out to see a funerall that was prepareing without the gate, which had drawn thither a great number of people.[71]

The *gabelle* was certainly a most unpopular indirect tax, particularly in those regions on which its full weight fell.

Another indirect tax about which Locke has something of interest to say is the excise duty or *aides*, levied chiefly on wine. This tax was unpopular not only with consumers, but also with the very numerous class of winegrowers. When he visited the Loire Valley in 1678, he picked up all sorts of grumbles about the catastrophically low prices being fetched by the wines of the region. At Angers he was told that 'the wine that was formerly sold here for 4 s. per pinte is now sold for 1 s.' and later at Orleans he noted: 'A tun of wine holding two poinsons which contein 400 pints, is sold here now, vessell & all, for £7, the vessell itself being worth neare the mony, & this is not bad or decayd wine, but that which is very good'. The poor returns received by the winegrowers after the heavy excise duty had been paid he had noted at Saumur: 'The white wine here of this towne is very good & wine soe plenty here that they sell it for 18 deniers la pinte at their boushons, i.e. where people in privat houses sell their owne wine by retail, & of these 18 deniers per pinte the King hath 10 deniers for excise & the proprietor 8d for his wine'.[72]

The war with Holland which began in 1672 brought about the introduction of new indirect taxes, particularly one on tobacco which Locke describes thus: 'For tobaco here they pay a livre a pound excise, for the Farmers who rent it of the King, sell now all the tobaco & sell it for 33s per lb, what they formerly bought for 13 or 15 s. per lb'.[73]

(b) The Towns, Trade and Industry

Nearly all our travellers explored Paris which by the seventeenth century had become the hub of a highly centralized country, the seat of the court and government and the undisputed cultural capital of France. They were generally very favourably impressed by what they saw of the city. While Evelyn, for instance, did not find it superior in every respect to those which he had visited in Italy, he certainly awards it very high marks:

I have seen Naples, Rome, Florence, Genoa and Venice; all stately Cities, and full of Princely Fabricks; but then I compare the extent, and here are many Centuries of Noblemens Houses, both within the Town, and the Environs, which althogether approach, if not exceed the best of them. This I will boldly affirm, that for the Streets, Suburbs, and common buildings, it infinitely excels any City else in Europe: for publick Edifices, some of the Hospitals are fair Foundations and handsome Piles; but the Convents and Churches come far short of the Towns before recited: yet that of the Sorbonne and Jesuites, are not much inferiour to some of the best and most modern Pieces of architecture extant.[1]

Reresby expresses even greater admiration: 'Paris, I must confess (although an Englishman), is the largest, fairest, and most populous city of all those I have seen in Europe (London not excepted), having twelve miles in compass, abounding with all things which can either render a town commodious or pleasant'.[2]

Yet they had their grumbles. There were many complaints about how dirty the streets were. It is true that, while making this criticism, Finch adds: 'Yet one may walke cleaner because the streets are better paved'.[3] However, this was a minority view. In the 1590s Fynes Moryson declared that the streets in the northern and eastern parts of Paris, 'either for the low situation, or by the negligence of the Citizens, are continually dirty and full of filth'.[4] Heylyn describes the state of their paving in his usual highly coloured style:

As it is now, the least rain maketh it very slippery and troublesome; and as little a continuance of warme weather, stinking and poisonous. But whether this noisomenesse proceed from the nature of the ground, or the sluttishnesse of the people in their houses, or the neglect of the Magistrates in not providing a sufficiency of Scavengers, or all, I am not to determine. This I am confident of, that the nastiest lane in London, is Frankincense and Juniper, to the sweetest street in this City.[5]

Evelyn makes the same point rather more soberly; after speaking of Paris as 'one of the most gallant Cittys in the World, and best built', he adds: 'but situat in a botome environd with gentle declivities, which renders some places very durty, and makes it smell as if sulphure were mingled with the mudd'.[6]

Earlier Howell had found 'the Streets generally foul all four Seasons of the yeer', a thing which he attributed first to the fact that 'having som of her Suburbs seated high, the filth runs down the Channell, and settles in many places within the body of the Citie, which lieth upon a flat'. A further cause was the large number of vehicles using the streets which created the sort of traffic jams which were to be vividly described in one of Boileau's satires a few decades later. In a striking passage Howell speaks of

> a world of Coaches, Carts, and Horses of all sorts that go to and fro perpetually, so that somtimes one shall meet with a stop half a mile long of those Coaches, Carts, and Horses, that can move neither forward nor backward by reason of some sudden encounter of others coming a crosse-way; so that oftentimes it will be an hour or two before they can dis-intangle: In such a stop the great Henry was so fatally slain by Ravillac. Hence comes it to passe, that this Town (for Paris is a Town, a City, and an University) is always dirty, and 'tis such a dirt, that by perpetuall motion is beaten into such a thick black onctious Oyl, that wher it sticks, no art can wash it off of some colours, insomuch, that it may be no improper comparison to say, That an ill name is like the *Crot* (the dirt) of Paris, which is indelible; besides the stain this dirt leaves, it gives also so strong a sent, that it may be smelt many miles off, if the wind be in one's face as he comes from the fresh Air of the Countrey.[7]

Although generally much impressed by Paris — Howell speaks of it in the same passage as 'this hugh Magazin of men, the Epitome of this large populous Kingdom, and rendezvous of all Forreners' — several of our travellers found its shops far inferior to those of London. This view is recorded from one end of our period to the other, starting with Dallington's observation in the 1590s that the shops were 'thick, but nothing so full of wares, nor so rich as they of London, in comparison whereof, these seeme rather Pedlers then otherwise: But for number, I suppose, there be three for two of those'.[8] When Coryate visited the Palais de Justice he found there

> the exchange, that is a place where the Marchants doe meete at those times of the day, as our Marchants doe in London. But it is nothing comparable to the place of our Marchants meeting in London, being a plaine pitched walke *subdio*, that is under the open ayre. As for their Exchange where they sell many fine and curious things, there are two or three pretty walks in it, but neither for length, nor for the roofe, nor the exquisite workmanship is it any way to be compared with ours in London.[9]

In describing this building, Heylyn makes the same point, but in a rather more forceful manner:

> Presently without the Chappell is the Burse, *La Gallerie des Merchands*; a rank of shops, in shew, but not in substance, like to those in the Exchange in London. It reacheth from the Chappell unto the great hall of Parliament; and it is the common throughfare between them. On the bottome of the staires and round about the severall houses, consecrated to the execution of

Justice, are sundry shops of the same nature, meanly furnished if compared with ours; yet I perswade my self the richest of this kind in Paris.[10]

In another passage he speaks scathingly of the poorly painted shop signs: 'Their houses are distinguished by signes as with us, and under every signe there is printed in Capitall letters, what signe it is: neither is it more than need. The old shift of This is a Cock, and this is a Bull, was never more requisite in the infancy of painting, then in this City'.

He goes on to speak disparagingly of the artisans and merchants of Paris, comparing them most unfavourably with those of a great seaport like London:

And indeed generally, the Artificers of Paris are as slovenly in their trades, as in their houses; yet you may finde nimble dancers, pretty fidlers for a toy, and a Tayler that can trick you up after the best and newest fashion. Their Cutlers make such abominable and fearfull knives, as would grieve a mans heart to see them; and their Gloves, are worse then they; you would imagine by their Gloves, that the hand for which they are made, were cut of by the wrist: yet on the other side they are very perfect at tooth-picks, beard brushes, and (which I hold the most commendable art of them) at the cutting of a seal. Their Mercers are but one degree removed from a Pedler; such as in England we call Chapmen, that is a Pedler with a shop. And for Goldsmiths there is little use of them, glasses being there most in request, both because neat, and because cheap. I perswade myself that the two severall ranks of shops in Cheapside can shew more plate, and more variety of Mercery wares, good and rich, then three parts of Paris. Merchants they have here, but not many, and they are not very wealthy. The river ebbs not, and floweth not higher then 75 miles or thereabouts, and the boats which thence serve the City, being no bigger then our Western Barges.

According to Heylyn 'the principall means by which the people do subsist, are the Court of the King, most times held amongst them; and the great resort of Advocates and Clients to the Chambers of Parliament. Without these two crutches the Town would get a vile halting, and perhaps be scarce able to stand'.[11] A similar view of Paris as a trading city was taken by Bromley much later in the century. Speaking of its large population — 'at present computed to be five hundred thousand Souls' — he adds: 'There is little Trade, excepting what is occasioned by the great confluence of Nobility and Persons of Quality, of this, and from most other Nations, who make Paris their centre'.[12]

Evelyn formed a poor opinion of French merchants. According to him, many of what he calls 'the People of Trade and Mechanicks' live 'very decently and handsomely in their houses, especially the better sort of Merchants who are better furnished then the rest; howbeit, in comparison with our Country-men of the same quality, to be esteemed, in truth, but as mean Mountebanks and inconsiderable Pedlers. Those of greatest Wealth and Commerce, being some crafty Italian or Portuguese, who (during the time of the late and present Cardinal) have amassed very considerable Estates, and great Riches'.[13]

Later in the century we finde Clenche describing Paris shops as 'not very good',[14] and although Ferrier was very impressed with the fine mansions of the capital, he too had no high opinion of its shops: 'It is adorned with abundance of fine pallaces there being scarce a nobleman but has his house in the City. There is severall indifferent good streets which would show a great deal better were they adorned as those in London with handsome shops, but there you shall scarcely see any but seems rather to be a Cobler's hole than of any trade, & pittifull signs to set them forth, they counting it a very noble one if it cost 15 or twenty livers'. On the other hand he was struck by the large barges on the Seine which he describes as 'worth the seeing, to see what huge flat-bottom boats they make use of to carry their marchandise up & down the river, there being some of them that will contain six or seven hundred tunns & whose rudders are four or five & twenty feet long'.[15]

Even Heylyn was struck by the advantages which Paris derived from the Seine:

> The river of Seine is also, no question, a great help to the enriching of it; for though it be not Navigable unto the Town, yet it giveth free passage unto boats of an indifferent big burden, into which the ships are unladen, and so their commodities carryed up the water. A profitable entercourse between the Sea and the City for the Merchants. Of these boats there are an infinite company that plie up and down the water.[16]

Veryard takes an even more favourable view of the value of the Seine to Paris, describing the river as 'its chief support, serving to import and export all sorts of Merchandize, and giving it all the advantages of other Cities that lie on the main Ocean; for this River is navigable from Rouen hither, and from hence divers Leagues up the Country, at least for large Boats and Barges'.[17]

Our travellers duly noted some of the new institutions which sprang up in Paris during the seventeenth century. In 1649 while visiting the Louvre Symonds came across the Bureau d'Adresse founded some twenty years earlier by Théophraste Renaudot, though the entry covers only one of its varied functions: 'Under the long gallery is a place is calld the Bureau d'Adresse. Here a man has bookes of Servants & Lacquais names. Every lacquay that wants a master for 5d. has his name enterd & condition, & those that want servants come to him & give 5d. also for the payment of helping them to him'.[18]

Coffee houses apparently flourished in London rather earlier than *cafés* were established in Paris. Edward Browne simply took their existence for granted when he arrived in Paris in 1664, but in so doing provides evidence for their existence at an earlier date than the reference books indicate. He speaks of visits to 'the Coffe house' on half a dozen occasions. A fortnight after his arrival he writes: 'I went to the Coffe house, which one Wilson, an Englishman, keeps in R. du Bucheries in Fauxbourg St.Germain, where I met divers English Gentlemen, They sell here likewise beere and Tobacco'. Later, he offers further details: 'I carried two French Gentlemen with mee to the Coffy house, that they might tast of some English beere and Ale, Coffe, & Chocolate'.[19] What he has to say about this coffee house would seem to suggest that the *café* which was to play such an important part in French social and intellectual life was introduced to Paris by an Englishman. These references certainly predate the visit of the special envoy from Turkey in 1669 which is said to have made coffee a fashionable drink.

Edward Browne also noted the existence of Paris's first experiment in public transport, the *carrosses à cinq sous*, with whose establishment two years earlier Pascal had been associated at the very end of his short life. Exploring Paris one Saturday, he came across 'the Bureau for the Carosses that goe about Paris. Here is one by the Palais d'Orleans,[20] which for 6 Sous marqué goes to Rue St. Honore, and to the Palais'.[21] Two years later Skippon offers a slightly less laconic account of this venture: 'Every hour of the day there passes a hackney coach from the Place Royalle to Luxemburg House, and another coach goes from Rue S.Honore to Rue S.Jacques, where the booksellers live. Every one pays five sols for his place, but goes with other company, and for that reason it is not usual for persons of any quality to go in them'.[22] This was no doubt one of the reasons why in the end the experiment proved a failure; the *carrosses* ceased to run in 1691.

Lister gives some account of various industries carried on in the Paris region. He describes, for instance, visits to the pottery works at Saint Cloud and the plaster works near Montmartre. He was particularly impressed by what he saw of glassmaking, one of the industries encouraged by Colbert:

The Glass-house out of the Gate of St.Antoine well deserves seeing; but I did lament the Fondery was no longer there, but removed to Cherborne in Normandy for cheapness of Fuel. 'Tis certainly a most considerable addition to the Glass-making. But I saw here one Looking-glass foiled and finisht, 88 inches long, and 48 inches broad; and yet but one quarter of an inch thick. This, I think, could never be effected by the Blast of any Man; but I suppose to be run or cast upon Sand, as Lead is; which yet, I confess, the toughness of Glass Mettal makes very much against.

There they are polished; which Imploys daily 600 Men, and they hope in a little time to employ a 1000 in several Galleries.

After going into a certain number of technical details, he adds: ''Tis very diverting to see the Joint Labour of so many Men upon one Subject. This has made Glass for Coaches very cheap and common; so that even many of the Fiacres or Hackneys, and all the *Remises*[23] have one large Glass before'.[24]

Writing about the same period, Joseph Shaw was equally impressed by this factory which he describes as 'the most considerable Sight in Paris, if not in all France'. He continues:

I had been searching into all their Manufactures, and impartially compared 'em with ours, and found the Advantage much on our side; till I came hither and found out the Lookingglass Manufacture which surpasses any thing in England, or perhaps in the Universe; I saw one Glass above Nine Foot long and Seven broad; there were above Eight hundred Workmen employ'd all together about this Manufacture, in a sort of a Colledge: I wish some of 'em were enticed over hither, to live better, and not in that Misery they now do.[24a]

On the other hand Lister found that by this date the *manufacture royale* at the Gobelins, established by Colbert and famous above all for its tapestries, was at a low ebb because of the state of the Treasury: 'The formerly so famous a Workhouse, the *Goblins*, is miserbly fallen to decay; perhaps because the King having furnisht all his Palaces, has little more to do for them'.[25] Earlier travellers had found the Gobelins in a more flourishing state. In 1675 Clenche offers a somewhat breathless account of the great variety of works produced there: 'Goblins, a House built for the Kings Artificers, such as Inlayers of Cabinets, Statuaries, Sculptors, Painters, Silver-Smiths, Tapestrymakers, &c. in all which, both great & small, the design is still the King's Tryumphs, &c'.[26] Locke mentions seeing only the tapestries, though he too remarks that they were made for the greater glory of Louis XIV; he refers in particular to 'Le renouvellement d'alliance avec les Suisses', one of a series designed by Le Brun: 'We saw the hangings at the Goblins. It being Fest Dieu, they remained exposd all day. Very rich & good figures. In every peice Lewis le Grand was the hero, & the rest the marks of some conquest, etc. In one was his makeing a league with the Swisse where he lays his hand on the booke to sweare the articles with his hat on & the Swiss Ambassador in a submissive posture with his hat off'.[27]

Other travellers, who visited the Gobelins in the 1680s before the outbreak of the Nine Years War, also depict it as a very active place. Ferrier who went to see it in 1687 was much impressed:

> We walked . . . to the Goblins, the place where all sorts of artificers at work for the King, there is doubtless the finest tapestry that eyes can look on, it being made of silver silk & gold, & so naturally done that no painting whatsoever can represent both men, women & all sorts of creatures more lively than they are there exprest. There is a gallery that is going to Versailles which is made of a certain stone every inch whereof is worth a great deal more than gold, it is of a white & grayish colour. There is also a man that is making a table of stone, he has been about it these 3 years & has not yet finished it, it is full of birds and beasts (onely at the corners where are to be the King's armes.) It is not painted, but stone inlaid so artificially that in ones judgment there is nothing wanting to set it forth.[28]

An even more detailed account of the varied activities of the Gobelins is provided by Northleigh:

> Here all the more curious of the French King's Artisans are at work. It was formerly fam'd for the making of Cloth and dying the best Scarlets, and has its name from the Gobelin that was excellent in that Work about the time of Francis 1st. It is at the King's Cost and for his Profit that they work, either in Silver or Tapestry for the furnishing his Courts; the fam'd Le Brun had abundance of his best Paintings here. For designs for Tapestry they employ Workmen of all Countries, the best they can get, as Flemings come from Flanders, where formerly at Antwerp the best were made, and indeed the richest that ever I saw for Gold and Silver I observed here, the best Artists in Gold and Silver Plates are here also, and those Rails and Balasters of Massy Silver that enclose the Alcoves of the King and Queen's Bed at Versailles, were first finish'd here; Mosaic Work, neat Iron, Copper and Brass-work, Statuary, Sculpture, Embroideries, and most curious Arts are here employ'd.[29]

Earlier Skippon had visited on his way to Calais the tapestry works at Beauvais: 'The royal manufacture here employs 400 or 500 men in weaving tapestry, having several looms in long chambers, and painters are invited hither, to draw the pictures that are to be woven. We observed those that weave, have the picture they work just underneath the tapistry they are weaving.[30]

Paris was not by any means the only French city visited and commented upon by our travellers; collectively they covered the greater part of the country. In the course of his travels Bromley correctly noted that 'the greater Towns' were 'more frequent, and larger than ours'.[31] Among northern cities Rouen was one which was frequently visited. As usual Clenche's comments could scarcely be described as objective: 'It is esteemed to have in it 60,000 souls, by which crowd of Sluttish People, ill Situation, and narrow streets, it is most abominable filthy; It has an ill-favoured Bourse, hung with ugly Pictures of their French kings, a small Trade with all sorts of Merchandize, but the most considerable commodity is English Lead'.[32] Ferrier gives a rather more favourable account of this city even if he 'found it, though bigger, neither so handsome nor so pleasant a place as Caen, the houses being old and the streets very narrow. It is a town of great trade, being full of shops from one end to the other'.[33] The author of *A New Journey to France* speaks fairly well of Rouen, though not without a rather sarcastic conclusion:

> There is a very beautiful, spacious Key; the Harbour is always fill'd with a great number of Ships. At the further end of the Bridge are curious Walks, and a Ring as in Hide-Park. I admire (this being the second City of all France for Ampleness, Riches, Trade, and Populousness) that they have not built a fine Exchange; for the Merchants are forc'd to meet without the Gate call'd *la Porte de laranguery*, in a Walk pav'd with small Pebble Stones along the Wall, having a row of small Trees at a considerable distance from one another between it and the Key. Were it pav'd with Free-stone and cover'd over to shelter them from the Rain, it would be pleasant enough; but when any Shower happens, they are forc'd to run to a little low Building within the Gate, where they are crowded like Hogs in a Stye.[34]

Those travellers who went as far down the Loire as Nantes were generally impressed with its trade. Thomas Browne, for instance, found it 'a very fair city' with 'very great suburbs, which are accounted bigger than the city ... Here is also great resort of merchants, English, Flemish, and other nations; and here are also embarked the Orleans, Blois and Anjou wines and commodities, to be transported into other parts'.[35] Reresby describes Nantes as 'the last place of note' on the Loire, 'though nothing inferior to any of the former, both for structure and riches, being a town of great traffic'.[36] Ferrier and his companions found it a pleasant place to rest in after a strenuous journey down the Loire. They 'had leisure to view the whole town which is indifferent large, high houses and a good key for their ships'.[37]

Another large port, Bordeaux, also drew some comment from our travellers. Reresby, who visited it in the 1650s, was much impressed by the city and by its trade in wine. Of his journey from Blaye to Bordeaux he writes:

> The passage was pleasant; the river (though larger than the Thames) some part of the way very calm. The banks planted with wines, afford those excellent well-bodied wines so much transported into England, called *Le Vin de Grâve*, and others. Bourdeaux, the metropolis of Guienne, is not without reason esteemed one of the prime cities in France. It stands on a plain, upon the river Garonne, being large and populous, and drives greater maritime trade (especially with England and Holland) than any other whatsoever. The best street is called *La Rue du Chapeau Rouge*, which, for breadth and length, I never saw a better.[38]

Mortoft who visited it shortly afterwards was equally impressed: 'Bourdeaux is a very faire and large Citty seated upon the River of Garonne there, belonging to the Citty, one of the fairest Ports in all France, which in Vintage tyme is fild with many hundred ships to receive the wine that is made in the Countrye of Guyin, the ground all about for many leagues together being planted with nothing else but Vines, so that they ship of at least every year at this Port a hundred thousand Tunn of Wyne'.[39]

Locke visited the city on both of his tours of France. In 1677 he commented on the high prices at which the best wines were selling thanks to demand from England: 'A tun (i.e. 4 hoghead English or perhaps 4 or 5 per Cent. more) of the best wine at Bourdeaux, which is that of Medoc or Pontac, is worth, the first penny, 80 or 100 crowns. For this the English may thank their own folly for, whereas some years since the same wine was sold for 50 or 60 crowns per tun, the fashionable sending over orders to have the best wine sent them at any rate, they have, by striveing who should get it, brought it up to that price. But very good wine may be had here for 35, 40 & 50 crowns per tun'. A year later he has a very different story to tell. The export of wine depended very much on the maintenance of peace, especially between England and France; in March 1678 Parliament had prohibited all trade with France, and for a few months the two countries were on the verge of war. Hence the depressed state of the wine trade in September of that year: 'They usually lade here in a year of the commoditys of this part of France, 2,000 vessels. The present prohibition in England much troubles them, which, joynd to the

Dutch warre, makes the wine here worth but about 25 ecus per tunneau, which formerly there sold for between 40 & 50, which was the price of the best sort of Graves wine, except Pontac which was sold for 80 or 100, & some others of a peculiar note'.[40]

The port which attracted most attention from our travellers was naturally Marseilles. It is true that Locke does not seem to have been greatly impressed by it except for the new *hôtel de ville*, the arsenal and the galleys (he describes the city as 'about as big as Montpellier'.) He had reservations about its amenities:

> The key is handsome & long & full of people walking, espetially in the evenings, when the best company, men & women, meet & walk, which is not soe safe in other streets nor sweet, for the houses being fild most of them with several familys living one over an other, have no houses of offices, but instead of that all is don in pots & thrown out of the windows, which makes the streets very ill sented always & very inconvenient anights.[41]

Other travellers, starting with Thomas Wentworth early in the century, were more enthusiastic about this Mediterranean port. He declares that it 'may well be esteemed one of the goodliest, safest and strongest of Christendome'. After quite a detailed description of the port and its defences he goes on: 'Itt is a towne that hath many privileges which itt doth maintaine. Itt payeth noe taxes nor any impost'. He ends a lengthy passage on Marseilles with an account of how the city was governed.[42]

Skippon who came there in 1665 writes rather briefly about it, but his companion, Ray, for once gives up his endless botanizing and embarks on a quite detailed account of his impressions of the city:

> Marseilles, an ancient City not great but well built with tall stone-houses for the most part, and very populous. We were told that the number of souls was about 120,000. The streets are narrow as in most of the ancient Towns in this Countrey, to keep off the scorching beams of the Sun in Summer time. The haven is the most secure and commodious that I have seen: the entrance into it is so strait and narrow that a man may easily cast a stone cross it, but the haven within large enough to contain 500 vessels or more; of an oval figure. On one side of this haven the Town is built which compasses it more than half round, having before it a handsome kay well paved, which serves the Citizens for a walk or Promenade. This haven is not capable of ships of above 600 tun.[43]

For the youth, John Buxton, Marseilles was 'a very noble town with magnificent buildings'. He was very struck by the spectacle of a street 'with stately and lofty houses on each side, and rows of trees so set in order, and the people so thick walking in their holiday dress, that methought I had not seen any town in France so pleasant to the eye', and he adds: 'In the town were many other streets well built but more narrow, good shops that seemed to be very well furnished'.[44] More impressive is Burnet's picture of the prosperity of the city. He was struck not only by the fine harbour — 'with respect either to Storme or Enemies the securest Port that can be seen any where' — but also by the volume of the port's trade: 'The Freedoms of this place, tho it is now at the mercy of the Citadel, are such, and its scituation draweth so much Trade to it, that there one seeth another appearance of wealth than I found in any Town of France, and there is a new street lately built there, and for the beauty of the buildings, and the largeness of the street, is the Noblest I ever saw'.[45]

Bromley too joins in this praise of 'the pleasant *Cour*, a very delightful, long and broad Walk, set with Trees on each side, and the Buildings lofty, handsome, and regular' and of the 'excellent Port, extraordinary safe', but what is more interesting is his remarks on the attitude of the inhabitants to trade:

> The Exchange is new built, not large, but very neat, where the Merchants meet; the Trading is chiefly countenanced by the English and Dutch, those of any condition among the French, disdaining the Profession, and others dealing only in little pedling matters. The Native Tradesmen of Marseilles are particularly observed never to be very rich, and seldom to have regard to posterity; but delight to live well, and enjoy themselves, in so much that no one that can afford it, will be without his Country as well as City-House.

Like many of our travellers Bromley was struck by the thousands of country cottages, known as *bastides*, to be found inland from the city, but only he gives an account of the use made of them by the inhabitants: 'About Four in the Afternoon in the Summer-time, when a Citizen has done his Days-work, and the Weather grown something moderate, he'll set his Wife on his Ass betwixt a pair of Panniers, in one of which shall be their Child, and in the other a little Wine, Oyl, and some Bread, and he himself drives, or follows at some distance to his Countrey-house; where they are entertained with Roots, Herbs, and Grapes, and their Ass with Vine-leaves till the next Morning that they return back'.[46]

Another, very different Provençal city which much impressed several of our travellers — Ray and Skippon as well as Locke and Bromley — was Aix. Locke wrote of it: 'It is round & something biger then Montpellier, but the streets much straiter, larger and handsomer than at Montpellier. The Towne House a pretty handsome building, but the Cours is the handsomest place, being a long strait street, 70 steps wide with two rows of trees on each side'.[47] Besides praising what is now the Cours Mirabeau, Bromley accounts for the prosperity of the town: 'Aix is the Capital City of Provence, the See of an Archbishop, an University, and Parliament-Town, which is of very considerable advantage to it, for the great concourse of people that are brought thither on that occasion, bring along with them a flourishing Trade.'[48]

Lyons which was visited by a great many of our travellers on their way either to or from the south of France or Italy naturally made a strong impression as a great trading city. When Howell arrived there from Italy in 1621, he described it as 'a stately rich Town, and a renowned Mart for the Silks of Italy, and other Levantin commodities, and a great bank for mony, and indeed the greatest of France'.[49] Some forty years later Ray describes Lyons as 'the second City in France for greatness, handsome building, trade, riches and multitude of people', adding: 'if any, setting aside Paris, may compare with it for any one of these, for altogether I am sure none can'.[50] His companion Skippon was struck by the amount of trade carried on there: 'Great merchandising here, and large shops full of all sorts of wares'.[51] Even Lassels who is generally in so much of a hurry to get his readers to Italy that he has little to say about what has to be seen on the way, devotes some space to this prosperous city: 'Lyons is one of the greatest and richest townes in France. It stands upon the rivers Saone and Rhosne, and intercepting all the merchandize of Burgondy, Germany, and Italy, it licks its fingers notably, and thrives by it. It expresseth this in its looks: for here you have hansome people, noble houses, great jollity, frequent balls, and much bravery: all markes of a good towne'.[52] Clenche, though normally determined to admire nothing on his travels in France, makes an exception for Lyons: 'The Buildings are high, Streets large, Shops better, People neater and richer much than in Paris. It Trades considerably with Germany and Italy; Prints Books and exchanges Money for all Europe ... The most extraordinary thing is the Towne-House which is equal to that of Amsterdam, with pretty walks behind it'.[53] Bromley was greatly impressed by its size, describing it as 'one of the greatest and chiefest Towns in the Kingdom of France, ordinarily reckoned to have 120,000 Souls'.[54] Veryard was also struck by the city's size and situation, it being 'so commodiously seated at the confluence of the Rivers Rhone and Soane, that it flourishes in Commerce above any other town in France. It's esteem'd the second City in the Kingdom for bigness, riches, and number of Inhabitants'. For him its 'stately Churches and Palaces' and its situation at the junction of the rivers

Rhone and Saône 'mutually concur to give it the pre-eminence above any other Inland City in Europe.'[55] For Berkeley, writing at the very end of our period, Lyons was 'a very noble city, and more populous and rich in proportion than Paris'.[55a]

When in the southern half of the kingdom and especially when they came to Lyons, several of our travellers were struck by the way in which paper replaced glass in many windows. Skippon found the houses in Lyons 'tall and well built, only defaced by the raggedness of their paper windows'.[56] Much earlier in the century Coryate had also observed that 'in many places of the city the whole window is made of white paper only, in some partly of white paper as the lower part, and partly of glasse as the higher part'.[57] While in Lyons Bromley also observed that, because of the heat there in the summer, 'the windows are generally of oyl'd Paper, which keeps out the Heat of the Sun better than Glass, but takes off from the Nobleness of the Buildings'.[58]

Some of our travellers remained long enough in one provincial town to offer interesting information about the way of life of the inhabitants as well as about local government and industries. Lauder provides a certain amount of detail about the feeding habits of the family he lived with at Poitiers. He was struck, for instance, by the important part played by bread in the making of the soup he was regularly given:

> Surely I fand it sensibly to be nourishing meat; and it could not be otherwise, since it consisted of the substance first of the bread, which without doute is wholesomer then ours, since they know not what barme[59] is their, or at least they know not what use we make of it, to make our bread firme, yet their bread is as firme without it: next the substance of the flech, which usually they put in of 3 sorts of lard, of mouton, of beef, of each a little morsell; 3dly of herbes for seasoning, whiles keel, whiles cocombaes, whiles leekes, whiles minte or others.[60]

A further entry on this subject reveals the carefulness of his Protestant landlady: 'In our soups, which we get once every day, and which we have descryved already, such was Madames frugality that the one halfe of it she usually made of whiter bread, and that was turned to my syde of the board, the other halfe or a better part she made of the braner, like our rye loaves, and that was for hir and her husband'.[61] In another note on this important item of diet he describes two ways in which soup could be made with this bread base:

> He that hes made ready boiled flech, he hath no more ado but to take the broth or sodden water with his flech and pour it above his cut doune loaves, which we proved to be very

nourishing. If a man would make a good soup without flech, he would cut me doune some onions with a lump of butter either fresh or salt, which he sall frie in a pan, then pour in some vinaigre, then vater, then salt and spice, and let al boil together, then pour it on your sup, and I promise you a good sup.[62]

Such entries throw considerable light on the feeding habits of the great majority of French families in this period. If we are to believe Evelyn, this item of diet was also popular with the upper classes. Comparing the consumption of alcohol and tobacco in England and France, he states: 'Fewer persons of quality use either in excesse: but what they do not in drink, they pay in bread, and are strange devourers of Corn; they adore a good potage (whatever the rest of the Repast be) as the Egyptians did garlick'.[63]

Among the curious scenes observed by Lauder in Poitiers was that of a man selling glasses of wine in the street:

To recknon over all the crys of Poictiers (since they are divers according to the diverse seasons of the year) would be difficult. Yet theirs one I cannot forgeet, a poor fellow that goes thorow the toune with a barrell of wine on his back; in his on hand a glass full halfe with win; in his other a pint stoop; over his arm hinges a servit; and thus marched he crieing his delicate wine for 5 souse the pot thats our pint; or 4 souse or cheaper it may be. He lets any man taste it that desires, giving them their loof[64] full.[65]

He also noted the primitive device which in the absence of street lighting poor people who were unable to afford a lantern were driven to use on dark nights: 'It is they take a peice wood that burnt only at one end, and goes thorow the toune waging it from one syde to the other, it casting a little light before him. It would almost fly[66] a man in a dark night to sie it at a distance, and always approaching him, til he keen what it is'.[67]

Locke's stay of over a year in Montpellier in the following decade produced many entries in his journals on life in this town. He has some interesting observations to offer on the decline in the authority of the six consuls who were nominally responsible for local government: 'Montpellier hath 6 Consuls who have the Government of the politie of the towne, order the building or repair of publique places, seeing the bread weight & flesh sold at its due rate, & looking after the weights and measures, & can determin all causes not exceeding five livres. They had formerly a considerable authority, but now they are little more then servants to the Governor of the towne'. The last governor, the Marquis de Castries, having died in 1674, his eleven year old son had been allowed to succeed him; this meant that affairs were in the hands of his mother, the sister of the powerful

Archbishop of Narbonne, Cardinal Bonzi. Locke duly recorded gossip about the corrupt manner in which she exercised her power:

> 500 escus made a year by Mme de Castres for a dispensation to tipling houses for breaking the rules of the town, which are that no townsman can eat or drink in cabarets which are for strangers, and if anyone be drunk or found in these houses on holydays in time of divine service, to pay so much. The Capitaine du Guet was the officer that looked after these formerly and was annuall and put in by the first Consul, but now by the Governor has been made perpetuall. She also makes a profit of the stores of the Cittadel and allowing bakers to sell light bread; and besides ploughing up the Splanade, which formerly belonged to the officers of the garison, she also sells the mud of the town ditches.

Locke also noted one picturesque detail about the Hôtel de Ville: 'The Towne House adornd with false weights, ballances & measures naild upon the outside. The same at Avignon'.[68]

Montpellier was much frequented by English travellers,[69] and both Ray and Skippon also left behind accounts of their stay there, in particular of its industries. Ray was surprised to find so many apothecaries: 'The number of Apothecaries in this little City is scarce credible, there being 130 shops, and yet all find something to do: their Cypres powder, sweet bags, Cassolets, Treacle, Confectio Alkermes, & Hyacintha having a name all France over. The Queen of Hungaries water (as they call it) made heer is likewise much bought up'.[70] Ray, Skippon and Locke all describe in varying amounts of detail the making of verdigris,[71] while both Ray and Locke showed particular interest in another important Montpellier industry, the preparation of kermes which was extensively employed as a dye before the advent of cochineal.[72] Both men also give a lengthy description of the making of olive oil and the blanching of wax, while Locke also mentions the manufacture of cream of tartar.[73]

While in Montpellier, Locke showed considerable interest in the production of silk. On 2 June 1676 he made the following entry in his diary concerning his landlady: 'This day Mme Fisket's silk worms began some of them to work. She took eggs and wrapped them up in a linen cloth on Good Friday and so wore them in some warm place about her night and day till the Monday following they were hatchd. They usually put the eggs hatching in Holy Week, but that which best governs the time is the budding of the mulberry trees, that the worms, when hatched, may have food'. For the next three weeks his journal contains numerous entries on the activities of the silkworms.[74]

On both his visits to Tours Locke made entries on the state of the silk industry there. In 1677 he gives a fairly optimistic account of it since he speaks of the town being 'well peopled & threiving, which it owes to the great manifacture of silke is there'. He also has an interesting note on the relative expense of becoming a master in different trades: 'Passer maistre or to have a licence to set up any trade, for haveing served an apprentiship (which is usually but of 2 or 3 year) gives not that priviledg, but it comes from the King, & they must have letters for it. The severall trades have severall regulated prices, & whereas about Tours & Amboise a Silke worker pays 100 escus for his freedome, a baker 50, those that would set up in the woollen manifacture pay but 6 livres. Marke the incouragement'.[75] When passing through Tours a year later, he gives a very different picture of the state of this industry, one derived apparently from a silk merchant named Gill, 'the son of an English man, that speaks himself good English, a merchant of silke that hath a very fine house & garden'. The picture is one of acute trade depression: 'Where as there were lately 6,000 silke weavers here in Tours, there are now but 1,200, & those that could gain 50s. an aulne for weaving of figurd silkes have now but 30s. or 35s. There have broke here since Easter last for above 6,000,000£'. On the following day Locke goes into more detail on this topic, adding: 'We saw the weaveing of figured silks. The worke men complain of want of worke, decay of trade & abatement of wages. In the house we saw it, were lately 12 looms & there are now but two'. He also offers some technical details, together with a remarkably compassionate sentence on the exploitation of a girl's labour:

> We saw also the way of Calandering & watering their silks which gives them a glosse & the water by drawing on them, being wound upon a rouler, a weight of 650,000 lib.
>
> A day's worke of figurd silke is about an aulne. We saw also the weaveing of velvet, the cutting whereof upon a little brasse wire with a little grove or noch in it all the length is very dexterous.
>
> We saw also the twisting and windeing of silke in one of their mills, which is drove about by a maid & turnes at once above 120 spooles & windes the silke off them. The maid works from 5 in the morning till night, only rests twice in the day an hour at a time, & has for her day's work 5s., a small recompence for drawing such a weight 7 leagues, for soe much they say she goes in a day. The wages was formerly greater.[76]

Earlier Evelyn had passed through Tours and had made a brief entry on the silk industry there: 'I went to see their Manifactures in silke (for in this Towne they drive a very considerable trade with Silke-Wormes) their pressing & watering the Grograns &

Chambletts: with weights of an extraordinary poyse put into a rolling engine'.[77] Although on his two visits to Lyons, the most important centre of this industry, Locke does not get beyond stating that the children received into the Charité were trained to work in it,[78] he made notes on machines which he observed in other places. At Orange, for instance, he writes: 'Here I also saw the way of windeing silk by an engine that turns at once 134 bobins. It is too intricate to be described upon soe short a view, but all these were turned by one woman, & they both twisted & wound off the silk at once'. At Nîmes, another important centre for the silk industry until it was severely damaged by the emigration of Huguenots after the Revocation, Locke was also struck by a similar machine: 'Here I saw also an engine to twist & winde the silke. Two winches going in a wheele turnd 3 engines where in were turnd at once 30 dozen of bobbins. It is too curious a thing to be described at large, & requires a longer time to observe all the parts of it'.[79]

Locke devoted a good deal of attention to the cloth industry, one of those which, during the period when he was in France, was being actively encouraged by Colbert, as he duly noted at Carcassonne when he visited the *manufacture royale* set up in 1666:

> Here is a great manifacture of cloth, and they use a great deal of Spanish wool which comes without any imposition. The finest medlys they sell for 30 escus per canne and the finest black £40 per canne, 1 2/3 aune de Paris makes just one canne which is the canne of Montpellier. One clothier there whom we talked with, makes 1200 cloths per annum. They pay no other tax but 5s. tournoys per cloth for laid mark.[80] They have got into this way of making fine cloth by means of 80 Hollanders which, about 5 or 6 years since, Mr. Colbert got hither. They are all now gone but about 12, but have left their art behind them.

He also noted two technical points concerning the woollen industry there: 'Instead of fuller's earth they use soap for their cloths' and 'At Carcassone I saw a wheel, turned by one ass, which twisted & wound at the same time 64 threads of yarn'.[81] At Lyons Skippon noted down particulars (complete with sketch) of a machine for raising a nap on cloth.[82]

It is mainly to Locke that we must look for information about other industries carried on in the provinces. His boundless curiosity led him to go from Angers to the nearby slate quarries where he noted once again the depressed state of the industry:

> We saw the quarrys of Ardoise. They employ about 100 men in diging, spliting & cutting these stones. Formerly there were 200, but the war as on other parts hath had an influence on this

vent to. The best workers in the quarre have about 13s. a day, & others on land that split & square them have 30s. per thousand, at which rate they can earn about 10s. per diem. The stones are dug out of the rock in great & large peices, but to make them more portable they break them into peices of a fit largenesse & soe with chisels they split them into that thicknesse they finde fitest for use & cut them square, those for Paris about a foot long & 8 inches over. The vaine of the rock runs towards the north east & lies perpendicular. That part of the rock that lies nearest the surface of the earth is not good, though it be also of a stone whose veine lies the same way & will split, but not soe well as that which lies lower. When they are come to the good, the lower they goe, the better, but they cannot worke it to the bottom of the rock, being dround out before they get soe low. It splits best as soon as it comes out of the quarre. After it is dried a month or two in the aire, it will split noe more. In frosty weather it splits best, but in a thaw they cannot worke it. One may have tables of it almost what largeness or thicknesse one will.[83]

On his travels he showed a similar interest in the metal industries carried on in the provinces. On a visit to the Arsenal in Paris he noted that the muskets which he saw were 'made at St. Etien in Forez & delivered here at the Arsenal for £8 – 10 – 0 a peice'. When returning to the capital for the second time he wrote that 'Moulins is famous for Cissars, razors & other little works in Iron'[84] — an observation made in one form or another by half a dozen of our travellers since many of them passed through this town. Bromley observed rather peevishly that it was 'famous for Scissors and Iron-work, as Razors, Knives, &c. which the Women take care in such quantities to carry to all Travellers that come in, and are so importunate to sell their Ware, that there is no quiet for them'.[85]

While in this same region, Northleigh made the somewhat bald observation that Cosne 'is noted among them a little for making knives; and they have some Mills hereabout for the polishing Iron and Steel'.[86] Locke provides rather more detail about the industry carried on there, stressing how it was favoured by the conjunction of coal and iron ore: 'Here at Cosne the King has a forge for Ankers & an other for musquets & pistols, etc. 'Tis a convenient place for it, there being an Iron mine & worke at Donzy, 3 leagues up the little river that falls here into the Loire, & colepits also from whence they have coles for their forge, though they are not very good'. Here as on many other occasions Locke shows his interest in ballistics, noting down the way in which gun barrels were bored:

A water mill boares their barrells. Each water wheele turns

two boariers, which is done by two cords of sheep's guts, each as big as one's thumb, which, from a solid wooden wheele fixed on the axis of the water wheele, goes to two other solid wooden wheels, each not above half the diameter of that which turns them, soe that they turne very quick. In the centre is a noch into which they put a borier as the wheele runs, & soe take it out & put in an other as they have occasion, & over against the end of the borier in the same line is fastend the barrell in a slideing peice of wood which a boy drives forward with his knees (for of that heigth it is above the ground) & thus one boy will boare 20 pistol barrells in a day. A litle spout from the water wheele conveys water upon the barell to keep it from heating in boaring.[87]

On his way up the Rhone to Lyons Skippon made notes, complete with a sketch, on 'the manner of blowing the bellows, using the hammer, and grinding', in use in a similar industry at Vienne: 'La Gierre is a little river here, that runs into the Rhône, and is useful to their mills, where they make swords, &c. They said many anchors and coutelaces were making now for Beaufort's fleet, and they counterfeit Olinda blades'.[88] Several of our travellers who passed through Abbeville on their way between Calais and Paris speak of its reputation for guns and pistols. Skippon, for instance, writes: 'Good guns and pistols made in this city'.[89] A very different view is expressed by Northleigh who writes of this town: 'It is much busied about making of Guns and Pistols, which after all its Repute perhaps are more fine than fit for Service, and far from that Strength and firmness of some of our English Work I have seen'.[90]

At Bordeaux Locke observed another industrial process, noting that the raw material was imported from England:

I saw them make shot thus. The lead being melted & scumd, they lade it with an iron spoon into an iron ladle peirced with holes (which is first well heated in the fire to neare the heat of the lead) which they hold over a bucket of water, & soe let it run into the cold water till the water be grown pretty warm, & then they change it into an other, for warme water does not soe well as cold. That which they let the warme lead thus strain into is not pure water, but there is about ½ bucket of lees of wine mixed with an hoghead of water which makes the shot as bright as peauter which in water would be black. They also, to polish it more, shake about 100 weight in a bag togeather. If the melted lead be too hot or too cold, it will not doe well. Each shot is at least twise as much in diameter as the hole the lead streams through. It is made of English lead which they buy now for 29 or 30 escus per 1000 lb., & they sell the shot for 2 1/4 or 2½s. per lb.[91]

We shall see that Locke has more to say on these matters when we come to deal with Colbert's efforts to build up the French navy.[92] Some generalizations about the state of trade and industry are occasionally made by our travellers. Reresby, for instance, writes: 'As to the people, they are very ingenious in improving what their country affords by manufacture, in exchange of which, and their wines, they have all foreign commodities brought them, the reason why they less addict themselves to navigation'.[93] Two decades later the author of *Popery and Tyranny* reviews in some detail the aims, successes and failures of Colbert's efforts to stimulate the economy. He speaks, for instance, of 'the erecting of East India and West India and Northern Companies, the encouraging and countenancing them with great Priviledges', though he claims that owing to the 'Want of able Merchants amongst them, and putting the Directions of all their present Companies, into the Hands of Persons ignorant in Trade, Favourites of the present Ministers . . . they have lost the third part of the Stock of the East India Company already'. He also mentions the encouragement given to existing industries and the attempt to introduce new ones with the aid of foreign workmen, though he criticizes 'making all the new Manufactures Monopolies, whereby most of them are come to nothing, as that of Silk-Stockens and Cloth'. His overall view of the progress so far achieved by the government's policies is not exactly favourable:

> Lastly, the natural Idleness and Luxury these People are addicted unto, but that Necessity forceth them to the contrary, together with the forcing them to enter into Companies of Trade, and imposing their new Manufactures upon Places and Buyers, with the evil Treatment of those Strangers, that teach them after they have once learned their Trade, and the difficulty of finding a Market and Credit, (which attends all new Beginners) especially where others are in possession of Trade, are Obstructions not easily conquered.[93a]

Veryard takes a rather different view, writing somewhat disgruntedly:

> The King has likewise, of late Years, mightily encourag'd and improv'd Trade, as well the Manufactures as Foreign Commerce. Their most advantageous Traffic is with England, Spain and Holland, which turns no less to their Profit than to the Detriment of these Nations; For having little need of the Product of these Countries, instead of bartering Goods for Goods, they have their returns, for the most part, in ready Money. With this Money they keep up their Trade in the Levant; for they carry little up the Straits but Silver and Gold, with what fine Cloth they make of our English and Spanish

Wooll. They have got all the Manufactures of their Neighbours. That of Weaving Stockings is gone thro' the whole Kingdom, and turns to a vast Account. They had it not long since from us by two English men, who were sent over by the French Embassadour, in the latter end of the Reign of Charles II.

Though the date of the introduction of this English invention into France appears to be wrong the loss of this secret obviously rankled. The large part played by luxury goods in French exports at this time is stressed by Veryard in a rather peevish passage:

> The foolish Curiosity of divers neighbouring Nations is arriv'd to such a pitch, that the French enrich themselves by such Toys as are sent out of the Kingdom, and fondly coveted by Strangers: tho' possibly they might find as good at Home, did not Fancy byass them from all things that are not far fetcht and dear bought. The French, 'tis true, are the usual Broachers of Novelties, and happy enough in their inventions, but are always beholding to the English to bring them to perfection. Their Ribands, Lace, Perfumes, Paints, and Womens Dresses, with an infinity of other Trifles (of which the greatest part goes out of the Kingdom) turn to their incredible Benefit; insomuch, that divers persons at Paris, that deal in these toyish Commodities, have been known to have got an Hundred thousand pound Sterl. in less than Ten Years time; which is a convincing Argument of their Neighbour's Dementation, and their own Dexterity in taking them on the blind side, and putting an high Value on their goods.

In this context Veryard pens a highly satirical passage on the taste of his own countrymen for all things French: 'My Lord's Perruque fits not well till Monsieur has had a hand in't; and my Lady relishes not her Victuals unless they're served in with a French Sauce. The Exchange Women would have a poor Trade, had they not the knack of Frenchifying their Wares; and the Courtier could hardly pretend to the Quality of Huff and Beau, unless he'd spent some time in a French Academy, and entertain'd Masters of Sciences of that Nation'.[94]

The shortage of coal from which France continues to suffer down to the present day is commented upon by several travellers, indeed as early as the 1590s by Fynes Moryson: 'For fier they use wood and coales, yet have they no pit coales or sea coales, but have their sea coales out of England for their Smiths Forges, and where they have lesse store of wood within land, there they burne straw, furres, and other kinds of stubble'.[95] This is echoed by Reresby in his account of the French people: 'Their fuel is usually wood, and charcoal. Sea coal they have in some places from England; the meaner sort burn stubble and furze'.[96] While at Aix-en-Provence Skippon noted down particulars of how olives could be used as a substitute for wood or coal: 'Here we were inform'd what that firing is they call *Mute*, viz. the oil being press'd out, the remaining part of the olives is made up with water into a paste, then squeez'd into round moulds like thick cheese-fats; and when they are dry'd in the sun, they are good firing like turfs'.[97] At Poitiers Lauder noticed how every Friday and Saturday the peasants brought in 'multitude of chariots charged with wood, some of them drawen with oxen, most with mules'. 'Wood', he adds 'is a passable commodity heir as in all France, wheir they burn no thing but wood, which seimes indeed to be wholsomer for dressing of meat then coall'.[98]

In seventeenth-century France there were a number of obstacles to the expansion of trade and industry. Our travellers often mention the tolls (*péages*) levied for the use of bridges, roads and rivers. Thus Skippon, in describing a journey by boat from Grenoble to Orange, noted: 'Many peages and tolls paid by the boatmen as we came along', adding that a league beyond Pont Saint-Esprit 'we landed at a peage or toll-place belonging to Orange'.[99]

They were even more struck by the existence of customs barriers between different provinces or groups of provinces inside France. These were not to be swept away until the Revolution. Alone of the numerous travellers going from the Channel ports to Paris Edward Browne mentions being held up at Montreuil: 'There they search my portmantle again, and I, not knowing I was to take a passe at Calais, was put to some inconvenience, and had like to lose my stockins, which were in my portmantle; but that one that travayled along with mee could speake both English and French, who perswaded [them] I was no merchant, and with fair words I got of'.[100] Travellers who entered France from the Spanish Netherlands and passed through the new territory in Flanders won by Louis XIV were disgusted to discover that when they arrived at the former frontier town of Péronne, they had to undergo a second customs examination. On arrival there, writes Veryard, 'we were very severely search'd at the Gate (as all Strangers are) to prevent the Importation of Commodities from Flanders without paying the Customs'.[101]

Northleigh was even more aggrieved by his experience at Péronne: 'Though you pay Duties to the French Government in Flanders for anything you bring in, that is obliged to pay Custom; here you arc search'd and examin'd again, and must pay additional Duty for things for which it is due, for here the King's Officers search'd us again as narrowly, and made us pay as rigorously'. The rest of his comments on this state of affairs, though rather crusty, are not lacking in humour:

I thought at first they might have offered us an hardship more than ordinary, and that their *Bureau*, or *Bourreau* (as I innocently, tho' perhaps justly in pronouncing it call'd him, which with them is Hang-man) had abus'd us with Impositions, but I found on my second Voyage through this Place, that their own Country-men fair'd no better than Foreigners: and that a French-man paid for a small trifling Toy that he brought in his pocket from Flanders, which he had bought at Paris, and paid duty for in this very place: at his carrying it out he made some stir and much Complaint, with as little Redress; and these Creatures places probably being bought from a Court that has always occasion for Money, they must be admitted to make the best of what they are forc'd to buy.

He was, or course, wrong on the last point; these customs officials were not government employees who had purchased their posts. They were hired and paid by the tax-farmers.

Many of our travellers encountered a customs post at Lyons, since the province in which it lay was not part of the 'cinq grosses fermes', the group of provinces which communicated freely with one another; it was one of the so-called 'provinces réputées étrangères' which from a customs point of view were cut off both from the 'cinq grosses fermes' and from the other provinces in this category. At Lyons Northleigh noted the presence across the River Saône of 'a Chain of Boats link'd together, to keep Barks from passing without paying Duty'.[102] Much earlier in the century Coryate had noted the existence of what he calls 'a Barracado of boates chained together' at this point,[103] while Finch speaks of 'two strong cittadels upon the water to hinder the passage when they demand the doanne'.[104] Symonds relates how on their arrival from Paris he and his companions were stopped at the entrance to the city 'where our Cloke baggs were opend';[105] Skippon's party, coming from the south, 'gave a piece of money to the searchers, who were desirous to see what we had in our portmanteaus'.[106]

Our travellers also encountered customs posts in other parts of France. On his way from Bordeaux to Paris Locke notes the presence of 'a Douan where my portmanteau was searchd', presumably when he was passing from Saintonge, a 'province réputée étrangère', into Poitou which was in the 'cinq grosses fermes'.[107] While travelling from Montpellier to Marseilles, Buxton was twice stopped at such posts, first on arriving opposite Arles where, he tells us, 'we were first stopt at the ferrying place by the King's officer to have our baggage examined; there we got a certificate'. On approaching Marseilles across the Étang de Berre, he adds, 'we met with a village and a Bureau or Custom house, where showing our certificates we had little stop'.[108]

In this period canals were much further developed in France than in this country. Traveller after traveller comments on the Canal de Briare, which joins the Loire and the Seine; it was begun in 1604, but not finished until 1642, the year of Richelieu's death. As often, Locke offers the most detailed account of it, throwing in a reference to plans for the Canal d'Orléans, constructed in the period 1682–92:

> Two leagues before we came to Gien we passed the Canale at Briare where by boats passe out of the Loire into the Sene, which communication betwixt these two rivers is of great convenience. The Canale cut is but 4 leagues longue & wants water in the summer. Cardinal Richleiue was the author of it & under his care it came to be perfected, but being in the hands of private men (under grants & priviledges from Luis 13) who have both the management & profit of it. The King is going to make a communication of these 2 rivers Lower to passe by Montargis. They pay here in the Canale of Briare 60s. per foot for the length of the boat when loaden with fish or such commoditys, when with heavier, v.g. wine, they pay more than a crown per foot.[109]

On his visit to the Calais region Kennet noted that a canal was already under construction to the recently annexed town of St. Omer: 'A river cutting out from Calais to St.Omers at the kings charge. Begun 1680, proceeded about 7 mile, expected to be finished in 1684'.[110]

Amongst travellers to the South of France the Canal du Languedoc aroused considerable interest. Described by one modern historian as 'the greatest feat of engineering in Western Europe since Roman times', this canal was another of the achievements of Colbert's administration. It was undertaken to link together the Mediterranean and the Atlantic, and with its construction was associated the creation of a new port at Sète (then known as Cette). Work was begun in 1667 under the direction of Pierre Paul Riquet (1604–1680) and it was finally opened to traffic in 1681.

In 1675 Clenche included a visit to Sète in his travels and speaks of the new port and the canal in his usual rather sneering fashion:

> Portsette, Where the King is making a Harbour in the Mediterranean, and has advanc'd a Mole already 600 yards, designs another Parallel to it, and the entrance to be just in the middle; the Stone they blow up out of a Mountain close by it, which is very good Marble: Here the famous Canal falls in, which is to join both Seas, but is scarce so large or deep as that in St. James's park; the Garonne that runs that way, has saved a great expence, yet is nevertheless excessive, but so wisely placed upon the provisions that Country spends, that his Majesty is a

gainer by it. There are two or three Basons and Reservoirs, one prodigious, being a Valley stopt up at one end, but the art to get water into them is not yet known.[111]

Locke's comments on both the canal and the port are more detailed as he spent much longer in the South of France at the time when both were being constructed and even had an opportunity to meet Riquet at Sète. He twice visited the new port, inspected part of the canal, including the basin at St. Ferréol where the waters were collected from the streams of the Montagne Noire, and soon afterwards travelled by boat down part of the canal from Castelnaudary to Toulouse.[112]

On his first visit to Sète in March 1676 he describes the mole as 'a mighty work', but adds that 'the sand in the port now & the breach made in the mole last winter shew how hardly one defends a place against Neptune which he attaques with great & small shot too'. When he returned there a year later, he met Riquet and was able to discuss with him the progress of both the port and the canal:

The long arme of the mole,which is that on the west side, runs out near east, as I think. It is now as far out into the sea as it is to be, as Mr. Riquet himself told me on the place. The farther end of it, which stands out into the sea, is of semented work, which is let down their quays. There were two others of like [size] of each side of this that is now standing, but the sea last December caried them both away, and they lost there by the weather goods to the value of 100,000£ Tournoys. They are now busy about repairing it by throwing in great stones on both sides, and so raise it of a breadth big enough to make a platforme on the top to be a fort for the defence of the port. This arme of the mole is about 1040 of my steps long and about 30 broad at the top. At the end of the mole they have 40 foot of water; farther in, where the vessels ride, 12 or 14: near the shore one or 2 where, when the mole began to be built, they had 18 or 20, and [we] saw [men] who told us that it fills every year with sand mightily. The other arm of the mole which runs near south, as I think, is not above 1/4 or 1/3 so long as the other. Riquet's draft in the printed book[113] agrees well with it, but that arm that points south is in print much longer than in port. From the Basin to Port Sette they have 80 Toyse fall & to Tholouse 40. The length of the Canal from Sette to Tholouse is 30 leagues and the passage will be of 4 days. The Canal is passable already from Toulouse to Castlenaudary & from Sette to Beziers. That of it which is yet to finish will not be done yet these 3 years. 1 Toyse is 6 foot of Paris & one league of Languedoc 2 of Paris. All this, except the increase of sand, I had from Riquet himself, and also that they hope not to have it for vessels above 100 tun. We saw about 12 of such or lesser in the port.

During the previous week, on this same trip from Montpellier, Locke had explored the finished stretches of the canal near Castelnaudary. He devotes some space to a description of the basin at Naurouze, giving particular attention to a water wheel which he saw there. He makes a certain number of critical comments on what he observed. Riding along the side of the canal between Castelnaudary and Naurouze at the watershed between the Atlantic and the Mediterranean, he notes that 'the earth of the bank falls in, but not much', and at Naurouze that 'the wall of the Basin is of ill stones which decay apace'. He also provides details about the section of the canal already in operation between Castelnaudary and Toulouse. The packet boat in which later in the month he was to travel, he notes, 'draws 3 foot water. Other boats of burthen need 5, which in summer they want and cannot go, but the packet boat goes always'. He adds that the transport of goods on this section cost $7\frac{1}{2}$ sous a quintal.[114]

In May 1681, by which time the canal is supposed to have been finished, John Buxton writes in a letter: 'I have been at a place called Port Cette, which I doubt not but you have heard of, where this great Monarch has attempted to make a communication between the Mediterranean and the Ocean by a canal which, if it be accomplished, history can never produce the like; for then there will be no need of his going about by Spain or danger of the Turks, because this canal is in his own territories and leads to Bourdeaux'.[115] Though Veryard who also saw the canal in the 1680s, calls its construction 'an extraordinary Enterprise' which 'shews something of the ancient Roman Magnificence', he has a rather lower opinion of its contribution to trade: 'It's capable of large Boats and Barges, which are carried over divers Hills by Sluces; but these Sluces are so numerous, and the Charge in passing them so very great, that Merchants choose rather to send their Goods by long Sea, in time of Peace, than make use of so expenseive a Conveniency; however, in time of War they will find the benefit of it; and the Country People have actually found it very commodious for transporting the Productions of their own Soil from one place to another'.[116] When Bromley visited Sète, he noted like Locke the menace which sand presented to the port: 'The Mole', he writes, 'is made of vast hard stones, that are blown out of the Rocks near by Gunpowder; but after all Endeavours, there is such a quantity of Sand constantly brought in by the Tide, that few Vessels of Burthen can ride there'.[117] Sand has always been a problem at Sète, and despite its fame the canal has never been much used for through traffic between the Atlantic and the Mediterranean.

We have already had some glimpses of wages and working conditions of the poorer classes in the towns. Another curious one is furnished by Locke during his stay in Montpellier: 'The women carrying earth at the gate in litle baskets on their heads, & singing & dancing in their sabots as they returned for new burthens'.[118] Somewhat conflicting views are expressed by the small number of travellers who mention the subject of begging. Skippon, for instance, states boldly: 'Few or no beggars in Paris,'[119] but this is contradicted by others, starting with Symonds who observes during his stay in the capital: 'Old Beggars will often say a Benediction & some prayers in Latine afore they begg'.[120] Northleigh speaks of the number of well dressed beggars he encountered: 'There is a great deal of appearance of Wealth in Paris, while at the same time there is a great deal less than appears: insomuch that you frequently meet with Beggars well habited, to whom I have sometimes pull'd off my Hat, till they desir'd me to pull out my Purse; and I saw that they had more want of Bread than of Ceremony or Compliment'. When in the provinces, at Nemours, he extends this observation to the whole of the country: 'I observ'd a Custom they had hereabout, that the Women of the Town, well habited and of some Fashion, us'd to visit all Inns, and especially all Travellers that came with their flying Coach, to collect Moneys for the Poor of the Place, and perhaps put in for it themselves; for Poverty as I have observ'd above, is the best clad and habited in France of any Place in Christendom'.[121] At the end of the century Lister offers a more realistic and compassionate view of the problem in Paris: 'The great multitude of poor Wretches in all parts of this City is such, that a Man in a Coach, a-foot, in the Shop, is not able to do any business for the number and importunities of Beggars: and to hear their Miseries is very lamentable: and if you give to one, you immediately bring a whole swarm upon you'.[122]

The problem of *mendicité* troubled the authorities, more especially in Paris which tended to attract beggars from all over France. In an attempt to deal with the problem the government set up the Hôpital Général in Paris in 1656: this had under its control ten charitable insititutions and houses of correction. Reresby who was in France shortly after its establishment is enthusiastic about it and somewhat naïvely imagined that it had actually managed to rid Paris of beggars:

> Before I leave Paris, I cannot but take notice of its Hospital-general, lately built at the public charge, out of the ruins of the Hospital of Pity, and very worthy of imitation. Here the whole impotent poor are relieved, and the more able set to work to some manufacture or other, by a stock yearly arising from the general contribution of the whole city, the king paying

his proportion as well as the meanest burgher. It received three thousand the first year it was erected, whereby the town in the world the most pestered with beggars is become the freest of them.[123]

Somewhat later in the century Veryard also devoted a passage to the subject. Though he gets wrong the number of institutions belonging to the Hôpital Général, he does bring out the fact that there were several:

> The Hospital General comprehends six distinct Houses, which are call'd but one, because the chief of them has the Superintendence over the rest. One of them is for poor old Women and Girls; another for Poor Families, Vagabonds, and poor little Children; in the third are poor Women with Child, sent hither to be brought to Bed; in the fourth, Beggars and Vagabonds; in the fifth, such as are troubled with scall'd Heads; and in the sixth, poor infirm Boys. All six entertain 8000 Persons.[124]

In his account of the Hôpital Général Northleigh stresses the very practical aim with which it had been set up:

> Their Hospital . . . call'd *L'Hopital General,* is a large piece of Building, and contains as they told us, six thousand Persons. It was founded or finish'd but about the year 1657. Cardinal Mazarine and some other Courtiers finding the Poor to perplex them with their troublesome importunity, and growing numerous, they further'd this Work to find Work for the Poor, where they are well look'd after; the Maidens are imployed in making their *Point de France,* so that those that are well are employ'd, and those that are sick are taken care for.[125]

The Hospice de la Charité at Lyons attracted the attention of several of our travellers. Bertie who visited it in 1662 was particularly enthusiastic, describing it as 'a goodly structure':

> In it are nine courts [and] fourteen corps de logis. Here are 1200 poor of both sexes, men and women, old and young, orphelins, debauched men and women, bastards, etc. Every one hath their own apartment. You see here the boulangeries, cuisine, grenier, the place where they work silk. Every flesh day the poor have 600 pounds of meat, every fish day 800 eggs and 100 pounds of cheese, every day 1900 pounds of bread, and two pipes of wine. Moreover every Sunday this house gives to the other poor in town 4500 loaves of bread, every one weighing five livres. They never stir out but once in a year at the great Procession. This is one of the best houses in France for the nourishment of the poor.[126]

Both Evelyn and Lassells have rather shorter descriptions of this institution.[127]

Locke was so impressed with it that he made two short entries on his visit to it in December 1675 and a longer and more detailed one when he came back in November 1678. On his first visit he could get no further than the outer court and the chapel where, he writes 'we staid & heard the women there sing Vespers which they did well, both in vocal & in instrumentall musick. They performed a great part of the evening service & were of those that had been bred up in that house'. He had the curiosity to go back the next day and see the inside of the building, including the huge granary, but his more detailed remarks are to be found in the entry he made three years later:

> We saw the Charitie, a very large & well regulated hospital where young children, male & femal, not under 7 years old, are taken in & set to worke. Their great imployment is about Silke. They are taught alsoe to reade and some of the girles to sing, & thus they are bread up. When they are of age, they may goe out or marry if they will, & then they give the maide that is maried £100 to begin the world with, or they may stay in all their lives, & of these there are usually in the house about 1,500 poore & orphans, & if they have any thing, as it happens to some of the Orphans, the principall is restord to them when they goe out & the house has the use for their breeding. Some of the girles are taught to sing & sing well enough.

The long hours of work and the frugal diet to which the children were subjected did not strike Locke as being at all unreasonable:

> They rise at 5 & worke till darke in winter, & in sommer till 6 at night, but, counting their masse & breakfast in the morning, collation in the afternoon & time of dinner, their worke is not hard.
> Their break fast & collation is bread & water. At dinner & supper they have a litle morsell of boiled flesh, each one about an ounce or two, & soope at dinner, but never roast meat, unless it be the singers who are treated better then the rest. They have all trades necessary for the house within them selves.

Bread being the main item of diet, there was a huge granary which Locke inspected for the second time:

> They bake, one week with an other, 100 asnes of wheat, partly for the use & consumption of the house, & partly to be distributed to the prisoners & poore of the towne, Though the portion of flesh be limited to every one, yet every one may have as much bread as he can eat.
> They usually have in their granary a provision of 6 or 7,000 Asnes of wheat which 10 or 12 men are dayly imploid in turning. It lyes about a yard or more thick & the roome open to the aire without glasse or paper to the windows.[128]

A decade or so later Ferrier also devoted some space to a description of La Charité which he found a much more impressive building than the Hôtel-Dieu:

> It is of a great circumference & being of stone seems [more] like some lord's habitation than the dwelling of inferme persons. It doe contain a vast number of people of all ages & conditions, there are at least two thousand bastards which are put out to nurse at its charge & almost as many that are continually there who, as they grow up, do work, some of whom twister, others net, &c.... We ascending some steps went into their corn chamber, we seeing it large measured it & found it an hundred and fifty paces long & twenty five broad. It was full of wheat from one end to the other, there is 60 ryemen to turn it every day, they eat very good victualls of all sorts & drink nothing but Ptisanne which an Apothecary (whome they there maintain) dos make. There number may be guest if you consider the quantity of bread they eat, there being baked every week six hundred loafs weighing six pounds a piece.[129]

Although the Hôtel-Dieu at Lyons is described by Ferrier as 'a handsome building', it is dismissed in a few words as 'the Hospitall where are all manner of sick & aged persons who knowing no ways to help themselves are taken in here'. Locke goes into a little more detail: 'I saw also the Hostel Dieu, a fair, large Hospital, containing, as they told me, 500 sick persons. They lye in a room which is a large crosse, & 3 rows of beds in each & in one part 2 in a bed, in the other but one, as I observed. Two of the arms of the crosse have men, the other two women. In the center is an alter'.[130] Bromley seems to have got his travel notes mixed up, as what he calls La Charité is clearly the Hôtel-Dieu. After visiting the Jesuits' College he went on to 'the Charité, a large well built Hospital, where all the poor sick Persons of the City are received, and carefully looked after during their Sickness. The Apartments for the Men and Women are distinct, conveniently contrived, and kept neat and clean. The Revenues are very considerable, as is necessary; there being generally five or six hundred People in it. Here also such Children are provided for, as are dropp'd in the Streets, or left at Doors: whereof, they said, they had then in the House near two hundred, and many more at Nurse out in the Countrey'.[131]

Locke almost certainly visited the Hôtel-Dieu in Paris, but all he chose to enter in his journal was one single line: 'People of good condition serveing the sick in the Hostel de Dieu'.[132] However, there is no lack of descriptions of this institution at various dates in the century. Heylyn who went to see it in 1625, rounds off his account of his visit to the hospital by rejecting the notion that such an expedition was somewhat foolhardy:

> One would imagine that in such a variety of wounds and diseases, a walke into it, and a view of it, might savour more of curiosity, then discretion, but indeed it is nothing lesse; for besides that no person of an infectious disease is admitted into it: which maketh much for the safety of such as view it; all things are there kept so cleanly, neatly and orderly, that it is sweeter walking there then in the best street of Paris, none excepted.

His description of what he saw inside the hospital is quite detailed:

> At the first entrance into it, you come into their Chappell, small, but handsome and well furnished; after, you passe into a long gallery, having four ranks of beds, two close to the two wals, and two in the middle. The beds are all sutable one to the other; their Valence, Curtains and Rugs being all yellow. At the right hand of it, was a gallery more then double the length of this first, so also furnished. At the further end of this a door opened into another Chamber, dedicated only to sick women: and within them another room, wherein women with childe are lightned of their burden, and their children kept till seven years of age, at the charge of the Hospitall. At the middle of the first gallery towards the left hand, were four other ranks of beds, little differing from the rest, but that their furniture was blew; and in them there was no place for any but such as were somewhat wounded, and belonged properly to the Chirurgeon. There are numbred in the whole Hospitall no fewer then 700 beds (besides those of the attendants, Priests, Apothecaries, &c.) and in every bed two persons.[133]

Symonds who visited this hospital in 1649 gives a good deal of interesting detail about the inside of it. He observes first that it was 'a large & Very Rich Hospitall having more Legacies bequeathed to it by the Riche sinfulle Citizens then any howse of France'. He went in at the front which resembled a church with its statues including 'that of our Saviour between the 2 dores'.

> Entering in that way, as the dores are open in the Holy Weeke, there is a large square roome with divers Roomes of Yellow Beds where Women Lye. This smells ranke notwithstanding the great industry & Cleanliness of the Nuns who helpe both these & the men. The other parts which are large & long have 3 and 4 Rowes of beds, divers beds having 4 men. Some 5 Boyes Lying heads & pownts. And the beds are not very large neither. On one side is divers small kitchens with Cisternes of water. The Offices below as large Kitchen that is neare River & is very convenient & Cleanly.
> Upon the Walls all about is written in Faire letters places of Scripture for Patience & comfort to the Sick & for Charity &

bounty for the Visiters the scripture Quoted, Preists catechise the boys lying in their beds & instruct them with much paynes. One man I saw dying & a Nun was praying in her booke by him laying a small crucifix upon him. By each bed is a deepe brasse Vessel like a kettle lett into a frame of Wood for their exputs.[134] One Vessel between every bed. Most have Ropes fastend aloft in the midst of the tester to ease the sick themselves by. In the middle of the Hospital is an altar rayle. In upon the wall is a large new picture where the Queen Regent that is presents her young son, to the V.M. The Crosse Ladder & persons as big as the life & well done.[135]

Though written in note form, this account of the Hôtel-Dieu, is in many ways the most vivid of all those produced by our travellers. The numbers of patients in a bed is given very differently by those who visited it. According to Finch who saw over this hospital two years after Symonds there were eight in a bed, while in 1660 Bertie declares that the sick 'lie three in a bed, two lying with their heads upward, and the third with his head downward in the middle, parting the heads of the other two with his feet'.[136] Shortly after his arrival in Paris in 1664 Edward Browne visited the Hôtel-Dieu which he describes as 'a brave Hospital indeed, in which there are four hundred sick persons. There are four rows of beds stande in a roome, very handsome ones'. Later in his stay he saw six men and boys undergo the operation of the cutting of the stone, and on this return from Italy in the following year he was allowed to watch an arm being amputated.[137] However, he has little to say about how the hospital was run.

Other doctors offer rather more information later in the century, though there continue to be remarkable differences between their accounts of the number of patients in a bed. Veryard gives a brief account of the various hospitals in Paris and continues:

The Hostel Dieu is the antientist, and receives all diseased Persons without distinction of Sex, Age, Country or Religion. Here are sometimes brought in fifty or an hundred in a day, and commonly the like number sent back to their Houses or to their Graves. The Sick are very carefully look'd to by an hundred Nuns, with divers other Servants, who told us that they had at least one thousand eight hundred under their Hands, and that the number sometimes exceeded two thousand. The greatest Incommodity we found here is, that the Place holds but a thousand Beds, so that they are often forc'd to lie two in a Bed, The Revenue of this Hospital amounts to at least twenty five thousand Pounds Sterling per Annum, besides the Alms which are daily collected for that Use.[138]

Northleigh offers a more detailed and livelier account, starting off with some remarks about the nuns who did the nursing: 'Their Hotel Dieu is a very large Hospital, and for the Sick the chief in Paris, said to contain sometimes Four Thousand; they are tended and look'd after by the Religious of the Order of St.Augustine, young perfect Nuns, and for the generality very comely Women, whom they venture among Men when infirm, though perhaps sometimes too far; for one of our infirm Irish-men was grown on a sudden so Lusty, that he made a shift to run away with one of the pretty Tenders'. Taking up Locke's point about the aristocratic ladies who helped to nurse the patients, he expresses some doubts as to this practice, instancing the death of the Duchesse de Nemours who contracted smallpox while fulfilling this pious duty: 'Such presumptuous Zeal, as it cannot be condemned in the Act, yet perhaps might be avoided without blame, but the Doctrine of Merit with them, makes that a part of Devotion, which with the people of another Persuasion, may be lookt upon as tempting the Almighty'.[139]

There follows a comparison with a much smaller Paris hospital, run by the Frères de la Charité who counted surgeons among their number. Earlier Finch had found this other hospital much superior to the Hôtel-Dieu: 'The Charité is the best accommodated that can be, as well as any gentleman in his own house. I beleive there's about 200, every man in a bed singly. The paynes of those religious persons which tend them is to be pitied', while Bertie too found it much superior to the Hôtel Dieu, adding: 'The sick lie every one in a single bed, and such clean sheets, so cleanly lookt to, that it is very remarkable and the manner of their attendance worth the seeing'.[140] Northleigh's comments on the two hospitals also favour the Charité; dealing first with the Hôtel-Dieu, he writes:

This place has great Revenues, and every Year continually encreases by new Benefactors. It is but like an ordinary Pile of our Building, and of no extraordinary Convenience for the Sick, being in a close place, and crowded too with Numbers, which I taking notice of to an experienced Chirurgion then with me, that such Houses should be seated in the Suburbs, in a freer Air, and not to be immur'd between other dwellings, made the Gentleman observe to me, that they generally made it their Remark, That in ill Symptoms and Affections occasion'd by Fractures or Dislocations, or cutting for the Stone or the like, they did much oftener miscarry here than in their other Hospital de la Charité; though I did allow that there might be some difference in the Excellency of the Chirurgions or Operators that belong's to one or the other; for indeed the Two places are not a quarter of a Mile asunder, and both built round by other

Houses, yet he assur'd me they seldom fail in the one, and seldom recover in the other, insomuch that they superstitiously believe an Æculapius in the one more particularly present; but then their Hotel Dieu would have the advantage, for not far from it stands his Statue; but one of these Places I think is better wash'd with a Current than the other, and so can be kept cleaner.

Of the Charité he has only this to say: 'The Hospital de la Charité, in which it seems they are more successful, does not seem to have more Conveniency than the other; it is serv'd by the Fryers of the Order of St. Jean, and as in the other, they lye all in long Rooms fill'd with three Rows of Beds'.[141]

We learn very little about the middle class inhabitants of the towns, perhaps because our travellers took them for granted. The guilds which played such an important part in the economic life of France before the Revolution appear mainly because they figure in the various religious processions held on Church feast days.

Locke does make it clear that, while many towns and cities were exempted from payment of the *taille*, this did not mean that the inhabitants were not taxed in other ways. Early in his stay in Montpellier he picked up grumbles (no doubt somewhat exaggerated) about the burden of direct taxation: 'Merchants & handicrafts men pay above half their gain'. Later on his travels he noted down more precise details about the means by which the Treasury extracted money from the townsfolk, partly through the guilds. At Tours, for instance, he wrote down the following details: 'They gave the King this year 45,000£ to be excused from winter quarter, which came to 1/10 on the rent of their houses. Wine, wood, etc. that enter the town pay tax to the King. Besides he sends to the severall companys of trades men for soe much mony as he thinks fit. The officers of each corps de mestier taxes every one according to his worth, which perhaps amounts to about 1 escu or 4£ to a man counted worth 100 escus'. In the following year he has a similar story to tell about how Orleans and Poitiers were made to contribute to the Treasury: 'The town of Orleans, though a free towne & by particular priviledges exempted from quartering any soldiers, yet the last winter, to be exempt from winter quarters, though noe soldiers were neare, were [*sic*] fain to compound at the rate of 52,000£: & Poictiers, a towne of extraordinary merit towards this very King, by whom it had that amongst other prviledges granted it, was fain also the last winter to buy its exemption at a round sum'.[142]

From one end of the period to the other our travellers comment on an important feature in the social history of France under the Ancien

Régime — the selling of official posts. These could be quite modest ones or, as with those in the Parlements and other higher courts, they could confer noble rank on the holder and his descendants. It is notorious that the attractions of these posts for members of the middle class led to a great deal of the wealth created in trade and industry being drained off into the coffers of the Treasury. 'All offices being vendible in this kingdom', wrote Sir George Carew early in the century, 'the merchants employ their money rather in buying offices than in exercising traffick, because officers' wives go before merchants' wives'.[143]

Similarly Dallington had spoken of the dangers arising from recourse to this expedient: 'There yet remayneth one other meanes (though extraordinary) to a Prince, to get money, which the necessitie of the times, and the want of other meanes, have forced the French Kings of late yeares to use. This is the vent or sales of Offices, a very dangerous & hurtfull Marchandize, both for the Prince & the subject'.[144] These posts could often be pure sinecures such as that of *secrétaire du roi*, an office frequently bought by wealthy *roturiers* in order to secure noble rank. 'To speak truth', writes Evelyn, 'the multitude of those who stile themselves Secretaries to the King, is such, that what with the greatnesse of their number, and inconsiderableness of most of their persons, the dignity of the charge is extremely eclipsed'.[145]

These offices had become hereditary on payment of an annual tax called *la paulette*, instituted in 1604 and continually renewed until the end of the Ancien Régime. Although Howell, writing in 1625, is wrong in thinking this tax was something new, he does give a clear account of it:

> There is a great businesse now a foot in Paris called the *Polette*, which if it take effect will tend to correct, at least wise to cover a great error in the French government: The custom is that all the chief places of Justice throughout all the eight Courts of Parliament in France, besides a great number of other offices, are set to sale by the King, and they return to him unlesse the buyer liveth fourtie daies after the resignation to another: It is now propounded that these casuall offices shall be absolutely hereditary, provided that every officer pay a yearly revenue unto the King, according to the valuation and perquisits of that office.[146]

In his description of the workings of the administrative machine Evelyn also observes that a post in it had become hereditary 'so that even the Widow of the defunct may delegate it to a Deputy or Proxy, the King only reserving a small annual rent, which they call *La Paulet*;

in default of which payment, or that person die without having resigned his office, these Treasurers dispose of it to the Kings use and benefit'.[147]

At the end of the century Lister penned a striking passage on the manner in which the holders of high judicial posts and their wives preened themselves on their exalted station, acquired either by their own money or that of a father or uncle:

> Amongst the Living Objects to be seen in the Streets of Paris, the Counsellors and Chief Officers of the Courts of Justice make a great Figure; They and their Wives have their Trains carried up; so there are abundance to be seen walking about the Streets in this manner. 'Tis for this that places of that nature sell so well. A Man that has a right to qualifie a Wife with this Honour, shall command a Fortune; and the carrying a great Velvet Cushion to Church is such another business. The Place of a Lawyer is valued a Third part dearer for this.[148]

The government could make heavy financial demands on its office-holders, particularly the wealthier ones, when it was hard pressed for money: it would inflict upon them an increase in salary ('une augmentation de gages'), which meant that they would be required to produce a large sum of money, often at very short notice, to pay for the increased value of their post; or else it would simply exact a loan from them. In 1676 at Montpellier Locke noted an example of the latter expedient: 'The King last year sent to all the officers of this province to lend him 2 years' profit of their offices. Some were fain to pawn their plate to have their money ready at the day. Otherwise they had lost their places. This got him two millions out of this one province'.[149]

Again and again our travellers denounce the corruption of justice which the sale of offices brought with it. 'Sales of offices cause sales of Justice', Dallington bluntly declares, while according to Overbury 'Concerning the Civill Justice there, it is no where more Corrupt nor expencefull . . . The King sells the places of Justice at as high a rate as can bee honestly made of them; so that all thriving is left to Corruption, and the gaine the King hath that wayes, tempts him to make a multitude of Officers, which is another burthen to the Subject'.[150] Sir George Carew was obviously taken aback by the French custom of soliciting one's judges: 'In every cause, little or great, there are solicitations and maintenance of potent men and women, not only tolerated, but expected, and in a manner exacted of the judges themselves'. He formed an unfavourable view of both the quality of the judiciary and the high cost of justice:

> Again, by the sale of their places of judicature it falleth out,

that old advocates plead causes, and young counsellors or judges determine them, who pass over matters in post, having for their ends, not the delivery of true and sound justice, but the gratifying of those men and women, who have solicited them in the cause, and the raising to themselves of huge and large Espices or fees; insomuch as a man of mean quality, that was reporter of a cause for some of your majesty's subjects unjustly condemned to the gallies at Rochelle (which sentence, at my suit, was afterwards overthrown in the parliament at Paris), taxed for his own pains in perusing the papers of this one cause, 24 *l*. sterling, besides all other officers: and had it not been for the hope of that gain, I doubt the cause would not have had so good an end.[150a]

In describing the *Présidial* court at Orleans Heylyn declares that the institution has now become burdensome: 'The reason is, that the offices are made salable, and purchased by them with a great deal of money, which afterwards they wrest again out of the purses of the peasants: the sale of offices drawing necessarily after it, the sale of justice; a mischief which is spread so far, that there is not the poorest under officer in all the Realm, who may not safely say with the Captain in the 22. of the Acts and the 28. vers., with a great sum of money obtained I this freedome'.[151]

Even Evelyn uses some unusually strong language on this subject:

The Justice of France (in the equal dispensation whereof should be the glory and diadem of a Prince in Peace, as is the multitude of people his visible strength in warr) is doubtless very good, but wonderfully ill executed, which happens through the sordid corruption of such as dispense it for mony and favour, without which there is nothing to be hoped for in this Kingdom: and good reason there should bee some gain made of that which the dividers thereof buy soe dear, purchasing their places and offices at such excessive charges, that they are constrained to sell their Vertue to him who bids most for it.[152]

Such comments, however, do not explain what drove multitudes of *roturiers* throughout the Ancien Régime to acquire the great variety of posts which were on offer, particularly the more expensive ones which conferred noble rank on their holders.

They lived in a society in which trade and the merchant were despised and in which the 1694 *Dictionnaire de l'Académie Française* offered the following examples of the disdainful use of the word *bourgeois*: 'Bourgeois veut dire encore, Un homme qui n'est pas de la Cour. *Cela sent bien son bourgeois*. En ce sens il est le plus souvent adjectif. *Une maniere bourgeoise, une conversation bourgeoise, il a l'air bourgeois'*. As Evelyn put it, 'no Gentleman will in France binde his youngest son to any Trade or Mechanique Calling whatever, under that of a Military life, as esteeming every Apprentisage and subjection, a stain and diminution to the Honor and Dignity of his Family; the like also, they for the most part observe in their Marriages and Alliances'. He adds that professions such as medicine and the law were also despised by the nobility: 'No Gentlemans necessity whatsoever shall easily engage him to seek any support either by Physick or Law: both which Professions are (as in truth they highly merit) in very laudable esteem and reputation amongst us in England'.[153]

A similar observation was made at about the same date by Symonds: 'When the sons of Gentlemen or Nobles are decayed in their fortunes, they use to serve another man of quality rather then goe to be apprentised to merchants or Burgeoys'.[154] Reresby has a very interesting passage in which he points out that on the one hand by engaging in trade a successful bourgeois could use his wealth to acquire noble rank, while on the other such an occupation was utterly despised by a nobleman, though he notes one amusing exception to this rule: 'Trading in France both procures and forfeits gentility; persons that have got good estates easily obtaining being ennobled by the king at cheap rates; when at the same time a gentleman born, is thought to degrade himself by traffic; and yet the best of them, in plentiful years, play the vintner, setting up huts at their gates, and selling a farthing's worth of wine to passengers'.[155]

The gulf between *gentilhomme* and *bourgeois* is described by Lauder when he writes that the French 'put a gentleman and burgoise as opposites; he cannot be a gentleman if a burgoise; but he may become on and then he ceaseth to be a burgoise. I urged whither or no a gentlemans sone by becoming a burgoise was not still a gentleman; the sayd not, for by becoming bourgoise (he is called Roturier) he seimes to renounce his right of gentleman'.[156] Locke has some interesting comments to offer on the legal position of noblemen who engaged in trade. He noted that here Brittany presented an exception: 'Gentlemen of Bretaigne have liberty to trade without losing their gentility, only entering their names and laying by their gentility for a time, which they resume again when they leave trade, but the rest of France cannot do so, but if they once trade, they lose their gentility'. He was well aware that this last statement required qualification. In 1665 Colbert had secured a royal edict reminding noblemen that it was only retail trade which involved loss of noble rank and that they could engage in the 'commerce de mer' without losing caste. This is reflected in an earlier entry by Locke: 'This King hath made an edict that those who merchandise, but do not use the yard, shall not loose their gentility'.[157]

Since the possession of noble rank conferred not only social status, but also the valuable privilege of exemption from the *taille*, the temptation to usurp it was great and often succumbed to. Colbert waged war on these *faux nobles* whose exemption from the *taille* increased the burden on others and diminished returns to the Treasury. In 1676 while Locke was in Montpellier, he picked up some information on the matter: 'One that gatherd it, told us that he collected in Bretaigne 215,000 [livres] for mulcts of those that pretended to gentility without title and consequently had worn swords. They paid 40 pistols each, and on the same score the King had 200,000 out of Languedoc'.[158]

(c) The Nobility

Several of our travellers belonged to the nobility and gentry and were entertained by their French counterparts. Thus Lord Herbert was welcomed, when he arrived in France in 1608, by the aged Duc de Montmorency and invited to make long stays to enjoy hunting on his estates at Melle and Chantilly.[1] Although other travellers often criticize sharply the treatment meted out by the nobles to the peasants on their estates, their attitude towards the second order in the state is much more objective than towards the clergy, the first order.[2]

They were clearly aware of the fundamental difference between the English and French nobility. Whereas in this country only peers and peeresses enjoy noble rank, in France before the Revolution the number of noble families, whether of the *noblesse d'épée* or the more recent *noblesse de robe*, was extremely large, their members totalling perhaps something of the order of two or three hundred thousand. Comparing conditions in the two countries in the reign of Henry IV, Dallington points out that 'we in England make two distinct orders of the Nobilitie and Gentry',[3] and some fifty years later we find Evelyn maintaining that 'the Noblesse of France comprehend the Gentry, under one and the same common term'. Naturally as a member of the gentry he was far from approving the distinction made on this side of the Channel; he goes on: 'Nor indeed is there in any Kingdome (save ours onely) that severe distinction of *Minores* and *Majores* amongst the Nobility: a difference which some think neither suits with true policy or justice'.[4] Reresby also points out that 'in France they make no distinction' between the nobility and gentry.[5]

The large number of men and women who came into this category is vividly brought out by Heylyn's hyperbole — 'Heaven hath not more Stars, then France Nobles'.[6] Our travellers were nevertheless conscious of the gap between a prince of the blood or a *duc et pair* and the great mass of noblemen. Thus Reresby ends his account of the *ducs et pairs* on a mildly satirical note: 'This title is the only one at this day considerable in France, those of earl, marquis, baron, and knight, being so common, a man needs not lands to acquire them; good clothes and a splendid equipage creates them daily'. He returns later to the same topic: 'Whereas titles used to be adherent to lands, so now lands are to titles; any gentleman that is owner of a piece of a manor, qualifying himself and children Counts, Viscounts, or Barons of the same, though it was never erected into that quality'.[7] Northleigh makes the same point later in the century when he writes of the noblemen: 'They have a Vanity among them of passing themselves for Counts and Marquesses, when indeed they are none; and so Monsieur *le Count* carries it many times by Courtesie, like an English Esquire'. He makes it plain, not without some exaggeration, that a large number of noblemen were far from wealthy: 'The Body of this vast people is not compos'd of the Gentry and Yeomanry, that with us, like Ziba and Mephibosheth, are to divide the Land; their Gentlemen have scarce the Demesne of our Yeomen, and 100*l.* per Annum makes about 1200 *Livres* a Year; and the Man that owns it a great Subject'.[8] That the nobility was by no means a closed caste, but that in the past its ranks had been replenished by the ascent of bourgeois and that this process was continuing is made clear at the beginning of the century by Overbury when he writes: 'That Gentrie was after made up by Advocates, Financiers, and Merchants innobled, which now are reputed antient, and are daily eaten out againe and repayred by the same kinde of men'.[9]

The gulf between the nobility and the mass of the population is vividly described by Evelyn: 'We are . . in this Dominion to take the *Noblesse* (that is the Gentry) for the sole visible body, and consequently the Plebeians of a far more vile and naturally slavish genius, then they really are in any part of Christendome besides; which meanness of spirit I easily conjecture to have been long since contracted from the over severity and liberty of their Superiors; their incomparable paucity,[10] and excessive oppression'.[11] While in Montpellier Locke made a laconic shorthand note on relations between *nobles* and *roturiers*: 'The nobility and gentry have very little trust in the common people'.

A small minority among those who frequented the court were men of great wealth, but even in the provinces Locke came across noblemen who were far from being the poverty-stricken *hobereaux* who were satirized by French writers of the time. Thus on a journey down the Loire, when he and his companions were held up by a strong wind and were compelled to seek a night's lodging in the château of Avary, they were well received by the owner, 'a gent. of 20,000£ per annum', and at Montpellier he mentions that one of the *lieutenants-généraux* of the province who lived at Nîmes was 'a dull man, but of great state, i.e. 20,000 escus per annum'.[12]

Wealthy as some of the noblemen were, their extravagant way of life often added their own debts to those which they had inherited from spendthrift ancestors. Already at the beginning of our period the French aristocracy had a reputation for extravagant living, as the following passage from Dallington shows:

> You had an example hereof in this your late voyage downe the River of Loire, at the Castle of Bury, a very goodly house, as any ye have yet seene in France, where ye heard it credibly reported, that Monsieur D'alluye, the owner of that place, had consumed above twentie thousand Crownes Revenue the yeere, onely in dyet and apparell, who now is forced to make his owne house his prison, and stand watchfully upon his gard, for feare of Sergeants, as we well perceived by his jelousy of us, when we came to see his house, until he was assured that we were strangers, and came for no such purpose.[13]

Evelyn points out that all the members of the nobility who could afford to do so preferred to leave their estates and to live in Paris, or failing that, provincial towns and cities:

> The Nobility and Gentry of this Kingdome differ much from the garb of living in England, both within (and till of late) without doors: They have many of them vast estates, either in Lands or Offices; the Revenues whereof they chuse rather to spend at Paris, and other great Cities, in a specious Retinue of Coaches, Pages, and Laquaies, then suffer themselves to be eaten up at home in the country in the likenesse of Beef and Mustard, among their unthankful Neighbours.[14]

This preference for town life is also stressed by Reresby and in somewhat satirical terms: 'The gentry there seldom live in the country, or when they do it is for recruit,[15] which makes them live very sparingly as to their bellies, to clap it on their backs when they return to a good town, where, howsoever they fare, they will be fine'.[16]

The extravagant way of living of the higher ranks of the nobility is also described by Evelyn: 'The Gentlemen are generally given to those laudable Magnificencies of Building, and furnishing their Palaces with the most precious Moveables, much of the *luxe* and excesse of Italy being now far entred among them, as may well serve to exemplifie, when in the Duchess of Chaulnes her Palace neer the Place Royal in Paris, the pennaches or tufts of plumes belonging to one of her beds onely, are estimated worth fourteen thousand livers, which amount to neer a thousand pounds sterling of our money'.[17] Such extravagant tastes were partly responsible for the court nobleman's increasing dependence on the favours which the King could bestow on him and his family. In his usual laconic fashion Locke notes an example of how a successful courtier, the brother of Mme de Montespan, Louis XIV's mistress, could contract huge debts and have them paid by the king: 'Yesterday morning at the Pallais in the Grand Chamber Mr. de Vivonne was received & sworne Duke & Paire de France & to day his son maried to Mr. Colbert's daughter. Mr. Colbert gave with his daughter £600,000 and the King gave them, to cleare the estate of debts, £900,000'. This striking example of Louis XIV's generosity towards a courtier was not, of course, entirely unconnected with the fact that Colbert was acquiring his third ducal son-in-law. At about the same time Locke made a note of a bill, recently posted in the streets of Paris, which reveals to what lengths a highly placed courtier would go to keep himself afloat financially: 'Within this year past were bills set up about Paris with a priviledg for a receit to kill lice where of the Duke of Bouillon had the monopoly & the bills were in his name:

      Par permission   Ks   et privilege du roy
      accordé a   arms   perpetuité, a Mr le
      Duc de Bouillion   Grand Chamberlan de
      France par lettres patentes du 17 Sept: 1677
      Verifiées en Parlm[i] par arest du 13
      Dec. au dit Ann.
         Le publique sera averti que lon vend
      a Paris un petit Sachet de la grandure
      d'une peice de 15 sols pour garantir
      toute sorte de personnes de la vermin
      et en retirer ceux qui en sont
      incommodes sans mercure &c.
         Il est fait deffenses a toutes personnes
      de la faire ny contrefaire a peine de
      trois mil livres d'amande.
      Extrait del afiche.[18]

   This dependence of the great nobles on all manner of favours which the king could bestow meant that by the end of the Fronde they had ceased to present the same danger to the Crown as earlier in the century. Their earlier behaviour towards the king is vividly described by Heylyn who was in France in the 1620s:

The Princes of this Countrey, are but little inferiour in matter of Royalty to any King abroad; and by consequence little respective, in matter of obedience, to their own King at home. Upon the least discontent, they withdraw themselves from the Court, or put themselves into armes; and of all other comforts are sure of this, that they shall never want partizans. Neither do they use to stand off from him fearfully, and at distance, but justifie their revolt by publick Declaration; and think the King much indebted to them, if upon fair terms and an honourable reconcilement, they will please to put themselves again into his obedience.[19]

Oddly enough, though writing in the middle of the Fronde, the worst civil war of the century — much more prolonged than anything which had happened during the reign of Louis XIII — Evelyn can state quite calmly of the nobles: 'Their Rebellions have been for the most part, though frequent, yet improsperous, so considerable a party ever remaining with the Prince'.[20] Certainly the divisions between the Frondeurs and the frequent changes of side brought about by personal rivalries and the absence of any clear aims were soon to lead to the collapse of the Fronde and to the establishment of Louis XIV's version of absolute monarchy.

As members of the *noblesse d'épée* except those destined for the Church embarked at an early age on a career in the army, the amount of learning which they acquired was generally small. 'The Gentlemen', writes Overbury, 'are all good outward men, good Courtiers, good Souldiers, and knowing enough in Men and businesse, but meerly ignorant in matters of Letters, because at fifteene they quit bookes, and begin to live in the world'.[21] Reresby makes the same point when he writes:

The gentry are well bred, but no scholars, being usually taken from their studies at about fourteen, then put into the academy to learn their exercises, as fencing, dancing, music, riding the great horse, and the like, and then sent into the army, where, if they purchase not some command, after a campaign or two (for the stoutest must pay as well as the rest) they return to such employments as their friends prepare for them elsewhere.

This upbringing gives such men great confidence, Reresby continues, but it 'often puts an handsome gloss upon mean parts, till further familiarity discover that they are the best to the outward'.[22]

Evelyn has an unusually sarcastic passage on the way great noblemen furnished their libraries:

Every great Person who builds here, however qualified with intellectuals, pretends to his Elaboratory and Library; for the furnishing of which last, he doth not much amuse himself in the particular elections of either Authors or Impressions; but having erected his cases and measured them, accords with a Stationer to furnish him with so many gilded Folioes, so many yard of quarto's and octavo's by the great, till his Bibiotheke be full of Volumes.

Yet he does concede that there were some learned noblemen, for he goes on: 'And yet some of them, both have excellent books, and are very polite Scholars'. In another passage on the nobility he returns to this topic: 'I cannot affirm that the youth of the Gentry and Noblesse of France are bred altogether so literate as most of our English and Dutch are . . . It is the Field and Court which the Gentry affect as the best of Education'.[23]

Two of our travellers met princes of the blood — one old and one young — and both were very impressed with their learning. On his visit to France in 1683 Burnet met the great soldier, the Prince de Condé, of whom he writes: 'He had a great quickness of apprehension, and was thought the best judge in France both of wit and learning'.[24] A few years earlier, while visiting a Paris library, Locke had encountered one of Condé's nephews, the Prince de Conti, who was to die before him. Locke was very impressed with this youth:

Here also I had the honour to see the Prince of Conti, now in his 17th yeare, a very comely young gent., but the beautys of his minde far excell those of his body, being for his age very learned. He speaks Italian & German as a native, understands Latin well, & Spanish & Portuguese indifferently, & is, I am told, going to learne English. A great lover of Justice & honour, very civil & obleigeing to all, & one that desires the acquaintance of persons of merit of any kinde; & though I can pretend to none that might recommend me to one of the first Princes of the Blood of France, yet he did me the honour to aske me severall questions there & to repeat his commands to me to wait upon him at his home.[25]

Unfortunately when two days later Locke went to wait upon the Prince, he had been suddenly called to Versailles, and Locke did not see him again.

One of the great occupations of the nobility as of the king and other members of the royal family was hunting, and among its privileges was its monopoly of hunting, the hated *droit de chasse*. Heylyn has a mildly sarcastic passage on the subject. 'By Brettaul in Picardy', he writes, 'I saw a post fastned in the ground, like a race-post with us, and therein an inscription: I presently made to it, as hoping to have heard of some memorable battell there foughten; but when I came at it, I found it to be nothing but a Declaration of the Prince of Condes pleasure, that no man should hunt in those quarters; afterwards I observed them to be very frequent'.[26] A rather more sombre tale is told by Locke when he visited Aigues-Mortes from Montpellier. The governor of the town was the Marquis de Vardes who in 1664 had been exiled from the court to this remote corner of France for his part in a plot to inform the Queen of Louis XIV's affair with Louise de la Vallière. Around Aigues-Mortes, Locke writes, 'we saw aboundance of partridges, and they say there are plenty of hares & other game preservd there by the strict order & severity of the Marquis de Vards who, not long since, clapt a towns man up in a litle hole in Constance's Tower, where he had just roome to stand upright, but could not sit or ly down, & kept him there 3 days for committing some small trespasse on his game'.[27]

Vardes's exile intrigued two of our travellers who were in Languedoc shortly after the event, and picked up conflicting rumours as to its cause. 'Marquis de Vards, governor of Agues-Mortes, captain of 100 Switzers, and formerly nigh the king's person', writes Skippon, 'is now prisoner here, and hath been for about five months; his refusing to take madam Vernouille, the king's mistrees, to be his wife, being supposed his greatest crime'.[28] Lister heard a different story from Sir Thomas Crew: 'The Letter for which the Baron of Wardes was thought to be imprisoned for, had this taint in it touching his Majestie of France, that since the Cardinal [*sic*] death, his Majestie had made noe other Conquest than that of Madame de Valliers'.[29]

Some of our travellers still speak as if what had formed the essential part of the feudal army — the King's vassala (*le ban*) and under-vassals (*l'arrière-ban*) — were still of importance, whereas in the course of the century this institution gradually faded out. In 1635 a royal ordinance had once again demanded from the *ban* and *arrière-ban* three months' service inside France and forty days outside its frontiers, but when summoned they proved of no military value. This obligation is stated by Overbury early in the century to be imposed in return for the privileges enjoyed by the nobility, particularly exemption from the *taille*. 'In recompense of this', he declares, 'they owe to the King the *Ban* and the *Arriereban*; that is, to serve him and his Lieutenant three Moneths within the Land at their owne Charges'.[30] Evelyn too speaks somewhat later as if this institution possessed a real military value: he maintains that in return for the privileges granted to the nobles by the king, 'there are none whieh render him such real and considerable service, upon all urgent and brisk occasions, as do the Gentry; especially, at what time the *Ban* and *Arrier-ban* be summoned to their several assignations'.[31] By the time Locke was in France in the 1670s, the institution was practically dead. 'The King having this present war raisd the arrear band', he writes, 'took occasion to exempt all that would for 100 crowns apeice, which stands establishd for all that think not fit to go to war hereafter in any such occasion'.[32] The summoning of the *arrière-ban* in 1674 to which he refers proved such a fiasco that in the following year the king demanded a money payment in its place in order to finance the levying of regular troops. The privileges of the nobility in the matter of direct taxation were to come more and more under attack since their military service which was held to justify such privileges was no longer obligatory for a nobleman.

(d) Justice

We have already seen that our travellers had come to the conclusion, not really backed by any clear evidence, that owing to the *vénalité des charges* the administration of justice at all levels was inevitably corrupt. They were also struck by the fondness of the French for litigation. At the beginning of the period Dallington contrasted the state of affairs in England and France:

> The processes and sutes in these Courts throughout France, are innumerable, wherein wee come nothing neere them; and yet there is no want of these in England: for I have heard of 340 *Nisi prius* betweene parties tryed at one Assise in Norfolk (as many I thinke, as in halfe England besides). But these are only twice in the yeare, that causes are tried at Assizes in our Countrey, whereas heere they are tried every day in the yere, that is not festivall: So that it is not much unlikely, that here as many Processes in seven yeeres, as have beene in England since the Conquest.[1]

Heylyn too had obviously read Camden's *Britannia*, for in speaking of the Normans' love of litigation, he makes a more detailed comparison between Normandy and Norfolk, quoting the same number of *nisi prius* at one assize in that county. He attributes what he calls 'the beggerlinesse and poverty' of the inhabitants of Normandy in part to 'their litigiounesse and frequent going to law', adding: 'They are pretty well versed in the quirks of the law, and have wit more then enough to wrangle'.[2] He then proceeds to compare Normandy and Norfolk from this point of view, attributing this common trait in the inhabitants to a similar geographical situation and soil. Certainly the Normans enjoyed among other French people a reputation for cunning and chicanery.

Evelyn too remarks upon this fondness for litigation, both in Normandy and in other parts of France, and to it as to the oppressive taxation system he attributes the poverty of so many *roturiers*:

That which addes not a little to their Ruine, is (for all this) their extraordinary litigious nature, and vindictive disposition, especially those of Normandy, Bretagne, Gascony, and Provence; so that, what with the premises, delay of their Process, and the abominable corruption of Justice, this rank of people seldom or never arrive at any considerable Fortune or Competency, by their own wit or industry, as do so many of our Yeomen and Farmers in England.[3]

One consequence of this frequent recourse to the law was that under the Ancien Régime France had multitudes of lawyers — *avocats*, *procureurs*, *notaires* and *tabellions* — scattered over its towns and even villages. The law student, John Lauder, was greatly struck by the number of *avocats* in Poitiers and by the low fees which they charged for their services compared with those paid in Scotland:

When we have had occasion to tel the Frenchman what our Adwocats would get at a consultation, 10, 20 crounes, whiles they could not but look on it as an abuse, and think that our Justice was very badly regulate and constitute. Thorow France a Adwocat dare take no more than a *quart escus* for a consultation, but for that he multiplies them . . . Ther is above 200 Adwocats at Poictiers. Of these that gets not employment they say, he never lost a cause, whey, because he never plaid one. Also, that theirs not good intelligence betuixt the Judge and him, whey, because they do not speak togither.[4]

Northleigh too was struck both by the number of lawsuits and by the excessive number and poverty of the practitioners whom he observed at the Palais de Justice in Paris:

Their Court Officers and Ministers of Justice, Advocates and Proctors, are too numerous to be either good or rich; their Gown is a Reproach of their ignorance, instead of the Badge of their Profession; their Poverty the scandalous Effect of the Idleness that attends it; their Palace at Paris is more crowded than our Westminster Hall; and there are more there that foot to it, because they can't afford Coach-hire; the multitude of law-suits, multiplied by their Number and Penury, Corruption and Bribery follow of Course, and the Sale of Offices excuses, almost necessitates their Knavery.

The same writer picked up two stories about the unconscionable length of lawsuits:

Tho' their manner of Process seem shorter than ours, many of their Causes continue as long depending as our Chancery Suits; and I was told walking among them by one of their Lawyers, a Person of good Parts and Ingenuity, that there was at that Time, a Cause depending between the Creditors of Philip de Comines, the famous Historian, who lies buried in their St. Augustin's Church, and his Executors; and a Cause that had continu'd down from his Time, who lived in the reign of Lewis the XI, a better Historiographer it seems, than a Pay-Master. And I remember at the same time the Count d'Antragues, a most civil and obliging Person that then lodg'd in the House with us, whose Grandfather by the Mother's-side, was kill'd in the Parisian Massacre, one of that unfortunate Gentleman's Causes that was kill'd so long ago, was then also depending; and they shew'd me the Papers and Writings that related to it, which the Count as the nearest Relative was prosecuting upon, or concerned in.[5]

As a law student Lauder made a note in his journal of various points in French legal practice which struck him. He does not always take account of the fact that French civil laws varied considerably from region to region until the Revolutionary assemblies and Napoleon provided a uniform set of laws for the whole country. His comments on primogeniture are somewhat oversimplified: 'As to the privilege of primogeniture in France its thus, that the eldest carries away 2 parts of thrie: as, for instance, the father is a man of 15,000 livres a year, the eldest hath 10,000, the other 5000 goes amongst the cadets'. The control exercised by French parents over the marriages of their children he summarizes thus: 'What concernes the consent of parents in the marriage of their children, the French law ordaines that a man within the age of 28, a woman within 25 sall not have the power of disposing themselfes in marriage without the consent of their parents. If they be past this age, and their parents wil not yet dispose of them, then and in that case at the instance of the Judge, and his auctority interveening they may marry tho their parents oppose'. He also observed that there were limits set to a father's ability to disinherit his son: 'The lawes of France wil hardly permit the father to disinherit his sone, unless he can prove him guilty of some hy ingratitude and disobedience against him, or that he hath attempted something against the life of his father; that he is debaucht he cannot'. The law excluding illegitimate children from a right to maintenance is another on which he comments: 'The Laws of France (this is the rigor) denies children begotten in Adultery or incest aliments which tho harsh, condemming the innocent for the guilty, yet they think it may serve to deterre the parents from sich illicit commixtions'.[6]

While in Paris in 1666, Skippon noted down details of a fairly recent *cause célèbre* involving what was called a *congrès* which is defined by the 1694 *Dictionnaire de l'Académie française* as 'Espreuve de la puissance ou impuissance des gens mariez, ordonnée par Justice':

The marquiss de l'Ange [Langey] a protestant, and reputed a stout man, was divorced not long since, from his wife, a very handsome and vertuous woman. She, after some years, complained to her friends, that the marquis was not able to get her with child: This made some disturbance among the relations; but at last (when physicians &c. had given in their testimonies, they could perceive no external fault in either) it was agreed by both parties, they should prepare themselves, and a day was appointed for the physicians to be not far off; but notwithstanding all the endeavours of the marquiss, it was concluded by a decree of parliament, that they might be divorced. The lady is since married to another, and hath children by him, and the marquiss hath another wife, and hath got her often with child.[7]

The *congrès* was abolished in 1677.

The only one of the travellers who mentions being involved in a civil suit while in France is Evelyn, and although he is one of those who criticize severely the amount of corruption in the French judicial system, he was handsomely treated when he had to make an appearance in court as a defendant at Tours:

My Valet de Chambre, One Garro, a Spanyard, borne in Biscay for some misdemeanors, I was forc'd to discharge; he demanded of me (besides his Wages) no lesse than 100 Crownes to carry him to his Country, which I refusing to pay, as no part of our agreement; he had the impudence to arrest me, and serve me with a Processe: so the next day I was call'd on to appeare in full Court, where both our Advocats pleaded before the Lieutenant Civile: but it was so unreasonable a pretence, that the Judge had not patience to heare it out, but immediately acquitting me, was so civil, as after he had extreamely reproch'd the Advocate who tooke part with my Servant, he rose from the Bench, and making a courteous excuse to me, that being a stranger I should be so barbarously used, conducted me through the Court to the very streete dore: This Varlet afterwards threaten'd to Pistol me.

The next day I waited on the Lietennant to returne him thanks for his greate humanity.[8]

Violence, and not merely threats of it, was a phenomenon which our travellers sometimes encountered in their persons. Evelyn himself recounts an extraordinary story of how in 1650 a party of English people, consisting of Evelyn and his wife, his father-in-law, Charles II's resident in Paris, and his wife, and various English noblemen, became involved in a violent fracas as they returned on foot from an excursion from Paris to Vanves. Evelyn does admit that the incident was provoked by some members of their party:

My Lord Ossorie stepping into a Garden, the dore open; There step'd a rude fellow to it, and thrust My Lord, with uncivil language from entering in: upon this our young Gallants struck the fellow over the pate, & and bid him ask pardon; which to our thinking he did with much submission, & so we parted: but we were not gone far, but we heare a noise behind us, & saw people coming with gunns, swords, staves & forks, following, & flinging stones; upon which we turn'd and were forc'd to engage, & with our Swords, stones & the help of our servants (one of which had a pistol), make our retreate for neere a quarter of a mile, when an house receiv'd us: by this time numbers of the baser people increasing, we got up into a turret, from whence we could discover their attempts, & had some advantage: however, my Lord Chesterfield was hurt in the face & back with a stone, his servant in the Eye & forehead, & Sir Richard Browne[9] protecting his Lady with his Cloake, on the shoulder, & his Lady with such a blow on the head & side of her neck as had neere fell'd her: I myselfe was hurt on the shoulder: my servant La Roch (a stoute Youth) much hurt on the reines: 'Twas a greate mercy that though they were so many, they durst not come neere us with their hookes, & that their gunns did no Execution amongst us, tho fir'd.[10]

In the end the English party was rescued by the authorities and enabled to return to Paris.

At Montpellier Locke noted a clash between members of the English colony there and the local inhabitants: 'For an accidental blow with a mall ball a quarrel begun by the French, and 50 or 60 set on 9 or 10 English with swords, malls and stones'.[11] Another Anglo-French dispute leading to violence was reported round about the same date from Saumur by Sir Philip Perceval's tutor:

Maybe you heard how within these twelve days my Lord Lorne was like to have been assassinated in Saumur by several young Frenchmen upon a slight ground. The day before the Lord walking in a public place, his sword was entermingled with another man's, and my lord, who has little of French,[12] having been told by a French servant who followed him how the other gentleman was angry, and he sent the same servant to desire his excuse, but he not being satisfied with that civility, said my lord himself ought to have come, and the next day that person meeting his lordship leading two women asked him whether he was called my lord, which he having owned, received from the Frenchman a box on the ear, and then several of the gang rushed upon him, and had he not got into a boat and crossed the water, he had been in great danger of being killed.

However, on this occasion the law intervened: 'Since that time the

magistrates have seized upon the goods of some of the offenders, and
I hear nearly five are taken. 'Tis said it will go hard with them'.[13]
Locke noted the prevalence of crimes of violence at Montpellier
and elsewhere in the South of France. Soon after his arrival in
Montpellier he wrote: 'One ran his sister into the head a little above
the temple in the house where I lay. The father was lately dead & he
had but a small legacy'. The very next day he wrote: 'A man shot dead
by another in the street some time before, & an other at Lyons when I
was there'. Soon after he tells of a crime committed a few years
earlier: 'Monsieur Reniac, a gent. of this towne in whose house Sir J.
Rushworth lay, about 4 years agon sacrificed a child here to the devill,
a child of a servant of his, upon a designe to get the devill to be his
friend & help him to get some mony'. He again refers to the crime
committed in the house in which he was living, adding: 'Severall
murders committed here since I came hither & more attempted'. This
was after he had been only ten weeks in the town. A fortnight later he
recurs to the same topic, showing incidentally how such crimes could
go unpunished: 'Many murders committed here. He that
endeavoured to kill his sister in our house, had before kild a man, & it
had cost his father 500 escus to get him off, by their secret distribution
gaining the favour of the Counsellors'.[14]

There were all manner of dangers to be faced in towns, sometimes
from rather unexpected quarters. In 1625 Heylyn launched a violent
attack on the behaviour of student gangs in Paris. After relating an
absurd quarrel over precedence amongst the dignitaries of the
University he continues;

> It were more for the honour and profit of the University, if the
> Rector would leave off to be so mindful of his place, and look a
> little to his office. For certainly never the eye and utmost
> diligence of a Magistrate was wanting more, and yet more
> necessary, then in this place. Penelopes suitors never behaved
> themselves so insolently in the house of Ulysses, as the
> Academicks here do in the houses and streets of Paris . . . When
> you hear of their behaviour, you would think you were in
> Turkie: and that these men were the Janizaries. For an Angel
> given amongst them to drink, they will arrest whom you shall
> appoint them: double the money. and they shall break open his
> house, and ravish him into the Gaole. I have not heard that they
> can be hired to a murder: though nothing be more common
> amongst them then killing, except it be stealing. Witness those
> many carkasses which are found dead in the morning, whom a
> desire to secure themselves and make resistance to their
> pillages; hath only made earth again. Nay, which is most
> horrible, they have regulated their villanous practises into a

Common-wealth: and have their captains and other officers, who command them in their night-walks; and dispose of their purchases. To be a Gipsie and a Scholar of Paris, are almost Synonyms.

He then proceeds to give an example of the misdeeds committed by a student and the punishment meted out to him:

> One of their Captains had in one week (for no longer would the gallowes let him enjoy his honour) stolne no fewer then 80 cloaks . . . For these thefts, being apprehended, he was adjudged to the wheel: but because the Judges were informed that during the time of his reign, he had kept the hands of himself and his company unpolluted with bloud: he had the favour to be hanged.

Heylyn suggests that those who criticize the behaviour of students in Oxford and Cambridge should go and see what happens in universities overseas: 'Then would they admire the regularity and civility of those places, which before they condemned of debauchednesse. Then would they esteem those places as the seminary of modesty and vertue, which they now account as the nurseries only of an impudent rudeness'.[15]

At about the same period in the century Howell relates an encounter which he himself had with malefactors in Paris: 'Being in som joviall company abroad, and coming late to our lodging, we were suddenly surprized by a crue of *Filous* or night Rogues, who drew upon us, and as we exchang'd some blows, it pleas'd God, the *Chevalier de Guet*, an Officer, who goes up and down the Streets all night a Horseback to prevent disorders, pass'd by, and so rescued us; but Jack White was hurt, and I had two thrusts in my Clook'. He then recounts the story of a misfortune which befell one of the Secretaries of State who, after having supper in the Faubourg St. Germain, was making his way home on foot across Paris, because his horse had been lamed while being fetched by a lackey to meet him:

> As he was passing the Pont-Neuf with his Laquay carrying a Torch before him, he might ore hear a noise of clashing of Swords, and fighting, and looking under the Torch, and perceiving they were but two, he had his Laquay go on: they had not made many paces, but two armed men with their Pistols cock'd, and Swords drawn, made puffing towards them, whereof one had a Paper in his hand, which he said, he had casually took up in the Streets, and the difference between them was about that paper: therefore they desir'd the Secretary to read it, with a great deal of complement, the Secretary took out his Spectacles, and fell a reading of the said Paper, whereof the substance was, *That it should be known to all men, that whosoever did passe over*

the Bridge after nine a Clock at night in Winter, and ten in Summer, was to leave his Cloak behind him, and in case of no Cloak, his Hat. The Secretary starting at this, one of the Camerades told him, That he thought that Paper concern'd him; so they unmantled him of a new Plush Cloak, and my Secretary was content to go home quietly, and *en Cuerpo*.[16] Howell compares the policing of Paris very unfavourably with what he calls 'the excellent Nocturnall Government of our Citie of London, wher one may passe and repasse securely all hours of the night, if he give good words to the Watch'.[17]

Even in daytime Reresby found that there were risks in crossing the Pont Neuf:

> One day, walking over Pontneuf, and haveing a belt with large sylver buckles, a man well dressed, as he came after me, rubbed a little upon me as he passed by, and soe persued his way, but I thought a little faster then ordinary. Another following after (but not of his company) tould me my belt was cutt behind, and the buckle was gone with the part which was cutt. This gave me presently suspicion that it was the man gone just before, though his appearance and dress (for he had a sword and a good cloake) spoake him noe man to doe such an action. However, I thought the best way to succeed was to be bould, soe overtaking him I drew my sword and bid him restoor my buccle which he had cut off, which without any denyall he produced and restoored, begging that I would not expose him to publique shame, but lett him goe. After some few stripes with the flatt of my sword I lett the rascall run his way, and the rabble shouting after him.[18]

At the end of the century Martin Lister in describing a visit to the Foire Saint Germain mentions the activities of professional pickpockets though here the culprit was caught:

> Knavery here is a Perfection as with us; as dextrous Cut-Purses and Pick-Pockets. A Pick-Pocket came into the Fair at night, extremely well Clad, with four Lacqueys with good Liveries attending him: He was caught in the Fact, and more Swords were drawn in his Defence than against him; but yet he was taken, and delivered into the Hands of Justice, which is here sudden and no Jest.[19]

The creation of the post of *Lieutenant de police* in 1667 is generally considered to have led to a great decrease in the amount of crime in Paris under its first two holders, La Reynie and D'Argenson. Yet, writing at the very end of the reign of Louis XIV, the author of *A New Journey* gives the impression that Paris could be a dangerous place to visit, particularly during the hours of darkness:

> It is very dangerous to be late out in the Streets of Paris, by

reason of the Filou's, who both Robb and Murder a Man if they find him alone, especially in a By-Street. The Englishman that travell'd with me, came early one Morning to tell me how narrow an escape he had the Night before; That coming Home between Eleven and Twelve a'clock thro' a lonesome Street, I saw, saye he, Three Fellows walking a pretty good pace towards me, where upon I cross'd the Way to avoid them; but they cross'd also, and the foremost coming up to me, endeavor'd to Collar me, but I happily slipt away from him and drawing my Sword, I scamper'd like a Devil.

It could even be dangerous to be out of doors during the hours of daylight:

They have another Way of Robbing even in the Day Time; when they meet a Man near some lonesome Alley, or Porch, they accost him with Hat in Hand after a civil Manner, pretending to speak to him, as if they knew him; and drawing him aside, they tell him they want Money, at the same Time shewing him a Pistol, threatening to Shoot him if he shou'd utter a Word; after he has deliver'd all, they order him to withdraw into the Alley, Porch, &c. until they are gone out of Sight, swearing, that if he shou'd attempt to raise a Hue and Cry, or pursue them, he wou'd turn back and take his Life, tho' they were sure to loose their own. Thus a Filou serv'd Mrs. Nicholson, an English Gentlewoman, some time ago; from whom he took a Gold-Watch, Chain, and Lockets, with Ten Pistoles, and what Silver she had.

There was also another danger, according to the same author: 'It is as dangerous to pick up a Whore, or go into a Bawdy-House; for they most commonly strip a Man, both of his Money, Cloaths, and Life, giving him the House of Office for a Grave'.[20]

If crimes of violence and various forms of robbery were prevalent during our period, it was not for lack of deterrents in the form of harsh punishments. As in this country the death penalty was used on a massive scale. In 1647 Evelyn records that 'my Valet de Chambre Hebert robbed me of the value of threescore pounds in Clothes & plate; but through the diligence of Sir Richard Browne his Majesties Resident at the Court of France ... I recovered most of them againe; obtaining of the Judge (with no small difficulty) that the processe against my Theife, should not concerne his life, being his first fault'.[21] Hanging was frequently the punishment for theft, and yet such a severe penalty did not necessarily deter. Edward Browne observed this when he was in Paris: 'I went over Pont neuf where I met with one carrying another man layd over his right Shoulder, his head dangling one way and his legs another. The Gippet was scarse taken downe where this man had been hang'd for robbery, but one had his hand just by mee in another's pocket, and had drawn his handkercher halfe out when as the man perceived him'.[22]

The punishment of hanging was so common on this side of the Channel that our travellers could scarcely have been surprised at the frequency with which they saw gibbets occupied. Yet they do seem to have been impressed by the number of executed criminals they saw strung together. Thus on his way south from Moulins Coryate observed 'one very ruefull and tragical object: ten men hanging in their clothes upon a goodly gallows made of freestone about a mile beyond Moulins, whose bodies where consumed to nothing, onely their bones and the ragged fitters of their clothes remained'.[23] Over a hundred years later the author of *A New Journey*, when passing through the forest north of Orleans, 'perceiv'd the Trees were loaded with very ungrateful Fruit, so rotten, that I was forc'd to hold my Nose from the confounded stink that proceeded from it; the Spectacle was very hideous, being above Twenty Highwaymen, that were hung to the Branches of the Trees in *Terrorem*'.[24]

Coryate was also struck by the practice of hanging in effigy a criminal who had fled from justice. On his way from Calais he observed at Clermont that

> in the middest of a streete there was erected a gibbet with the picture of a certaine fellow called Antony Peel, who was painted hanging on a gallowes in the same picture. Under the which his offence was mentioned by way of a proclamation for apprehending of him. The reason why his picture was set forth in that manner, was this: That as his picture was there hanged, so should he also if he might be apprehended. This custome is observed in many places of France.[25]

For his part Skippon was impressed by the speed with which once it had been pronounced, a sentence of hanging was carried out: 'Malefactors receive their sentences on their knees, which pronounced, the hangman presently ties a rope about their necks, and conveys them to the prison, whence, after confession, they are immediately hauled to the gallows; so that sometimes they are condemned in the morning and hanged before night'.[26] While in Paris, the medical student, Edward Browne, describes in some detail the method of hanging which, he declares, was different from that employed in England:

> I saw a man hang'd for robbing his master. The manner is different from ours in England, for after they have turned the person to bee executed over the ladder, his hands being tyed together, the hangman (a very Gentile blade) puts his feet

between his armes and so standing, with one hand on the ladder, the other on the Gallowes, his whole weight being upon the Condemned person, hee Jumps, lifts himself up and down, [and] shakes the hanged man after such a violent manner that I began to dought after I saw the rope hold out, wether the Cordage of his neck was as strong, and did expect that by this violence hee should bee as well beheaded as hangd. The hangman untied the rope and let him slip on to a man's shoulders that carry's him away.[27]

Two of our travellers describe in some detail a much more painful form of capital punishment, not abolished until the Revolution, breaking on the wheel. On his way from Boulogne to Montreuil Coryate observed 'a place of execution made of timber, at the toppe whereof there is a wheele, whereon the bodies of murderers only are tormented and broken in pieces with certaine yron instruments, wherewith they breake their armes first, then their legs and thighes, and after their breast: If they are favoured their breast is first broken. That blow on their breast is called the blow of mercy, because it doth quickly bereave them of their life'. At a later stage in his journey the same writer saw near Montargis 'a very dolefull and lamentable spectacle: the bones and ragged fragments of clothes of a certaine murderer remayning on a wheele, whereon most murderers are executed: the bones were miserably broken assunder, and dispersed abroad upon the wheele in divers places'.[28]

Other travellers were not too squeamish to attend such a brutal form of execution when they had the opportunity to do so. During his stay at Poitiers the law student, John Lauder, describes in considerable detail the breaking on the wheel of a criminal 'who was the first we ever did sie in France':

> About 12 acloak on that day he was to be execut he was conveyed to the Palais to hear his sentence, wheir it was read to him on his knees, the hangman *bourreau* at his back with a tow in his hand. The sentence being read he puts the tow about his neck with thir words, *le Roy wous salou, mon amy*, to show him that its the King that causes him dy. His sentence is read to him again at the foot of the Palais ... and then a third tyme on the schaffold.
>
> Their ware mo then 10.000 spectators at the Marcher Vieux. In the middle of it their was a little *eschaustaut* erected on which was nailed 2 iests after the forme of St. Androws crosse, upon whilk the poor fellow was bond on his back, with his 2 armes and his 2 thigs and legs on the 4 nooks of the crosse, having bein stript naked to his shirt. After he had prayed a little and the 2 carmes that assisted him, the *bourreau* made himself ready to

execute the sentence, which was that he should get 2 strooks quick and the rest after he was strangled.

At Paris in breaking great robbers, for the better exemple they do not strangle them at all; but after they have broken all their bones to pieces almost, they leave them to dy on the rack. To return to our poor miserable, the *bourreau* with a great baton of iron began at the armes and brook them with tuo strooks, then his knees, then a strook on every thigh, then 2 on the belly, and as many as on the stomack; and after all thir, yea after the 20 strook, he was not fully dead. The tow brak tuice that was ordained to strangle him. In sying what this cattiff suffered made us conclud that it was a cruel death to be broken in that sort.[29]

What Locke's feelings were when he and his pupil witnessed such a barbarous method of execution in Paris we cannot deduce from the laconic entry in his journal: 'The danceing master broke on the wheele. Chamber room 3 - 0 - 0'.[30] Neither Lauder nor Locke witnessed the penalty of being burnt at the stake being carried out, though both record recent examples of this punishment being inflicted. Lauder notes the case of a man 'who brunt his mother because she would not let him ly with hir, and was brunt quick himselfe at the place in Poictiers some 5 years ago',[31] while Locke noted that 'Pomey & Chauson were burnt at Paris about the yeare '64 for keepeing a baudyhouse of Catamites'.[32]

A public whipping must have been too common a sight in this country for it to arouse much interest in our travellers. Even so, two of them do mention this form of punishment. Coryate saw 'a fellow whipped openly in the streets of Lyons', but adds that the criminal was 'so stout a fellow, that though he received many a bitter lash, he did not a jot relent at it'.[33] It is not clear that Lauder actually witnessed such a spectacle, but he at least mentions this form of punishment as well as branding: 'They that commits any pitty roobery of theifte are whipt thorow the toune and stigmatized with a hote iron marked with the *flower de lis* on the cheik or the shoulder. If any be taken after in that fault having the mark, theirs no mercy for them under hanging'.[34]

Considerable interest was aroused by the galleys as a penal institution as well as part of the French navy. Occasionally the condition of the men sentenced to this punishment aroused some pity among our travellers. This is how the author of *A New Journey* describes the spectacle of men chained together as they were being conducted from Rouen to the galleys: 'We met with fifteen poor Wretches condemn'd to the Gallies; some for having Salt conceal'd in their Pockets, others for deserting the King's Service during the late

War; they were all link'd together with Chains, and under a Guard of Soldiers'.[35] Among Veryard's reasons for taking a strong dislike to Marseilles he puts the sight of 'the poor Slaves, loaden with Chains and groaning under the heavy Yoke of Servitude'.[36] Several of our travellers who visited Marseilles give a fairly detailed account of the condition of the galley-slaves, not all of whom were convicted criminals. Among them were a large number of prisoners of war (especially Turks), not to mention the Huguenots who were condemned to this punishment after the Revocation of the Edict of Nantes. Locke devotes little attention to them: 'The slaves are in very good plight. Their food is only 1½lb. of bisquet per day & thrice a week beanes boild in salt & water, & their drink noe thing but water. They have sometimes tried what flesh & wine would doe with them, but found that with that food they were neither so healthy nor strong'.[37] Some thirty years earlier Evelyn had penned a description of the slaves' lot which was both much fuller and more compassionate. Being on board a galley in motion was to him 'the newest spectacle I could imagine, beholding so many hundreds of miserably naked Persons, having their heads shaven close, & onely red high bonnets, a payre of Course canvas drawers, their whole backs & leggs, in Cupples, & made fast to their seates: and all Commanded in a trise, by an Imperious & cruell sea-man'. He goes on to expand this last remark:

> Their rising forwards, & falling back at their Oare, is a miserable spectacle, and the noyse of their Chaines with the roaring of the beaten Waters has something of strange & fearfull in it, to one unaccostom'd. They are ruld, & chastiz'd with a bulls-pizle dry'd upon their backs, & soles of their feete upon the least dissorder, & without the least humanity: Yet for all this they are Cherefull, & full of vile knavery.

There were other sides to the slaves' life, as Evelyn noted. Not only did some of them perform music while the captain of the galley received him and his companion in his cabin, but they were sent to their inn to play for them during dinner. The slaves were allowed to earn money: 'There was hardly one but had some occupation or other: by which as leasure, in Calmes, & other times, permitts, they get some little monye; in so much as some have after many Yeares of cruel Servitude been able to purchase their liberty'. Evelyn was also struck by their presence in the streets of the city: 'There is nothing more strange than the infinite number of slaves, working in the Streets, & carrying burthens with their confus'd noises, & gingling of their huge Chaynes'.[38]

This account is supplemented by later travellers. In describing the harbour at Marseilles John Buxton noted that 'on the side that the galleys lie, all along next the water are huts, which are shops for the slaves, who there exercise several crafts and sell divers commodities'.[39] To this Bromley adds these details about the galleys:

> The Slaves that row in them, are a melacholy Sight; they are kept under strict Discipline when they row, and at other times fare hardly, the King's Allowance being not very considerable; but then they have liberty to get what they can by their Labours, and go about the Town chained together, with a Soldier to watch them; and many of the Turks have little Shops upon the side of the Port, to which they are chained, where they work at several Trades and Merchandize.[40]

These onshore occupations of the slaves are described in rather more detail by Veryard:

> The Slaves have little Shops or wooden Boxes all along the Key where they work at their respective Trades, and all sell their Goods, whilst the Gallies continue in the Port; but they are fastned to a Block with a Chain of eight or ten Foot long, which keeps them from budging thence, till the Officer comes at Night to loose and conduct them to their Vessels. Such of them as have no Trades learn to knit Stockings, and others serve as Porters in the City, but are chain'd two and two together, having a Guard always following them, who share in what they get.[41]

Although this punishment continued to be inflicted down to the Revolution, by then the galleys had long ceased to put to sea as part of the French navy.

Lauder noted other brutal punishments during his stay in Poitiers. This particular entry is largely based on information from his Protestant landlord: 'Even the wery papists heir punisheth greivously the sine of blasphemy and horrid swearing. Mr. Daillé saw him selfe at Bordeaux a procureurs clerk for his incorrigibleness in his horrid swearing after many reproofes get his tongue boored thorow with a hot iron'. From the same souce Lauder obtained information about the treatment meted out to women taken in adultery: 'Adultery, especially in the women, is wery vigorously punished in many places of France. In Poictou, as Mr. Daillé informed, they ignominiously drag them after the taile of a mule thorow the streits, the hangman convoying them, then they sett them in the most publick part of the toune to a stake, with their hands behind their backs, to be a object of mockery ther to all that pleases'. Apparently the wrongs inflicted upon battered husbands did not go unavenged: 'The punishment of women that beats their good men in Poictiers is that they are monted on an asse with their face to the taile, in this posture conveyed ignominiously thorow all the toune; the hangman accompanying them'.

As later under the Napoleonic penal code, the law allowed a good deal of licence to the husbands of adulterous wives: 'The Laws of France permits, or at least forgives, a man to slay his wife if he take hir in the wery act of adultery'. However, here a curious distinction was apparently made for he goes on: 'But if he slay hir after a litle interwall, as if he gives hir lieve to pray a space, he is punished as a murdrer, since its to be praesumed that that just fury which the willanous act of his wife pouses him to, and which excuses his fact (since according to Solomon even wery Jalousie is the fury of a man) is layd in that interwal, so that he cannot be excused from murder. Both hath bein practised seweral tymes in France'.

Lauder notes the different treatment meted out, according to social class, to men as a penalty for getting an unmarried woman pregnant:

> In France a man wil do weill to take heid what woman he medles with; for if get a woman of degre below himself with child he most ether mary hir or tocher[42] hir; if his aequal, ether marry hir or be hanged (which few chooses); if she be far above his condition (especially if a valet engrosse his masters daughter or sister not married) he is hanged without al process *brevi manu;* the maid is thrust unto a convent to lead repentance their for her lifetyme, since she hath prostrat hir honor so basely.[43]

Our travellers have little to say about criminal procedure. This is scarcely surprising since so much of the investigation of a crime and of the trial of an accused person was carried out in secret. However, Lauder describes various forms of torture in use in the different parts of France to extract a confession:

> At Paris the hangman takes a serviet, or whiles a wool cloath (which I remember Cleark, in his Martyrologie discovering the Spanish Inquisition also mentioned),[44] which he thrustes doune the throat of him as far as his wery heart, keiping to himselfe a grip of one end of the cloath, then zest with violence pules furth the cloath al ful of blood, which cannot be but accompanied with paine. Thus does the *burreau* ay til he confesses. In Poictou the manner is with bords of timber whilk they fasten as close as possibly can be both to the outsyde and insyde of his leg, then in betuixt the leg and the timber they caw in great wedges from the knee doune to the wery foot, and that both in the outsyde and insyde, which so crusheth the leg that it makes it as thin and broad as the loafe[45] of a mans hand. The blood ishues furth in great abondance. At Bourdeaux, the capital of Guienne, they have a boat full of oil, sulfre, pitch, resets and other like combustible things, which they cause him draw on and hold it

above a fire til his leg is almost all brunt to the bone, the sinews shrunk, and thigh also al streatched with the flame.[46]
In contrast to these secondhand and not necessarily accurate accounts we have Evelyn's description of the various forms of torture which he saw with his own eyes applied in Paris in 1651. In the end even he had not stomach to see more than a certain amount:

> This morning I went to the Chastlett or prison, where a Malefactor was to have the *Question* or Torture given to him, which was thus: They first bound his wrists with a strong roope or small Cable, & one end of it to an iron ring made fast to the wall about 4 foote from the floore, & then his feete, with another cable, fastned about 6 foot farther than his uttmost length, to another ring on the floore of the roome, thus suspended, & yet lying but a slant; they slid an horse of wood under the rope which bound his feete, which so exceedingly stiffned it, as severd the fellows joynts in miserable sort, drawing him out at length in an extraordinary manner, he having onely a paire of linnen drawers on his naked body: Then they question'd him of a robery, (the *Lieutennant* Criminal being present, & a clearke that wrot) which not Confessing, they put an higher horse under the rope, to increase the torture & extension: In this Agonie, confessing nothing, the Executioner with a horne (such as they drench horses with) struck the end of it into his mouth, and pour'd the quantity of 2 boaketts of Water downe his throat, which so prodigiously swell'd him, face, Eyes ready to start, brest & all his limbs, as would have pittied & almost affrited one to see it; for all this he denied all was charged to him: Then they let him downe, & carried him before a warme fire to bring him to himselfe, being now to all appearance dead with paine. What became of him I know not, but the Gent: whom he robbed, constantly averred him to be the man; & the fellows suspicious, pale lookes, before he knew he shold be rack'd, betraid some guilt.

Why Evelyn and his companion or companions should have been allowed to be present on such an occasion, is a mystery, but he then reports some conversation with the *Lieutenant criminel:*

> *The Lieutennant* was also of that opinion, & told us at first sight (for he was a leane dry black young man) he would conquer the Torture & so it seemes they could not hang him; but he did use in such cases, where the evidence is very presumptuous, to send them to the Gallies, which is as bad as death. There was another fat Malefactor to succeede, who he said, he was confident would never endure the Question; This his often being at These Trials, had it seemes given him experience of, but the spectacle was so uncomfortable that I was not able to stay the sight of another.[47]

His account of the proceedings would seem to confirm La Bruyere's well known observation: 'La question est une invention merveilleuse et tout à fait sûre pour perdre un innocent qui a la complexion faible, et sauver un coupable qui est né robuste'.[48]

(e) Leisure

One of the liveliest passages in Evelyn's account of the periods which he spent in France is his description of the Jardin du Luxembourg and the crowds which frequented it. He visited the palace and gardens on 1 April 1644 and concluded his description with the following:

In summ, nothing is wanting to render this Palace, & Gardens perfectly beautyfull & magnificent; nor is it one of the least diversions, to behold the infinite numbers of Persons of quality, & Citizens, & strangers who frequent it, and to whom all accesse is freely permitted: so as you shall meete some walkes and retirements full of Gallants & Ladys, in others melancholy Fryers, in others studious Scholars, in others jolly Citizens; some sitting & lying on the Grasse, others, running, & jumping, some playing at bowles, & ball, others dancing and singing; and all this without the least disturbance, by reason of the amplitude of the place; & what is most admirable, you see no Gardeners or people at Worke in it, and yet all kept in such exquisite order, as if they did nothing else but worke; It is so early in the mornings that all is dispatch'd, and don without the least confusion: I have been the larger in the description of this Paradise, for the extraordinary delight I have taken in those sweete retirements.[1]

Another meeting place, but this time only for the aristocratic and wealthy inhabitants of Paris, was the Cours-la-Reine, created by the Regent, Marie de Médicis, along the Seine close to what is now the Place de la Concorde. Lister was much taken with it, though he also notes its drawbacks:

Coaching in Visits is the great and daily Business of People of Quality: But in the Evenings, the Cours de la Reyne is much frequented, and a great Rendezvous of People of the best Fashion. The Place indeed is very commodious and pleasant, being three Allies set with high Trees of a great length, all along the Bank of the River Seine, inclosed at each end with noble Gates; and in the middle a very large Circle to turn in. The middle Alley holds four lines of Coaches at least, and each side Alley two a-piece: These eight lines of Coaches, may, when full, supposing them to contain near 80 Coaches a-piece, amount to about 6 or 700. On the Field side, joyning close to the Allies of the Coaches, there are several Acres of Meadow planted with Trees, well grown, into narrow Allies in Quincunx Order, to walk in the Grass, if any have a mind to light; and this must needs be very agreeable in the Heats of Summer, which we staid not to enjoy.

One thing this *Cours* is short of ours in Hide-Park, for if full, you cannot in an hour see the Company twice you have a mind to see, and you are confined to your line; and oftentimes, the Princes of the Blood coming in, and driving at Pleasure, make a strange stop and *embarras*.

Besides, if the weather has been Rainy, there is no driving in it, it is so miry and ill gravelled.

Lister also greatly admired the Tuileries gardens, not only for their layout, but also for the company which he saw there:

Towards 8 or 9 a Clock in June most of them return from the *Cours*, and land at the Garden Gate of the Tuilleries, where they Walk in the cool of the Evening. This Garden is of the best Ordonnance, and now in its full Beauty, so that Mons. Le Nostre has seen it in its infancy, for it is all of his Invention, and he enjoys his Labours in perfection. Certainly the Moving Furniture of it at this time of the Evening, is one of the Noblest Sights that can be seen. The Night I came away from Paris, a Lady of Quality Madam M—— when I took my leave of her, askt me, What I had seen in Paris that most pleased me; I answered her Civilly, as I ought to do; but she would not take my Compliment, but urged for a further Answer: I told her, (since she would have it so) that I just then came from seeing what pleased me best; that was, the Middle Walk of the Tuilleries in June, betwixt 8 and 9 at night; I did not think there was in all the World a more agreeable place than that Alley at that hour, and that time of the year.[2]

Several of our travellers give an account of an entertainment which attracted a broad cross-section of the population, even including Louis XIV himself in the early part of his personal reign — the Foire Saint-Germain. Skippon visited it in 1666:

The fair of St. Germain begins the 3d of February and holds all the Lent; the place the fair is kept in, is a large square house with six or seven rows of shops, where customers play at dice when they come to buy things; the commodity is first bought, and then they play who shall pay for it. After candle-lighting is the greatest gaming, sometimes the king comes and dices.[3]

Some years later Clenche describes the fair as 'a large piece of ground under an ordinary cover of posts and tyles, divided into eight small Walks, or streets; and the pleasure and benefit of it is to cheapen[4], and then play for a Toy: it belongs to the Abbot, and yields him a very great Rent'.[5]

Lister who visited the fair in 1698 provides sufficient detail to give a clear notion of what this annual event was all about:

We were in Paris at the time of the Fair of St. Germain; It lasts six weeks at least: The Place where it is kept well bespeakes its Antiquity; for it is a very Pit or Hole, in the middle of the *Faubourg,* and belongs to the great Abbey of that Name. You Descend into on all sides, and in some places above 12 Steps; so that the City is raised above it 6 or 8 Foot.

The Building is a very Barn, or Frame of Wood, Tiled over; consisting of many long Allies crossing one another, the Floor of the Allies unpaved, and of Earth, and as uneven as may be; which makes it very uneasie to Walk in, were it not the vast croud of People which keep you up: But all this bespeaks its Antiquity, and the rudeness of the first Ages of Paris, which is a foil to its Politeness in all things else now.

The Fair consists of most Toy-shops, and Bartholomew-Fair Ware; also Fiance and Pictures, Joiners Work, Linnen and Woolen Manufactures; many of the great Ribban Shops remove out of the Palais hither : No Books: Many Shops of Confectioners, where the Ladies are commodiously Treated.

The great Rendezvous is at Night, after the Play and Opera are done; and Raffling for all Things Vendible is the great Diversion: no Shope wanting two or three Raffling Boards. Monsieur[6], the Dauphin, and other Princes of the Blood come, at least once in the Fair-time, to Grace it.

Here are also Coffee-Shops, where that and all sorts of strong Liquors above-mentioned are to be Sold.

Just before this, Lister inserted a passage on the fashionable pastime of gaming, so often and so vigorously denounced by French moralists in this age:

Gaming is a perpetual Diversion here, if not one of the Debauches of the Town: But Games of meer Hazard are strictly forbid upon severe Fines to the Master of the House, as well private as Publick, where such Playing shall be discovered, This was done upon the Account of the Officers of the Army; who, during the Winter used to lose the Money, which was given them to make their Recruits, and renew their Equipages in the Spring. And indeed, such quick Games, as Basset, Hazard, &c. where Fortune in a manner is all in all, are great Temptations to Ruine, by the sudden Passions they are apt to raise in the Players: Whereas Games, where Skill and Cunning, and much Thought are imployed, as well as Luck, give a Man time to Cool, and recover his Wits, if at any time great Loss shall have Dismounted his Reason; for he must quickly come to himself again, or forfeit his Skill and Reputation in Conducting the Game, as well as Husbanding his Money.[7]

None of our travellers gives a firsthand account of the goings-on in Paris during the carnival. Symonds who arrived there in January 1649 during the first phase of the Fronde, recorded that in the circumstances it could not be observed in the usual manner:

> Next follows the time of *Carnaval* which begins *in die Regum* & continues *ad diem Cinerum* which we call *Ashwednesday:* about 3, 4 or 5 weekes. The last day is the chiefest & then they eate & talke & sing most freely. By reason of the War no *carnaval* now in Paris. There was wont to be publique shows in the streets on the last day, the eve of Ashwednesday. Bacchus riding in state in his lofty charyott, a liberty of musicians to enter into any chamber & speak with any lady or person.

The same writer, after noting how many shops were open on Sundays, describes briefly a street scene: 'A Mountebanke & his boy on Sunday hanging his Crocodyle Skins & selling his medicaments with his quack confidence to the people under the brasen Horse of Henry IV upon Pont Neuf'. [8] Another entertainment for the populace was provided by bonfires and fireworks. In Paris on 23 June 1678 Locke made this entry in his journal: 'Fire works at the Greve[9] & bonfires all the town over as it is always Midsomer Eve in all Catholique Countrys'.[10] 'They have a Custom in this Town', wrote Northleigh, 'of making a sort of sacred and holy Bonfire on St. John's Eve, and what they call'd St. John's Fire; some of the best Quality go in Procession to it; Priests sing their Anthems at it, and while 'tis quenching, the People supersitiously dance around it'.[11] In summer when the weather turned hot, one could leave Paris and indulge in the pleasures of river-bathing. Evelyn relates how in the summer of 1651 his wife and he went to Conflans where the Marne joins the Seine: 'I went with my Wife to Conflance, where were aboundance of Ladys & others bathing in the River: The Ladys had their Tents spread on the Water for privacy: it being exceeding hot weather, we also bathed & returned next day by boate to Paris'.[12]

In his account of France at the beginning of our period Dallington devotes several pages to the way in which people over the country as a whole spent their leisure, to what he calls their 'exercises'. He begins with some remarks about the ancient game of tennis which was extremely popular in France in the fifteenth and sixteenth centuries:

> I am now by order to speake of his Exercises, wherin, me thinks, the Frenchman is very immoderate, especially in those which are somewhat violent; for ye may remember, ye have seene them play Sets at Tennise in the heat of Summer, & height of the day, when others were scarce able to stirre out of dores. This immoderate play in this unseasonable time, together with their intemperate drinking and feeding, is the onely cause, that

heere ye see them generally itchy & scabbed, some of them in so foule a sort, as they are unfit for any honest table.

A page or so later he returns to this topic:

As for the exercise of Tennis play, which I above remembred, it is here more used, then in all Christendome besides, whereof may witnesse the infinite number of Tennis Courts throughout the land, insomuch as yee cannot finde that little *Burgade,* or towne in France, that hath not one or more of them. Here are, as you see, three-score in Orleans, and I know not how many hundred there be in Paris: but of this I am sure, that if there were in other places the like proportion, ye should have two Tennis Courts, for every one Church through France. Me thinks it is also strange, how apt they be here to play well, that ye would thinke they were borne with Rackets in their hands, even the children themselves manage them so well, and some of their women also, as we observed at Blois.

Dallington concludes his remarks on the subject with laments at the popularity of this sport among the lower orders and a technical detail about the game as it was played in France:

There is this one great abuse in this exercise, that the Magistrates do suffer every poore Citizen, and Artificer to play thereat, who spendeth that on the Holyday, at Tennis, which he got the whole weeke, for the keeping of his poore family. A thing more hurtfull then our Ale-houses in England, though the one and the other be bad ynough. And of this I dare assure you, that of this sort of poore people, there be more Tennis Players in France, then Ale-drinkers, or Malt-wormes (as they call them) with us.

You observe here, that their Balles are of cloth, which fashion they have held this seven yeeres: before which time they were of lether, like ours. Much more might be said of this exercise, but I will not reade you a Lecture in the Schoole of Tennis, whom I confesse the better Scholler.[13]

The popularity of the game had begun to decline by the seventeenth century; thus companies of actors including Molière's had no difficulty in finding on their arrival in Paris a disused *jeu de paume* which they could speedily turn into a theatre. This perhaps explains why none of the later travellers mentions the game.

Dallington next turns his attention to the game of pall-mall which, as he points out, had not yet been imported into England where in due course it was to give its name to a famous London street:

Among all the exercises of France, I preferre none before the *Palle-maille*, both because it is a Gentleman-like sport, not violent, and yeelds good occasion and opportunity of discourse, as they walke from the one marke to the other. I marvell, among many more Apish and foolish toyes, which we have brought out of France, that wee have not brought this sport also into England.[14]

Our travellers offer a good many comments on this sport, though often they refer rather to other uses to which the space in which it was played was put. Thus Heylyn simply lifts the above lines on the game from Dallington and then goes on to describe what he calls the 'Palle-Malle' at Orleans;

> Into this walke, which is of a wonderful length and beauty, you shall have a clear evening empty all the Town: the aged people borrowing legs to carry them; and the younger, arms to guide them. If any young Dame or Monsieur, walk thither single, they will quickly finde some or other to link with them: though perhaps such with whom they have no familiarity. Thus do they measure and re-measure the length of the *Palle-Malle*, not minding the shutting in of the day, till darkness hath taken away the sense of blushing. At all hours of the night, be it warm and dry, you shall be sure to finde them there, thus coupled: and if at the years end, there be found more children then fathers in the Town; this walk and the night are suspected shrewdly to be accessaries. A greater inconvenience in my opinion then an English kisse.[15]

After noting that this was 'a game much used in France', Mortoft writes of Tours: 'The suburbs are great and faire; there is also the place where they play at Mall, which is a thousand paces long, and shadowed with 7 Rowes of trees, and is esteemed to be the fairest in all France'.[16] The game was also popular in the South as was noted at Montpellier by Skippon who endeavours to explain the rules:

> At Montpelier they play at mall in the highways; the players agree first how far to play, and what stone &c. to touch, which is the usual *terminus* of this sport: *A* that strikes first, plays the pair, *B* plays *le plus*, but if *B* strikes beyond *A*. then *A* plays *le plus*; if *B* gets another stroke, *A* plays at two, and *B* rests at one, &c.[17]

During his stay in the same town Locke also noted the popularity of the game. A few days after his arrival he wrote: 'All the highways are fild with gamesters at Mall, soe that Walkers are in some danger of knocks'.[18] We have in fact already seen his account of how an accidental blow from a mall ball caused a free fight between English and French in Montpellier.[19]

Dallington next lists what he calls 'Shooting with the Peece', the last word in its old sense of 'firearm'; he no doubt exaggerates when he describes such a competition as taking place everywhere in France:

> Once in a yere, there is in each city a shooting with the Peece at a Popingay of wood, set upon some high steeple (as also they doe in many places of Germany.) He that hitteth it downe, is called the King for that yere, and is free from all taxe: besides, he is allowed twenty crownes towards the making of a Collation for the rest of the shooters. And if it happen, that three yeres together he carry the Prize, he is free from all taxe and imposition whatsoever, all his life after.

Dallington strongly recommends that this practice in the use of firearms should be introduced into England since, as he puts it, 'our Countreymen would grow more perfit & expert in the use thereof, at whose unaptness and aukwardnesse in their first trayning, before they come to have served some time, I have often marvayled'.[20] During his stay in Orleans Lauder watched a competition of this kind:

> During my abode heir, about the end of May, I had occasion to sie another custome of the city. At that tyme of the year the tounes men put upon the other syde of the bridge a pole as hie as the hiest house in Edenborough: on the top of it they fasten a bird made of brasse at which they, standing at the feet of the pole, shoot in order, beginning at the better, with gunes, having head peices on their heads, to sie who can ding it down. I went and saw them shoot but no man chanced to shoot it doun that year I was their.[21]

No doubt the laconic entry in Locke's journal for Monday, 15 June 1676 at Montpellier — 'Shooting at Target'[22] — refers to the same sort of competition.

Dancing, again according to Dallington when he generalizes about the French, was a pastime 'in which they most delight, and is most generaly used of all others', and to this he attaches their fondness for music and songs:

> I am persuaded, were it not for this, that they of the Reformed Religion, may not Dance, being an exercise against which their strait-laced Ministers much inveigh, that there had long since many of the Catholikes turned to their side; so much are they all in general addicted hereunto. For yee shall not onely see the *Damoiselles* (Gentlewomen) and them of the better sort but every poore *Chapperonieze* (draggletayle) even to the Coblers daughter, that can Dance with good measure, & Arte, all your *Quarantes, Levalties, Branles*, & other Dances whatsoever: not so much but the *Chambriere* (Chamber-maid) and poore Citizens wife, Dance usually in the Citie streets, in a round, like our countrye lasses on their towne greene, about the May-pole, making musick of their own voices, without any instrument. And rather then faile, the old women themselves, both Gentle &

base, who have more toes then teeth, and these that are left, leaping in their heads, like Jacks in Virginals, will beare their part. This argueth (I will not say a lightnes & immodesty in behaviour) but a stirring spirit, & livelynesse in the French nature: whereof also the Musicke and songs they have, is no small argument: For there is not almost a tune in all France, which is not Ionicke, or Lydian, of five or seven tunes: a note forbidden youth by Plato, and Aristotle, because, sayth Bodin, it hath great force and power to soften and effeminate mens minds. The tune Doricke, which is more grave musicke, and was commaunded for the singing of Psalmes in the Primitive Church, their inconstant and stirring humor cannot brooke by any meanes.[23]

Heylyn furnishes another vivid passage to demonstrate the popularity of dancing with all classes and all ages. This is the spectacle which he observed at Étampes on his way from Paris to Orleans:

> Without the town, they have a fine green medow, daintily seated within the circlings of the water; into which they use to follow their recreations. At my being there, the sport was dancing; an exercise much used by the French, who do naturally affect it. And it seemeth this natural inclination, is so strong and deep rooted; that neither age nor the absence of a smiling fortune can prevail against it. For on this dancing green, there assembled not only youth and Gentry, but age also and beggery. Old wives which could not put foot to ground without a Crutch, in the streets; had here taught their feet to hoble; you would have thought by the cleanly conveyance of their bodies that they had been troubled with the Sciatica; and yet so eager in the sport, as if their dancing daies should never be done. Some there were so ragged, that a swift Galliard would almost have shaked them into nakedness: and they also most violent to have their carkasses directed in a measure. To have attempted the staying of them at home, or the perswading of them to work, when they had heard the Fiddle, had been a task too unwieldy for Hercules. In this mixture of age and condition, did we observe them at their pastime; the rags being so interwoven with the silks, and wrinkled browes so interchangeably mingled with fresh beauties: that you would have thought it, to have been a mummery of fortune: As for those of both sexes, which were altogether past action; they had caused themselves to be carried thither in their chairs, and trod the measure with their eyes.[24]

If Locke watched the King and courtiers dancing at Fontainebleau, he also found that the same amusement was very popular in the South of France. While in Provence he made this entry in his journal: 'At St. Giles a congregation of men & wenches danced heartily to the beating of a drum for want of better musick; nay, their natural inclinations wrought so effectually that it helped them to dance even when the dubing of the drum faild them'. At Avignon he found 'Danceing here by moonshine in the streets'. Back in Montpellier he noted: 'After a rainy day dancing along dirty streets in the night to a hobboy'. His picturesque account of the carnival at Montpellier contains an amusing reference to the part dancing played in it: 'Shrove Tuesday, 18 Feb. The heighth & consummation of the Carnival. The town fild with mascarades for this last weeke, danceing in the streets in all manner of habits & disguises, to all sorts of musick, brass kettles & frying pans not excepted'.[25] Skippon had been present at the carnival in Lyons, though he does not seem to have been very much entertained by what he saw:

> March 9. being Shrove Tuesday, N.S. in Bell-Cour were many masquers on horseback, who had mallets with little hatchets fastened to them, with which they struck at a wooden cage, wherein was enclosed a lamb; and he that first broke the cage and kill'd the lamb, was adjudged king; then the trumpets sounded, and he at the head of the rest, rode up and down the streets. The carnival seemed very mean.

Skippon also gives an account of acrobatic performances at which he was present in Montpellier:

> We saw here a Valachian walk up a sloping rope, then he danc'd on a strait rope as high as the top of a tennis court; after that he danc'd with two naked swords, one tied cross the right, and the other cross the left leg; then he had two ropes tied to his feet, and a boy hanging by the middle in those ropes was swung to and fro as he walk'd up the high strait rope; at last he cut capers, and stood upon his head on the top of a pole as high as the tennis court roof.
>
> A Dutchman danc'd without a pole in his hand on a lower rope, and three or four times slip'd down and straddled the rope, and up again presently on his feet; he also cut high capers.
>
> Another fellow tumbled upon a bending rope.
>
> Another on a scaffold threw himself backward, and landed on his feet; he threw himself through three hoops which were held up as high as his head, but he had the advantage of a sloping board, which he ran up, before he went through the hoops; he made use of the same advantage when he tumbled over a boy's head, who sat upon a tall fellow's shoulders, the boy's head was higher than he could reach with his hands.[26]

During his long stay in the same town Locke made further notes on popular entertainments. On a Sunday in January he wrote: 'All the world at Mall & the Mountebank at's tricks.' He observed the popularity of bonfires which were used to celebrate the capture of towns in the war with Spain. On 14 May 1676 he wrote:

> Bonfires all over the towne for the takeing of Condé. The Consuls walked about that cock of brush before the Towne House in their scarlet with drums, trumpets & violins before them & then each with a torch kindled it. The other bonfires through the towne not soe big. One fagot of sermans often made one. In other places a little tod of straw or piece of bedmat wherein perhaps some of their enemys were destroied, made a flame which sometimes an unlucky boy with one kick extinguished. I lost my way amongst these will-o'-the-wisps, as soon out as in.

About a fortnight later he noted: 'Bonfires for the taking of Bouchain', and when mentioning the usual bonfires for St. John's Day, he adds, 'but bonfires made only by papists'.[27]

So far we have mentioned only entertainments available to the different social classes in the towns. Fortunately Locke provides us with a picture of the amusements of the peasants in Celleneuve, a small village to the west of Montpellier to which he retired in the summer heat. This is how he describes what he calls their 'annual Olympiad':

> Men run at Selneuf about twelve score[28] or some thing more over ploud land, very stony, barefoot, and maidens the same, about half so far. There were also races of boys together and girls in other course. He that won among the men had a hat, among the maidens a ribbon, and less fry smaller matters, all which were given at this annual Olympiad by the Cardinal[29] who is Seignure of the place, and was all tied to the end of a pole which was held up at the end of the race. The whole prize thus exposed was a hat, severall ribbons and tagged laces, 2 or 3 purses and a few pennies. Jumping also was another exercise, and after all, what never fails, dancing to hoboy and tabor.[30]

Evidently dancing was as popular in the countryside as in the towns.

III KING, COURT AND GOVERNMENT

Most information on the political structure and personalities of seventeenth-century France is provided by our travellers for the high point of the reign of Louis XIV from his assumption of power in 1661 down to the 1680s. The period of Henry IV and the early part of the reign of Louis XIII, though much less well covered, are not almost a blank as is the age of Richelieu. The period of Mazarin, no doubt partly because it coincided with the Civil War and the Commonwealth which drove numbers of people into exile on the Continent, is fairly well dealt with, in contrast to the end of the reign when for long periods wars made visits to France almost impossible.

Fynes Moryson offers a vivid account of the state of France at the moment when Henry IV was striving to pacify the country after several decades of civil war. When he arrived in Paris in 1595 he noted that opposite the gate of the Palais de Justice 'stood the house of John Chastell, which was pulled downe in memorie of a young man, his sonne, brought up among the Jesuites, and a practiser of their wicked doctrine, who attempting the death of King Henrie the fourth, did strike out one of his teeth'.[1] His journey to Paris from the frontier with Lorraine had been very dangerous because of the unsettled state of the country. At the first French village he and his guide came to, 'a French Gentleman dwelt, who the same day had there proclaimed the Peace', but all around them in the countryside of Champagne they saw signs of the ravages of war. The fields 'seemed apt to beare great store of Corne, but now in the time of Civill warre they lay unploughed, and the Husbandsmens houses were fallen to the ground'.

Before entering France with so many soldiers on the loose at the end of the war, he had been advised to sell his horse and go on foot. The warnings he had received were rapidly justified:

> When I had passed halfe this dayes journey, I met with some dozen horsemen whose Captaine demanded of me my name and Countrey, I answered, that I was a Dutch man, and the servant of a Dutch Merchant, who staied for me at Chalons, whether I was then going. He (as it seemed to me) thinking it dishonourable to him, if he should himselfe assault a poore

fellow, and a stranger, did let me passe, but before I came to the bottom of the hill, I might see him send two horsemen after me, who wheeling about the mountaines, that I might not know they were of his company, suddenly rushed upon me, and with fierce countenance threatening death, presented their Carbines to my brest.[2]

This encounter cost him his sword, cloak and shirts, and most of his money though he did manage to hide some of it from the robbers. Even when he reached Châlons-sur-Marne and took 'a long waggon' to Paris his fears of trouble were not over, 'The second day we were carried 12 miles to Nangi, being as yet not freed from the cries of poore people, driving their cattell from Troopes of Souldiers, but for my part I made the proverbe true, that the passenger having nothing, sings before the thiefe. Yet was I not without feare of a greater mischiefe then robbing, by the losse of my life, having no money to redeeme it from the cut-throat souldiers'.[3]

Perhaps a sign of the unsettled state of France in the 1590s, though the same observation was made by other travellers even at the high point of Louis XIV's reign, is what in his summing up on the French people Dallington calls 'their liberty of speach', something he greatly disapproves of: 'It is incredible to beleeve, and odious to heare, how the Frenchman will talke, and impudently utter what hee foolishly conceiveth, not only of all forraine States and Princes of the world, but even of their own State and King himselfe; of whom hee will not spare to speake whatsoever hee heareth, and sometimes also more then the trueth; which insufferable vice of theirs, I heere put in the first place, because I holde it of all others the most disloyall and unlawfull'.[4]

Lord Herbert boasts of the warm reception which he received from Henry IV during his first visit to Paris in 1608: 'Sometimes also I went to the Court of the French King, Henry the Fourth, who upon information of me in the Garden of the Tuileries, received me with all Courtessie, embracing mee in his Armes and holding mee some while there'.[5] Sir George Carew who, as ambassador, had occasion to get to know the king rather better, had no high opinion of the man. After speaking of his 'want of true magnanimity', he goes on:

> Those, who hazarded their lives and fortunes for settling the crown on his head, he neither rewardeth nor payeth; those, who were of the league against him, he hath bought to be his friends, and giveth them preferments. And to myself he hath affirmed, that he found them his most trusty servants. The Jesuits, who sought to take away his life, he cherisheth most of all the Roman orders, for fear lest they should do the same again.

Nor did he form a high opinion of his intellectual powers;

> Touching the strength of his apprehension and conceit, it is held rather to consist in certain starting holes and short ends of wit, than in any sound suffieiency of discourse. And therefore those of his court say of him, that for defaites and repartees he is excellent, but that he is nobody at enterprises or consultations *de longue haleine*; the which, in mine own negotiations with him, I have observed also to be true.

Yet when Carew comes to deal with the ruler of France, he offers a very different verdict: 'Estimating him as a king, his virtues are much more eminent, having brought his realm, that was utterly shaken, and ready to rend in pieces, to the greatest wealth, union and strength, that it hath been in for this many hundred years'.

Sully, Henry's most famous minister, is criticized for his morals, though Carew found that in negotiations he was 'open, substantial, and ingenuous, despising the affectation or seeming wise by petty subtilities, and close retiredness', and he accepted his account of how he had restored the royal finances:

> When Sully came first to the managing of the revenues, he found (as himself told me) all things out of order, full of robbery of officers, full of confusion, no treasure, no munition, no furniture for the king's houses, and the crown, indebted three hundred millions; that is three millions of pound sterling. Since that time, that is February 1608, he had acquitted one hundred and thirty millions of that debt, redeeming the most part of the revenues of the crown that were mortgaged; that he had brought good store of treasure into the bastille, filled most of the arsenals with munition, furnished most of the king's houses with rich tapestry, and other moveables; and where the farms of the whole realm amounted then but to 800000 l. sterling, this year 1609, he had let them out for 1000000 l. and that without exacting any more upon the people than was paid before, but only by reducing that to the king's coffers, that was embezled by under-officers.[5a]

Whether writing towards the end of his reign or after his assassination, both Overbury and Howell speak of Henry in glowing terms. In his account of the state of France in 1609 Overbury praises every aspect of his policies both at home and abroad:

> Concerning the King himselfe, hee is a person wonderfull both in War and Peace: for his Acts in Warre, he hath manumized France from the Spaniard & subdued the League, being the most dangerous plot that hath bin layd, weakening it by Armes, but utterly dissolving it by wit, that is, by letting the Duke of Guise out of Prison, and Capitulating with the heads of

it every one a part, by which meanes hee hath yet left a continuall hatred among them, because every one sought, by preventing other, to make his conditions the better; so that now there remains little connexion of it amongst the Gentrie.

He does, however, somehow suggest the atmosphere in which Ravaillac was to perpetrate his deed in the following year when he goes on: 'Onely there continues some dregges still among the Priests, and consequently the people, especially when they are angered with the increase and prosperitie of the Protestants'.

Henry's internal policies receive further praise:

For his Acts of Peace, hee hath enriched France with a greater proportion of Wooll, and Silke, erected goodly Buildings, cut passages betwixt River and River, and is about to do the same betwixt Sea and Sea,[6] redeemed much of the Mortgaged Demaynes of the Crowne, better husbanded the Money, which was wont to be drunke uppe two parts of it in the Officers hands, got aforehand in Treasure, Armes and Munition, increased the Infantrie, and supprest the unproportionable Cavalry, and left nothing undone but the building of a Navie.

All this, according to Overbury, can be attributed to Henry alone 'because in a monarchy, Officers are accordingly active or carelesse, as the Prince is able to Judge and distinguish of their labours, and withall to participate of them somewhat himselfe'.

Yet the passage concludes on a note of foreboding about what would happen when the reign of such a strong personality came to an end:

Sure it is that the Peace of France, and somewhat that of Christendome it selfe, is secured by this Princes life: For all Titles and Discontents, all factions of Religion there supresse themselves till his Death; but what will ensue after; what the rest of the House of Bourbon will enterprise upon the Kings Children, what the House of Guise upon the House of Bourbon; what the League, what the Protestants, what the Kings of Spaine, and England, if they see a breach made by civill Dissension, I chuse rather to expect then Conjecture, because God hath so many wayes to turne aside from humaine fore-sight, as hee gave us a testimony upon the Death of our late Queen.[7]

Here Overbury clearly anticipates the period of disorder which was to follow the king's assassination.

Writing about 1620, in the midst of this disorder, Howell not only provides a detailed account of Henry's assassination, but praises him in terms which reflect the beginnings of this king's legend:

Never was King so much lamented as this, ther are a world not onely of his Pictures, but Statues up and down France, and ther's scarce a Market Town, but hath him erected in the Market-place, or ore some Gate, not upon Signe-Posts as our Henry the eight; and by a public Act of Parliament which was confirmed in the Consistory at Rome, he was entitled, Henry the Great, and so plac'd in the Temple of Immortality. A notable Prince he was, and of an admirable temper of body and mind, he had a gracefull facetious way to gain both love and aw, he would be never transported beyond himself with choler, but he would passe by any thing with som *repartie,* som witty strain, wherein he was excellent.[8]

More than a page of examples of such witty remarks follows.

Apart from what Overbury has to say about the king himself, he has some interesting comments to make on the development of Absolutism during this reign. In his conclusion on the French people, he describes them as 'loving to the Prince, and so they may have liberty in Ceremony, and free access to him, they will be the better content that he shall be absolute in matter of substance'.[9] Arriving from Holland, he found in France

of Monarchies the most absolute, because the King there, not only makes Peace and Warres, Calls and dissolves Parliaments, Pardoneth, naturalizeth, Innobleth, Names the value of Money, Presseth to the Warre; but even makes Lawes, and imposes Taxes at his pleasure: And all this he doth alone: for as for that forme that his Edicts must be authorized by the next Court of Parliament, that is, the next Court of soveraigne Justice; first the Presidents thereof are to be chosen by him, and to bee put out by him; and secondly, when they concurre not with the King, he passeth any thing without them, as he did the last Edict for the Protestants; And for the assembly of the three Estates, it is growne now almost as extraordinary as a general Counsell; with the loss of which their Liberty fell, and when occasion urgeth, it is possible for the King to procure, that all those shall bee sent thither, shall be his Instruments: for the Duke of Guise effected as much at the assembly of Bloys.

The establishment of absolute monarchy in France since the fifteenth century, Overbury goes on to argue , was the result of the division between the two privileged orders and the Third Estate: 'The Clergie and Gentrie did not runne the same fortune with the people there, as in England; for most of the Taxes falling only upon the people, the Clergie and Gentrie being forborne, were easily induced to leave them to the Kings mercy. But the King having got strength upon the Peasants, hath been since the bolder to invade part of both their liberties'.[10]

Our travellers offer two contemporary accounts of Louis XIII as Dauphin. In 1608, when he was seven, Coryate saw him at Fontainebleau on his way to Mass; his account would seem to err on the side of exaggeration: 'His face full and fat-cheeked, his haire black, his look vigorous and coragious, which argues a bold and lively spirit. His speech quick, so that his words seem to flowe from him with a voluble grace.'[11] Sir George Carew, as ambassador, was likely to know him rather better, especially as one of his sons had often been in the Dauphin's company:

> The Dauphin resembleth his mother much more than the king. He is like to prove of a tall, and strong body, and a fierce and imperious mind. He sheweth to those youths, who are brought up with him, somewhat a cruel and vindictive disposition; though the king one day pain'd himself to tell me many pretty stories, that argued the meekness of his nature. He is yet heavy and dull in conceit and discourse, and timorous and dastardly in his courage; at the which the king hath been much troubled, when he hath seen or heard the tokens of it, saying *Fault il donc que je soy pere d'un poltron?* but his education is like to polish and amend both these faults. [11a]

Lord Herbert who, as ambassador from 1619, frequently encountered Louis XIII, offers in his *Life* a very different account from Coryate's of the king's physique and ability to express himself:

> His words were never many as being so extream a Stutterer, that he would sometimes hold his Tongue out of his mouth a good while before he could speak so much as one word. He had besides a double Row of Teeth, and was observed seldom or never to spit or blow his Nose, or to sweat much though he were very laborious, and almost indefatigable in his exercises of Hunting and Hawking, to which he was much addicted. Neither did it hinder him though he was burst in his body, as we call it, Herniosus, for he was noted in those sports though often times on foot to tire not only his Courtiers but even his Lacquies; being equally insensible as was thought either of heat or cold.

Of his mental capacity and moral character Lord Herbert formed a fairly favourable opinion:

> His Understanding and natural parts were as good as could be expected in one that was brought up in so much ignorance, which was on purpose so done that he might be the longer governed; howbeit he acquired in time a good knowledge in Affairs as conversing for the most part with wise and active Persons. He was noted to have two Qualities incident to all who were ignorantly brought up, Suspicion and Dissimulation .. Howbeit I must observe that neither his fears did take away his courage, when there was occasion to use it, nor his dissimulation

extend itself to the doing of private mischiefs to his Subjects either of one or the other Religion.[12]

In 1625 Heylyn also saw Louis XIII, though no doubt from a greater distance than an ambassador. He was obviously not impressed by the king's physical appearance:

> For person he is of the middle stature, and rather well proportioned then large, his face knoweth little yet of a beard, but that which is black and swarty, his complexion also much of the same hew, carrying in it a certain boisterousnesse, and that in a further measure then what a graceful majesty can admit of, so that one can hardly say of him, without a spite of Courtship, which Paterculus did of Tiberius, *Quod visus praetulerit principem*, that his countenance proclaimed him a King. But questionlesse his greatest defect is want of utterance, whch is very unpleasing, by reason of a desperate and uncurable stammering; which defect is likely more and more to grow upon him.

After pointing out that the king was now twenty-four, Heylyn continues, 'an age which he beareth not very plausibly; want of beard, and the swarthinesse of his complexion, making him seem older'. Speaking of his childless marriage to Anne of Austria, he adds, 'It is thought by many, and covertly spoken by divers in France, that the principall cause of the Queens barrennesse proceedeth from Spain'. After explaining that her marriage contract laid it down that neither Anne nor any of her children could succeed to any of the dominions of the king of Spain and that she herself had had to make an act of renunciation, he goes on to explain the meaning of his words: 'This being not sufficient to secure their fears, it is thought, that she was some way or other disabled from conception before ever she came into the Kings imbraces'.[13]

The period of disorder through which France passed in the early part of this reign is reflected in the writings of our travellers. When Howell arrived in France in 1619, he described to a correspondent the unsettled state of the country in the years after the assassination of Concini, the Maréchal d'Ancre, and the exile of Marie de Médicis, the Queen Mother and former Regent, to Blois:

> I am but a freshman yet in France, therefore I can send you no news, but that all is here quiet, and *tis no ordinary news, that the French should be quiet:* But som think this Calm will not last long, for the Queen Mother (late Regent) is discontented being restrain'd from coming to the Court, or to the City of Paris, or the Tragicall death of her Favourit (and Foster-Brother) the late Marquis of Ancre, lieth yet in her stomach undigested: She hath the Duke of Espernon, and divers other potent Princes, that

would be strongly, at her devotion (as 'tis thought) if she would stir.[14]

In another letter he describes in detail how Concini was assassinated and his body disinterred and dragged through the streets. After briefly relating the trial and execution of his widow, he concludes: 'This was a right act of a French popular fury, which like an angry torrent is irresistible; nor can any Banks, Boundaries, or Dikes stop the impetuous rage of it. How the young king will prosper after so high, and an unexampled act of violence, by beginning his Raign, and embruing the Walls of his own Court with blood in that manner, there are divers censures'.[15] Heylyn also gives a good deal of space to these events, but his sources were obviously hostile to the Concinis. According to him the Maréchal d'Ancre 'made a shift to get into his own hands an authority almost as unlimited, as that of the old *Mayre* of the Palace', and while he cannot conceive that he could have had designs on the throne of France, he concludes that 'the Spanish gold had corrupted him to some project concerning the enlargement of that Empire, upon the French dominion'.[16]

The person who, outwardly at least, profited most from the assassination of Concini was Louis XIII's favourite, Charles d'Albret, who had all sorts of honours heaped upon him; he was made Duc de Luynes and finally *Connétable*. Lord Herbert got on with him so badly that for a time, until death removed Luynes from the scene at the end of 1621, he was recalled from the Paris embassy. Naturally Luynes is dismissed somewhat contemptuously in the *Life*: 'His favourite was one Monsieur De Luynes, who in his Nonage gained much upon the King by making Hawkes fly at all Little Birds in his Gardens, and by making some of those Litle Birds againe catch Butter Flies. And had the King used him for no other purpose, he might have been tolerated; but as, when the King came to a Riper Age, the Government of Publick affairs was drawn cheifly from his Counsells, not a few Errors were committed'.[17] According to Howell who was in France in this period Luynes was far from popular. 'The Favourite Luines strengthneth himself more and more in his minionship, but he is much murmured at in regard the accesse of Suiters to him is so difficult, which made a Lord of this Land say, That three of the hardest things in the World were, *To quadrat a Circle, to find out the Philosophers Stone, and to speak with the Duke of Luines*'. Howell watched the progress of the favourite until he was able to announce in another letter: 'The Duke of Luynes is at last made Lord high Constable of France, the prime Officer of the Crown, he hath a peculiar Court to himself, a guard of 100 men in rich liveries, and a hundred thousand livers every year Pension'. He follows this with an account of how Luynes won the young king's favour and of how he had secured dukedoms and aristocratic marriages for himself and his two brothers.

Howell furnished his correspondents with news about the clash between Louis XIII and the Queen Mother after her escape from Blois. When her adviser, Richelieu, had negotiated for her the governorship of Anjou, she was joined at Angers by the Duc D'Épernon and other disaffected great noblemen; their army was, however, quickly routed in August 1620 by the royal troops. 'France is now barren of news', writes Howell, 'onely there was a shrewd brush lately twixt the young King and his Mother, who having the Duke of Espernon and others for her Champions met him In open field about pont de Ce, but she went away with the worst; such was the rare dutifulness of the King, that he forgave her upon his knees, and pardon'd all her complices; And now there is an universall Peace in this Countrey, which tis thought will not last long, for there is a war intended against them of the reformed Religion'.[18]

The clashes between the Crown and the Huguenot minority are best dealt with in another place.[19] Heylyn who visited France in 1625, shortly after Richelieu came to power, has a number of shrewd comments to make on political conditions there at that date. He draws attention to the existence of a figure who was to play an important part in the second half of the reign, Louis XIII's younger brother, Gaston d'Orléans. As long as Louis's marriage with Anne of Austria remained childless (a Dauphin was not produced until 1638), Gaston remained heir presumptive, and for more than a decade he was to be a centre of opposition to Louis XIII and Richelieu. Heylyn was obviously more impressed with Gaston's appearance than with that of his brother since he describes him as 'a Prince of a brave and manlike aspect: likely to inherit as large a part of his Fathers spirit, as the King doth of his Crown'. No doubt Heylyn was deceived by appearances since Gaston proved a weak and irresolute opponent of Richelieu who, after the failure of each conspiracy, had him pardoned by the king on more and more humiliating terms; but Heylyn does describe the duke's position accurately when he writes: 'He seeth his elder brother as yet childlesse, himself the next heir to the Crown, and it is likely he will look on a while, and expect the issue of his fortune'.[20] In 1658 Mortoft saw Gaston in his château at Blois; although Louis XIV's uncle, he was now in disgrace after his slippery behaviour during the Fronde: 'Wee had that morning that wee were in the Duke's house the honour to see him, who is a very bigg and grosse man, having a very red Countenance'.[21] Gaston died there less than eighteen months later.

Like Dallington, Heylyn was scandalized by the disrespectful fashion in which a Frenchman would speak of his king: 'I never heard people talke lesse reverently of their Prince, nor more sawcily of his actions. Scarce a day passeth away without some seditiious Pamphlet printed and published, in the disgrace of the King, or of some of his Courtiers. These are every mans mony, & he that buyeth them is not coy of the Contents, be they never so scandalous; of all humours the most base and odious'. Although Heylyn is well aware of the challenge which the power of the great nobles presented to the authority of the Crown during this reign, he also stresses the contrast with conditions in England 'wherein the King hath his full Prerogative, the Nobles all due respects, and the People, among other blessings perfect in this, that they are masters of their own purposes, and have a strong hand in the making of their own Laws'. In France, on the other hand, 'the government of the King is meerly, indeed, regal, or to give it the true name *despoticall*; though the Countrey be his wife, and all the people are his children, yet doth he neither governe as a husband or a father; he accounteth of them all as of his servants, and therefore commandeth of them as a Master. In his Edicts which he over frequently sendeth about, he never mentioneth the good will of his Subjects, nor the approbation of his Councell, but concludeth all of them in this forme, *Car tell est nostre plaisir*'. In France, he adds, 'the Subject frameth his life meerly as the Kings variable Edicts shall please to enjoyn him; is ravished of his money as the Kings taske-masters think fit; and suffereth many other oppressions'.

On paper the Parlements and the Estates General limited the King's power, but this, Heylyn argues, is illusory: 'Though the Court of Parliament doth seem to challenge a perusall of his Edicts, before they passe for Laws yet is that but a meer formality. It is the *car tel est nostre plaisir*, which maketh them currant'. Although the Estates General had been sitting only ten years earlier, they were not to meet again until 1789, so that Heylyn, after comparing this institution with the English Parliament, can say with some reason:

But these meetings are now forgotten, or out of use; neither, indeed, as this time goeth, can they any way advantage the State; for whereas there are three principall, if not sole causes of these conventions, which are, the deposing of the Regency during the nonage or sickness of a King; the granting Aides and Subsidies; and the redressing of Grievances, there is now another course taken in them. The Parliament of Paris, which speaketh as it is prompted by power and greatnesse, appointeth the Regent; the Kings themselves with their officers determine of the Taxes; and as concerning their Grievances, the Kings eare is open to private Petitions.[22]

Although the reasons given are at times a trifle odd, the eclipse of this potential check on the royal authority was definite enough.

As his trip to France took place not long after Richelieu came to power, Heylyn's comments on him are somewhat perfunctory. Indeed he treats him as a mere 'assistant' to Marie de Médicis to whom he attributes an extraordinary influence over Louis XIII: 'For indeed during her Sons minority, and after since her reintegration with him, she hath made her selfe so absolute a mistresse of his mind, that he hath intrusted to her the entire conduct of all his most weighty affaires'. According to Heylyn the Queen Mother had 'all the virtues of Katherine de Medices, and some also of her vices'. His verdict on her is generally very favourable; he declares that France was 'never more quietly and evenly governed, then first during her Regencie, and now during the time of her favour with the King'. He concludes his account of her with words which no man would dare pen today: 'An heroicall Lady, and worthy the report of posterity; the frailty and weaknesse of her as a woman, not being accounted hers, but her sexes'.

Though Richelieu appears here as a mere appendage of the Queen Mother, Heylyn does show some recognition of his qualities, describing him as 'a man of no great birth, were Nobility the greatest parentage; but otherwise to be ranked among the noblest'. He goes on: 'Of a sound reach he is, and a close brain; one exceedingly well mixt of a lay understanding, and a Church habit; one that is compleatly skilled in the art of men, and a perfect master of his own mind and affections.'[23]

Relatively few other travellers were in France during the period 1624–1642. It is true that Sir Thomas Abdy was in Forges in 1633 when Richelieu accompanied the king and queen to this resort, but he did not catch even a glimpse of him since he was 'by reason of some certaine indisposition not to be sene'. However, when Abdy visited Le Havre shortly after he picked up an interesting piece of gossip. This town which came under the control of Richelieu as *Amiral de France* he found 'almost imprenable', adding 'All this has bin so strong made by the meanes of Monsieur le Cardinal and that upon policie, as some thinke, there to retire himselfe upon the least frowne'.[23a]

Howell has only a few rather scrappy comments to make on the events of these years. In 1635 he reports that the execution, three years earlier, of the Duc de Montmorency for his part in another of Gaston d'Orléans's revolts still aroused strong feelings: 'Ther is yet a great resentment in many places in France, for the beheading of Montmorency . . . He died upon a Scaffold in Tholouse, in the flower of his yeares, at 34, and hath left no issue behind; so that the noble old Family extinguished in a snuff'. Yet Howell does stress the seriousness of his crime: 'His Treason was very foul, having received particular commissions from the King to make an extraordinary Levie of men and money in Languedoc and then turn directly against the King, against whose person he appear'd arm'd in open Field, and in a Hostile posture, for fomenting of Monsieurs Rebellion'. Howell is the only one of our travellers to claim to have seen Richelieu and even to have spoken with him. In 1641 he published in Paris a French translation of his *Dodona's Grove*, a political allegory in prose, under the title *Dendrologie, ou la Forest de Dodone*. The author is named on the title page as 'M. Jacques Howel, Gentilhomme Breton Anglois'. The work appeared with the imprint of the well-known publisher, Augustin Courbé, but 'aux dépens de l'Auteur'. This is how he relates the story of his encounter with Richelieu in a letter to Lord Herbert of Cherbury:

> I send herewith Dodonas Grove couch'd in French, and in the newest French; for though the main version be mine, yet I got one of the *Académie des beaux Esprits* here to run it over, to correct and refine the Language, and reduce it to the most modern Dialect. It took so here, that the new Academy of Wits have given a public and far higher *Elogium* of it then it deserves. I was brought to the Cardinal at Ruelle, where I was a good while with him in his privat Garden, and it were a vanity in me, to insert here what propositions he made to me.

One is not, of course, compelled to take at his word this 'Gentilhomme Breton Anglais', but he does add some interesting remarks on the sycophantic verses in Latin and French addressed to the Cardinal and concludes with a reasonably balanced judgment on his period in power: 'Certainly he is a rare man, and of a transcendent reach, and they are rather miracles then exploits that he hath don, though those miracles be of a sanguin Dy (the colour of his habit) steep'd in blood; which makes the Spaniard call him the gran *Caga-fuego*[24] of Christendom'.[25]

Perhaps the most interesting comment on this period of French history is furnished by Lord Herbert. Writing in the 1640s, he tells how he warned the Duc de Guise of the consequences for the great noblemen of the government's treatment of the Protestants during the period when Luynes was in power:

> The Duke of Guise, coming to see mee one day, said that they should never be happy in France, 'till those of the Religion were rooted out, I answer'd that I wondred to hear him say so, and the Duke demanding why, I replied that whensoever Those of the

Religion were put down, the turn of the Great Persons and Governors of Provinces of that Kingdome would be next; and that though the present King were a good Prince, yet that their Successors may be otherwise, and that men did not know how soon Princes might prove Tyrants, when they had nothing to fear; which Speech of mine was fatal, since those of the Religion were no sooner reduced into that weak condition in which now they are, but the Governors of Provinces were brought lower, and curbed much in their Power and Authority, And the Duke of Guise first of them all, so that I doubt not but my words were well remembred.[26]

The Duc de Guise (1571–1640) fell out with Richelieu over his support for Marie de Médicis: in 1631 he retired to Italy and died there. In view of the way Richelieu strengthened absolutism by reducing the power of the great noblemen, Lord Herbert's warning was indeed prophetic.

There are naturally scattered references to Richelieu in the writings of travellers who came to France after his disappearance from the scene. Two writers have something of particular interest to say about him. When Finch was in Paris in 1652, he picked up the following piece of gossip about Richelieu's unpopularity when he died ten years earlier:

One Bonaville that sells wine at Navarr College Gate, and is one of those that have the monoply to hang the churches with black at funeralls, told me that he distributed with his own hands above 12,000 pistolls at Cardinall Richlieu' death, for masses and offices to be said for him and yet that was not the tenth part, but when his body was to be buried and was carried from the Sorbon there was above 4,000 Covisters[27] that would have taken the corps and thrown it into the Seine had it not been well defended.[28]

More significant are Evelyn's comments on the strengthening of absolutism under Richelieu, though they were made, oddly enough, in the middle of the Fronde, when the power of the monarchy was gravely threatened. Whereas in the past, he maintains, 'the Nobility of France were in a manner free and independent Princes' with 'so many fortified Towns, Governments, and Places of importance ... notably bridling the head of Majesty', now thanks to Richelieu the monarch is absolute:

The defunct and great Cardinal de Richlieu found out a speedy and fortunate expedient to reduce them to obedience, and that not onely by subjugating the Posts themselves, which he performed by strength, but likewise by so dextrously interesting the Gentry and refractory Nobility, both by honours and blood, to the Court and his faction, which he did by policy: in fine, he so handled the Cards, that the better sort of people became tractable out of mere respect to their Relations; so that now the Sovereignty of France is become so independent and absolute, that albeit it do still reteine a shadow of the ancient form, yet it is, duly considered, a thing heavenly wide and different.

As a result of Richelieu's policies 'in the Kings sole power it is to resolve of, and dissolve warrs; by him are the Laws interpreted; Letters of grace, of Naturality, and other Acts given out; he it is imposeth Taxes from which (by a speciall decree) the Church her selfe is not exempt.' It is true that there still remains the empty formality that the king 'permits none of his Edicts to passe as authentick until the Court of Parliament (who is absolutely at his devotion) have first verified them', but this is merely 'the handsomer to disguise and apparell these his volunties'.

Despite the turmoil of the civil war which raged as he was finishing his *State of France* in Paris in February 1652, he concludes his observations on the position of the monarchy with a striking passage: 'In a word, he who would perfectly, and without more adoe, understand by what Law and Rule the Kings of France impose on their Vassals, may see it summarily, yet very legibly ingraven by that forementioned Cardinall, upon that excellent Artillery, which defend his Majesties Citadell at Havre de grace, in Normandy, where you may run and read the best of Tenures, as the times are now, in this Epigraph, – *Ratio ultima Regum*.[29]

The death of Louis XIII on 14 May 1643 plunged France once more into a minority with all its threats of disorder and civil war, as his successor had not yet reached the tender age of five. On Christmas Eve Evelyn who had recently arrived in Paris caught a glimpse of the child at Notre Dame: 'The young king being now there with a greate and martial Guard, who enter'd the Nave of the Church with their drums & Fifes, at their ceasing was entertaind with the Church musique, and so I left him'.[30] In June 1648, just before the outbreak of the Fronde, Lord Willoughby, according to John Pridgeon, had the privilege of seeing in the gardens of Richelieu's mansion at Rueil the Regent, Anne of Austria, together with Louis XIV and his younger brother. After paying his respects to the Prince of Wales and Henrietta Maria at St. Germain, 'my Lord came home by Ruelle, where he saw the Kinge of France with his mother, and the Duke d'Angeau his brother in the Cardinalls garden with their attendants'.[31] In May 1651 Evelyn was present when the young king and his brother along with selected courtiers danced a ballet; 'the King', he declares, 'performing to the admiration of all'. Later in the same year he witnessed a much more important ceremony; now that Louis XIV had entered his fourteenth year, the regency was theoretically at an end: 'The 7th of September I went to Visite Mr. Hobbs the famous Philosopher of Malmesbury, with whom I had long acquaintance: from whose Window, we saw the whole equipage & glorious Cavalcade of the Young French Monarch Lewis the XIVth passing to Parliament, when first he tooke the Kingly Government on him, as now out of Minority & the Queene regents pupilage'. Though Evelyn's account is derived from Théophraste Renaudot's *Gazette,* he does add one touch of his own when he compares the king to 'a young Apollo'. In the following week he went with his father-in-law, Charles II's envoy in Paris, to the court: 'I accompanied Sir Richard Browne my Father in Law to the French Court, who had a favourable Audience of the French King & Queene his Mother, congratulating the one his coming to the exercise of his royal charge, & the others prudent, and happy Administration during her late Regency, desiring both their Majesties to conserve the same Amitie for his Master, our King, they had don: which they both promis'd, with many civil expressions & words of Course upon such occasions'.[32]

Although the Italian cardinal, Mazarin, was to dominate the French scene from the beginning of this reign down to his death in 1661, he is barely mentioned by our travellers except by Eveyln in his *State of France.* Writing in the middle of the Fronde at a time when Mazarin had already been compelled to leave the country once, Evelyn could be excused for expressing some doubt as to his chances of clinging to power:

> The Government of France doth at present rather totter then stand upon the late great Cardinals substruction; the Queen Mother having ever since his decease continued in the principall ministry of State affairs her favourite, Mazarini, a person of (to speak with the world) farre greater fortune, then either extraction or vertue; however, he hath steered this great vessel of Monarchy a long time, and that amidst so many stormes, and in such foul weather, as whether his craft or courage exceeds it is not yet decided: certaine it is, that as he hath longer held in, then by some wise men it was judg'd he could, so some late actions of his (interpreted to have been ingratefull enough) make others daily confident of his absolute ruine: and in truth he doth play so hazardous a game at present, that as the hand is universally turned, it were great odds to lay on Confusions side, so prodigious a fatality now threatning Princes, that if France compose not suddenly, these calamities, I am confident, will

epidemically visite Europe for a time.[33]

However, Eveyln had seen Mazarin at a very low point in his fortunes; he could scarcely foresee the position of power which he was to occupy after the collapse of the Fronde.

In his diary he makes one or two references to events of the Fronde, but for a vivid account of Paris during its first phase, the so-called Fronde Parlementaire, we must turn to the travel notes of Richard Symonds.[34] He landed at Calais on 5 January 1649. During the following night Anne of Austria, the Regent, and Mazarin removed themselves from Paris to Saint-Germain taking the young king with them, and using the Prince de Condé's army to blockade the capital. When Symonds arrived at St. Denis, he found that 'this was now the head quarters of the French army, for they & the Parisians begin to quarrel, both being upon their guards, & the paisants as we passt had barricaded the villages'. He later explains more fully the situation which he found on his arrival in the capital:

> At my being at Paris was the very heate of the beginning of their Civill warr between their Parlement & the Army Royal, which army was for Cardinal Richleu's favorite Secretary, successor & minion Cardinal Mazarino, an Italian, who togeather with the Queene Regent governe the kingdome during the minority of the King, and now the Parisians are raysing & forming an Army; many of the Parliament men rayse companys & march to the guards at the head of them in martiall & ostentous garb.

He offers a good deal of information about the troops recruited in Paris under the leadership of the Prince de Conti. Condé's younger brother, and various great noblemen such as the Duc de Beaufort. The attitude of the population of the capital to the generals on both sides is conveyed in a vivid passage:

> Sometimes when a Convoy had brought in much provisions & that Monsieur de Beaufort who commands now the forces of the Citty, this Monsieur Beaufort le plus grand homme de tout le monde, and so, when the newes that he had taken St. Dennis; but when after 2 or 3 dayes it appeared St. Dennis was not taken & bread which was in time of peace at 20d came to be 50 pence and that the newes was that the Prince de Conde had recruited his Army for the King, then Monsieur le Prince de Conde le tres fameuse General de l'universe. Peste le bougre de Borgois [*sic*].

He records how a seditious placard was put up in the capital: 'An Officer in an English Regiment of the Royal army told me that in Paris a picture was in publique viewe where they painted an Asse sadled & the Cardinal Mazarin mounting her, being help't up & lifted by the Prince of Conde & written with this word. L'asne d'Austrich. The Queenes name is Ann of Austria'. He also relates a well-known episode in the first Fronde which illustrates the haughty manner in which the Parlement treated the Court:

> During the heate of the Warr in this Towne A herald was sent by the king in his Velvette Coate of blew & Gold with Trumpets. The sentry had him staid. He desird to be admitted, saying Je suis Herauld de Votre Roy, je demande entrance. The Captaine of the guard told him he should not come in. Then the herauld began to tell his businesse. The Captaine told him if he told his businesse afore he knew the Parlement's pleasure, he would shoot him. The Captaine of the Guard sent to the Parlement, but he was not sufferd to enter.

Symonds also records the only serious military engagement of the war — the capture of Charenton by the Prince de Condé:

> The Parisians putt in 800 men to man the towne of Charenton 3 english myle, one league, down the River of Seyne. Prince de Condé about 4 of the clock in the morning Monday Feb. 7 with 6000 surprisd it & putt them to the sword. The Parisians marcht out with a vast company of armes, but the Prince was in readinesse to receive them & they returnd . . . Since tis reported that about 300 was killed in the place at Charenton.

However, as both the Court and the Parlement were anxious to bring the conflict to an end, negotiations opened at Rueil on 4 March and a final agreement was registered by the Parlement on 1 April.

When Robert Montagu arrived back in Paris in November of the following year, at a time when the position of Mazarin was becoming increasingly desperate, just before he was driven into exile, he noted the cardinal's unpopularity in the capital:

> The day I came heere some of the inhabitants did hange up the Cardinal Mazarine's effigies with a rope about his necke in sev[er]all places of the citty with these following verses at it
>
> Voicy une Harpie, habilé en Cardinal,
>
> Qu'on depende la copie, pour pendre l'original.[34a]

Finch too was in France during the Fronde, though at a later date. His comments concern the opening months of 1652. While still in Paris, he made the following notes: 'The coadjutor, Bishop of Corinth, [Retz] was made Cardinal about February 12; he expected his cap so long that he told the Pope's Nuncio he would make a cardinall's capp so poore a thing that the meanest abbott in France should not desire it. Cardinall Mazarin's library was sold when I was there about March 2'.[35]

In the middle of March Baines and he set out for Lyons and rapidly found themselves in the path of various armies engaged in the civil war in the provinces. In a letter to his sister from Lyons Finch describes various encounters with these armies. On the first day of their journey, he explains, 'the Count Grandpré and my Lord Digby were within three leagues of us, with 5,000 of the King's men'. On the third day, at Auxerre, they found public transport entirely disrupted by the war: 'Although a coach and messenger used to go from Auxerre to Chalons, we could get none to conduct us, by reason of the soldiers, who were all over Bourgogne, and who robbed all they met, and behind us was the Count Grandpré, who marched after us'. After being robbed by soldiers when they continued their journey on foot, they eventually met an officer with 300 infantry who escorted them to Dijon. On their way from there to Beaune, he relates, 'I passed by 3,000 foot, within a league, beseiging Bellegarde'. Some idea of the dangers of travel in France in these days of civil war may be gleaned from his remarks on the difficulty another Englishman would have joining them from Rouen:

> I have received a letter from Mr. Austin from Rouen, and if he knows how to come to us in safety, he is a wise man; for though he may escape by fortune, yet I cannot meet with one man of 40 that does. Seven merchants that went with guns were set upon, and six slain, and a gentleman from Paris met 40 stripped as naked as they were born. The armys of the Duc de Nemours, Beaufort, Marshal Turenne, Prince of Condé, Count Harcourt, and the Duc de Lorraine, all lie in the way between this and Paris, and if Mr. Austin can charge through them all, he is a valiant man.

Finch explains that he has now decided to travel to Italy through Geneva instead of Marseilles and Genoa as he had intended, 'the former being for the Prince of Condé and Toulon for the King, it is impossible to pass that way'.[36]

There are references to the Fronde in the writings of travellers who came to France long after this civil war was over. When Skippon visited Marseilles in 1665, he noted how Louis XIV had shown his displeasure at the way the city had behaved during the civil war: 'About eight years ago[37] the king was here in person, but being much displeased with the town, refused to enter the gates, but commanded a breach to be made in the wall, which is not yet made up, and where at present most people go in and out: At the same time the king gave order for the razing the house of monsieur Glandeve de Nevizeles,[38] who was suspected as chief of the discontents, and a pillar of infamy is erected where his house stood. He lives now at Barcelona'.[39] On his return from Poitiers to Paris in 1666 Lauder observed the destruction caused during the Fronde at Étampes which he describes as 'a ruinous toune, their no being so meikle as a whole house standing in all the fauxbourgs, and that since the late troubles raised by Mr. le Prince, who defended the toune against the King'.[40]

Louis XIV's resentment at the disorders in Paris during his minority is stressed, even to the point of exaggeration, by later travellers, who seem to ignore the fact that the removal of the court to Versailles was only a very gradual process which was not completed until 1682; they speak as if Louis XIV never spent one night in the city after the end of the Fronde.[41] In the early 1680s Veryard has this to say of Louis XIV's attitude to his capital: 'When he passes through it, he never stops; and notwithstanding all the endeavours that have been us'd to reconcile him, he still continues the marks of his Displeasure. They have paid dearly for their Revolt, have been, and are still, more burthen'd with Taxes than any other part of the Kingdom. His Statue stands erected in the Town House, treading on the Necks of the principal Magistrates that were concern'd in the Rebellion; but they say he has of late consented to the taking of it down, and that they are about to do it'.[42] Northleigh, who was in France a few years later, speaks of a reconciliation being effected when Louis XIV, after recovering from his operation for a fistula, visited Paris on 30 January 1687 and dined at the Hôtel de Ville:

> The Government of Paris instituting some solemn Prayers and Procession with Thanksgiving for the King's Recovery, from his late dangerous Disease, he came afterward in Person to the Town-house to return the Senate Thanks for their Concern and Care for his Health; and seeing in their Senate-house where he was entertain'd, some Hangings, in which was wrought the Submission of the Senators with Halters about their Necks, and also his Statue trampling upon one of the Citizens, Marks of Indignity for their Rebellion, He as a Mark of his Favour, order'd the one to be burnt, and the other to be taken down; and so took away those monumental Reproaches they had continually before their Eyes, in Memory of which gracious Condonation they instituted an annual Festival with Fireworks for that day.[43]

This was over thirty years after the end of the Fronde.

Reresby who came to France after the civil war was over, in a period when Mazarin had succeeded in re-establishing the authority of the Crown, continually stresses the absolute nature of the French monarchy. After describing the Estates General, he continues, 'The kings of France are now too absolute to use this way of advising with their subjects, consulting only their own wills, which they have always a standing army ready to execute. This so overawes the common people that they dare scarce so much as reflect on their past liberties'. This state of affairs, he argues, could only be achieved by securing the support of the nobility: 'And yet it would seem impossible for a king so to govern, did he not by the same way raise and engage to himself the gentry, that he depresseth the commonalty; first rendering the privileges granted to the gentry more considerable by denying them to those of meaner quality'. In short, Reresby concludes, 'himself is the channel through which flow all the streams of favour and reward to such as he would fix to his own interest, whilst the poor countryman sinks under the weight of his oppression'.[44]

Reresby was at least as much impressed as any previous traveller with the absolute power enjoyed by the king of France:

> The French kings have a most absolute power; when they would have anything done or confirmed by parliaments, they speak to them in these terms:
> 'We, of our free grace, full power, great knowledge, and royal authority, have willed, appointed, and ordained, that do so and so'. And to shew they are obliged to give nobody a reason for what they enjoin, they end with, 'for such is our pleasure'.
> They dispose of all governments of towns and countries, and of all the offices belonging to the crown, whether justiciary or military. They lay what taxes they please upon the people, alter the rate of money, making it greater when their coffers are low, and less when full. They make the laws, and interpret them; dispose of all ecclesiastical preferments, which the pope confirms; declare war, enter into leagues and confederations, levy soldiers, and, in fine, whatever they please.[45]

Like Evelyn Reresby offers some account of the royal councils, starting with the most important of all, the *Conseil d'en haut*, and of the *Secrétaires d'État*,[46] but, unlike Evelyn, he makes no mention of the increasingly important role played by those *maîtres des requêtes* who were sent out into the provinces as *Intendants* to administer them in the king's name. Evelyn does at least get as far as mentioning that some *maîtres des requêtes* were despatched from Paris 'as Commissioners for his Majesty in the Cities and Provinces, where they judge and determine upon all affairs of the Crowne, with most absolute power and authority'.[47]

Quite a number of our travellers describe, in varying degrees of detail, how they caught a sight of Louis XIV at the height of his power, first as a quite young man and later in his maturity. Shortly after his arrival in Paris in 1664 Edward Browne noted in his journal: 'This day I was at the Louvre to see the king of France as hee tooke

L

coach to goe to Verseilles', and a few days later he could write: 'As I came home I met the King of France in a Chariot with two other nobles with him. The Chariot was open before and hee drove it himselfe. His Guarde of Suisse waited in their armes from the Louvre to Port de la Conférence'.[48] When he was back again in Paris in the following year he had a more interesting scene to describe; in a letter to his father he relates what he saw at the end of a short tour of the surroundinds of the capital: 'Returning to Paris, the King overtook us in chaise roulante with his Mistress La Valière with him, habited very prettily in a hat and feathers, and a just aucorps. Hee had dined that day with his brother, at a house of his in the country; and had left his company and came away full speed to Paris. Upon the news of the King of Spaines death, they prepare apace'.[49]

Looking back in the *History of his own Time* on his first visit to France in 1664, Burnet writes of his arrival from Holland:

> From thence, where evry thing was free, I went to France, where nothing was free. The King was beginning to put things in great method, in his revenue, in his troops, in his government at home, but above all in the increasing of trade, and the building of a great fleet. His own deportment was solemn and grave, save only that he kept his Mistrisses very avowedly. He was diligent in his own counsels, and regular in the dispatch of his affairs: So that all things about him looked like the preparing of matters for all that we have seen acted since.[50]

Skippon in 1666 records only a glimpse of the king at Versailles: 'Here I saw Louis XIV and his queen, attended by a foot company of Swiss, armed with back, breast and head-peice, a company of Swiss with halberds, and a company of French foot, besides his guard in livery on horseback arm'd with carbines'.[51]

A decade or so later some more lively accounts of glimpses of the king, as well as of other members of the royal family and the *maîtresse en titre*, were furnished by Locke. On his first visit to Versailles in 1677, after describing the fountains in the gardens, he continues: 'We had the honour to see them with the King, who walked about with Madame Montespan from one to an other, after haveing driven her & 2 other Ladys in the coach with him about a good part of the garden in a coach and 6 horses,' He then adds a sarcastic passage for which he made prudent use of shorthand: 'The King seemed to be mightily well pleased with his water works and severall changes were made then to which he himself gave sign with his cane, and he may well be made merry with this water since it has cost him dearer than so much wine, for they say it costs him 3s. every pint (i.e. 2 lbs.) that run there'.

In September of that year his pupil and he followed the court to

Fontainebleau. At a performance of Lully's opera *Alceste* they saw various members of the royal family: 'At the opera the King & Queen sat in chaires with armes. On the right hand the King sat Mme. Montespan &, a little nearer the stage on her right hand, Mademoiselle, the King of England's niece. On the left hand of the Queen sat Monsieur, & of his left hand, advanceing towards the stage, Madame, & soe forward towards the stage other Ladys of the Court, all on Tabourets except the King & Queen'. The next day after seeing over the palace Locke and his pupil were present at a ball: 'At night we saw a ball where the King & Queen & the great persons of the Court danced, & the King himself took pains to cleare the roome to make place for the dancers. The Queen was very rich in Jewells & there needed her stiffness to support so great a treasure, & soe were several of the Ladys. The King, Queen, etc. were placed as at the Opera'. Another point which Locke noted before they left Fontainebleau three days later was that 'the King & Court went a stag hunting in the afternoon, & at night had an opera, at all of which Madame appear'd in a peruke & upper parts dressed like a man'. Lest the reader should form too high an opinion of the elegance and refinement of Louis's court, another of Locke's comments on Fontainebleau must be quoted:

> On the farther side the parterre is a moat which bounds the garden which would be very fine , were it not turned into filthy suds by those who continually wash there. The gardens are everywhere full of nosegays, especially under the long gallery windows, & there was one laid at Monsieur's back stairs to mark, I suppose, the good housekeeping rather than the cleanlynesse of the place, and at all the stairs one is sure to meet with a parfume which yet hath nothing of Vespatian's good savour.[52]

Before setting out from Paris on his second tour of France Locke saw the king hold a review of the household troops near St. Germain. A few passages of general interest may be extracted from his description of the occasion:

> The King came to take a view of these troops between 11 & 12, which he did soe narrowly that he had made them, squadron after squadron, march in file, man after man, just before him, & made the number in each squadron, as they passed, be counted, takeing in the meane time a strict survey of their horses & them. The King, when he light out of his coach, had a hat laced about the edg with gold lace & a white feather. After a while he had been on horseback, it beginning to rain, he changed it for a plaine hat that had only a black ribbon about it ... The Queen towards the latter end came in a coach & 8 horses. The King led

her along the head of all these squadrons, they being drawn up
all in a line 3 deepe with little intervals between each squadron.
At going off the field, which was about 3 in the afternoon, the
Grenadiers were made exercise before him ... When this was
don, the King went alone into his chariot, takeing his best hat
again, & soe returned.

No doubt of greater interest to many a reader is the note which Locke
made a few days later when the king left for a secret destination,
Ghent, which was besieged and captured by the French a month later:
'King of France passed through Paris to go to   .[53] He was
in the Queen's coach with 8 horses. In the coach with the Queen
Madam Montespan'.

At the end of 1678, on his return to Paris, Locke offers a faintly
sarcastic account of the king's behaviour at his *lever*: 'At the King's
Levé which I saw this morning at St. Germans, there is noe thing soe
remarkable as his great devotion which is very exemplary, for as soon
as ever he is dressed, he goes to his bed's side where he kneels downe
to his prayers, severall preists kneeling by him, in which posture he
continues for a pretty while, not being disturbed by the noise & buz of
the rest of the chamber, which is full of people standing & talking one
to an other.' One last glimpse of Louis XIV is afforded by Locke's
description of another review of the household troops:

> As the King passed at the hed of the line as they stood drawn
> up, the officers at the heads of their companys & regiments in
> armer with pikes in their hands saluted him with their pikes &
> then with their hats, & he very courteously put of his hat to them
> again, & soe he did again when, he takeing his stand, they
> marchd all before him. He passed twise a long the whole front of
> them forwards & backwards, first by himself, the Dauphin etc.
> accompanying him, & then with the Queen, he rideing along by
> her coach side.[54]

Covel who was in France at this time gives a description of the
furnishings of the King's apartments in his account of Versailles: 'The
hangings of the King's appartment green velvet lined with green
tafety, paned with Green cloth of Gold embroyderd, no pictures. We
saw the King's bedchamber, bed inside and counterpaine cloth of
gold and side like the hangings of the roome; his council chamber the
same, two cupboards and cabinets with philegrin silver flower'd, little
knacks, trunkes, flowerputs &c.' Then follows a lively account of the
royal family eating in public:

> We saw the King at dinner, the room furnisht after same
> manner but other colours. He sat of the entrance side, the
> Queen on his left hand. At the right End the Daulphin, with

Monsieur on his right hand. At the end over against them sat Madam Montpensier all alone. She is daughter of the old Duke of Orleans, aunt to this King,[55] and he will not let her marry &c. On the side opposite to the King at the corner sat Madmeselle, the Monsieur's daughter. Madame was not there. When the King or any one would drink, they bawl out A boir pour----, and his taster an ordinary clad fellow give the King to drink, reaching a *sotto coppa*,[56] over the table with wine and water to him without any further ceremony. The Queen had the richest necklace of pearl that ever I saw, and the brightest.

Covel then relates how a petition was presented to the King: 'Then came a poor gentlewoman (with three sons) and presented a petition to the King at table about her Husband lost in the warres; he received it with abundance of sweetnesse mixt with majesty'.

In the afternoon Covel saw the King and courtiers, male and female, engaged in their favourite sport of hunting:

The King & Court went to hunt the stagge in his park which is round about the Garden; many Ladys like Monsieurs accompanyed him. Madame d'Epinoy[57] let fall her muffe. We saw the whole chase with about 30 couple of English hounds which would trayl half a mile at least. The Stagge soild himself[58] at last just by us and there was pull'd down and half eaten up before the huntsman came to him, but they hunted him onely for sport, and gave all his flesh to the dogs, as it was fit for nothing else.[59]

In 1687 Ferrier visited Versailles; he offers a fairly detailed account of what he saw in the palace, down to the unimpressive menu of the royal family's dinner:

After having walked about the garden & viewed the vast number of strange flowers & plants that were there, we went into the Pallace, where we had the honour to see the King, Monsieur, & the Dauphinesse at dinner with abundance of the nobility standing round the table. The Dauphin was that day gone a hunting the wolf, a sport he takes great delight in ... The dinner the King had was but ordinary, there being a dish of soupe, some chickens & a quarter of lamb, of all which he made no scruple to eat though on a Friday. Before our entrance into the Chamber we had a caution given us by one of the company to take care of our pocketts, though the same person, before he stir'd out of the chamber, had six or seven guineas & a louis d'or taken out of his.[60]

Much closer contact with Louis XIV was made by Burnet, though in the *History of his own Time* he rather plays down his reception at Versailles in 1683. There was something, to say the least, paradoxical in this prominent Whig being so well treated by Louis XIV after he had thought it better to go abroad for his own safety in the period of Tory domination in the last years of Charles II:

> The exterior of the King was very solemn: The first time I hapned to see him was, when the news came of the raising of the seige of Vienna, with which, Schomberg[61] told me, he was much struck, for he did not look for it. While I was at Court, which was only for four or five days, one of the King's coaches was sent to wait on me, and the King ordered me to be well treated by all about him, which upon that was done with a great profusion of extraordinary respects: At which all people stood amazed. Some thought it was to encourage the side against the Court by this treatment of one then in disgrace. Others more probably thought, that the King, hearing I was a writer of history, had a mind to engage me to write on his side. I was told a pension would be offered me. But I made no steps towards it: For tho' I was offered an audience of the King, I excused it, since I could not have the honour to be presented to that King by the Minister of England.[62]

The envoy in question was furious at the reception which Burnet met with at court where he had at least one unofficial meeting with the king.[63]

A more distant relationship with the king is implied by the portrait of him furnished by Northleigh who also visited France in the 1680s:

> The King himself is a well made Person, and of a Majestic Meine, the Reverse of that effeminate Part that appears in his Brother, with an Air of Gallantry in his Face, and 'tis to be wish'd that it were to be seen too in all his Actions; full of aspiring Thoughts, which could be a Virtue in a Prince, did they not swell to Ambition. He is reported a just Dispenser of Rewards and Punishments, in both which the Laws as well as his Will make him absolute; so that the two Extremes both of Fear and Love force an Obedience from his Subjects; but with them generally, notwithstanding their Oppressions, he is more beloved than fear'd. He is observed to be very affable, pleasant and courteous in Discourse; his greatest Weakness seems to lie, in being so strongly Bigotted, and that to a religious Society whose Maxims help only to undermine his State, as well as they have been publickly condemn'd by some of the Gallican Church; and what makes it seem more surprising at the same time, that he appears a discerning Prince, quick in Observation and resolute in Execution; and by his long and early Reign has that Advantage over other Princes, to be more vers'd in the Reasons of State and the Arts of Government.

However, for this observer Louis's good qualities were cancelled out by his persecution of the Huguenots and his aggressive foreign policy, for he concludes: 'He might have made himself much more the Admiration of Europe, had he made himself less the Scourge and Terrour of it'.[64]

As we have already seen, Louis's mistresses attracted the attention of several of our travellers. We meet one of them again in the 1680s in the guise of a Carmelite nun — the discarded Louise de La Vallière, who entered a convent of this strict order in 1674. Burnet visited her in 1683 as, he explains, a pious courtier 'thought instances of devotion might have some effect upon me: So he made the Duchess La Valiere think that she might be an instrument in converting me: And he brought a message from her, desiring me to come to the grate to her. I was twice there: And she told me the steps of her conversion, and of her coming into that strict order of the Carmelites, with great humility and much devotion'.[65] At about the same date a fresh female figure in the King's entourage makes her appearance in Veryard's account of his travels: 'We had here a sight of the famous Madam De Maintenon. The People fancy her married to the King; but on what Grounds I know not. Her Age and Features are not so charming; but her parts are so very extraordinary that she passes for the wisest of her Sex. She is Widow to the late ingenious Mons. Scarron. She lives at Court, and when she goes abroad, has the King's Equipage and Attendants'.[66]

The renewed building activity at the Louvre naturally attracted the attention of Christopher Wren when he came to France in 1665 and spent several months 'surveying the most esteem'd Fabricks of Paris, and the Country round'. He observed Colbert as *Surintendant des Bâtiments* supervising the work which was going on in the palace, and he also met Bernini who had been invited to Paris to produce plans for completing the building:

> The Louvre for a while was my daily Object; where no less than a thousand Hands are constantly employ'd in the Works; some in laying mighty Foundations, some in raising the Stories, Columns, Entablements, &c. with vast Stones, by great and useful Engines; others in Carving, Inlaying of Marbles, Plaistering, Painting, Gilding, &c. Which altogeather make a School of Architecture, the best probably, at this day in Europe . . . Mons. Colbert, the Surintendant, comes to the Works of the Louvre, every Wednesday, and, if Business hinders not, Thursday. The Workmen are paid every Sunday duly. Mons. Abbé Charles introduc'd me to the Acquaintance of Bernini, who shew'd me his Designs of the Louvre, and of the King's Statue . . .
> Bernini's Design of the Louvre I would have given my Skin

for, but the old reserv'd Italian gave me but a few Minutes View; it was five little Designs in Paper, for which he hath receiv'd as many thousand Pistoles: I had only time to copy it in my Fancy and Memory; I shall be able by Discourse, and a Crayon, to give you a tolerable Account of it.[66a]

While the Louvre along with the other sights of Paris drew our travellers in large numbers, another great attraction was Louis XIV's new palace at Versailles.

Locke who went there altogether six times was certainly impressed with what he calls 'a fine house & a much finer garden', and he provides elaborate descriptions of the palace, gardens and especially the 'water works'.[67] Other travellers criticized severely the choice of the site. Northleigh concedes that 'the back part which fronts the Garden, surpasses the Beauty and Magnificence that is commonly reported of it; and the Garden all the Delight that Fancy can give, or Thoughts imagine; all that I have since seen in Italy is much short of it'; but he begins his account by declaring that it 'is certainly the finest Seat in the foulest Place that Europe or the World affords'.[68] Veryard similarly says of Versailles: 'Did its Situation answer the Magnificence and Beauty of the Architecture, nothing of this nature could exceed it. I could not but admire that so much Money should be spent in beautifying a Bogg'.[69] Ferrier was equally impressed with the splendour of the palace and gardens, but he makes the same complaint: 'The greatest fault that can be found with it, is in its situation, which is extraordinary bad, it being in the summer time nothing but dust, & in the winter but dirt'.[70] Lister who visited Versailles in 1698, later than any of these travellers, noted that 'what of it was first built, and much admired 30 years ago, is now no longer relisht', but he plays down the unfavourable position; though it is 'plac'd in a very ungrateful Soil, without Earth proper for Herbs or Water', the king 'hath brought that to it in abundance, and made the Ground too to be fruitful'. The palace for him is 'without dispute the most magnificent of any in Europe'.[71]

Lister also visited in the ambassador's suite the king's retreat at Marly which was destroyed during the Revolution. He was informed that Louis 'left Versailles every Tuesday night, and came hither with a select Company of Lords and Ladies; That he returned not till Saturday night, and sometimes intermitted 10 or 14 days; so that he spent half of his time here in Repose'.[72] Impressed as he was by Marly, Lister still thought that in his old age Louis would do well to move his court to Languedoc. The author of *A New Journey*, writing at the very end of the reign, in 1714, gives a rather different version of the use which Louis made of his retreat at Marly: 'Hither the French

King comes generally upon Friday, and stays till Monday, or sometimes longer; withdrawing himself from all manner of State affairs, and indulging himself to Pleasure and Repose'.[73]

In view of the gross flattery bestowed on Louis XIV by courtiers, clerics and writers, it is difficult to decide how sincere admiration for him really was. A recurrence of the old complaint about the disrespectful way in which French people spoke of their king is to be found in Lauder's *Journals*. It is true that these lines were written early in Louis's personal reign, in 1665: 'A man may live 10 years in France or he sy a French man drink their oune Kings health. Amongs on another they make not a boast to call him *bougre*, *coquin*, *frippon*, etc. I have sein them in mockery drink to the King of Frances coachorses health'. Yet he also relates how the execution of Charles I, which had caused such a sense of outrage on the Continent, 'a 1000 tymes hath bein casten up to me . . . I cannot forget whow satyrically they have told this, saying that the peaple of great Britain keip their Kings at their beck, at their pleasure not only to bereave them of their croune but also of their life'.[74]

Veryard and Northleigh who were in France in the 1680s when the cult of Louis le Grand was at its height are particularly critical of the flattery lavished upon him. If Veryard describes without comment the statue of the king in the Place des Victoires with its inscription 'Viro Immortali', he speaks scornfully of the adulation bestowed on Louis by the clergy:

> No People have a better Opinion of their King than the French, which is owing in a great measure to the Clergy; for his Reputation is blazon'd in every Pulpit, and his great Actions are a principal part of their Sermons. They are told, That the Glory of God is the sole end of the Wars, and that, tho' the Taxes may seem irksome, yet since they are expended in extirpateing Heresies, and propagating the Faith, they ought to shew their Zeal and Forwardness in promoting such pious Resolutions. I was once in company with a Priest at Paris, who hearing his King's Conduct blam'd, left the Room, passionately uttering the words of the Roman Orator, *Sit sacrilegus, sit fur, sit flagitorium omnium princeps; at est bonus imperator:* Let him be Sacrilegious, a Thief, and Ringleader of all Vice; he's nevertheless a good Prince.[75]

Northleigh's condemnation of all the flattery of the king which he saw and heard around him in France was much more outspoken. He speaks sarcastically of the 'Flights their flatterings have aspir'd to upon their present Monarch':

> *Viro Immortali*, more than Mortal, is the common

Monumental Epithet, they give their mighty Man, who as great
as he is, cannot baffle or be above the Grave; and who with all
his *Pays conqui* must at last be encompast in that narrow space:
To which I may also add with an augmented Profaneness the
Abusive or Blasphemous Application to him which I observ'd
on one of their Prints, or Sculptures. *Replebitur Gloriâ suâ
omnis terra*, and that with a Glory about his Head. 'Tis to be
hoped his Majesty (a Prince truly Great) is not affected with
these profane Hyperboles, and though his Pharisees or Parasites
tell him he has the Voice of a God and not of a Man, that he will
give God the glory, and that his Modesty may be more than
Herod's, for fear of his Fate.

In the conclusion to his account of his travels in France Northleigh
has more to say of this adulation of Louis. The French, he declares,
'shew so much Affection for him, that they seem not to feel that
Slavery, which our Humanity and Compassion seems to feel for
them: *Louis le Grand, le Dieu donne, l'august, & le conquerant*, are
the common Titles they give their Royal Hero'. He rounds off a
highly critical account of Louis's aggressive foreign policy and
persecution of the Huguenots with the words: 'His Court and
Church-flatterers magnifie that, which other people call inglorious.
They make him their Augustus, for that which other people think him
an Attila; and care not how little he hath of his Father *the Just*, so long
as they can make him their *Louis le Grand*'.[76]

In this connection a curious point is made by Veryard. He
maintains that, unlike his father, the Dauphin was extremely popular
in Paris, and that he cultivated this popularity:

> The Citizens are wonderfully fond of the Dauphin, flattering
> themselves with the Ease they shall enjoy under his reign, and
> hoping that he will reside here: And he, on the other hand, to
> keep up the good Opinion they have of him, is frequently here,
> and converses very familiarly with them. He seems to be a Man
> of a very sweet temper, and is the darling of the People in
> general; insomuch, that the King keeps him always near him. If
> he permits him to go and view the Army, he soon countermands
> him; for, tho' possibly there might be no danger, it may be of ill
> consequence to give the occasion.[77]

The Dauphin, however, seems to have been generally regarded as a
man of very limited intelligence who spent his days in hunting and
gaming. Covel who saw him at Versailles when he was about
seventeen, compares him very unfavourably with his father: 'The
Dauphin fat, feeds unreasonably & lookes like a soft, peevish, self
conceited, il natured boy, effeminate enough, and I cannot conceive
he will ever arrive to (if maintein) the King's greatnesse, who is a

jolly, lusty, strong, souldjerlike man, and there is more of goodnesse then fury in his aspect'. [78] Among the courtiers Burnet met during his stay in Paris at this period was the Duc de Montausier to whom Louis had entrusted the upbringing of his only legitimate son. The duke told him that to this task 'he had applied himself with great care, tho', he very frankly added, without success'. [79] What sort of a king the Dauphin would have made we do not know; he died four years before his father.

Absolutism at its height in these decades naturally made a strong impression on our travellers. Burnet later claimed that when he paid his first visit to France in 1664, the spectacle of this form of government 'established me in my love of law and liberty, and in my hatred of absolute power'. [80] Two years later Skippon was struck by the fact that French people, despite their grumbles, were actually proud of the political system under which they lived: 'At this time most people complained of their king's imposing taxes, &c., yet they seemed to boast of him, and were proud to think themselves subjects to an absolute monarchy'. [81]

Travellers in the 1670s are less given to generalizations of this kind, but confine themselves to points of detail. 'The King of France', Locke wrote in a shorthand note, 'is so far aquainted with the grant of all offices that the hangman's place of Tours hath his hand in the margent to the grant of it'. When visiting the new town and naval port of Rochefort he observed that it was being surrounded by strong walls, though 'being now frontier & the 3 leagues to the sea being difficult to passe in 2 or 3 tides by their owne vessells, they have no reason to apprehend any forraine attaque, & these walls are strong enough to keepe out any suddaine insurrection of the people'. [82] Similar precautions against popular uprisings were taken at Bordeaux which had caused the monarchy trouble by revolts not only in 1635 and especially during the Fronde, but once again in 1675. In that year Clenche speaks there of 'a new Cittadel, called Chasteau Trompette, design'd more to awe the City than defend it, which makes the Inhabitants hate the name of it'. [83] Three years later Locke noted more accurately that work was proceeding to extend the defences of this ancient citadel: 'We saw the Chasteau Trompett, a very strong fort on the river's side, of 4 bastions, which, without shouting off one gun, has shooke down 4 churches & one side of the fairest & best street of Bordeaux in which one only house belonging to the Abé [84] that was pulling down when we were there, had cost lately the building above 50,000 ecus. All this ruin has been made to set this cittadell in a faire open space, free from incumbrance. There are in Garison in it about 500 French soldiers &

200 Swisse'.[85] Veryard speaks more bluntly of the cause of these precautions against popular uprisings in this city: 'The New Citadel, built in the place of Chasteau Trompette, was not long since erected by the Kings Order, to curb the Inhabitants, and hinder the Tumults and Disorders which have lately much disturbed the public Tranquility in these Parts; and of which the People of Bourdeaux were commonly the Ring-leaders'. He also notes the punishment inflicted by Louis XIV on the city's Parlement which was exiled to remote places: 'The Parliament is likewise remov'd to La Reaule, a small town about 12 Leagues higher on the River; and tho' they are in daily expectation of its return, yet 'tis believ'd the King designs to mortify them, till he finds them better dispos'd and affected towards the Government'.[86] It was not until 1690 that the Parlement was allowed to return from La Réole, its second place of exile.

As both Northleigh and Veryard added to the account of their travels in France in the 1680s general observations on what they had seen there, they naturally have more to say directly on the subject of absolutism. Although Northleigh had been a supporter of James II, he speaks with some scorn of the form of government in France: 'They themselves thought their Monarchy the best, because the most absolute; and tho' they are Slaves for it, pride themselves in the Chains they wear: They will call this Absolute Power a just one, tho' it reduce the Subject to just nothing; and tho' they groan under it, will hardly suffer a Stranger to whisper against it'. Northleigh found French reproaches for our civil wars and revolutions hard to bear:

> And what is more extravagant, after all this exalted Absoluteness, even to Tyranny it self, some of their Authors shall tell us, that this is accompanied with all the sweet Mixture of a compleat Commonwealth; that their Counsellors of State make an Oligarchy; Their Parliaments and Officers of their Courts of Judicature, compose an Aristocracy; Their Provosts, Mayors and Merchants, make up a Democracy; pleasant Rattles indeed and Chimes for Children, when all the while this pompous Mixture makes but one Tyranny, and is as insignificant, as the Representation of it is ridiculous and incomprehensible; quite contrary to the Practice; and all this swadling-Clout of Limitations, is always swallow'd up in the Absolute and Despotick Power of the Prince: The Counsellors of State are his Creatures; the Parliament and Officers of Justice his Dependants; Provosts and Mayors his Vassals; and though perhaps I may be found to have said as much for Monarchy as most Men of my Age; yet it has still been with a Respect to that Species of Monarchial Government which I think the best; not the Excesses of it, which are still the worst.[87]

In his general observations Veryard is equally struck by the absolute nature of Louis XIV's rule: 'The Government is, at present, wholly arbitrary and unlimited, for *sic volo, sic jubeo,* is the usual reasoning of State, and all Procedures of the Civil Magistrate presuppose an *ultima ratio Regum'*. However, in contrast to Northleigh, Veryard holds that, given the unruly nature of the French people, such a regime is necessary:

> Cardinal Richelieu and Mazarin laid the Foundations of this absolute Sovereignty, which they saw could not be attain'd to but by impoverishing the People, and therefore left such Methods behind them as have, in process of time, produc'd such extraordinary effects, that Liberty, Property, and such like other Topicks of Mutiny and Rebellion, so zealously asserted heretofore in France, are quite laid aside and forgotten. They found this Course absolutely necessary; for the French being naturally hot, unstable and ambitious, on every light Occasion were apt to find fault with the Government, and shew their distast by very frequent Revolts. What suited not with their Humour pass'd for Oppression, and suffic'd to hurry the giddy Multitude into rash and extravagant Enterprizes, by reason whereof the publick Tranquility was very often disturb'd, and the Course of all Affairs turn'd topsy-turvy.

The French people, he continues, 'seem well enough satisfy'd' with this regime', though, he adds, they 'dare not for their lives murmur; for he that has taught them to obey, has the whole power in his own hands, to keep them within the Bounds prescribed'.

Veryard goes on to declare that there is no longer any need for a Richelieu or a Mazarin 'since the King himself is the main, if not sole, Politician that acts, and leaves no more to his Ministers than the bare Execution of his Orders, in which they are extream careful and sedulous, striving to out-do one another in the exact Performance of what belongs to their respective Stations'. He notes the wealth which, following in Mazarin's footsteps, such ministers are allowed to accumulate while in office. He stresses the secrecy with which affairs are conducted: 'Secrecy is so religiously observ'd amongst them, that the Debates in Council are never publickly known, unless they happen to be printed by Authority. The King, it must be confess'd, is a very judicious Prince, and knows it as well; so that in Affairs of greatest Importance he hears his Council, 'tis true, but keeps his Designs within his own Breast 'till things are ready to be put in Execution; so that all the great Enterprizes are done with a surprize, and consequently seldom or never fail'.

This surprisingly favourable view of Louis's control over events is followed by a somewhat inaccurate account of the system of royal councils. More to the point is what Veryard has to say about the abasement of the Parlements: 'They represented heretofore the States-General of the Nation, but their Priviledges have been considerably retrench'd by the present King; insomuch, that at present, tho' they act in matters belonging to the Government to give them a gloss of Equity, yet they only work on Materials ready cut out to their hands, and put the King's positive Commands in Execution'.[88] Stated rather more precisely, what Louis had done was to render the Parlements' right of remonstrance useless by insisting that they register his edicts before they presented their objections to them.

The Bastille, the fortress which a century later was to become the symbol of despotism, figures somewhat luridly in several of our travellers' accouns of Paris. It is true that Symonds who was allowed to go over it in 1649 treats of it essentially as a somewhat antiquated fortress when he describes it as 'an old building of the old fashion of Castles'. It is only incidentally that he mentions its use as a State prison: 'Here they put Prisoners of Quality . . . A Cordelier was lately a Prisoner here'.[89] Skippon clearly took a less neutral view of the Bastille when a Scotsman whom he calls 'Dr. Du Moulin of Aberdeen' and with whom Ray, Lister and he had travelled to Paris, was suddenly whisked off there:

> After dinner, and just as Mr. Howlet, Dr. Ward, Mr. Wray, Dr. Moulins, Mr. Lister and myself were going out of our lodgings . . . one of the French king's officers, a captain *de Guet,* asked for monsieur Moulins, and while he exchanged two or three words with him, he set his baston (which he had under his cloak, in two or three pieces) together, and presently came in eight or ten musqueteers, who seized on Dr. Moulins, and hurried him away in a sedan to the bastile; the captain first read the order or warrant commanding him to apprehend one Moulins, wheresoever he could find him.[90]

Skippon and Lister stayed on in Paris for a few days, but they could learn nothing about the prisoner's fate. An attempt to communicate with him met with a rebuff as Skippon explains: 'Dr. Moulins sent a note for some linnen to our lodging, and Mr. Lister returned by the messenger a little billet, which only condoled his misfortune, but the captain of the guard at the Bastile tore it in pieces. All the while we heard no crime laid to his charge'. However, he does add: 'He was kept a prisoner at the king's charge, and well dieted.'[91]

A more sinister mention of the Bastille is to be found in Clenche's account of his travels: 'Bastil, A little old square Castle, with four

Towers, serving for great mens Prison, like the Tower of London, but more fatal to its Prisoners'.[92] This is nothing compared with the accounts which later travellers give of executions being carried out secretly in the Bastille. Presumably these reflect popular belief in Paris about the fate of persons imprisoned there. Veryard gives an account of what went on inside the Bastille which makes one's flesh creep:

> All such as have been any ways obnoxious to the Government are sent hither, where their Examination, Tryal, and Execution, is commonly manag'd with so much Secrecy, that their Friends and Relations seldom hear more of them, unless they chance to be set at Liberty, or brought to an open Punishment, when the Crime is too publick to be conceal'd. They are commonly put to Death privately within the Castle, and the Keepers tell such as enquire after them That they are in Health, or Dead of a natural Death; when, perhaps, they were beheaded or Hang'd ten or twenty years before.[93]

Writing at the end of the reign, the author of *A New Journey*, mingles fact and fiction in his account of the Bastille. He begins by decribing it as 'a small Castle . . . wherein Persons of Note are imprison'd for High Treason &c. as here in the Tower of London'. He continues:

> but with this difference, that here they have a fair and publick Trial, as well as a publick Execution; there, both Examination of Witnesses, Trial, and execution; is manag'd privately, so that several, after being committed, are reported to be alive Twenty Years after their Death; several are committed upon Suspicion, who if look'd upon only as disaffected Persons, do remain there during Life, bury'd in Oblivion, for from thence there is seldom or never any Redemption.

The account given of an execution in the Bastille is certainly the product of a lurid imagination:

> The manner of Execution in the Bastille, is very extraordinary; after the Person is thought Guilty by the King, Council, &c., without any publick Trial or the Liberty of Confronting or Cross-examining the Witnesses, a Confessor is sent for to prepare him for the other World; which after he has done for several Days, he at last attends him with the Executioners, and as they walk together in a spacious room where there is a Trap Door in the Floor, known by a certain mark to all the rest except the criminal, they make him go over the same, so that he drops down of a sudden, and falling upon certain Wheels and Engines underneath (the weight of his Body putting them into a Motion), he is in a Minute cut into a thousand Pieces'.[94]

Prisoners did die in the Bastille, often after years of imprisonment, but no modern historian writes of executions being carried out behind its walls.

One very important development in France in these years — the strengthening of the authority of the central government by the establishment of its agents, the *Intendants,* on a permanent footing in every province — is seldom touched upon by our travellers, though the author of *Popery and Tyranny* does mention this point. Writing in 1679, he shows how 'the Nobility of all sorts are very much Oppress'd', being excluded from all part in government, in the provinces as well as at the centre: 'Governours of Provinces, Towns, Fortresses, are eclips'd . . . by Intendants who are Superiours, placed in every Province, who usurp the whole Power under the Notion of Intendants, over Justice, Policy, and Finances, at first only ordained for Finances'.[94a] Even so shrewd an observer as Locke mentions this agent of the central government only three times — once for his part in the assessment of the *taille,* another time for the speech made by one of them at the opening ceremony at a session of the Estates of Languedoc, and finally in a shorthand passage with the marginal note 'Politia Galliae': 'In France there are Governors of Provinces as formerly, but they have no power at all. Leiutenants of provinces are watch and guard upon them and on the least occasion can seize them, and the King's man is spy and guard on them both. Besides the Intendant gives constant intelligence of all things to the Court'.[95] Though Locke exaggerates the power of the *Lieutenants généraux,* he does make clear the governors' loss of all effective influence and its transfer to the *Intendant.*

In contrast he gives very full information about the role of the Provincial Estates of Languedoc since he happened to be in Montpellier while they were meeting there in 1676 and again in 1677. This was one of the few provinces which still had such a representative body, and it was regarded there as a great privilege not to be subject to the direct taxes exacted from those provinces which did not have Estates, but instead to furnish the king with a so-called *don gratuit* and to raise the money itself. Earlier the Estates had often proved very recalcitrant. 'One of the States', writes Locke, 'told me that he was at an Assembly 20 yeares agon when, the King asking for 7 or 800,000 Livres Tournois, they thought it too much and gave nothing at all, but that they dare not do so now'. Locke clearly discerned that, despite the measure of autonomy which Languedoc enjoyed through the part played by its Estates in the assessment and collection of taxes, they were now impotent in face of a monarch who was determined to wield absolute power. Even in the 1660s there had been occasions when the assent of the deputies to increases in taxation had been secured only by the secret distribution of bribes. By the time Locke arrived in the province, the Estates could do nothing but offer prompt compliance with the ever-growing demands of the Crown, which were swollen by the heavy cost of the war with Holland. Ceremony there was in plenty during the four months in which the Estates with their 22 bishops, 22 noblemen and 44 representatives from the towns were in session (all this is described in considerable detail), but the emptiness of it all is revealed in Locke's dry summing up on the functions of this body: 'They . . . have all the solemnity & outward appearance of a Parliament. The King proposes & they debate & resolve about it. Here is all the difference, that they never doe, and some say dare not, refuse whatever the king demands'.[96]

Three of our travellers record having seen Louis in the last part of his reign. Two of them visited France during the uneasy peace between the end of the Nine Years War and the beginning of the War of the Spanish Succession. Joseph Shaw wrote of Louis: 'He is of the largest size, and well-made, has an imperious Look, a commanding Air and Mein, and his Actions bespeak his Genius'. Those actions are harshly judged in the dedication to Shaftesbury, the philosopher; he denounces

> that despotick arbitrary Government, where the Lives and Estates of so many Millions of Mankind are subjected to the lawless Will of one single Prince, whose extravagant Profusion has expended above Fifty Millions Sterling in his delicious Palaces at Versailles, Marli, Trianon, &c. rioting himself in the utmost licencious Excesses; while Thousands of his poor unhappy Subjects are rotting and starving in the Streets for want: And whose boundless Ambition and faithless Perjury, has thrown away and sacrificed the lives of 2500000 Men, besides the Loss of their Product, and Sums, as incredible as they are numerous.[97]

The other traveller in this period between the wars was Lister who visited Paris in the suite of Lord Portland, ambassador extraordinary to the French court at the end of the Nine Years War. Lister had seen Louis XIV much earlier in the reign; he describes his illegitimate daughter, the dowager Princesse de Conti, as 'one of the most graceful and handsomest Women in France, and methinks exceedingly like the King her Father, as I remember him in his full beauty, when I first saw him in the year 65'. Lister had opportunities of seeing the king, now in his sixtieth year, as he went in the

M

ambassador's suite to receptions at Versailles and Marly: 'All the Paintings and Prints made of late years of the King make him look very old; which in my mind is not so; for he is plump in the Face, and is well coloured, and seems healthy, and eats and drinks heartily, which I saw him do; This is certainly an injury to him, and possibly in complaisance to the Dauphin, or worse'.[98]

At Marly the courtiers offered Lister a eulogy of Louis XIV which he summarizes without comment:

> As for their own King they were much in the Praise of him, as one can easily imagine ... That he was the most affable Prince in the World, and never out of Humour, of a pleasant and open Conversation where it pleased him; easie of access, and never sent any one away discontented; The most Bountiful Master in the World, of which there were Ten thousand Instances; nothing of Merit in any Kind, but he most readily and chearfully Rewarded, ever, of late years at least, preferring the Virtuous; so on the other hand, he never spared the Rebellious and Obstinate; That the Government of his People could not be carried on with less severity and strictness; nor the Taxes which was necessary to support it, raised; That he delighted not in Blood or Persecution; but that the Art of Government had different Rules, according to the Climate and Nature of the People, where and upon whom it was to be put in practice. His great Wisdom appearing in nothing more, than in preserving himself amidst his Troops, his Converts, his Court and numerous Family, all in a manner fit for the Throne. The greatness of his Mind, and Magnificence, in his Buildings. This was the Sum of the Discourse these Gentlemen were pleased to entertain me with.[99]

When it comes to expressing his own views on the France of Louis XIV, Lister declares that the splendid palaces and gardens which he had visited 'are the best and most commendable effect of Arbitrary Government'. He goes on to give a somewhat odd reason for this view: 'If these Expenses were not in time of Peace, what would be this Kings Riches, and the extream Poverty of the People? For it is said, that every 3 years, some say much oftener, he has all the Wealth of the Nation in his Coffers; so that there is a necessity he should have as extravagant and incredible ways of expending it, that it may have its due circulation amongst the People'.

Louis's aggressive foreign policy which other travellers condemned is considered by Lister to have had its good side:

> But when this vast Wealth and Power is turned to the Disturbance and Destruction of Mankind; it is terrible; and yet it hath its use too: We and all Europe have been taught by the

Industry of this great King, mighty improvements in War; so that Europe has been these 12 years an Over-match for the Turk; and we for France by the continuation of the War. The 40 Millions Sterling which the late War hath, and will cost England, before all is paid, was well bestowed, if it had been for no other end, than to teach us the full use and practice of War; and in that Point to equal us with our Neighbours.[100]

These lines were, of course, written in the brief interval of peace between the end of the Nine Years War and the outbreak of a fresh Anglo-French conflict in the War of the Spanish Succession the end of which Lister did not live to see.

At the end of that war Berkeley speaks in his letters from Italy of the sad state of France where he spent several weeks late in 1713. 'I could assure you', he writes to one correspondent, 'that the French nation is so impoverished and dispeopled by the war, that we need not entertain any apprehension of having a Pretender imposed upon us by their power. I speak this of my own knowledge having passed through the heart of France, and been an eyewitness of its misery'. To another correspondent to whom he suggests a journey to Italy he offers this advice 'Your best way is to come through France; but make no long stay there; for the air is too cold, and there are instances enough of poverty and distress to spoil the mirth of any one who feels the sufferings of his fellow-creatures'. He then contrasts the state of the aged Louis XIV with that of his country: 'The king indeed looks as he neither wanted meat nor drink, and his palaces are in good repair; but throughout the land there is a different face of things'.[101]

IV THE ARMED FORCES

Early in the century Overbury set out the strengths and weaknesses of France from the military point of view. As listed by him its strengths were very impressive:

> For the strength of France, It is at this day the greatest United force of Christendome; The particulars in which it consists are these: The shape of the Countrey, which being round, no one part is farre from succouring another; The multitude of good Townes and places of strength therein are able to stay anArmy, if not to waste it, as Metz did the Emperours; the masse of Treasure which the King hath in the Bastile; The number of Arsenals distributed upon the Frontiers, besides that of Paris, all which are full of good Armes and Artillerie: And for ready men, the 5 Regiments bestowed up & down in Garrisons, together with the 2000 of the Guard; the Troupes of ordinary and light Horse, all ever in pay; besides their Gentrie all bred Souldiers; and of which they thinke there are at this present 50000 fit to beare Armes; And to Command all these, they have at this day the best Generalls of Christendome, which is the only commodity the Civill wars did leave them.

Amongst France's weaknesses Overbury puts first 'the want of a sufficient Infantry, which proceeds from the ill distribution of their wealth; for the Peysant, which containes the greatest part of the people, having no share allowed him, is heartlesse and feeble, and consequently unserviceable for all Military uses, by reason of which, they are first forcd to borrow ayde of the Swissers at a great Charge, and secondly to compose their Armies for the most part of Gentlemen, which makes the losse of a battaile there almost irrecoverable'. Another weakness, he declares, is the excessive amount of land owned by the Church, 'for, as they say, *The Church will loose nothing, nor defend nothing*'. Two further weaknesses according to him are that all its land frontiers are menaced by Spain and that the country is divided in matters of religion which must 'cause the weaker to stand in neede of forraigne succours'.[1]

Writing after the end of the Thirty Years War, but while the long struggle with Spain still dragged on, Evelyn penned an almost poetic passage on the advantageous geographical position occupied by France:

The Frame and Positure of the Continent, situated as it were in the Navel of all the Christian World, qualifies it to collect, unite and dispose of her forces; for it hath Spain and Italy before it, England behinde; The Seas upon the right, and Germany upon the left-hand; at one corner the Neatherlands, and the Cantons of the Suisse at the other; all of them potent, considerable, and active Neighbors, and where they intermit, it is a worthy prospect to behold how Nature hath served and defended her with the Pyrenees, Alps, Ocean and Mediterranean Seas, whilest she sitting secure from any subitaneous irruption or natural pretension, may well be pronounced a fair and most Just Empire.

He goes on to point out how greatly France has been strengthened by the unification of the country under one king,

since the later accession of Bretagne, Guyenne, Normandy (once the goodly portion of the English), and Bourgogne, who are now all of them under one Prince, as having enjoyed heretofore every one their proper Dukes; by whose favour or spleen there was always a facile entrance for any potent stranger to disturbe the rest of the Kingdom; the consequencies whereof have filled almost every Chronicle. And to the stronger twisting of this Cord, such prudence hath been had of late times, that all those great and powerful houses remain now no more divided (as still among the Princes of Italy and Germany), the Cadets and yonger Brothers minding for the most part no greater preferments then what they cut out with their Sword, and merit in Field by being Soldiers of Fortune.

According to Evelyn the chief strength of the French land forces lies in the cavalry of which he speaks very highly, describing it as 'a strength and spectacle both of Admiration and Gallantry, they being for the greater part composed of Gentlemen, who generally so bequeath themselves to this Service, that hee who (amongst them) hath not made two or three Campagnes (as they use to term it) by that time he is 18 years of age, is esteemed as a person *lasche*, that is, of a soft education and small repute'. On the other hand the French infantry is inferior to the Spanish. The reason is the same as that given by Overbury — 'the Peasants of France (of whom they should naturally consist) are thought (and that upon good grounds) to be more than accidentally improper and *mal-adroict* for that service'. However, Evelyn suggsts that things have now changed; while the Spanish infantry has not recovered from the battering which it received from Condé at Rocroi in 1643, the French peasants now make better soldiers: 'Howbeit, we finde (and that by quotidian experience) that Custome or something else more propitious hath much altered and reformed their natures, even in this particular instance: and for ought I perceive, they keep what they have gotten, and become as good Souldiers as those who brag so much of their lowsie and tenacious epitheton'.

France's military strength, he continues, is due in part to its large population and its fertile soil which can produce so much food. 'Adde to these Advantages their store of good Armes and Munitions; in sum why should I further tire you with particulars, when their present Exploits, and almost continual Triumphs, have planted the Flower de lyces where ever they break ground?'[2]

Writing much later in the century, after the military successes won by Louis XIV, Northleigh was greatly impressed by the French army: 'Their infantry is good and their Horse better, and both for near this hundred years from Henry IVth's time train'd up in War, the Discipline of which descends among the soldiers and survives their Persons; and for the particular Men that now compose their Regiments, they are most of them Veteran Soldiers, that have served the King in the Sieges he has form'd and the Battles he has fought'. Perhaps somewhat optimistically Northleigh considers the troops to be well paid and even attributes their discipline in part to the regularity with which they receive their pay: ''Tis observable among his vast Armies still a foot, which in Garison and Camps they boast to be no less than 400,000, we now a days hear nothing of any mutiny; to the regularity of the Discipline, to their punctual pay, and their perpetual Action it must be imputed'. He too was impressed with the way in which 'their Magazines and Stores' were 'conveniently distributed in such parts of the Kingdom, and their Conquests, as may upon all occasions be easily brought where they are wanted, which facilitates their Designs, and forwards their Expeditions'. War seemed indeed to be a national industry, for, as Northleigh observed, 'some of their Politicians think War as necessary among them and their Troops, as the old Romans did among their Legions to keep their Arms from Rust, and the Men from Rebellion; and their Peace indeed is so precarious that they look on War only like breating a Vein and drawing blood to prevent a Fever; or that Peace is but a breathing time for the better preparation for the next War'.[3]

When we turn from these generalities to the detailed observations made by our travellers, we get a rather less impressive picture of the French army, particularly in the reign of Louis XIV. Locke twice comments unfavourably on the French troops he saw during the war with Holland in the 1670s. '5 Companys of the Regiment of Champagne at Aix, poore, weak, tatterd fellows' he writes, and '2 or 3 days last passed through Montpellier a regiment of horse and another of foot from Catalonia for Nîmes. The horse were good men, but the horses poor and lame, but the foot miserable little boys'. He also comments on the corrupt way in which Cardinal Bonzi's mistress disposed of commissions in the regiment of dragoons which Louis XIV had demanded of the province of Languedoc: 'Cardinal's Mis[tress]. 50 pistols the way to have a captain's place in the new regiment of dragoons. Mistresses get money all the world over. This made men of worth and good soldiers miss places'.[4]

The author of *Popery and Tyranny* produced his account of the state of the French army at a moment when a considerable part of it had been disbanded after the Treaty of Nimeguen, reducing it, he declares, to 'fifty or sixty thousand Horse and Foot'. This measure, he maintains, gave rise to various weaknesses.

> 1. The Discipline and Duty being so rigorous, that for want of five men, the Captain shall be cashiered, though they ran away, and he not able to supply it.
>
> 2. The Pay is small, that neither Officer nor Souldier can scarce live upon it, besides Deduction to Horse and Foot for Clothing, Hay and Oats; and the pay of a Captain of Foot, *per diem* being fifty Soulz; a Lieutenant thirty Soulz; Ensign fifteen Soulz; Souldier five Soulz; a Captain of Horse six Livres, Lieutenant three, Cornet two Livres 5 Soulz.
>
> 3. The great Discouragement of old Officers, and new ones too, by the late Disbandment without Pay, and keeping only such in Pay, as were able at their own Charges to keep up their Company; and taking away all Priviledges in Muster or otherwise, for so many Horses, for so many Servants, and their allowance for Table, besides most of their old Bo[d]yes are spoiled by Disbandment of part.

On the other hand the author does concede that the king 'entertains all retired Officers at half Pay' and that, among other things, he was generous with pensions.[4a]

The first impression of the French army which the author of *A New Journey* received when he landed at Calais at the end of the War of the Spanish Succession was highly unfavourable: 'When I saw the Soldiers that were there in Garrison, (poor, punie, ragged Shabberoons, whose Cloaths, formerly White, were so tater'd that they were not sufficient to hide their Nakedness) I did admire that such Troops durst look our Jolly Britains in the Face; I thought indeed that France must be very ill defended by such shabby Champions, but upon inquiry I found that these were only the Militia of the Country, who were soon to be dismiss'd, and therefore not cloathed'. Shortly afterwards at Hesdin he encountered some much more impressive-looking soldiers: 'There was in Town a French Regiment of Carabiniers, all comely Men, of a very good size and well accoutred; their Livery was Blue fac'd with Red, and brass Buttons; they were very unlike the shabby, despicable Dogs I saw at Calais'. At this point in his travels the same author had a curious encounter with Irish soldiers who, after serving in the British armed forces, had now been recruited by France:

> Amongst the Soldiers, I saw several who had serv'd the Government in England during the late War, and having ask'd them why they put themselves into the French Service, after having taken the Oaths to the Queen their natural Sovereign, they answer'd, That they had served the Queen faithfully, some by Sea, and some by Land, whilst the War lasted; that they did not desert the Government, but were deserted by it; that being broke, they would neither Steal nor Rob, and cou'd not bear to Starve, and that since there was no further occasion for them in England, they having neither Money, Estate, nor Trade, only their Sword to get their Bread by, they thought they were not to blame to go and seek a livelihood elsewhere; that however they preferred the English service before the French.[5]

A resolution neither to steal nor rob was fairly uncommon in the French army in the seventeenth century. Locke was told by the famous botanist, Pierre Magnol, of the kind of recruits which it obtained: 'Wars are often necessary to the King of France to take away by this fermentation the scum of the people, for before these last wars Montpellier was so full of idle fellows that one was not safe in the evening going out in the streets, and he that carried out a cloak, was not sure to bring it home'. While in Montpellier Locke recorded a minor riot caused by the recruiting methods in use at that time:

> Here was in the street a bustle to day, the cause this. Some that were listing soldiers slid mony into a country man's pocket, & then would force him to goe with them, haveing, as they said, receivd the King's money. He refused to goe & the women, by crowding & force, redeemed him. These artifices are necessary in a country where presseing is not allowed & where volunteers come not forwardly to the beat of the drum, & 'tis a usuall trick, if any one drink the King's health, to give him presse money & force him to goe a soldier, pretending that haveing drank his health, he is bound to fight for him.

Two days later he noted: 'Drums beat for soldier, & 5 Luis d'or offered to any one that would list himself'.[6]

Civilian contacts with soldiers tended to be extremely unpleasant, not to say dangerous. We have seen that having troops billeted in a region was a disaster and that the threat of billeting troops on towns was used by the government to extract large money payments from them.[7] Northleigh has a curious passage about the country between Lyons and the frontier with Savoy:

> Between Lyons and Savoy, all that part of Dauphiny is as fine a country as most Parts of France; and yet so few live in it, that you would think it uninhabited. Upon Discourse with some intelligible Person from whom I inquired the Reason, I came to understand that these Counties hereabouts were allotted for the Winter-quarters of their Horse; so that the Peasants only come from the adjacent Parts to sow their Seed, and reap their Corn, and then retire, and leave the Land to the Forragers of their own Countrey, and the Incursions of their Friends instead of foreign Force; but that I think they have since felt too: But from the Burdens of their own Armies, they have form'd their Backs the better to bear those of Savoy.[8]

The reaction of a town when troops were quartered on it is described by Locke with his usual gift for understatement: '33 Companys quartered at Moulin upon free quarter, which the people like not. Their companys are about 50 men a peice, officers & all'.[9]

Evelyn's *Diary* contains several references to the marauding habits of French soldiers. When he first arrived in France, his party was compelled by a snow storm to spend the night in a village between Calais and Boulogne: 'This night we none of us went to bed, for the Souldiers in these parts leaving little in the Villages, we had enough to do to get ourselves dry by morning, between the fire and the fresh straw'. In describing the journey from Montreuil to Abbeville, he relates how they 'passed all the way in continual expectation of the Volunteers as they call them' — an obvious euphemism for marauding soldiers. When doing the same journey six years later, Evelyn lost a spaniel which he had brought with him from England, 'taken up I suppose by the Souldiers', as he puts it, adding: 'We were in all this Journey greately apprehensive of Parties, which caused us to alight often out of our Coach, & walke separately on foote with our Guns ready, in all suspected places'.[10]

When in 1659 Lady Fanshawe escaped from England to join her royalist husband in Paris, she made the same journey from Calais 'in a waggon-coach'. At Abbeville she received a message from the governor that, in view of the number of robberies being committed, 'he would advise me to take a guard of the garrison soldiers, and giving them a pistole a piece they would convey me very safely'. She relates with dry humour how this protection worked out:

> The next morning he sent me 10 troopers well armed, and when I had gone about 4 leagues, as we ascended a hill, says

some of these, 'Madame, look out, but fear nothing'. They rid all
up to a hill and met a well mounted troop of horse, about 50 or
more, which after some parly wheeled about in the woods again.
When we came upon the hill I asked how it was possible so many
men so well armed should turne, having so few to oppose them;
at which they laughed and say'd 'Madame, we are all of a
company and quarter in this town. The truth is, our pay is short,
and we are forced to help ourselves this way, but we have this
rule, that if we in a party guard any company, the rest never
molest them, but let them pass free'. I haveing past all danger, as
they said, gave them a pistole each man, and so left them and
went on my journy and met my husband at St. Denis, God be
praysed.[11]

These dangers continued on the Calais-Paris route even in time of
peace. Lauder, for instance, writes of making the journey in 1665:
'The great number we meit of souldiers all the way begat in us great
fears of robbing, yet it pleased God to bring us most safely to Paris'.[12]
Soldiers did not, of course, confine their criminal activities to the
highways of France. Sir Philip Perceval's tutor wrote from Angers in
1677: 'The soldiers quartered here have been very troublesome with
their robberies and abuses at night till one of them, who killed a
townsman, hath been hanged, so that now they are quiet enough
within the gates, but without they rob people of what they are
bringing to market'.[13]

It was in the seventeenth century that the wearing of military
uniforms began. When Locke was present at two reviews of the
household troops by Louis XIV, he was interested not only by the
part played in them by the king and other members of the
royal family, but also in the uniforms of these troops which he
describes in some detail. Thus at the first review, that of the Gardes
du Corps, Mousquetaries and Grenadiers, he pays attention not only
to their weapons, but to their costume, stressing, for instance, that the
Gardes du Corps were 'well clad, all in blew, new & alike even to their
hats and gloves':

> The Gards du Corps were 11 or 12 squadrons & might be
> about 12 or 14 hundred men, all lusty, well horsed & well clad,
> all in blew, new & alike even to their hats and gloves, armed with
> pistols, carebins & long black swords with well guarded hilts.
> The Musquetaires were 4 squadrons, about 400 men, clad all
> alike in red coats, but their clokes blew, but with distinction
> from those of the Gards du Corps, but half (i.e. all one company)
> horsed on black horses & half on grey, their coats & belts laced,
> the grey with gold galoon & the black with gold & silver, their
> hats and gloves to all the same, even to the ribbans on their hats

and crevats. At least, I am sure the Gards du Corps were so, some squadrons haveing all yellow ribbans & others all skie. The Grenadiers were but one squadron of the same size neare with the others, but their clothes different, their coats being red, but with loops distinguished from the Musquetars, & soe their blew clokes too, but that which did most soe, was an odde fashion cap that was the cover of their heads, made of red cloth turned up with fur, the fashion when on, something like a Mountro, but standing out much more before & behinde, & standing up with a peake upon top of their heads which turned backwards. These caps both soldiers & commanders all wore & which seemed an uniformity.[14]

Another innovation of the reign of Louis XIV — the founding of the Hôtel des Invalides in 1670 for aged and disabled soldiers — attracted a good deal of attention when our travellers visited Paris. When Locke arrived there in 1675, this was the only building which he mentioned in his account of his ten days in Paris before he made his way south to Montpellier: 'In Paris I saw the great hospital which this King of France has built for his maimd soldiers, called Les Invalids. 'Tis a magnificent building capeable, as they told us, when finished, of 1000 soldiers'. The building had been completed except for the dome which was added later, by the time he returned to Paris in 1677. His first note on the subject indicates a wave of economy in the administration: 'At the Invalids they had at the first Institution 1 pint of wine, $1\frac{1}{2}$ lbs. of bread per diem & half a pound of flesh per meale, but now it is abated and they have but half so much. They have a new suit of clothes and 2 pair of shoes once every 2 years and a half'. This is followed by a detailed account of the building (complete with a sketch). Locke endeavoured to work out for himself how many people it could hold, but seems to have been unable to secure any reliable figure since he concludes his entry: 'They say there are at present about 15 or 1800 in it'. He was also interested to know how the foundation was financed:

One double p. lib.[15] amounts to £1,700 per diem for the building the Invalids. Abbays & priorys & monastarys were formerly obleiged to enterteine, some one, some 2, some 5 lay brothers which were maymed soldiers. This maintenance in kinde came to be changed into a pension of 100£ per annum for each person. This, some few years since, was augmented to 150£ per annum & presently after taken from the present possessors & applied to the Invalids, besides which all the maladries or lands and revenues belonging to the hospitals for leapers are appropriated to the said Invalids, & whatsoever accrues from the Knights of St. Lazar, an order newly revivd.[16]

A lively account of the inmates is furnished by John Buxton's cousin, John Herne, who visited Paris in 1681, and described 'the Hospital for disabled soldiers' in a letter to his father:

> It can entertain no less than 2,000 at one time ... At every pair of stairs, at each   [17] and every gate there is a good watch kept by men with a wooden leg or without an arm, so unfit for such postures as you would think they did it only for their recreation. They are fed very well, and in their halls (for they have two) there is a large map of every town that the King has conquered, where every soldier may place himself by that city that made him an object fit for that place; for I believe that many of them are pleased with old age or to part with one limb to make the rest happy. And because the King will not take care of their bodies only, he has built them a chapel and is about to build them a stately church; and being they are not good walkers, he intends to build them a fine bridge over the river to give them a shorter cut into the city. They are all clothed with blue lined with scarlet, and those that have been officers have their coats laced with silver.[18]

Ferrier who visited Paris six years later was much impressed by the Invalides, describing it as 'a building of all the Hospitals in France, I daresay even in Europe, the most noble, it seeming to be rather the pallace of a great Prince than what it really is'. He adds further details about how it was run: 'There is in it at present 2,600 soldiers, every one of whom has his bed by himself, and is served every flesh-day with a quarter of pound of meat both noon & night, every fish day with four eggs at each meal, a pint of wine, and for bread they have a pound for two days. They are kept in very good order, being governed by officers that are in the same condition with themselves. They keep a good guard there, being continually six hundred in armes'.[19]

Veryard who also visited Paris in the 1680s adds further details of interest:

> The Invalides is likewise an Hospital for old and maim'd Soldiers, and one of the most superb Structures in France, where there are usually about 200 Officers, and 3,000 Common-Soldiers, all decently entertain'd according to their degree, The Officers lie two in a Chamber, and the private Sentinels six or seven; but every one has a Bed to himself, and may follow what Trade or Occupation soever he can manage to his own Advantage. They eat in common, in large Refectories, each having his portion of Meat and Drink serv'd in; and such as are Sick are taken care of in the Infirmary. They are permitted to go our to visit their Friends, and negociate their Affairs abroad, but two days a Week, for which they get Billets in their turns, or cannot pass the Sentinel at the Gate. The Governour, who has

the whole Management of the House, is a Person of Quality, and has his Lodgings within the House.[20]

Northleigh too was greatly impressed by the Invalides, considering it much superior to Wren's Chelsea Hospital and describing it as 'Their fairest and finest Foundation of all':

It far out-does the Chelsea College founded for the same design, it containing and taking care of maimed Emerited Souldiers; the King rais'd it at a vast Expence, and that in the midst of a War. About 1670 they began it, and till '78 when they finish'd it. I think that Crown was deeply engaged in an expensive War; it has a dry Ditch like a Castle, round a great square Pile, a great Quadrangle in the midst, Flankt with two other Courts on each side, so consists of five, with Piazza all under, and fair Corridors or Galleries upon them all round the great Court; and that which makes it look more majestick than our Chelsea Square, is their Stone, making besides a better show than our Brick ... Their Kitchen is Noble and Great, their Refectorys where they eat have all the Sieges exactly painted on their Walls, in which that Crown has been in their late Wars so successful, so that the old Soldiers that serv'd in them, have continually before them a little comfortable prospect of their fair Labours. Their Pharmacopaeum, or Apothecarys Apartment, is the prettiest of that kind, that I have ever yet seen, and as well furnish'd.

Northleigh cannot resist making the same joke as in his description of the Hôtel-Dieu: 'The Sisters of St. Lazarus are assign'd to serve all the poor old Soldiers, of which some of them are stout enough to make Mistresses of these Holy Maids'.[21] Clearly if Lous XIV's aim in founding the Invalides had been to impress, he had certainly succeeded with all our travellers who visited it.

Living in an age which saw rapid advances in artillery, Locke showed a great interest in guns. He seems to have spent many happy hours in Paris with his friend, Nicolas Thoynard, examining models of guns and making detailed notes on them in his journal.[22] He also took the trouble to visit the Arsenal while in Paris and noted down various technical details: 'At the Arsenall, as they told us, always armes for 100,000 men, though there seemed not half soe many. They now make their musquets 3 foot 10 inches longe in the barrell & of 18 bullets to the pound ... The carbines of the gardes are scrued'. In his travels in the provinces he also made occasional notes on such matters. Thus, when he visited the citadel at Tain on the Rhone, he observed that it contained only 'one great gun, which was left behind, when the King lately took away all the rest for his ships, for a fault very frequent in this country, viz. in the touch hole'.[23] Later at Cosne on the Loire he describes in detail the making of pistol barrels.[24]

When Bromley visited Toulon a few years later, he saw some fearsome engines of war:

> Here I also saw two vast great Bombs cast in Bronze, to be sent to Genoa, when the French bomb'd it;[25] of an oval Figure, each two Fathom long, and proportionaly broad, and held an hundred Kintals of Powder; besides divers lesser Bombs. They are of such Dimensions, that they cannot be thrown out of Mortar-pieces like others, but are intended to be placed as near the Walls of the Town besieged, as they can be brought, and to be fired by a Train of Powder, and when either flies in pieces, 'tis expected it will not only rend & tear all within its reach, but will cause such a *Terra-motus* as to dismantle the Town, and shake down the Houses. The Experiment has never yet been made; so it is uncertain whether it will answer expectation or not; however it will certainly occasion great Confusion, and strike Terror. One of them, they say, will hold eighteen Men together. The lesser Bombs receive generally 100 1. of Powder. The French, I was assured, throw them three, and sometimes four Miles, and at great certainty; whereas ours seldom go more than one and a half, which made me the more narrowly view the Mortar-pieces, which I observed to be all Chambered.[26]

From the middle of the century onwards several of our travellers show considerable interest in the growth of the French navy. At the beginning of our period one of the rare criticisms which Overbury had made of Henry IV was that he had 'left nothing undone but the building of a Navie', a point which he develops further when he speaks of one of the weaknesses of France being 'the want of a Competent number of Ships and Gallies, by reason of which defect, first the Spaniard overmasters them upon the Mediterranian, and the English and Hollander upon the Ocean, and secondly it renders them poore in forraine Trade, so that all the great actions of Christendome for these fifty years, having beene bent upon the Indies, they only have sate idle'.[27] Writing at the same date, Carew records remarks of Sully on this subject: 'Mons. de Sully hath sundry times told me, that if he were admiral of France, he would be in hand with setting up of a navy royal; which, if they had once done, they might easily prove ill neighbours to Great Britain'. Carew was obviously not worried by this threat; he goes on complacently: 'But till that happen, the controversy will be, what we may conquer on them, not what they might get upon us'.[27a]

Yet before the century was out, the English and their Dutch allies in the Nine Years War had reason to regret that France had changed its policy and had devoted a considerable amount of effort and money to building up a navy strong enough to challenge the combined fleets of the two maritime powers.

Already in 1652 Evelyn was becoming alarmed by the increase in French naval power:

> At this instant, their Maritime strength is not totally so contemptible, having a very stately and considerable Armada of handsome Gallies in most of their Mediterranean Ports, as at Toulon, Marseilles, and other places, which are Vessels of excellent use and service upon those Seas. On the Ocean, I confess, both their Shipping and Traffique have been alike trivial; and yet of late, they have greatly augmented their Fleet, especially since the time (to our Nations egregious shame and dishonour) that they have made so large inroads and gaps in Flanders, towards the Sea Coasts; Witness those strong towns and havens of Dunkirk, Mardike, &c. Stout Forts, and very commodious Harbours for shipping; so that a little time (if we will still suffer it) may likewise furnish them with Ships enough to make them stand in a bolder competition with their Neighbours.[28]

Later writers such as Northleigh and Veryard look somewhat resentfully on the growth in French naval power under Colbert. The former writes with a mixture of anger and sarcasm:

> A Ship is not so soon rigg'd out in France, as with us in England, notwithstanding they have the Vanity to compare with us; and for these late Years to swagger it on the Ocean too: Our English Oak was once wont to teach them more Modesty; till of late Years by Neglect or Design, we have help'd them to turn our own Timber upon us, tho' they have good Planks too in France, Cordage, Sails, and Iron, and almost all other Materials; but when great Quantities and Supplies are required, they must be beholden to their Neighbours. And 'tis but of late Years that Navigation has been brought to that Perfection among them; 'tis within this Twenty Years, some of this King's Politicians put him upon augmenting his Navy; and 'tis well they did, or else with all the glittering Glory of his Royal or Rising Sun, he could never have faced a Fleet of English and Dutch.[29]

Veryard devotes rather more space to French sea power and deals less in generalities, since he refers to something which he had observed at the Mediterranean port of Toulon:

> Their Fleet consists of about Ninety Ships of the Line, with divers smaller Frigats and Fifty Gallies. The present King uses all Means imaginable to encourage Navigation and encreases the number of Seamen, by erecting Publick Schools for that Science in the most considerable Sea-Ports, and divers other

ways unpractic'd heretofore in France ... Their Ships of War
are not so high built as formerly, and the Decks of divers old
ones are taken down lower, by means whereof they are not so
much expos'd to Shot. They use none but Brass Guns; and in
their Sea-Fights rarely or never risque their Men by Boarding,
their chief aim being to disable their Enemies, and so to sink or
burn them. To exercise their Gunners, when the Fleet is not at
Sea, the King gives certain Prizes to be shot for every Week on
the Water, by mounting their Guns on a Barge, and placing a
Mark on another at a convenient distance: He that makes the
best Shot carries the Prize, which is usually a Hat and Feather, a
Sword and Belt, or some such like thing that is worn; and
inspires others with an Ambition of carrying the Marks of their
King's Liberality. This I have seen practic'd at Toulon.

Veryard was very much aware of the importance which the French
attached to privateering, the only form of action which they were to
take in the Nine Years War after the failure of their battle fleet's
challenge to the combined English and Dutch naval forces. He
stresses the encouragement given by the French government to this
form of sea warfare: 'In time of War, the Privatiers have the Tenths
given them to encourage Merchants to set out their Ships, and Men to
enter into the Service; and such as behave themselves well on Board,
are usually preferr'd to some Station in a Man of War, proportionable
to their Merit'. The profitability of this type of warfare is emphasized
by Veryard:

Privatiering is become so usual a thing in France in the time of
War, and withal so beneficial by reason of the commodious
Situation of the Country, that Merchants employ their whole
Stocks that way, which turns more to their Profit than if they
risq'd them in any other sort of Commerce; insomuch, that
divers Sea-ports enrich themselves more in two or three Years
of War, than they could do in Seven or Eight Years of Peace;
and likewise the number of Seamen is considerably
augmented.[30]

French privatiers were long to continue to exact a heavy toll from the
shipping of their enemies, particularly the English.

Before Anglo-French rivalry ended in the Nine Years War English
travellers visited the Mediterranean ports and examined the ships
and shore installations there, apparently with considerable freedom;
none of them met the fate of Edward Lhwyd and his companion who
were arrested as spies in Brittany on the eve of the War of the Spanish
Succession. The galleys and their slaves at Marseilles were a great
attraction for foreign tourists, not only English.[31] Early in the century
Thomas Wentworth makes the curious point that not all the royal

galleys actually belonged to the king:

> Within the haven upon the bankes hear lieth all the kings galleys which weare 13, not bycause they are all his, but have ther allowance from him for ther was one of the Duke of Epernons which had 250 slaves within itt, one that was Mr de Gundés, general of the Galle[y]s, one of Mr le Marquise d'Ancre, one of Mr de Créqués, one of the Queen. I was aborde the Admiral Galley which had 23 ores on a side; they goe out commonly with the general once a yeare, but do seldome inconter with any ennymie.[31a]

We have half a dozen later accounts of the galleys, ranging from Evelyn's in the 1640s to those of Bromley and Veryard in the 1680s. As this was a period when the fleet was still being expanded, the figures which they give for the number of galleys continually rise. Evelyn speaks of 'about 25', while in the 1680s Bromley writes: 'Here are already thirty six Gallies, and the King intends to make them forty' and Veryard puts the figure at 'about forty'. English tourists had apparently no difficulty about going on board the galleys. 'The Captaine of the Gally royal', writes Evelyn, 'gave us most courteous entertainment in his Cabine, the Slaves in the interim playing both on loud & soft musiqu very rarely. Then he shew'd us how he commanded their motions with a nod, & his Wistle, making them row out'.[32]

Locke and his companion were able to go on board the show Galley, *La Grandé Réale*, built in 1675, and he provides some technical details about this vessel:

> We went aboard the Royal, the Admiral Gally, the slaves clad in the King's livery, all in blew, the rest of the slaves in the other Gallys in red. This Gally had twenty-nine oars of a side, 280 slaves, 60 seamen, soldiers & volunteers as many as added to the former make 500. They usually go victauld for 50 or 60 days ... There goe out 25 Gallys this year, the least hath 26, the biggest 29 oars on a side. There rides at the Key a very large Gally, cald also the Royal, of 32 oars, most curiously carved. All the carved work is to be guilt; the gold for the guilding it is agreed for already & will cost 36,000 livres. The Royal we were in carrys 5 guns, all before; that in the middle lyes in a case & is a very large one, cald the chase gun.

He was also free to inspect the docks and arsenal.

> Just at the end of the Key is a yard & 2 docks to build gallys. The docks are coverd to work out of the rain & sunshine, & lower then the sea water which they pump out, & when the gally is built, instead of launching her, they let in water at a hole which takes her off the stocks, & then open the gate and let her out. 3

sides of the yard are beset with buildings which with several other large, square courts make the Arsenal, which is stord with all necessarys for the Gallys, ever gally having its particular store house. Within this arsenall are imploid also smiths, sayle makers, carvers, joyners & all other trades necessary for the building & furnishing the gallys, great bake houses and large store houses fild with meale, bread & bisquit & a gallery in it, 120 fathom long, to make ropes & cables, an armory very well furnishd, & a large hospital for sick slaves, all very fit & magnificent.

Locke concludes his account of the galleys and their shore installations: 'Indeed all the buildings of the Arsenall are soe great, soe well contrived & made with so little saveing of charges that one cannot but thinke it is to carry on the businesse with great care & intention'.[33]

Buxton provides a description of the slaves' hospital which is not without interest:

Near this is the hospital for the slaves. We entered the room where they were kept, a boy going before us with a pan of perfume to entertain our nose and to prevent a worse savour. Over the door coming forth is the King of France, his picture as big as life; right against the door is the door into the Apothecaries' room, which is large and square and well furnished with pots; in the middle a very fine marble table inlaid with curious art; all things seemed very neat; they say there are in this hospital 120 slaves.[34]

Unlike other travellers who were much impressed with Marseilles, Veryard was repelled by both the inhabitants and the slaves with the constant clanking of their chains. He ends his account of the city with this bitter outburst:

When we first entred the City we verily thought our selves in the Suburbs of Hell, for the continual Noise and ratling of Chains was a harsh sort of Musick we had hitherto been little us'd to; and I am apt to think, that if any place upon Earth may be said to resemble the Infernal Kingdom, it must be this; for as the inhabitants are meer Devils incarnate, inhuman, crafty, deceitful, and superlatively base, so the poor Slaves, loaden with Chains and groaning under the heavy Yoke of Servitude, seem to symbolize with the Damned in all things but the duration of their Pains.[35]

Like several other travellers Veryard moved on from Marseilles to the great naval port of Toulon, though strangely enough he has nothing to say about the ships which he must have seen there. In 1665 Skippon had visited Toulon at a time when England and France were on the verge of war; he writes indignantly of the capture of English merchant vessels in the Mediterranean and of the ill-treatment of their crews. Although he gives a favourable account of the harbour, he was not very impressed with the warships or the skill of their officers:

> At this time almost all the French king's ships of war belonging to this (Mediterranean) sea, were in port ... The men of war belonging to this sea are 22. The admiral, named *Philip*, carries 72 guns, and hath about 700 men aboard. Six new bottoms were now upon the stilts, and one of them may possibly be launch'd the next summer; but the rest will hardly be finish'd in some years, unless more workmen be employ'd. Four or five of these ships are esteem'd able to engage in a battle; but the rest of them, if our English seamen may be believ'd, are not considerable. Chevalier de Paul is reputed a good soldier, but no skilful seaman. Marquis de Martel is another French captain; was formerly a slave in Barbary, and there learn'd the Turkish cruelty, which he now exercises on all the prisoners he takes. Some say the French on the Mediterranean understand little of navigation, and that the best pilots and seamen are fetch'd from west France; but others say that the Provençals are the best seamen in France.

A significant additon to this account is the sentence: 'A Flemming or Hollander is now the master workman in building the new men of war'.[36]

Some ten years later Locke also visited Toulon. He was very impressed by the harbour:

> The port is very large, capable of the bigest fleet in Europe & to spare, & in the basin its self roome for a great fleet. It is separate from the rode (as they call it) by a mole made within these 4 or 5 years, & hath a narrow entrance continually chaind. The water in both in most places deepe, the bottom mud with some shelves in it, the entrance wide between 2 castles at least $\frac{1}{2}$ a league on sunder. To fortifie it more, there is another platform of 28 guns made on the S.W. side the whole port.

Locke was able to inspect the arsenal and docks, though like Skippon, he was not impressed by the speed with which warships were being constructed:

> Adjoining to the port is the Arsenal, not soe fine as that at Marseilles, but every ship hath its particular store house, & there are within it offices for all that is necessary for the Navy: hemp dressers, cabels, smiths, bakers, etc. In the same place also is the dock where there are now 3 ships upon the stocks of 40 guns a peice, began last yeare, but at present goe not on very

vigerously, & the timber they build with seems not to be very excellent.

He and his companions were able to go on board one of the smaller warships, but he does not seem to comment very favourably on the larger vessels: 'In the Basin rode the Royal Louis which is admired there, but was never at sea, but serves for a receptacle for Soldiers & seamen as they are brought thither for the maning of other ships ... The Sterne is mightily adornd with gilded figures. The guilding, as they say, cost 150,000 livres. She hath portals for 120 guns, 8 foot one from another, but was never yet at sea, nor is never like to goe. The Dauphin Royal lyes by her, of 100 guns, but of noe more service'.

Locke notes without comment the inscription on the *Royal Louis*:

> Je suis l'unique sur l'onde
> Et mon roy l'est dans le monde.[37]

Bromley who visited Toulon a decade or so later also notes it, describing it as 'this pompous Motto'.[38] He states that the number of men of war there was 'generally Sixty, though the King's Navy (as I was told) consisted ordinarily of three hundred ships'. He was particularly impressed by the dock installations and by the amount of money which Louis XIV was putting into building up a strong navy:

> Round about this Port they were Building, when I was there, Storehouses of all sorts for the Ships, which are disposed in admirable Order, every Ship having her Cable fastened to an Iron-Ring that is a Lion's Head of Brass, before her respective Store-house, and a little Canal is made for Boats to go round to these Houses, without coming in among the Ships. This was a work of so prodigious Expense, as not to be compassed, but by a Prince who had Money at Will, and valued neither Charge nor Pains to accomplish his end. Strong Fortifications are building about this Town.[39]

Only two of our travellers — Clenche and Locke — visited the new town and naval port which Colbert and his cousin, Colbert de Terron, had constructed between 1665 and 1668 on the River Charente. Clenche is, as usual, fairly caustic about what he saw:

> Rochfort, The Place where the King builds and lays up his lightest Ships of 40, 50, 60 and 70 Guns; the Charante a little dirty River, or rather Ditch, not so large as Puddle-dock, being the Harbour wherein they ride; and so shallow, as well as narrow, that they cannot sail with their Guns in them; at the mouth of it is a little Fort, and by the side of it is a fine Store-house built of Freestone, the length of 20 ships, with several Apartments for such a number which lye every one over-against their own dressing-room, and have their Terrible

Names upon black Marble, in Golden Letters over every door:
The country thereabouts Marshy and bad.[40]

Locke who was invited to dine with the *Intendant*, 'a very civill &
obleiging person' (he had a letter of introduction to his secretary),
formed a much more favourable impression of both the new town and
the port. Although he considered the situation unhealthy because of
the river overflowing, he concluded 'that if the building & peopling
the place mend the aire, a few years will probably make this one of the
finest towns in France, for the imployment is here to be had & the
freedome from impost on wine, salt & all other provisions cannot
faile to people it & beautifie it with handsome buildings'. He rejects
one of Clenche's criticisms of the situation of the port: 'The
narrownesse of the river (which some object) seems not to me to be
any great inconvenience, the water being deepe & the banks soft, soe
that if a ship should chance to run a ground, it can receive noe harme,
for the rocks that are in it are well known to their pilots, & I see noe
great need there is to turne a ship in the river'.

Locke was clearly impressed by the port installations:

> The magazins here for all things are exceeding large &
> commodeous, placed all along the river side where there are
> stores of all sorts. In the yard which is of a large circuit, there is a
> generall store house for all things for ships, &, joyning to it, in a
> long range of building, particular stores for 60 ships, the names
> of each ship set over the dore. Besides this, a large building to
> keep Masts in, another for planks, great forges for Ankers &
> other iron worke. In the yard there are now 5 vessells on the
> stocks, 2 large frigats of about 40 or 50 guns, 66 or 68, & 2 lesse,
> with a large vessell they call a flute. There is also rideing in the
> river a very large ship which carrys 110 guns, called the
> Victorieuse, built here, but not yet quite finished. She is masted.
>
> Up higher in the river, but within the walls of the towne, is the
> Corderie, a long building like a gallery, for makeing cables &
> cordage. It is 2 storys & the length is 200 brases (1 Brasse is 5
> foot 2 inches & the toise is 6 foot), & above that the Magazin of
> provisions & place for casting of Cannons. These are all large,
> substantial, handsome buildings & at the Fondery there is this
> good invention that, a vault being made all under the furnaces,
> there is a pent house on the outside of the building at each end
> which, being made with wooden shuts, they open them on the
> side which the winde blows & shut them on the other, which
> serves to blow the fire with great force.[41]

Locke certainly seems to have been allowed to inspect all these
installations pretty thoroughly.

Writing towards the end of the century Northleigh has some

pungent observations to make on the aggressive foreign policy which France's military might allowed Louis XIV to pursue. ''Tis pleasant', he declares, 'to observe some French Statesmen reflecting upon the House of Austria for once aspiring to an Universal Monarchy, and for their Violations of the Treaty of Nimeguen; when the House of Bourbon is as much now to be feared for the former, in this age, as the other was in the foregoing; and for the Observation of that Treaty, all Europe knows where to lay the Violations'. Examining the reasons why Louis XIV had been able to extend the territory of France, he concludes:

> That which has facilitated the French Conquest is the want of Money in those Neighbouring Countries they have attackt; and where they can't pay for their own defence, they alway want hands and hearts to fight for it.
>
> 2ndly. Another reason may be the willingness of a People in an undecided War, and doubtful success, to put themselves under the protection of that power that seems most to promise to protect them, and from being under it, is safe from any former Insults and Successes it has had upon them.
>
> 3ly. The Uniformity in Religion the French bring with them in all the places they reduce, being Roman Catholic Countries, where the Priests say the same Mass, keep the same Monasteries that they did before, and so are more apt to convert the People to the French to keep their Convents from being Bomb'd and Batter'd down. And this might be truly the Case of the Countries the French so easily conquer'd on the frontiers of Germany, and their *Pays Conqui* of Flanders, where I have often heard the Flemings wish themselves under the Government of that Enemy, who was laying them waste and desolate, which made me think that the Death of the King of Spain would some time or other, give us further proof of their good inclination to France.

The means used by the French to keep the territories which they had annexed are summed up by Northleigh as follows:

> 1st. By the immediate improving of the necessary Fortifications of the place they reduce.
>
> 2dly. By busying the meaner sort of the Vanquisht in the building up their own Slavery and Subjection.
>
> 3dly. By drawing the better sort of them into France.
>
> 4ly. By Demolishing all Places in the Country they possess themselves of, that are not necessary to cover it.
>
> 5ly. By the Mixture of Marriages and Alliances.
>
> 6ly. By the Progress the French Tongue has made upon all that border upon them, insomuch that even in Brussels it self there is two to one, that talk French instead of Flemish.[42]

In the revised version of the early part of his diary, his *De Vita Propria*, which Evelyn produced towards the end of his life, about 1700, there is a bitter passage on the means by which French influence had been spread in Europe. The starting-point is an admiring account of the *académies* in which young French noblemen were trained before going into the army:

> There is scarse a Prince in Europe, but what have ben scholars in the French Academys, & which by Consequence has leven'd them all, with the mode as well as the Language of France, & disposed them to an undervaluing of their owne Countrys, with infinite prejudice to the rest of Europ; The French, naturaly active, insinuating, & bold, having with their trifles & new modes allmost debaucht all the sobriety of former times, Continualy aspiring to inlarge their Tyranny, by all the arts of dissimulation; & tretchery: Tho' it cannot be deneyed; that there are many worthy persons of probity, & greate Learning among them, who are weary of the intollerable yoake under which they Groone.[43]

Discontent with the France of Louis XIV had to await his death and the reaction of the Regency before it could come out into the open.

V THE ROMAN CATHOLIC CHURCH

Our travellers could scarcely be expected to offer a completely objective account of Roman Catholicism in the France of their day since with one exception — that of Lassels who was a Catholic priest — they view from the outside its doctrines, rites and ceremonies and are frequently extremely hostile to everything to do with Popery. Yet even hostile writers can contribute to an understanding of the phenomena they are describing, and the degree of hostility varied considerably from one traveller to another. On arriving at Calais from Edinburgh John Lauder began his account of his travels in France with the words: 'About 5 in the morning we landed on France the land of graven images'.[1] On the whole Anglicans took a less prejudiced view, though we shall find considerable variations; some wrote fairly objectively, while others gave free rein to their feelings of revulsion and disgust.

The Catholic clergy's position as the first order in the state was duly noted, especially by Heylyn: 'In the generall assembly of the three Estates the Clergy hath authority to elect a set number of Commissioners, to undertake for them and the Church; which Commissioners do make up the first of the three Estates, and do first exhibit their grievances and Petitions to the King'.[2] The great wealth of the Catholic Church struck our travellers very forcibly, so much so that they tend to considerable exaggeration on this point. Overbury, for instance, describes it as 'very rich, being estimated to enjoy the third part of the Revenew of France',[3] while according to Heylyn it owned 'almost a fourth part' of the land. Like Overbury Evelyn concludes that the Catholic clergy possess 'one third part of the Revenue of France'.[4]

Lauder starts off with an even wilder generalization — 'The halfe of France with its revenues belongs to the Ecclesiasticks, yea, the Beautifullest and the goodliest places' — but he does offer an interesting estimate of the wealth of the clergy, particularly the regulars, in Poitiers: 'To confine our selves within Poictiers, the rents of whosse convents, men and women togither, wil make above six 100 thousand livers a yeare, besydes what the bischop hath, to wit, 80,000 livers a year. The Benedictines, a wery rich order as we have marked, have 30,000 livres in rent; The Feuillans, 20,000; besydes what the Jacobins, Cordeliers, Minims, these de la Charité, Capucyns, Augustins, the Chanoines of Ste. Croix. St. Radegunde, St. Peter, the cathedral of Poictiers, Notre Dame la Grande, St. Hilaires, with other men and al the women religious have, being put togither wil make good my proposition'.[5]

Skippon claims to summarize a 'calculation made by order of the assembly of the clergy of France, held in the Augustines convent, at the end of Pont-Neuf, in Paris, the 16th of November 1635', and another summary is to be found in *Popery and Tyranny*.[6] In his journal Locke twice reproduces in French a similar document, though without indicating its source.[7] It has to be borne in mind that the Assemblée du Clergé consisted of representatives of only the so-called Clergé de France, that is, of the clergy belonging to the provinces which formed part of France in 1561. The clergy of provinces acquired since that date were known as the 'Clergé étranger'. In other words any figures concerning the wealth of the Clergé de France do not cover the whole of the Church's wealth. It cannot be said that these three versions of this document are of any great help to the reader, as, apart from other considerations, the figures they give for the annual income of the Clergé de France are widely different: '312 Millions of Livres' according to *Popery and Tyranny*, '120000 crowns' according to Skippon (i.e. 360,000 livres) and according to Locke 'trente six millions'. Strangely enough, Locke adds 'which is 24 millions sterling'; if this last figure is correct, then at 13 livres to the pound, it would be the equivalent of 312 millions livres, that given by *Popery and Tyranny*. Though historians cannot regard as any more reliable other contemporary estimates of the income of the French clergy which correspond roughly with this sum, there is no doubt that our travellers were struck by their enormous wealth.

The fiscal privileges which they enjoyed were duly commented on. Heylyn for instance, writes: 'To the King they pay only their Dismes'[8] or Tithes according to the old rate; a small sum if compared unto the payments of their neighbours; it being thought that the King of Spain receiveth yearly one half of the living of the Churches; but this I mean of their livings only, for otherwise they pay the usuall gabels and customes, that are paid by the rest of the King's liege people'.[9] Reresby makes the same point in general terms: 'They pay no subsidies, more than a tenth to the king, which they only term and allow as a charitable contribution'.[10] In his account of the royal revenue Locke merely notes that 'the Church gives the King every now and then a round sum',[11] but he does enter into some detail about the exemption of the clergy from the *taille*.[12]

It is notorious that the considerable wealth of the clergy was very unevenly distributed among its members. In seventeenth-century France it was rare for a man to reach high office in the Church unless he either belonged to a great noble family or was the son of one of the king's ministers. Since the Concordat of 1516 which had given the Crown the right to appoint to almost all high posts in the Church, the king had the means, as Heylyn puts it, 'of binding to himself his Nobility, by the speedy preferring of their children'.[13] After declaring that the noblemen's sons who were destined for a career in the army were no scholars, Reresby adds: 'Such as are designed for the Church are brought up another way, and find good preferment for some bishop's see, abbey, priory or convent; into the best of which, persons of the best quality, not parts, are commonly chosen'.[14] The same point is made later by Veryard in speaking of the careers open to the sons of noblemen: 'On such of them as apply themselves to the Study of Divinity, he confers Bishopricks and Abbacies; for Learning rarely qualifies, unless they are likewise nobly descended, and consequently more capable of strengthening the Court-Party'.[15] At the end of the century Lister describes thus his impression of the bishops whom he saw in Paris (non-residence made these very numerous):

> No sort of People make a better figure in the Town than the Bishops, who have very splendid Equipages, and variety of fine Liveries, being most of them Men of great Families, and preferred as such, Learning not being so necessary a Qualification for those Dignities, as with us, tho' there are some of them very Deserving and Learned Men. I say, they are most Noblemen, or the younger Sons of the best Families. This indeed, is for the Honour of the Church; but whether it be for the good of Learning and Piety is doubtful. They may be Patrons, but there are but few Examples of Erudition among them. 'Tis to be wisht, that they exceeded others in Merit, as they do in Birth.[16]

Lister is putting the matter fairly tactfully, as is Burnet when writing of the Archbishop of Rheims, the son of Louis XIV's chancellor, Le Tellier, and the brother of the Secretary of State, Louvois, whom he describes as 'a rough boisterous man', adding: 'He seemed to have good notions of the episcopal duty, in all things except that of the setting a good example to his Clergy: For he allowed himself in Liberties of all kinds'. Of his discussions with theologians at the Sorbonne (this was at the height of the clash between Louis XIV and Innocent XI), he records: 'They spoke to me of the Bishops of France, as men that were both vitious and ignorant'.[17]

Many bishops indulged in the same worldly pursuits as the lay members of their social class. Hunting was one of the main occupations of French kings and their nobility, and many high clerics regarded this sport as quite compatible with their position in the Church. When in the 1680s Ferrier visited the country house of the archbishop of Lyons, he found that hunting was the great interest of its aged occupant, Camille de Neuville de Villeroy:

> Tis an old Castle though no ways fortified, there is on the backside a park of at least three leagues about & for all its great circumference it is walled round with a very high wall. There are in it abundance of deer of the largest size. He is a great lover of hunting & to that end he keeps a stable with a great many horses & a hundred & fifty hounds the finest that I ever saw, some of them as high as an ordinary greyhound. We saw him as he was walking in his garden after dinner, he is a little old man clothed like the meanest Paisant of all; every thing he had on, if at a mart, I dare say would not have sold at ten shillings; he is about 80 years old & is also much troubled with the gout & yet he is one of those that follow the stagg the closest, & for the most part is nearest him at his death.[18]

Locke gives a very unflattering picture of the behaviour and morals of Cardinal Bonzi, the Archbishop of Narbonne, who presided over meetings of the Estates of Languedoc. At the mass which preceded the day's sitting 'the Cardinall sat uppermost, nearest the altar, & had a velvet quishon, richly laced with broad silver & gold lace; the bishops had none at all. He also had his book and repeated his office apart very genteelly with an unconcearned look, talking every now & then & laughing with the bishops next him. He keeps a very fine mistress in the town, which some of the very papists complain of, and hath some very fine boys in his train'.[19] In the end the scandal caused by the archbishop's liaison with Jeanne de Gévaudan contributed to the decline of his influence in the province when Louis XIV became devout and strait-laced.

The scions of the great noble families were often appointed to high posts in the Church in their early twenties, and at the beginning of the century some were appointed even younger, as Heylyn noted in 1625, when he wrote: 'The third of the Kings naturall brethren, is Mr. Henry now Bishop of Metz in Lorreine, and Abbot of St. Germans in Paris; as Abbot he is Lord of the goodly *Fauxbourg* of St. Germans, and hath the profit of the great Fair there holden, which make a large revenue. His Bishoprick yeeldeth him the profits of 20000 Crowns and upwards'. Henri de Bourbon, the son of the Duchesse de Verneuil, had been made a bishop at the age of seven, though much later he was created a duke and married. Heylyn also noted that the Archbishop of Rheims was 'son unto the Duke of Guise, by name Henry de Lorraine, of the age of 14 years or thereabouts, a burden too unweildie for his shoulders', and he added that he was abbot of both Cluny and St. Denis. He too finally left the Church and succeeded to the dukedom of Guise.[20] Heylyn also notes the protest made to Louis XIII in 1617 by the Assemblée du Clergé: 'That whereas his Majesty was bound to give them fathers, he gave them children; that the name of Abbot signifieth a Father; and the function of a Bishop is full of fatherly authority: that France notwithstanding was now filled with Bishops and Abbots, which are yet in their Nurses armes, or else under their Regents in Colledges; nay more, that the abuse goeth before their being; Children being commonly designed to Bishopricks and Abbacies, before they were born'.[21] Later in the century Finch speaks of a youth of eighteen having just been made Archbishop of Rheims,[22] but this turns out to be wrong: Henri de Savoie-Nemours was twenty-seven when he was appointed in 1652; he was never consecrated and five years later he renounced the Church and married after his elder brother had been killed in a duel. Even twenty-seven seems to us nowadays rather on the young side for such an appointment; certainly mere boys or even youths were not given such posts after the early part of the century.

There were naturally considerable variations in the incomes of the higher clergy. Those who were appointed to some of the smaller bishoprics (these were particularly numerous in the South) received relatively modest incomes while those who held the real plums were very highly paid, especially as they often added to the stipend they received from their diocese the income from one or more wealthy abbeys. Locke collected a good deal of information on the subject. He maintains, for instance, that of the twenty-two bishops who attended the Estates of Languedoc '17 have revenues to about 3,000 l. sterling & upwards, the other 5 much more. The Bishoprick of Alby is worth 40,000 ecus per annum'.[23] It would seem that his figures are rather too high; but it all depends on whether one is talking about the income from the diocese or the total income of the occupant of the see. For instance, Cardinal Bonzi as Archbishop of Narbonne drew 90,000 l. from his diocese and another 29,000 l. from three abbeys. When Locke visited Narbonne, he noted that the Cardinal's income from the archbishoprick came to 100,000 l., which is certainly an exaggeration, but understates the cardinal's total income from the Church. Locke noted a few more figures on his travels — 45,000 l. for St. Pons, 40,000 l. for Castres — and while in Paris he suddenly made an entry concerning two southern bishoprics which brings in a factor which must not be forgotten in assessing the wealth of the higher clergy: that they sometimes had to pay out of their income pensions to other people. 'The Bishoprick of Cahors', writes Locke, 'is worth 12,000 ecus per annum, & there is on it a pension of £10,000'. The figure which he gives for the income from the diocese is approximately correct, though whether there was such a heavy charge on it is uncertain. Unfortunately what he says about Lavaur does not make sense: 'The Bishoprick of Lavor is worth £2,500, and a pension on it of £1,700',[24] since the income from this diocese was at least ten times the figure which he gives. However, there is no question but that Locke, like other travellers, was impressed by the affluent state of many members of the higher clergy.

About the great mass of the secular clergy they have in contrast remarkably little to say. Dallington was much impressed by the variety of casual fees paid to the *curés*, what in the language of the time was called *le baisemain*, defined by the 1694 edition of the *Dictionnaire de l'Acadmie française* as 'L' offrande que l'on donne au Curé, parce qu'autrefois on luy baisoit la main': Besides the clergy's income from land, Dallington writes:

> they have their *Baise-mani* [*sic*] (as is said) that consisteth in Churchings, Christnings, Marriages, Burials, Holy-bread, Indulgences, Vowes, Pilgrimages, Feasts, Processions, Prayers for cattell, for seasonable weather, for children, against all maner of diseases, and infinite such purposes; for which the superstitious people will have a Masse said, which they pay the Priest for, particularly: over and besides all this, there is scarce that Arpen in all France, upon which there is not some *Dirige*, or *de profundis*, some *libera me, Domine*, or some reckoning or other liable.[25]

Even if Heylyn seems at times to be merely copying Dallington, he does offer a somewhat more realistic view of the financial position of the lower clergy:

> As for the vulgar Clergy they have little Tithe and lesse Glebe, most part of the revenue being appropriated unto Abbeys and other Religious houses; the greatest part of their *Baisse-maine* [*sic*], which is the Church-offerings of the people at Christenings, Marriages, Burials, Dirges, Indulgences, and the like; which is thought to amount to almost as much as the temporall estate of the Church, an income able to maintain them in good abundance, were it not for the greatnesse of their number; for reckoning that there are (as we have said) in France 130000 Parish Priests, and that there are only 27,000 Parishes; it must of necessity be, that every Parish one with another must have more then four Priests; too many to be rich.

Heylyn has a very low opinion of the learning of the Catholic clergy: 'The common Priests of France, are so dull and blockish, that you shal hardly meet with a more contemptible people. The meanest of our Curates in England, for spirit and discourse are very Popes to them; for learning they may safely say with Socrates, *Hoc tantum scimus quod nescimus*; but you must not look they should say it in Latine. Tongues they have none but that of their Mother and the Masse book: of which last they can make no use except the book be open, and then also the book is fain to read it self'. According to Heylyn the progress made by the Reformation in France was due in part to the stupidity of the Catholic clergy: 'And certainly there is nothing that hath prepared many of this Realm more to imbrace the Reformation, then the blockishnesse of their own Clergy'.[26]

Locke has surprisingly little to say about the parish clergy. The only relevant entry of any significance in his journal was derived from his friend, Nicolas Thoynard:

> *Sacerdotium.* It is not only looked on, but in some places treated as a mariage, for at St. John de Luz the preist, the day he says his first masse, gives a ball & he himself leads up the first dance, & the preist who the last immediately before him had don this exercise, is invited as a principall guest & leads up the dances as King of the ball. Mr. Thoynard has been present at such a solemnity where the preist gets noe small credit if he can cut capers well.[27]

The regular clery attracted a great deal more attention, most of it fairly hostile. Given the proliferation of the new religious orders and the expansion of existing ones in the Counter-Reformation, this aspect of Catholicism was bound to strike our travellers very forcibly. 'France hath too many Religious' Northleigh declares bluntly.[28] When Lauder was in Orleans, he saw the commemorative ceremony for Joan of Arc and, in describing the procession through the town, he gives a very vivid and useful account of the principal male religious orders. It would be a pity not to reproduce the diatribe with which he begins to speak of what he calls 'all that swarms of grassopers which we are fortold sould aschend out of the bottomless pit: al these filthy frogs that we are fortold that beast that false prophet should cast out of his mouth, I mean that rable of Religious orders within the body of that Apostolical and Pseudo-apostolicall Church of Rome'. Having got that off his chest, he goes on to describe this part of the procession:

> Only the Jesuits were wanting; the pride of whose hearts will not suffer them to go in procession with the meaner orders. In order went the Capuchines, then the Minimes, which 2 orders

tho they both go under the name of Cordeliers by reason of that cord they wear about their midle, on whilk cord they have hinging their string of beads, to the end of their string is hinging a litle brazen crosse, tho also they be both in on habit, to wit long broun gowns or coats coming doune to their feet, a cap of that same coming furth long behind just like a Unicornes horne, tho the go both bar leged only instead of shoes having cloogs of wood (hence when I saw them in the winter I pitied them for going bar leged; on the other hand, when I saw them in the summer I pitied them that they ware necessitat by the first institution of their orders never to quate their gounes which cannot be but to hot for them; yea, never to suffer any linnen only wooll to come neirest their skine), notwithstanding of this its easy to distinguish them by the Clerical Tonsure, you sall never find a capuchin but with a very liberall bard: for the Minime he must not have any. Again in their diet and other such things they differ much: the Minime must renounce for ever the eating of fleche, their only food is fishes and roots; hence Erasmus calls them fischy men (homines piscosos). Not so with the Capuchines. Their be also many other differences that tyme must discover to me. Thir 2 orders our Bucanan means when he names *nodosa canabe cinctos*. To returne to our purpose their came also the Dominicans or Jacobins, which are but one order having 2 names; then came the Chartereus or Carthusians: both which go in a long white playding robe. Only the Jacobins hood is black; the Carthusians is white: then followed the Franciscans, who are now called Recollects because being al banished France by reason of their turbulency and intromitting with the state (of which wery stamp they seim to have bein in the tyme of our James the 5, when he caused Buchanan writ his Franciscani against them) by the praevalent faction the Pope had in France then, they were all recalled, so that France held them not so weil out as Venice do'es the Jesuits. Then came the Peres de l'Oratere, who goes allmost in the same very habit with the Jesuits. Then cames the Augustines with their white coat and a black gown above, after them came the moncks of the order of St. Bennet or the Benedictin friers, who goes in a white coat indeed, but above it he wears a black cloak to his heels, with the Jesuits he wears also a hat as they do.[29]

In Paris Lister was shocked by the uncomfortable dress and the meagre diet of some religious orders:

Here is also daily to be seen in the Streets great variety of Monks, in strange unusual Habits to us Englishmen: These make an odd Figure, and furnish well a Picture. I cannot but pity the mistaken Zeal of these poor Men that put themselves into Religion, as they call it, and renounce the World, and give themselves most severe Rules of Living and Diet; some of the Orders are decently enough Cloathed, as the Jesuits, the Fathers of the Oratory, &c., but most are very particular and obsolete in their Dress, as being the Rustic Habit of old times, without Linnen, or Ornaments of the present Age.

He condemns the asceticism for which some orders stood:

Wantonly to persecute our selves, is to do violence to Christianity, and to put our selves in a worse state than the Jews were; for to choose the worst of Food, which is sowre Herbs and Fish, and such like Trash, and to lie worse always rough, in course and nasty Woollen Frocks upon Boards; To go Barefoot in a cold Country, to deny themselves the Comforts of this Life, and the Conversation of Men; this, I say, is to hazard our Healths, to renounce the great Blessings of this Life, and in a manner to destroy our selves.[30]

That was not the aspect of monasticism which most impressed Heylyn. Not only does he stress the large incomes drawn by the abbots of the wealthier monasteries; he also considered that the lot of the Franciscan friars whom he saw in Paris was not particularly hard:

It was my chance to be in a house of the Franciscans in Paris, where one of the Fryers upon the intreaty of our friends, had us into the hall, it being then the time of their refectory; a favour not vulgar; there we saw the Brothers sitting all of a side, and every one a pretty distance from the other, their severall commons being a dish of pottage, a chop of Mutton, a dish of cherries, and a large glasse of water: this provision together with a liberall allowance of ease, and a little of study keepeth them exceeding plump and in a good liking, and maketh them, having little to take thought for, as I said before, passing good company.

Another encounter with members of religious orders did not give him a high opinion of their morals, though he was impressed by their cheerfulness:

As I travailed towards Orleans we had in our Coach with us three of these mortified sinners, two of the Order of St. Austin, and one Franciscan; the merryest crickets that ever chirped, nothing in them but mad tales and complements; and for musick, they would sing like hawkes. When we came to a vein of good wine they would cheer up themselves and their neighbours with this comfortable Doctrine, *Vivamus ut bibamus, & bibamus ut vivamus*. And for courtship and toying with the wenches, you would easily believe that it had been a trade with which they had not been a little acquainted; of all men, when I am marryed, God keep my wife from them, till then, my neighbours.[31]

When Lauder inquired why members of the religious orders were never seen in the streets except in pairs, he got an answer which revealed that such suspicions were shared by many French people: 'They know the thoughts of the common people, that they be litle faworable to them, the orders being talkt of as the lecherousest people that lives'.[32]

The custom of appointing as commendatory abbots or priors men whose connection with the Church was often of the slightest aroused some comment. 'One may be of the clergy. and yet marry' wrote Finch in 1652, 'for to have the *tonsura prima* is enough for that and by vertue of that cutting off a little lock of haire a man may possesse any ecclesaistical preferment, as the Prince of Conté who hath at least 40,000l. in church preferment per annum'.[33] In practice the Prince de Conti gave up his posts in the Church when he married one of Mazarin's nieces in 1654. Later in the century Veryard is more to the point when he stresses the use which the King made of such appointments to reward service to the Crown, though, numerous as abbeys held *in commendam* were, they were not quite so common as he seems to suggest: 'The French Monks had formerly Abbots of their own Order, and vast Revenues which were usually spent in Riot, with little Benefit to the Publick: But the King has reform'd them in their way of Living, and taken off a considerable part of the Income for the honourable Maintenance of Gentlemen of slender Fortunes and good Families; whom he qualifies with the title of Secular Abbots. They are oblig'd to Celibacy, but not to the Rules of the Order'.[34]

While in France, several of our travellers visited out of curiosity convents of English nuns established there since the Reformation. Thus at both Gravelines and Dunkirk Ray and Skippon went to convents of the order of St. Clare and were struck by the austere lives led by the nuns.[35] In Paris Edward Browne was present at the ceremony in the convent of Augustine nuns at which two women took the veil, and afterwards had a conversation in the parlour with a nun who had lived in the convent for twenty years and who 'much commended her manner of living, and the innocent pleasures of a Monastery'.[36] Northleigh went to a different convent of English nuns in Paris, that of the Benedictines, founded in 1657; he noted its educational role: 'In this Nunnery also several of the young Ladies Children of our Popish Parents are educated and instructed in the Accomplishments proper to their Sex: besides the Language that they learn of Course by Conversation'.[37]

However, they also visited convents of French nuns. Locke, for instance, gives a detailed account of the ceremony of a nun taking the veil in the convent of the Visitation at Montpellier, and he also describes an earlier visit to a very genteel convent at Hyères: 'Above the towne is a nunnery, of the order of St Bernard, of persons of quality. They all eat alone in their chambers apart, & keepe a maid servant & a lacquey, & goe out of the Nunnery, & walke abroad when they please, The situation is very pleasant, overlooking the towne, the orange gardens, the vally & the sea'.[38] The youth, John Buxton, was mildly surprised at the way in which he and his companions were received by the nuns of this convent. In a letter he relates how, after arriving at Hyères,

> walking about it, accidentally looking into a church, as it is the custom in these countries to leave the door open, we saw some nuns in it; upon that we made towards 'em. They perceiving us to be strangers, vouchsafed the like in some measure. After a little discourse with 'em about our own country and several other things, we were permitted to go into the convent, where we saw the Lady Abbess in her closet, which was beautifully adorned, and many delicate nuns in a chamber near it; they immediately surrounded us and demanded some questions, one of which I remember was this: 'Do you not think it very strange of us to let men come into the nunnery?' We answered them thus: 'The favour was so great that we could not expect it or can be so ungrateful as to forget it'. We afterwards understood that this place particularly had that privilege, being persons of great quality. When our eyes were fully dazzled with beholding their charming objects, we expressed our gratitude in the best manner we were able, and so made our obeisance.

He rounds off his account of their visit to these flirtatious nuns with a rather coarse remark: 'Had you been there – being a stout man – you might have been half tempted to turn friar'.[39] During the three months which he spent in Lyons Reresby formed a friendship which he describes in rather enigmatic terms: 'I made a particular acquaintance with a nun of the Carmelite Convent, a woman of witt and beauty, which helped to pass away the time whilst I stayed there'.[40]

However, by far the most striking accounts of a French convent produced by our travellers concern the strange goings-on in that of the Ursulines in the Protestant stronghold of Loudun in the 1630s. Nearly half a century later, in 1678, Locke picked up one view of the whole matter current in the learned circles of the capital:

> The story of the Nuns of Lodun possessed was noe thing but a contrivance of Cardinall Richlieu to destroy a man Grandiere he suspected to have writ a booke against him, who was condemned for witchcraft in the case & burnt for it. The scene

was managed by the Capucines, & the nuns plaid their tricks well, but all was a cheat.[41]

None of our travellers joined in the rush to Loudun before the end of 1635, more than a year after the *curé*, Urbain Grandier, had been burnt at the stake. Though they have nothing to offer about his trial and execution, three of them have a great deal to say about the exorcism of the nuns being carried out by Jesuit fathers.

Writing from Orleans on 7 December 1635, only a few days after leaving Loudun, the playwright, Thomas Killigrew, provides a vivid account of what he had seen of these exorcisms. He was accompanying a somewhat elder man, Walter Montagu (1603–1677), son of the first Earl of Manchester, a convert to Catholicism, who was later to become the commendatory abbot of a monastery near Pontoise. Killigrew relates to an unknown correspondent how on the previous Thursday morning they had gone to the Ursuline convent and had seen in the chapel five of the possessed nuns, who were accompanied by five fathers praying while a priest said Mass:

> This for the space of halfe an houer was all we saw, but on a suddaine two of them grew unruly & would by force have left their Seates, but the Friers made them keepe them, which they did, but one left not with rediculous Motions to abuse the Frier, thrusting out her Tonge, & then catching him about the neck to have kist him. The others rage was Anger, for she tooke her Preist by the Throte, & Struke him, & then got from him & ran roring & talking to the Preist that was saying Masse, where she committed some extravigances before the Frier could take her away. Noe other strang things hapned in the Chappell at this tyme that I saw, or heard, but sad Cryes that came from the Grates of the Nunnerie.

At this point they were advised to come back in the afternoon 'for it was Holiday & there was noe Exorcismes used there in the fore noone by reason they were to goe to the Churches'.

In a church (unspecified) they saw in succession three nuns being exorcised. Killigrew obviously found some of them quite attractive. Of the first he writes: 'When we saw her, her selfe, she was a lusty younge woman, browne har'd, & black ey'd, & tall of Stature, but now soe violently possest, that her strength was above five woemens, for being by in her rage, the Preist desired me to hold one of her hands, which was all I could without rudenesse doe'. He describes 'her eyes soe strangly turn'd asquint, as nothing but white appeared' and how 'her Tonge brake out', its colour being 'as strange as the proportion, it looked as if her eyes had bine broke upon it'. While 'this poore wretch lay tortured thus on the Ground, breathing nothing but Grones & Oathes', the priest 'stood treading on her brest, & holding the Host over her, commaunding the Devill to worship it, calling him Dog, Serpent, & other names'.

Killigrew did not wait to see what happened there, but went to another chapel where a second nun was being exorcised. His account gives rise to several sceptical observations, for instance:

> The Preist then commaunded her or the Devill to prostrate her selfe at the feete of the Alter, & then to put on a body of Iron; but he refused to doe it, till the Preist had Charmed him by Psalmes & Prayers; then he reared & lay downe, all the Body shot out straight & the Armes thrust out, & soe lay the whole Body of one peice as the Preist said, & bad me feele, which I did, but I must tell you the truth; I only felt firme flesh, Stronge Armes & Leggs held out stiffe; but others affirme that felt it that she was all stiffe & heavy as Iron, but they had more faith then I, and it seemed the Miracle appeared more visable to them, then to me.

Killigrew noted without comment a point to be taken up by a later traveller: 'The Preist Speakes only in Latin to him, the Devill only French'. He then continues his account of this exorcism, again expressing his scepticism:

> One Miracle I had mist if Mr. Mountague had not sent for me, which was to obey what the Preist commaunded him Mentally without speaking it to him, to confirme me it was the Devill by the knowledge of his thoughts, which I confesse had bin Strange if I could have bine satisfied by his telling me mine, but I was refused. But to my Story: when I came into the Chappell Mr Mountague tould me I should see the Devill obey the Preists thoughts, And that I might be sure it was the Devill, the Preist had tould him in his eare what he thought. Whilst we were in this discourse, the Devill lay in a great deale of torture by the Strange signes that he gave of the turning of his Body & Head, but in all this accions I saw little above Nature, or a Tumblers expression. The Preist then commaunded him to tell him his thought, but the Stubborne Devill would not, . . . till another Jesuite came & layd a Purse of Reliques on his head, with which, as if she had bine Thunder stouck, she sunke to the ground & there lay groveling, & his eyes were on the Purse, & said (Let me kisse your Thumbs) which was (it seemeth) the thought, and then, being demaunded why she was soe longe obeying, she said there were Herit[i]ckes there, but she hoped they would not believe what they saw. The Preist then gave one bout more for my sake, being loath that I should Continue an Heriticke, & it was to show how the Hugonets should be used, & being a greate

while Charmed, at last he told them, like Calvin their head, & being asked how that was, exprest his torture in Ugly faces. This last, I confesse, I was glad to see, for it confirmed me in beleiving nothing this Devill did or said. The Frier then layed the Devill and the woman was within a Minute well, & being asked where the Devill was, the Frier & she Confest in her (Thinge) which is the place he hath ever kept since he came into her. I gave soe little faith to what he said, as I offred (contrary to my resolution) to doe more then I have done yet or intend to doe, & it was to try if the Devill Possesses all or none, but I was refused.

Killigrew ends his account of this second exorcism with the ironical reflexion: 'You would have wondered to see how lively the Frier was & with what Dexterity he commaunded the Devill, how with a word he raised him, & layed him with another, with such ease that I Conclude, that the Devill is but an Asse to a Jesuite'.

Leaving the company 'in admiration of these Miracles', Killigrew went to see a third nun being exorcised. Though he found her 'sitting in a melancholy posture', he was struck by her beauty:

She was very younge & handsome, of a more tender looke & slender shape then any of the rest. When she sat still, you would have thought you could not have strokt her breasts too softly, her armes & hands soe small & white, as she shewed a breeding not answerable to the estate she was in. You would have thought her servant Could only have led her by that hand & not have hurt her. The lovelinesse of her face was clothed in a sad sable looke which, upon my coming into the Chappell, she hid, but presently unvailed againe, & though she stoode now bound like a slave in the Friers hand, you might see through all her misfortunes in her black eyes, the unruined Arches of many Triumphes.

Seeing this young woman roughly handled by the Jesuit and two peasants who held her arms while she was in her fit, was too much for him. He returned with Montagu to their inn for dinner.

As soon as they had finished their meal, they were summoned back to the convent where they witnessed two exorcisms. Although he does not mention her by name, the second of these was of the Mother Superior, the famous Jeanne des Anges (1602–1665). He was fortunate too in that he had the privilege of being present on the day when the first of the names – that of St. Joseph — was to appear miraculously on her hand, to be followed in due course by those of Jesus, Mary and St. François de Sales. Here, as we shall see, Killigrew's scepticism was swept away in the general enthusiasm at this miracle.

Lying on a special couch in the chapel, the prioress

like the rest fell into extravagant talkings, & violent beating of
her selfe as she lay, her face drawne into Horrid & Strange
Postures, & her Belly swelled to the bignesse of one with Child
& then fell flat againe, & at the same instant her breasts swelled
to the bigness that her Belly was; but these Accidents continued
not in one place of her body longe, but removed sometymes to
her Leggs, sometymes to her Hands, & still as the Priest perceived the parts afflicted, he applyed his Relique there, &
prayed, signing the place with the Signe of the Crosse, &
immeadiately it was well.

After she had torn off her headgear, 'she lay Cursing the Preist &
the Sacrament & the power they had thus to Torment her'. ; then the
Jesuit ordered the devil 'to pay an Adoration to that he soe Curst,
groveling on the Ground, which at last after a greate many Curses he
obeyed in the manner that followeth':

She slidd from her Seate backwards upon the Ground, &
there lay, but refused to pay reverence to the Host, till by
prayers & touching her with Reliques, & shewing her her God
(as he called it), she at the last obeyed, And as she lay on her
back, she bent her wast like a tumbler, & went soe, shoving her
selfe with her Heeles on her bare head, all about the Chappell,
after the Frier, and many other Strange unaturall Postures
beyond any that ever I saw or could believe possible for any man
or woman to doe. Nor was this a sudaine motion & away, but a
Continuall thinge which she did for above an hower together.

Then came the famous miracle which impressed even the sceptical
Killigrew:

While this Nunn lay as I have discribed for the space of an
hower, her Tonge swelled to a most incredible bignesse, & never
within her Mouth from the first falling into her fitt. I saw her in
an Instant Contract it, & I heard her, after she had given a Starte
& Scrich that you would have thought had torne her in peices,
she spake one word & that was (Joseph), at which all the Preists
starte up & Cryed, That is the Signe, looke for the Marke, which
one seing her hold out her arme, look't there for it. Mr.
Mountague & my selfe did the same very earnestly, & on her
hand I saw a Collour rise a little Ruddy, & run for the length of
an Inch upon her Veine, & in that a greate many Redd specks, &
they contracted into Letters, which made a distinct word, & it
was the same she spake (Joseph). This Marke, the Jesuite said,
the Devill promised, when he went out he would make, & from
the tyme he promised this, to this day was four Moneths. This as
I live I saw, nor could I finde the least argument to question the
reality of this Miracle. The Preist then told us, that the Devill
would have wrote his owne name when he went out, but that he
enjoyned him to write (Joseph), for to that Saint the Preist had

addrest him selfe with a Vow, to have his ayde in the expelling of him. While we were in admiration, she Came to her selfe, & pulled her hand from us & kist the Marke, & fell to prayers.

Killigrew ends his letter by declaring that what he had seen was 'strange & above Nature', adding: 'All that I have written here, of the last woman aboute the Name, I have by a President of Mr. Mountague, sett my hand to, and soe did all the Preists that saw it, & t'is sent to the Kinge of France & will be printed'.[42]

Two other travellers who were present as quite young men at these exorcisms were decidedly more critical of what they saw. It is true that they were not writing down their immediate impressions, but looking back at an earlier period in their lives. In a letter which the future Duke of Lauderdale wrote in 1658 to Richard Baxter from Windsor Castle where he was a prisoner, he describes how, in view of the stir events in Loudun were causing in Paris in the spring of 1637, he went there to see for himself. It was not that he rejected all belief in spirits: 'I, who was perswaded such a thing might be, and that it was not impossible the Devill could possess a Nun as well as another, doubted it as little as any body'. He was rapidly undeceived. He went first to the convent: 'When I had seen Exorcising enough of three or four of them in the Chapel, and could hear nothing but wanton Wenches singing baudy Songs in French, I began to suspect a Fourbe'. When he expressed his disappointment to one of the Jesuits, he was directed to exorcisms in the parish church. There he saw 'a great many people gazing, and a Wench pretty well taught to play Tricks, yet nothing so much as I have seen twenty Tumblers and Rope-dancers do'. Back in the convent chapel, he saw Jeanne des Anges, but was not in the least impressed: 'I saw the Mother Superior exorcised, and saw that Hand on which they would have made us believe, The names I.H.S. Maria Joseph, were written by Miracles: (but it was apparent to me it was done with *Aqua Fortis*) then my Patience, was quite spent, and I went to a Jesuit and told him my Mind freely'. His encounter with this man had a hilarious conclusion:

> He still maintained a real Possession, and I desired for a Tryal, to speak a strange Language. He asked, What Language? I told him, I would not tell; but neither he or all those Devils should understand me. He asked, if I would be converted upon the Tryal (for I had discovered I was no Papist). I told him that was not the Question, nor could all the Devils in Hell pervert me; but the Question was, if there was a real Possession, and if they could understand me, I shall confess it under my hand. His answer was, *These Devils have not travelled*, and this I replied to with a loud Laughter, nor could I get any more Satisfaction.

The next day he met at Saumur another Scotsman, Mark Duncan, who, in addition to being a professor of philosophy and principal of the Protestant Academy there, was also a physician; in 1634 he had published his *Discours de la possession des Religieuses Ursulines de Loudon*. Duncan told him

> how he had made a clearer Discovery of the Cheat in presence of the Bishop of Poitiers, and of all the Country, how he had held fast one of the pretended Nuns Arms, in spite of all the Power of their Exorcisms, and challenged all the Devils in Hell to take it out of his Hand. This, with many more Circumstances, he told me, and he printed them to the World.[43]

Sir George Courthop's verdict was not quite so downright though obviously he was more than sceptical about what he saw. Late in 1636 he had left Oxford for Paris and after two months there he moved on to Loudun where he spent thirteen months. After a long and severe illness he was on the point of leaving the town when he decided he must first see something of the exorcisms of which he had heard so much. At this point an ardent Catholic, Lady Purbeck, who was utterly convinced of the nuns' possession, asked him to accompany her to the exorcisms. Somewhat reluctantly he agreed, 'provided she would ask the Nun that was possessed and exorcised that day, to tell me what was wrote in a Paper that I should hold in my hand, and her Honour should see what I wrote in it before I went, on condition she should not reveal it to any of the Fathers'. This is how he relates their visit to the Ursulines' convent:

> When I came to the place, one of the Nuns cries out, *Le voila un Hugenot* (Yonder is a Protestant) meaning me. I saw all the people fastening their eyes upon me, and demanded in Latin of the Father, if I might be permitted to ask one question: he answered me I might, for the Devill would answer any question in any language.
> I then went on and told the Father that by the same reason the Devil knew me to be a Protestant he might know another man to be one. I demanded whether there were any more standing there, knowing Mr Covell who went with me to be one. After many prayers said and conjurations to make the Devil give me and the company satisfaction I was told I could not be answered till the Nun had received the wafer and an Honourable Lady (a stranger) had made her confession and received the Eucharist, which being done and the exorcism of the Devils going on I was called upon by the Lady Purbeck and one of the Fathers to come and remove the Nun's head (as she lay flat on her back) from the ground, Mr Covell and I at one side and two Papists and the Lady Purbeck on the other side: but though all five of us lifted

together we could make no motion in her head, but it remained as immovable as a Church: The Father told us the Devil was entered into her head and that was the reason it was fixed to the floor of the room but by his Prayers and the form of exorcism he used he would get it out and then one of our fingers could make it stir: this we saw performed, by what juggling tricks was not made known to us. Upon this the Lady Purbeck came and asked if this were less than a miracle, I answered it might be a matter of wonder but no miracle: she demanded if I would stay to know what was in the paper in my hand and she would know of the Father if I should have satisfaction: She asked him and his answer was *Nimia curiositas in facie populi post miraculum fatum*. After I had received this answer I went home and left them that were there to see the end of the exorcism of the day.

Being determined to discover the truth of the matter, Courthop then proceeded to interrogate both Catholics and Protestants in the town. Finally he was referred to his own landlord, named Strachan, who was 'Master of the Academy' and was 'reputed to be a learned man (as indeed he was)'. Strachan would only agree to state his opinion provided he could accompany Courthop on the first day of his journey out of Loudon and reveal it to him in their inn in the evening. After Courthop had sworn never to reveal his views or return to Loudun,

he then told me Cardinal Richlieu, who was the great Minister of State in those days, was resolved to build a town where he was born and call it by his name; this place of his birth was some eight miles from Loudoun, and he finding this town full of Protestants and a city where was a Castle, Courts of Justice and a great trade driven was resolved to depopulate it and carry the Garrison of the Castle, the courts of Justice and the trade to his town called Richlieu, all which he lived to see performed: and finding no better way to effect it, sent down these Jesuits and Nuns to make an exorcism there, whereby the Protestants' Religion might be disgraced; and such who turned to be Papists upon sight of this wonder, if they would leave the town and go to inhabit in his town they sho'd be seven years free from all imposition and pay two capons a year during that time for rent: these privileges and the other juggle so effectually wrought, that the Castle was demolished, the courts of Justice removed and all ways and means that brought profit to the town were carried to Richlieu and that being peopled and his work done the Jesuits and Nuns left the town.

Courthop goes on to relate how in 1644 his landlord's son visited him in England and told him 'that the vizard was taken off and the juggle manifest to all the world, and, though he was a Papist, he could not but acknowledge to me he never had faith enough to believe it to be a truth'.[44]

Whatever the truth concerning Richelieu's part in the affair, it is certainly untrue that the Ursuline nuns left Loudun. Down to 1660 a number of our travellers had the curiosity to inspect the marks on the hand of Jeanne des Anges. Indeed Lord Willoughby went twice to the convent to see her — in December 1648 when he saw 'the nun there that shewes a certaine writing on the back of her left hand . . . . ., a marke, as they say, the divell gave her when he quitt her, havinge beene formerly possessed', and he went back again in the following August.[45] In 1649 Robert Montagu visited the convent though his flat adolescent style would seem to indicate that, unlike his uncle Walter, he was not swept off his feet by the sight of the marks on her hand: 'I saw likewise in the cloister of St. Benoist one of the nuns which had written on her hand Jesu Marie Joseph, the which she told us that the devil in going out of her had marqued it so, having bin possessed by him almost two years, as also she sayed that every eeve of our Ladys day it goes away and next day comes againe'.[46] The last word on the subject belongs to Bertie who visited Loudun in 1660. After relating how Grandier was burnt at the stake, he speaks slightingly of the 'miracle (a cheating one I believe)' of the devil's departure from Jeanne des Anges leaving 'written on her hand, Jesus Marie, Joseph Français de Salle, which can never be got out again. It seems as if it were scratched with a pin, and it is very probable that these holy sisters made the miracle themselves. Thus when she showed me her hand she told me looking on it that it was a veritable oeuvre de Dieu, though I had not faith enough to believe it'.[47]

None of the monasteries visited by our travellers provided them with such sensational material. Indeed though they saw over a great many monastic libraries both in Paris and the provinces, they have surprisingly little to say about monastic life. The only monasteries of which they offer any sort of description are those of the Carthusians. While at Avignon, Locke crossed the Rhone to visit the Charterhouse at Villeneuve-lès-Avignon on which he made this rather jocular entry:

> Their chappell well adorned, their plate, copes & reliques very rich, amongst the rest a chalice of gold, given by Rene, the last King of Naples of the Anjou race. I was going to take it in my hand, but the Carthusian withdrew it till he had put a cloth about the handle & soe gave it into my hand, noe body being sufferd to touch these holy things but a priest. In their chappell Pope Innocent the 6th lies interd; he died 1362, & in a litle chappel in their convent stands a plain, old chair where he was infallible. I

sat too little a while in it to get that priviledg. In their devotions they use much prostrations & kisseing the ground. They leave no more hair on their heads but one very little circle going round, which is cut as short as one's whiskers. After shaveing they confessd they finde it somewhat cold & inconvenient. The Cell we were in had 3 litle rooms below, a litle garden & a litle cloister on the far side of it. In the roome above we were not. Such an habitacion hath each of them apart. Their chappel, refectory & the Cell & other parts are all kept very cleane, & yet on the walls of one of their cloisters we saw a litle, black scorpion.

He later added another entry on the same subject. This mainly deals with a topic which was of considerable practical importance when the heir presumptive to the English crown was a Roman Catholic:

Over the entrance into the Carthusians' cloister we saw this morning is writt: Janus Caeli. The Carthusian that shewd us the convent seemed not very melancholy. He enquird after their houses & lands in England, & asked whether, when we came to be papists, they should not have them again. I told him yes, without doubt, for there could be noe reconciliation to their church without restitution. He told me I was a very good divine & very much in the right. They have in their chappell several pictures of the execution of some of their order in England in Henry 8's reign.[47a]

Several of our travellers who ventured into that remote corner of France describe in some detail their visit to the Grande Chartreuse. Probably the best account is that given by Skippon who made the journey along with Ray in 1665:

At a narrow passage between two high precipitous rocks, we passed over a bridge cross a torrent, and knocking at a gate, were let in by a servant belonging to the monastery of the Chartreuse; then we ascended a mountainous way above a quarter of a league, till we passed by a large building, where persons of all trades live, and who are habited like the fathers of the Carthusian order, and work for the convent. A good distance further up, we arrived at the Grande Chartreuse, where the porter ask'd us whence we came, and called a lay brother, who introduced us into one of the halls appointed to receive strangers in. At the gate we left our swords and pistols. Seven hours riding from Grenoble hither.

This convent is seated under one of the highest mountains in these parts, and discovers far and near into the adjacent countries.

As soon as we came into the hall, wine, bread and cheese were set before us; and one of the fathers, a very intelligent man,

visited and discoursed some time with us about the news of
Europe, which he was no stranger to. A boy guided us up into
the mountain, and shewed us a neat chapel dedicated to S. Maria
de Casalibus, which is prettily adorned with the letters of her
name in gold, and with scripture epithets: beyond this we saw S.
Bruno's chapel built on a rock.

At night we had our supper and beds prepared for us.

We observed the friars at evensong bowing their heads, as
they sat, at the saying the Gloria Dei, &c. Sixty fathers, and as
many lay brothers here.

No women, but those of the royal blood can enter this cloister.
There are two ways more to come to this convent, besides that
from Grenoble, viz. one from Lyons and the other from
Chambery.

In their stables they keep about 60 horses, besides mules and
asses.

Skippon's entry is continued on the following day which happened
to be a Friday:

We saw their church, a dark and narrow building; before the
altar stand four tall brass candlesticks; within the choir the
fathers sit, and without sit the lay brothers. The fathers rise to
their devotions at midnight, and are in the choir three hours; but
then they sleep till seven or eight in the morning, when the
masses begin. The cloister is a very long and narrow square; we
went into one of their cells, which are not kept so neat as those
we saw at Venice. At meal-time, several servants bring bread,
wine, &c. and open a little window by the side of the cell-door,
and there put in the provisions. On Fridays they fast strictly, and
this day we saw what they ate viz. two or three spoonfuls of cold
pease (boil'd), four or five pears, and a few stew'd prunes, and
raw plumbs, besides a small pittance of bread and wine, and at
night they had no supper.

In the *Refectorium* are two tables, besides the prior's at the
upper end; they dine here together only on Sundays and great
festivals. In the general of the order's lodgings, we observed the
pictures of S. Martin's at Naples, the *Certresa* of Pavia, and the
convent nigh Avignon, &c. places belonging to this order. In the
chapel is an altar-piece of great value. In the chapter-room is a
large picture, how seven of this order were executed for treason
(they say for religion) in Henry VIII's days in England. Cardinal
Richelieu professed himself first of this order. The lodgings to
entertain princes in are neat; the chapel there is within crusted
over with marble.

We gave the cook a quart d'escus, and having taken our
break-fast, and written our names in a book kept by a porter, we
mounted and rode back to Grenoble the same way we came.[48]

The mendicant orders are generally treated with less respect. It is true that Lauder was impressed by the poverty of the Capuchins at Poitiers:

> Their poverty is such that they have nothing to sustain them but others charité when they come begging, and that every 24 hours. They having nothing layd up against tomorrow, if their be any day amongs others wheirin they have gotten little or nothing, notwithstanding of this they come al to the Table, tho' nothing to eat. Each man sayes his grace to himselfe, their they sit looking on one another, poor creatures, as long as give they had had something to eat. They fast all that day, but if their be any that cannot fast it out, then he may go doune to the yard and houck out 2, 3 carrots to himselfe, or stow some like some cibows,[48a] beets or such like things, and this is their delicates. If their be any day wheirin they have gotten more then suffices them all, the superplus they give to the poor. The convent hath no more rent then will defray their charges in keiping up their house about their ears. Al this do thir misers under the hopes of meriting by the samen: yet I would be a Capuchin before any other order I have sein yet.

The conclusion is somewhat unexpected.

Lauder had an opportunity to see two men admitted to the order:

> To sie the ceremony of their matriculation unto the order I went with my good sire, wheir the principal ceremony was that they cast of their cloathes wheirwith they were formerly cloathed and receaves the Capuchines broun weid, as also they get the clerical tonsure, the cord about their west, and the clogs of wood on their bare feet. A great number of speaches being used in the intervalls containing as is probable, their dueties, but we could not understand them for the bruit. At the point of each of them all the people cried Amen. Finaly we saw them take al the rest of their brethren by the hand, all of them having burning torches in their hands.

Later during his stay in Poitiers Lauder noted a couple of stories which gave a much less favourable view of members of this order,[48b] but, as they were secondhand, they need not detain us.

While Locke admired the water cistern at the Capuchins' house in Paris (they acted as volunteer firemen), he was critical of the harshness of their rule and of the effect which this had on members of the order. After visiting Father Chérubin, a friar distinguished for his researches in optics, he made this entry in his journal:

> The Capucins are the strictest & severest order in France, soe that to mortifie those of their order they often command them seeming unreasonable things which, if not considered as

conduceing to mortification, would be very irrationall & ridiculous, as to plant cabbage plants the roots upwards, & then reprehend the planter because they doe not grow. As soon as they finde any one to have any inclinations any way, as P. Cherubin in opticks & telescopes, to take from him all he has don or may be usefull to him in that Science, & imploy him in something quite contrary; but he has now a particular lock & key to his cell which the gardian's key opens not, by order of the King. Sometimes also they order a brother to enter the refectoir on all fours with an ass's pad on his back and a bridle in his mouth for humiliation, which happening once when a stranger was there, was like to have cost the Gardian his life. This severity makes them not compassionate one to an other, what ever they would be to others.[49]

Locke's two references to the Carmelites are not particularly flattering. The first concerns a service which he attended in their chapel in Montpellier shortly after the beatification of the Spanish Carmelite, St John of the Cross:

At the Carmes' Church this day was an end of their octave of open house, as one may say, upon the occasion of the canonization of St John de Croix, one of their Order lately canonized at Rome, dead 80 years agon. During the 8 days of their celebration there was plenarie Indulgence over the door of their chappell & at the doore a pavilion of bays with emblems set round & his picture in the midle. This being the close of the solemnity, there was a sermon which was the recital of his life, virtues & miracles he did, as preserving baptismall grace & innocence to the end of his life, his driveing out evil spirits out of the possessed, etc.

Later in Paris he picked up an amusing story about Jean Pierre Camus (1582-1652), Bishop of Belley, who wrote several works attacking monks:

A devout Lady being sick & besiged by Carmes made her will & gave them all. The Bishop of Belly comeing to see her as soon as it was don, asked her whether she had made her will. She answerd yes & told him how. He convinced her 'twas not well &, she desireing to alter it, found a difficulty how to doe it, being soe beset by the Friers. This Bishop bid her not truble her self for that, but presently tooke order that 2 Notarys, habited as Physitians, should come to her, who being by her bed's side, the Bishop told the company it was convenient all should with draw, & soe the former will was revoked & a new one made & put into the Bishop's hands. The Lady dies. The Carmes produce their will & for some time the Bishop lets them enjoy the pleasure of the inheritance, but at last, takeing out the other, says to them:

Mes freres, you are the sons of Eliah, children of the Old Testament, & have noe share in the New. This is that Bishop of Belly that hath writ soe much against Munks and Munkery.[50]

It is obvious that Locke thoroughly enjoyed writing down this story.

Lauder gives a somewhat critical account of a sermon delivered by a Dominican in Poitiers on St. Dominic's day. 'For the vertues that are relative to God', he writes, 'he numbered them up to 13, and that out of Thomas, whom they follow in all things; amongs which were piety, sanctité, zeal for Religion, which broke out to that hieght that he caused sundry of the poor Albigenses, over the inquisition of which he was sett, to be brunt; but this he mentioned *no*.' Lauder continues in this sarcastic tone down to the end of the entry: 'His epiloge was that St. Dominick was worth all the Saincts of them. And to speak the truth, believing him he made him on of the perfectest men of the world, subject to no imperfection. I should discover no difference he made betuixt him and Christ'.[51] During his stay in Paris Locke recorded an account of recent disorders in the Dominicans' house in the Rue St. Jacques:

The Jacobines in Paris fell into civill war one with an other & went to gether by the ears, & the battail grew soe fierce between them that the covent was not large enough to contein the combatants, but they severall of them sallied out into the street & there cuffd it out stoutly. The occasion, they say, was that the Prior endeavoured to reduce them into a stricter way of liveing then they had for some time past observd, for which in the fray he was soundly beaten.

This story was not invented by Locke; six days before he made this entry Colbert had written to the Archbishop of Paris about 'le désordre des Jacobins de la rue Saint-Jacques'. Later Locke returns to this topic in speaking of the secular priests of the Oratory: 'Les peres del'Oratoire live togeather in society, but are under noe vow nor noe obedience to their superior but what respect & civility obleiges them to, which gave just occasion to a Jacobin to demand of one of them if their superior had noe authority over them, who it was parted them when they went togeather by the ears'.[52]

Another order which attracted some attention was that of the Minims. Evelyn visited their house at Chaillot to see one of their number who had a considerable reputation as an apothecary and physician:

I went to visite Frier Nicholas at the Convent at Challiot, who being an excellent chymist shew'd me his Laboratoria, & rare collection of Spagyrical remedies: He was both Physitian & Apothecarie of the Convent, & insteade of the names of his drogues painted his boxes & potts with the figure of the drug or simple contained in them: he shew'd me as a raritie some Mercury of Antimonie: he had cur'd Monsieur Seneterre of a desperate sicknesse for which there was building a monumental Altar, that was to cost 1500 pounds.[53]

A less favourable account of another house of the same order is given by Locke in describing the stone coffins which he saw in the Alyscamps at Arles:

By the side of this place & on some part of it stands a covent of the Minims, where in we were shewd severall of these toombs, dug up in severall places hereabouts, of eminent saints, one whereof, as well as St.Denys, caried his head in his hands a good way. They shewd us also one of these toombs which was always wet on the outside & that under it always drie, for they piled them one upon another, & had always water in it which increased & decreased with the moon. This the Frier that shewd the toombs said was a constant miracle. He dipd in his cord at a little hole to give us demonstracion, & I thought it noe lesse then a miracle to beleiv upon such a proof.[54] The Frier shewd us these & other things very courteously, & as civily at parting desired something to say Masse for our good journey, which a Swisse that was then there understood to be mony to drink our healths, & said it was the first Frier he had ever observed to aske mony to that purpose, & some thought his mistake not soe far out of the way, saying soberly thinking of it, it was to aske mony to drink.[55]

Locke was not the only traveller to take notice of the Oratorians, a very different order of secular priests who do not take vows. At Poitiers Lauder noted the hostility to the Jesuits of 'the Peres de l'Oratoire, who are usually all Jansenists, so that ye sall seldome find these 2 orders setled in one city, tho they be at Orleans'.[56] Lister visited the Oratory in Paris in order to see Father Malebranche and comments: 'They live very neatly together in a kind of Community, but under no Rule: He was very handsomely lodged, in a Room well furnisht'. The absence of the asceticism of many religious orders which he abhorred makes Lister speak with approval of this order. He concludes his account of his visit to this house: 'The Freedom and Nature of this Order puts me in mind of what I heard of a certain rich and learned Man, Monsieur Pinet, of the Law: who put himself at length into Religion, as they say, amongst the Fathers; but first persuaded his Cook to do so too; for he was resolved not to quit his good Soupes, and such Dishes as he liked, whatever became of his Penance and Retirement'.[57]

It goes almost without saying that the religious order which attracted most attention throughout our whole period was the Society of Jesus. Jesuits were not popular figures on this side of the Channel, and various travellers note with satisfaction that they were not all that popular in France. Lauder even goes so far as to declare: 'They contemne and disdain all the rest of the orders in comparation of themselves ... whence they get nothing but hatred again from the other religious, who could with ease sy them all hanged'.[58] Both Locke and he observe that the Jesuits never appeared along with the other orders in processions held for Church festivals:[59] and on his way back to England, Locke noted at Abbeville: 'There are here in this towne of all the orders but Jesuits, whose establishment here the magistrates of the towne have always opposed & prevailed hitherto'.[60]

At the beginning of the century Dallington had warned the traveller to have nothing to do with such men: 'I must precisely forbid him the fellowship or companie of one sort of people in generall: these are the Jesuites, underminders and enveiglers of greene wits, seducers of men in matter of faith, & subverters of men in matter of State, making of both a bad christian, and a worse subject'. He does, however, make an exception for their preaching, since, as he put its it, 'being eloquent, they speake excellent language; and being wise, and therefore best knowing how to speake to best purpose, they seldome or never handle matter of controversie'.[61]

In his account of the Jesuit house in the Rue St.Antoine in Paris Heylyn embarks on some general reflections on the nefarious activities of the society:

> And indeed out of this Trojan horse it is, that those firebrands and incendiaries are let out to disturb and set in combustion the affaires of Christendom, out of this forge come all those stratagems and tricks of Machiavellianism, which tend to the ruine of the Protestants, and desolation of their Countries. I speak not this of their house of Profession here in Paris, either only or principally; wheresoever they settle, they have a house of this nature, out of which they issue to overthrow the Gospell.[62]

For Lauder the Jesuits were 'one of the most pestilent orders that ever was erected, being ever a republick in a republick wheir ever they be', and he then proceeds to describe how they have acquired so much wealth:

> The Jesuits be the subtilist folk that breathes, which especially appears when under the pretext of visitting they fly to a sick carkcass, especially if it be fat, as ravens does to their prey. Their insteed of confirming and strenthening the poor folk to dy with the greater alacrity, they besett them with all the subtile mines

P

imaginable to wring and suck money from them, telling them that they most leive a dozen or 2 of serviets to the poor Cordeliers; as many spoones to the godly Capuchines who are busie praying for your soul, and so something to all the rest; but to us to whom ye are so much beholden a goodly portion, which they repeit wery oft over; but all this tends as on the one hand to demonstrate their inexplebible greediness, so on the other to distraict the poor miser with thoughts of this world and praejudice or defraudation of his air.

This explains how 'the Jesuits, who, above 50 years ago, entred Poictiers with their staffes in their hand, not a 100 livres amongs them all, since have with their crafty dealings so augmented their Convent that they have 40,000 livres standing rent'.[63]

Locke rakes up in his journal a scandal of the 1660s — the misconduct of two Paris Jesuits, Fathers Le Clerc and Faverolles:

P. Clerk, procurator of the Jesuits at Paris, cozened the Society of 100,000 crowns or more, and having too much familiarity with an Abbess, was in the year '66 sent to their convent at Orleans, kept there 2 years a close prisoner, with bread and water 2 years, and died a prisoner in that convent. The King since gave them £100,000 to repair that and a trunk in their church in the Street St.Antoine yet stands as a mark of it.

P. Favarol of the same convent was well whipped and then turned out for keeping a Mistress, an other man's wife.[64]

Veryard offers a rather more detailed and objective account of the society. He explains why its members did not process with the other religious orders: 'They pretend that, by their Institution, they are a Regular Clergy, and consequently claim a place next to the Secular Priests, who take it of all the rest; but this being deny'd them, as being the last confirm'd Order, they go not at all'. They were freer from the restrictions imposed on members of most religious orders:

Indeed their Founder has, in his Rule, left out all that he thought troublesome or rigorous in other Orders, the easier to engage, by these Baits of Liberty and Ease, Men of great Families (whose too delicate Education might deter them from such Austerities) by whose Interest they keep themselves in at Court, and in vogue amongst the People. They neither keep Quire in their Churches, nor have they half as many Fast Days as are kept by other Orders.

Veryard describes the lengthy training which the members of the society received, and he also stresses the dangers which such a body of men present:

Their Priests are profess'd, as they call it, after seventeen

Years standing, in which they renew their former Vows of Chastity, Poverty forsooth, and Obedience, and are not 'till then made privy to the Secrets of the Order, nor admitted into the principal Employments. Neither can they be profess'd, unless their Professors that examine them deposit on Oath, that they are capable of teaching Philosophy or Divinity publickly in any part of the world. At their Profession they likewise make an additional Vow of blind Obedience to the Pope, which no other Order does; and on this account they have been suspected, and expell'd from divers States: and not without reason, since so powerful and intriguing a Body of Men, being link'd by stricter ties to a Foreigner than to their own Prince, may be capable of doing a great deal of mischief.

He does, however, conclude these general observations on the society by conceding that its members 'are better Govern'd, and live freer from Scandal, than any of the other Orders' and, that judging by their constitutions, their founder must have been a wise man.[65]

English visitors to Paris were much struck with the Jesuits' church in the Rue St.Antoine. Evelyn was particularly impressed by it during his first visit to France in 1643–4:

We found the Fathers in their Church at the rüe St.Anthoine, there one of them shewd us the body of that noble fabrique which indeed for its Cupola, pavings, incrustations of marble; the Pulpit, Altars (especially the high-Altar) Organ, Lavatorium, &c. but above all the richly carvd, and incomparable front, I esteeme for one of the most perfect pieces of Architecture in Europ, emulating even some of the greatest now at Rome it selfe.[66]

He was less pleased with the sermon which he heard there some years later: 'I heard a Jesuite preach (at their Greate & magnificent Church) on their patron Xaveriu's day, on I. Cor: 9. 19: Eloquently shewing, how he became all things to all men, to gaine some; the chiefe discourse of his whole Sermon, was Elogies on their Saints: representing their owne patron to be one of the most flattering timeservers that ever was'.[67] Finch takes us behind the scenes to the financial problems which this building caused the Jesuits: 'The church of St. Louis of the Jesuits built by the Prince of Condé, the King and Cardinall Richlieu is a very fine structure; but Pere Barton an English Jesuit there sayes that they ow 5,000 l. English for that building which the King hath not yet payed, for which they pay use. The altar is too low there and not possible to be altered with convenience'.[68] Northleigh visited all three Jesuit establishments in Paris, accompanying his descriptions of them with appropriately sarcastic comments. In 1682 the Jesuits changed the name of their college in the Rue Saint-Jacques from 'Collège de Clermont' to 'Collège Louis-le-Grand'. Northleigh comments on this change (it will be noticed that the Latin distich was given him by a passer-by):

> The next Thing of Note is, that of their noted Society the Jesuits; who have on the front of their College in great Capitals this Inscription. *Collegium Ludovici Magni*; and these Fellows are so much his Creatures too, That they might also call themselves St.Lewis his Society instead of our Saviours, especially since they are said here or at the Town Clermont[69] to have put this Inscription but lately, and to have put out the Name of Jesus, and that of their Founder, to make room for their King's; upon which this satyrical Distich was pasted upon their portal:

> > Abstulit hinc Jesu, posuitque insignia Regis:
> > Impia gens alium non habet illa Deum.[70]

> A Papist of good Parts upon our passing by repeated me these, and seem'd to observe: That this Order, tho it has much of the King's Favour, is not much in the general Esteem of the Subjects, tho so much favour'd by the Prince: which puts me in mind of another couplet of Verses that the Wits of this Country have afforded them, and as biting a Satyr.

> > Arcum Nola dedit Patribus, dedit Alma sagittam
> > Gallia; quis funem quem meruere dabit?[71]

Northleigh then moved on to the professed house in the Rue St. Antoine of which he writes: 'They have another Foundation in the Rue St. Antoin for those good Fathers, that in all Governments do the greatest hurt; and this is indeed dedicated to their old S.Lewis, as the former wholy devoted to this present new one; This their Church is a good magnificent Pile after the modern manner; Cardinal Richelieu carried on this work under Lewis XIII as appears in Capitals on the Front'. His account of a visit to the noviciate, the third Jesuit establishment in Paris, is introduced by the words 'Another foundation of this Order, and another too much'.

In his account of the Jesuits in Paris Northleigh does refer to Fathers Rapin and Bouhours (the latter's name being printed as 'Boucheurs') as 'good writers'.[72] During his visit to France in 1683, Burnet tells us, 'I was carried by a Bishop to the Jesuites at St.Anthoine's. There I saw P. Bourdaloue, esteemed one of the greatest preachers of the age, and one of the honours of his order. He was a man of sweet temper, not at all violent against Protestants: On the contrary, he believed good men among them might be saved, which was a pitch in charity that I had never observed in any of the learned of that Communion'. Burnet was much less favourably impressed by another Jesuit whom he met: 'I was also once with P. de la Chaise, the King's Confessor, who was a dry man. He told me, how great a man they would make me, if I would come over to them'.[73]

Apart from their important activities in the educational field[74] we learn little from our travellers about the Jesuits in the provinces except in Lauder's journal. He visited their college in Orleans and tells us that he 'discoursed with the praefectus Jesuitarum, who earnestly enquiring of what Religion I was, for a long tyme I would give him no other answer but that I was religione christianus. He pressing that he smeled I was a Calvinist, I replied that we regarded not these names of Calvin, Luther, Zuinglius, yea not their very persons, but in whow far they held the truth. After much discourse on indifferent matters, at our parting he desired me to search the spirits, etc'.[75]

Lauder, no doubt well trained in Scotland in listening to sermons, records (with his own comments) no fewer than three delivered by a Jesuit in Poitiers. The first of these was preached soon after his arrival there in July 1665:

> About 8 dayes after I had bein in Poictiers was keipt be the Jesuits Ignatius Loyola their founders day, whence in the Jesuits Church their was preaching a fellow that usually preaches, extolling their patron above the wery skies; evicting whow that he utstripped infinitly the founders of all other orders, let it be St. François, St.Dominick, or be who he will, by reason that he founded a order to the universal good of Christendome; the order not being tyed to one place, as other religious are, but much given to travelling up and doune the world for the conversion of souls, which truly may be given as a reason whey all that order are usually so experimented and learned; for their are of them in Americk itselfe. From all this he concluded that Ignatius was and might deservedly be named the universall Apostle of the Christian World. He showed also the manner of his conversion to that manner of life; whow he had bein a soger (he was a Spaniard by nation) til his 36 or 40 year of age. One tyme in a battell he had receaved a wound right dangerous, during the cure of this wound one tyme being somewhat veary and pained he called for a Story or Romance. They having none their, some brought a devot book termed the Saints Rest, not that of Baxters; in which he began to read with a sort of pleasure, but without any touch. At lenth continuing he began to feel himselfe sensibly touched, which wrought so that he wholly became a new man; and with the permission and confirmation of the Pope then instituted the order.

On 15 August he heard another Jesuit sermon, this time for the feast of the Assumption. Like other travellers from this side of the Channel, Lauder was struck by the violent gestures used by French preachers, and having in the meantime seen performances by strolling players,[76] he makes some obvious comparisons:

> I went and heard the Jesuite preach, a very learned fellow, but turbulent, spurred and hotbrained; affecting strange gestures in his delivery mor beseiming a Comoedian than a pulpit man. Truly ever since in seing the Comoedians act I think I sy him. He having signed himselfe, using the words *In nomine patris, filii*, etc., and parfaited all the other ceremonies we mentioned already he began to preach. The text was out of some part of Esay, thus, *Et sepulcrum ipsius erat gloriosum*. He branched out his following discourse unto 2:–1. the Virgines Death; 2. hir assumption. As to hir death he sayd she neided not have undergoon it but give she liked, since death is the wages of sin, *mais Nostre Dame estoit affranchie de toutes sorte de peché, soit originell, soit actuell*. In hir death he fand 3 priviledges she had above all others: first she died most voluntaryly, Willingly, and gladly; when to the most of men Death's a king of terrors. 2ndly, she died of no sickness, frie of all pain, languor or angoisse. 3dly, hir body after death was not capable of corruption, since its absurd to think that that holy body, which caried the Lord of Glory 9 moneths, layes under the laws of corruption. For thir privilegdes he cited Jean Damascen and their pope Victor. But it was no wonder she putrified no, for she was not 3 dayes in the grave (as he related to us) when she was assumed in great pomp, soul and body, unto heaven, Christ meiting hir at heavens port and welcoming hir.
>
> He spoke much to establish monstrous merite; laying doune for a principle that she had only merited heaven, and indeed the first place their, being the princess of heaven: but also had supererogated by hir work for others to make them merit, which works the church had in its treasury to sell at mister.[76a] He made heaven also *a vendre* (as it is indeed amongs them), but taking himselfe and finding the expression beastly and mercenarie he began to speir, but whow is it to sell, is it not for your *bonnes oeuvres*, your penances, repentances, etc. This was part of his sermon.

On the feast of the Virgin's birth (8 September) he returned once more to hear the same preacher:

> I went and heard our Comoedian the Jesuit preach hir panegyrick, and his oune valedictory Sermon (for they preach 12 moneth about, and he had ended his tower). He would have had us believing that she was cleansed from the very womb from that wery sin which all others are born with, that at the moment of hir conception she receaved a immense degrie of grace infused in her. If he ware to draw the Horoscope of all others that are born he would decipher it thus, thou sal be born to

misery, angoiss, trouble and vexation of spirit, which, on the wery first entering into this walley of tears, because thou cannot tell it with they tongue, thou sal signify by the weiping. But if I ware, says he, to cast our charming Ladies Horoscope I would have ascertained then, that she was born for the exaltation of many, that she [was] born to bear the only sone of God, etc.

The sone he brought in as the embleme of Justice ever minding his father of his bloody death and sufferings, to the effect that he take vengeance for it even on these that crucifies him afresh. The mother he brought on the stage as the embleme of mercy, crying imperiously, *jure matris*, I inhibite your justice, I discharge your severity. Let mercy alone triumph. Surely if this be not blasphemy I know not whats blasphemie. To make Christ only Justice fights diamettrally with the Aposle John. If any man hath sinned he has a Advocat with the father. Christ the righteous, he sayes, is not Christ minding his father continually of this passion; its true, but whey; to incite God to wrath, sayes he. O wicked inference, horrid to come out of the mouth of any Christian save only a Jesuite. Does not the Scripture language cut thy throat, O prophane, which teaches us that Christ offereth up to his father his sufferings as a propitiatory sacrifice; and consequently to appaise, not to irritate.

His inference at lenth was this: since the business is thus then, Messieurs, Mesdames, mon cher Auditoire, yeel do weill in all occassion to make your address to the Virgin, to invock hir, yea definitivly I assert that if any of you have any lawfull request if yeel but pray 30 dayes togither once every day to the Virgin ye sal without faill obtain what you desire. On whilk decision I suppose a man love infinitely a woman who is most averse from him, if he follow this rule he sall obtaine hir. But who sies not except thess that are voluntary blind whow rash, inconsiderat, and illgrounded thir decisions are, and principally that of invocking the Virgin, since without doubt its a injury to Christ, whom we believe following the Scripture to be the only one Mediator betwixt God and Man. Also, I find Christ calling us to come to him, but never to his mother or to Peter or Paul.[77]

Though Lauder's summaries of the sermons he heard are far from objective, they do give some idea of the content of those preached by a French Jesuit in the 1660s.

Most of our travellers attended Catholic services, either on Sundays or on other occasions. Coryate, for instance, on his arrival at Calais went to a Whit Sunday service and he has some strong comments to make on what he observed:

There are two Churches in this towne, to the greatest whereof I went on Whitsun-day, where I saw their Masse (but not with that superstitious geniculation, and elevation of hands at the lifting up of their consecrated Wafer-cake, that the rest used) and many ceremonies that I never saw before. This amongst the rest: about the middle of the Masse there was an extreme crackling noise from a certain hollow place in the vault of the middle of the Church. This is the same place, as I take it, where they let up and downe their Bels. After the noyse there was powred downe a great deale of water, immediately after the water ensued a great multitude of Wafer-cakes, both white, redde and yellow; which ceremony was done to put them in minde of the cloven tongues, that appeared that day of Pentecost to the Apostles in Hierusalem. Here I observed a great prophenation of the Lords supper, committed by their irreligious ἀρἰολατρεἱα which in steed of Christ doth worship the God Maozim.[77a] Also I saw their mutilated Sacrament, whereof I much heard before. For I saw the Priest minister the Sacrament to the lay people under one kind only, namely that of bread, defrauding them of the Wine, contrary to the holy institution of Christ and his Apostles, and the auncient practise of the Primitive Church ...

The high Priest being in very rich copes, went abroad in Procession round about the Church-yard, after one of their Masses was done (for that day many Masses were said in the Church) having a rich silver Crosse carried before him, and acompanied with many that carried silke banners and flags after a very Ethnicall and prophane pompe.[78]

While waiting for an opportunity to leave Calais for Dover, Kennet describes what happened there on All Saints Day: 'This festivall of all Saints celebrated with lighted candles in the church & the ringing of bells the whole night. A custom for dying persons to impose their surviving friends the task of procuring so many pair of penitentiall psalms to be said successively for so many years on this day, which piece of devotion is performed by boys who run about the church in quest of customers who give 1 penny or more & name the person for whome the psalms are to be repeated'.[79]

Edward Browne describes a service which he attended at Notre Dame on the Whit Sunday he was in Paris:

After Dinner I went to Nostre Dame to Vespres, where the Archbishop of Paris was present. Hee had his mitre on and his Coape; he was led in by two, his footboy following him; his Cross and Crosier were carried before him. Hee had red gloves on, and a ring upon the fore finger of his right hand, in which was set an Agurmarine the largest I ever saw. When hee gave the blessing, hee made a crosse three severall wayes. Upon the Altar were huge silver Candlesticks and a silver crucifix. The whole manner of the service and the many ceremonies would be too tedious to recite.[80]

Like Lauder, Locke was obviously struck by the violent gestures employed by Catholic preachers when he speaks of a friar preaching in Carcassonne cathedral 'with great action'.[81] Lister too makes the same remark about a service which he attended during Lent at La Charité. While he concedes that the preacher 'had many good Arguments about the necessity of Grace, and the means to attain it', he disapproved of both the preacher's delivery and of the language he used:

> I was strangely surprised at the Vehemency of his Action, which to me appeared altogether Comical, and like the Actors upon the Stage, which I had seen a few days before: Besides, his Expressions seemed to be in too Familiar a Style: I always took a Sermon to the People to require a grave and ornate kind of Eloquence, and not *Verba Quotidiana*, with a certain dignity of Action; but 'tis possible this way here best suits with the Customs and Manners of the People; who are all Motion, even when they say the easiest and most intelligible Things.[82]

No doubt there was a difference between the style of the ordinary sermon and the high flown eloquence of, say, Bossuet's funeral orations.

Lauder offers an interesting account of such an oration, that for Anne of Austria, at which he was present in Poitiers:

> A little after was the Queen Mothers panegyrick or *funebre oraison* made at St. Pierre in a prodigious confluence of people of al ranks; the Intendant, the President and the Conseillers, the Mair, the Eschiwines, and the Maison de Ville assisting; also many of the religious orders. The Cordelier who preached the Advent before and the careme after made the harangue. He deduced hir glory and commendation, 1^0, from that she was Anne of Austria, which is the province in which standes Vienne, the Metropolis of Germany; that she was Philip the 3d of Spaines daughter; next that she was Queen or wife to Lewis the Just, 13 of that name in France; 3dly that she was mother to Lewis the 14th, so hopeful a Prince, after she had bein 23 years barren. Whence he took occasion to show that the virginity and coelebat was very commendable, yet that it was no wayes so in the succession to crounes. He had also heir a senseless gasconad which nobody approved of, that St. Gregorie sould say that as far as Kings are exalted above other men, that in so far the Kings of France ware above al other Kings. In the 4th place he fand a large elogium to hir in that she falling widdow she becam Regent of hir sone and the Realme during his minority. Hir last and principal commendation was that she was a Princesse most devot and religious.[83]

Heylyn was struck by one curious custom — that of churches bearing special marks of mourning for a nobleman. Of the town of Arpajon (then known as 'Châtres' which he gives as 'Castres') he writes: 'Nothing else remarkable in it, but the habit of the Church, which was mourning: for such is the fashion of France, that when any of the Nobles are buried, the Church which entombeth them is painted black within and without, for the breadth of a yard, or thereabouts; and their Coats of Armes drawn on it. To go to the charges of hanging it round with cloth is not for their profits: besides, the counterfeit sorrow feareth no theef; and dareth out-brave a tempest'. He adds: 'The like Funeral Churches, I saw also at Tostes in Normandye; and in a village of Picardie, whose name I minde not'.[84] Lister was also struck by this custom: 'I saw in some Country Towns near Paris, the Church Wall near the Top, had a two foot broad Mourning List, which compassed the whole Church like a Girdle, and on this was at certain distances, painted the Arms of the Lord of the Manner, who was dead'.[85] The practice was finally swept away by the Revolution along with other honorific rights of the nobility.

Even if, while in France, our travellers had never set foot in a church, they would none the less have encountered Catholicism on the streets in the processions made on Church festivals. Those for Corpus Christi day, in both Paris and various provincial towns, naturally drew their attention. Coryate, for instance, met the procession as it emerged from Notre Dame:

> No sooner did I enter into the Church but a great company of Clergy men came forth singing, and so continued all the time of the procession, till they returned unto the Church againe, some by couples, and some single. They walked partly in coapes, whereof some were exceeding rich, being (in my estimation) worth at least a hundred markes a peece; and partly in surplices. Also in the same traine there were many couples of little singing choristers ... The last man of the whole traine was the Bishop of Paris,[86] a proper and comly man as any I saw in all the city of some five and thirty yeares old. He walked not *sub dio*, that is, under the open aire, as the rest did. But he had a rich canopy carried over him, supported with many little pillers on both sides. This did the Priests carry; he himselfe was that day in his sumptuous Pontificalities, wearing religious ornaments of great price, like a second Aaron, with his Episcopall staffe in his hand, bending round at the toppe, called by us English men a Crosier, and his Miter on his head of cloth of silver, with two long labels hanging downe behind his neck. As for the streets of Paris they were more sumptuously adorned that day then any other day of the whole yeare, every street of speciall note being on both sides

thereof, from the pentices of their houses to the lower end of the wall hanged with rich cloth of arras, and the costliest tapistry that they could provide. The shewes of our Lady street being so hyperbolical in pomp that day, that it exceeded the rest by many degrees. And for the greater addition of ornament to this feast of God, they garnished many of their streets with as rich cupboords of plate as ever I saw in my life. For they exposed upon their publique tables exceeding costly goblets, and what not tending to pompe, that is called by the name of plate. Upon the middest of their tables stood their golden Crucifixes, with divers other gorgeous Images. Likewise in many places of the city I observed hard by those cupboords of plate, certaine artificiall rocks, most curiously contrived by the very quintessence of arte, with fine water spowting out of the cocks, mosse growing thereon, and little sandy stones proper unto rockes such as we call in Latin *tophi*: Wherefore the foresaid sacred company , perambulating about some of the principall streets of Paris, especially our Lady street, were entertained with most divine honours. For whereas the Bishop carried the Sacrament, even his consecrated wafer cake, betwixt the Images of two golden Angels, whensoever he passed by any company, all the spectators prostrated themselves most humbly upon their knees, and elevated their handes with all possible reverence and religious behaviour, attributing as much divine adoration to the little wafer cakes, which they call the Sacrament of the Altar, as they could doe to Jesus Christ himselfe, if he were bodily present with them.[86]

Coryate remarks that there were dangers for any Protestants who happened to be in the streets at such a moment: 'If any Godly Protestant that hateth this superstition, should happen to be amongst them when they kneele, and forbeare to worship the Sacrament as they doe, perhaps he may be presently stabbed or otherwise most shamefully abused, if there should be notice taken of him'.[87]

Other travellers who were in Paris for Corpus Christ day provide rather briefer, but none the less interesting accounts of the processions. Thus Evelyn writes: 'There was this day a grand Procession, all the streetes tappissri'd: & severall Altars erected in the Streetes, full of Images & other rich furniture, especially that befor the Court, of a rare designe & Architecture: There were abundance of excellent Pictures, & huge Vasas of silver'.[88] Edward Browne offers his version of what Paris looked like on such an occasion:

> The streets were stroud with hearbs, the houses hang'd with Tapistry, and in some Places the Streets canopied for a good way together as you walked, most delightfully. At the Palais

d'Orleans were Good Hangings. But none so rich, so large, or so fine as those of Hostel de Condy. I saw divers processions; that of the Cordeliers and one which Passed by whilst I was looking on the Hanging in Rüe de Condy, were the greatest, and indeed did make a noble show with their Singing, and the Infinite numbers of People which followed. In Hostel de Condy stood a very noble Altar.[89]

Similar processions for this festival were observed in the provinces. At Tours, for instance, Evelyn saw 'a goodly Procession of all the Religious Orders, the whole streetes hung with their best Tappissrys, and most precious moveables expos'd, silkes, Damasks, Velvets, Plate & Pictures in abundance, the Streets strew'd with flowres, and full of pageantry, banners & bravery'.[90] While he was at Orleans on his way to Poitiers Lauder noted the problems which such celebrations posed for Huguenots: 'Such is the fury of the blinded papists, the Hugonots are in very great hazard if they come out, for if they kneel not at the coming by of the Hosty or Sacrament they cannot escape to be torn in peices'. From his account of what he saw there emerges another difficulty faced by Protestants:

> The most part of all the city was hung with tapistry, especially the principall street which goes straight from one end of the toune to the other, which also was covered all above in some parts with hingings, in other with sheits according to the ability of the persones; for every man was obliged to hing over against his oune house, yet the protestants ware not, tho John Ogilvy[91] was also called before the Judges for not doing it; yet producing a playdoyes in the Hugonets faveurs they had nothing to say against it; yet they caused the wals of his house to be hung with publick hingings that belonged to the toune. For to sy the procession I went with the other pensioners to a place wheir when all others went to the knees, to wit, when the Hosty came by, we might retire out of sight. I retired not so far as they did, but boldly stood at a little distance that I aen might sy it the better.[92]

A detailed account of the procession at Montpellier is provided by Locke:

> The day being, as they call it, Feste Dieu, the Host was carried about the town by the Bishop, the canopy over it carried by the 6 Consuls. Several companys of tradesmen, each with a banner wherein was a picture of their saint and some tools of their trade before them. After each banner followed a piper, or fiddlers played before them all the way, and after the musick followed a thing like a garland dresed up fine with heron's plumes etc., and after this company thus went all the companys, each with its

banner, musick and garland, each garland having also cakes of
bread about it. After the companys marchd the severall orders
of Friers, each with a cross before them. There were no Jesuits
who, it seems, never use to assist at such occasions. After the
friars followed a great many little boys in blue frocks with great
white flambeaux lighted. After them the Chainons of St. Peter's
here in their surplices who sung. Then came the Bishop and the
Host, 2 in surplices going by it, one each side, with censors in
their hands, every now and then incensing it. After the Host
followed Praesidents, Intendants, Conseilers, Treasurers,
proctors and other officers in their robes with lighted tapers in
their hands, and after all a crowd of people, tradesmen of
company and caried lighted tapers. In this order they set out for
St. Piere's church, and so, fetching compasse through several
streets of the town, returnd thither again, the streets all hung
where they passed.

Locke rounds off this entry with a characteristic observation: 'This
is the most solemn procession of the year, but if one judge either by
the habits of the tradesmen or the hangings of the streets which were
in many places blankets & coverlids, one is apt to think that either
their fortunes or devotions were very scanty'.[93]

Not all our travellers were as determined not to be impressed with
what they saw in the provinces at this festival. Ferrier, for instance,
obviously enjoyed the spectacle at Lyons:

We saw on the Feste Dieu . . . the great procession which is
constantly every year made on that Feast: first there went four
or five thousand men, each one carrying a lamp in his hand, next
went the Priests in their surplices singing as they passed, two of
the last of them cast Incense before the host which after was
carried by a Priest under a Canopy supported by four more;
after them went almost as many men as there were before; it
shew very finely & that which added to its setting forth were the
streets, which were hung & adorned with Altars and Crucifices.

It should be added that Ferrier was not always enthusiastic about
the Catholic processions which he saw. Earlier in Paris, he relates, 'we
met with a great procession of Priests who carried the thigh of Saint
Honoré which the Pope had sent thither, it cost a hundred thousand
livers, it delivers all women from their pains when they pray to it, &
does many more miracles which I have now forgotten'.[94]

Our travellers witnessed various other religious processions
besides those on Corpus Christi day. Somewhat surprisingly Heylyn
almost approved of a procession which he saw at Boulogne — one for
deliverance from the plague:

But that which made this low Town[95] most pleasing to me, was a solemn procession that passed through the streets of it, intending to pacifie Gods anger, and divert the plague, which at that time was in the City. In the first front there was carried the Crosse, and after that the only or sanctified Banner; next unto it followed all the Priests of the Town bare-headed and in their Surplices, singing as they went the Services destinate to that occasion. After them followed the men, and next to them the women of the Town, by two and two, it being so ordered by the Roman Rituall, *Ut laici a clericie, foeminae a viris prosequantur separatae*. On the other side of the street went the Brethren *De la Charitè*, every one of them holding in his hand a little triangular Banner, or, a Pennon;[96] after them the boys and wenches. In this method did they measure solemnly every lane and angle of the Town; the Priests singing, and all the People answering them in the same note. At the Church they began it with prayers, and having visited all the Town, they returned again thither to end it with the same devotion. An action very grave and solemn, and such as I could well allow of, were it not only for one prayer which is alwayes said at the time of this performance, and the addition of the Banners.[97]

The prayer which offended him was one for the intercession of the Virgin, St.Sebastian ('their Æsculapius or tutelary Saint against Sicknesse') and all saints.

Though apparently objective, Locke's descriptions of other processions which he saw in the South of France are clearly unsympathetic. After visiting Aix-en-Provence, he made the following entry in his journal:

Aix, whilst we were there, was fild those 2 days with processions of the villages round about, the Archbishop, Cardinal Grimaldi, having obtaind of the Pope the benefit of the last year's Jubilee to his diocesse, which they are to receive upon processions, soe that the whole towns come in these processions, scarce leaving people enough to look to their houses. From Brignole there will come 4,000. Some parishes come ten leagues, & severall of them in the processions walke bare foot with banners fild with pictures of Our Saviour, the Virgin & other saints, statues of saints & heads in silver, etc. & soe march through the streets with lighted tapers in their hands, 2 & 2, great numbers of them clad as Penitens Noirs, Blancs & Gris, etc.

The *pénitens* were members of *confréries* which flourished in the South. Back in Montpellier, Locke observed another religious procession on the Wednesday of Rogation Week:

To-day went by a large procession of severall orders of friers, litle children dressed up fine & carying litle banners by some of the crosses, & after the friers, following among the adults, a great company of children, some walking, some carried, dressed up to their best abilitys & hung about with little pictures, etc. This is Rogation weeke & for a blessing on the fruits of the earth, which, though the children cannot pray for, yet the prayers being made in their names & offerd up as from them by the parents or friends of these innocents, they think they will be more prevalent.[98]

The sceptical detachment of these entries is not always to be found in Locke's comments on Catholicism.

Lauder has a characteristically pungent comment to make on the practice which he observed in Poitiers of sprinkling houses with holy water on the eve of the principal Church festivals:

The day before great fests, as *les Roys*, *Toussaints*, etc., their fellows that with white surplices and a pigful of holy water with a spung in it goes thorow al the Catholick houses be-sprinkling the persons as also the house, and so sanctifieing them that the Dewill dare not enter their; passing by the Protestants houses as infected; or rather, as the Angel who smote the first born of the Egyptians past the Israelits. At *Toussaints* al are in their best cloaths.[99]

Relics and the miracles associated with them are one aspect of Catholicism in seventeenth-century France on which practically all our travellers comment scathingly. Lassels as a Catholic priest naturally offers a very different account of the shrine at St.Maximin from that given by Protestant travellers. He writes: 'Neare to Saincte Beaume stands the towne of S.Maximin famous for the Church of S.Maximin governed by Dominican Fryers: In this Church are to be seen many famous Relicks of S.Mary Magdalen; as her head in a Chrystal case enchased in gold: her body in a guilt *chasse*; and divers other rich things'.[100] Somewhat surprisingly Locke does not apply his usual sarcastic treatment to these particular relics although he devotes a short entry to them;[101] but a few years later John Buxton writes of what he saw with obvious scepticism:

Being enterd, this friar and another fall on their kness for some time before a cupboard to say (as I guess) a prayer, then they open the cupboard and after that mumble something and then pull forth the head of Mary Madgalen, silver and gilt chased, beset with jewels of great price. Opening this silver head or case they take out the true head or skull as they say of Mary Magdalen, which is enclosed in a glass; on the forehead of the skull is a long spot of a different colour from the skull which they say is the flesh and skin of Mary uncorrupted, also there seems to be something about the nose which they say is the flesh too, and the reason, that our Saviour when he said to Mary 'touch me not' laid his hand on her face, his thumb [on this] part and finger on the other, which parts are not consumed. They showed us a glass in which they said was a little of Christ's blood which Mary picked off the ground and never would part with it whilst she lived, this blood (as they say) boils up every Good Friday. Her tomb was there likewise, but not her body, for having given some parts to other churches, the dust left they took up and put in an urn. They also showed the arm of St. Maximin in gold, also his tomb, etc.

And in another little chapel of the same church was an arm of Mary Magdalen, and a very long one it was, without doubt she was a proper woman, for it was much longer than the friar's, who was a tall man; there was the head of the woman who said 'blessed is the womb that bare thee', this it seems was Martha's maid. Also the head of the woman who touched our Saviour's garments and was cured of the bloody issue. Also the hearts of two innocents murdered by Herod, and the man's head that had his eyes and sight restored when He spat on the ground and made the clay.

This was the Eve of Mary Magdalen's Day, the next day therefore these things were to be carried in procession.[102]

The tone of this passage is fairly typical of those written by our travellers on this subject.

As the Abbey of St.Denis could easily be visited either on their way to Paris or while they were staying there, both its saint and its relics receive a good deal of attention. Evelyn called in on his way to Paris and reports how on the last part of the journey he observed 'divers faire Crosses of stone erected, and carv'd with flower de Lyces, at every furlong's end, where they affirme St.Denys rested, and layd downe his head after Martyrdome, carrying it from the Place where this Monastery is builded'. In his tour of the abbey he was shown an amazing number of relics:

> In a Tabernacle of Silver gilded is shew'd a pretended naile of the real Crucifix, this is supported by an Angel, and in a box of Gold full of precious stones. There is likewise a greate Crosse of Silver garnish'd with jewells, and a multitude of other Crosses full of Reliques which I had not time to take notice of: A Crucifix of the true Wood of the Crosse carved by Pope Clement the 3d which was inchas'd in a Chrystal coverd with Gold . . . A Box wherein is preserv'd some of the B:Virgins haire, also her Image in Silver guilt, bestudded with faire stones; another where she holds a box of Chrystal in which lyes some of the Linnen our B: Saviour was envelop'd in at his Nativity . . .Then they brought out a huge Reliquary model'd like a Church of rare

workemanship, in this he shew'd us some thing staind red, which
the Father would have us believe was of the natural blood of our
Saviour, as also some of his haire, Cloaths, Linnen with which he
wip'd the Apostles feete: Something of the Crowne of Thornes,
a piece of the Sponge, of the Title, all these in Chrystal'd, &
Phiols set in gold: In another faire Reliquary coverd also with
Chrystal, he expos'd some of the B: Virgins milke; with other
Sacred toys.[103]

And so the list of relics continues. Other travellers express
themselves more pungently on what they were shown at St.Denis.
Heylyn, for instance, waxes sarcastic about 'the Lanthorn which
Judas used when he went to apprehend his Master': 'A pretty one it is
(I confesse) richly beset with studdes of Crystall, through which all
the light cometh; the main of it being of a substance not transparent.
Had it been shewed me within the first century of years after the
passion, I might, perhaps, have been fooled into a belief; for I am
confident that it can be no older. Being as it is, I will acknowledge it to
be a Lanthorn, though it belonged not to Judas'.

In Paris Heylyn greatly admired the stained glass of the Sainte
Chapelle, but he speaks scathingly of the relics which were exhibited
there:

> I was there divers times to have seen them, but (it seemeth)
> they were not visible to an Hugonots eyes; though me thinketh,
> they might have considered, that my money was Catholique.
> They are kept, as I said, in the lower Chappell, and are thus
> marshalled in a Table, hanging in the upper; know then you may
> believe that they can shew you the crown of thornes, the bloud
> which ran from our Saviours brest, his swadling cloutes, a great
> part of the Crosse (they also of Nostre dame have some of it),
> the chaine by which the Jewes bound him, no small peece of the
> the stone of the Sepulchre, *Sanctamtoelam tabulae insertam*,
> which I know not how to English. Some of the Virgins milke,
> (for I would not have those of St.Denis think, that the Virgin
> gave no other milk, but to them) the head of the Lance which
> pierced our Saviour, the purple Robe, the Sponge, a piece of his
> Shroud, the napkin wherewith he was girted when he washed his
> Disciples feet, the rod of Moses, the heads of St.Blase,
> St.Clement, and St.Simeon, and part of the head of John
> Baptist.

He sums up his view of all these relics in the words — 'venerable
ones I durst say they were, could I be perswaded there were no
imposture in them', and, after quoting two of the Fathers,
St.Ambrose and St.Jerome, on the subject, he asks: 'Had they lived in
our times, and seen the supposed remnants of the Saints, not

honoured only, but adored and worshipped by their blind and infatuated people; what would they have said? or rather, what would they not have said?'[104]

Our travellers did not have to wait until they arrived in the Paris region to encounter relics and miracles. When Skippon and Ray landed at Calais, they visited the Minims' convent where, Skippon relates, they were shown 'a piece of our Saviour's cross brought out of England, and a piece of the spunge us'd at the passion'. Before this, he writes,

> we saw a poor maid in the church, who (they say) was three years before miraculously cured of a palsy and asthma in a quarter of an hour's time, by praying before St.Francis his picture, she herself telling us that she was thus suddenly restor'd to her health and use of her limbs, after she had been four years distemper'd; her picture hangs up there, praying to that saint, and underneath are her crutches. And we also observ'd a great many legs, arms, hearts, &c of wax, being resemblances of such parts as were cur'd.[105]

In other parts of France our travellers made similar notes on what they saw. Thomas Browne visited Chartres cathedral (he describes it as a 'magnificent piece of antiquity') and went to the treasury

> where, in a box adorned with diamonds and precious stones, crosses and such like, is said to be the shift or smock of the Virgin Mary, remarkable for many miracles; namely for miraculously causing Rollo, duke of Normandy, not only to raise his siege, but also to change his religion. There is also a phial, in which they hold that there is the milk of Our Lady; and that they also have the flesh, bones, teeth, and hair, and innumerable reliques of Romish saints. We had the favor to touch the *Chemise de Chartres* in a small silver box made in the fashion of Our Lady's shift.[106]

Several travellers commented on the relics in Angers cathedral, though none as fully or as sarcastically as Locke:

> We saw also at St.Maurice, the Cathedral of Angers, aboundance of reliques, the tooth of one Saint, the bone of another, etc. whose names I have quite forgotten as well as he had, of some of them, that shewd them us, though they were his old acquaintance, but it served our turns as well when he put St. Martin for St.Moril; but the things of most veneration were a thorn of the crown of Our Saviour, some wood of his crosse which I beleive was there, though I saw noe thing but the gold & silver that coverd it. There was also some of the haire, a peice of the petticoat & some of the milke of the Virgin, but the milk was out of sight; and one of the water pots wherein Our Saviour

turnd water into wine. That which made this morcell pretty hard of digestion was that it was porphyre, a sort of furniture a litle to costly for the good man of the house where the weding was kept, & which made it yet worse, was a face in demy releive on that side that stood outwards, a way of ornament not much in use among the Jews. However, I could not but wish for the pot because of its admirable effects to cure diseases, for once a yeare they put wine into it, consecrate it & distribute it to beleivers, who there with cure feavers & other diseases.[107]

The church of Notre Dame des Ardilliers at Saumur, a famous place of pilgrimage because of the miraculous cures wrought there, attracted the attention of several of our travellers. Reresby describes it 'as a place of great devotion, for the cures she is cried up to do the lame and diseased, which leads many a blind man to see miracles'. 'In the church', he adds, 'hang up arms, legs, and almost all sorts of members, in white wax, which they tell you such persons as came indisposed into those parts, and returned sound from this pilgrimage, left behind them, in commemoration of their cures'.[108] Thirty years later Ferrier visited the same church where the Virgin, as he puts it, 'is worshipped & dos work a great many more miracles than ever our Saviour did in curing all sorts of distempers'.[109]

Travellers who visited the Benedictine monastery at Marmoutier near Tours were not impressed by the relics they were shown. The Calvinist, John Lauder, who had never seen relics before, treats the whole subject with scorn:

> Their we saw the heart of Benedictus, the founder of their order, enclosed in a crystall and besett with diamonds most curiously. We of our company, being 6, were all of the religion.[110] whence we had no great respect for the relict, but their ware som others their that ware papists; who forsooth bit to sit doune on their knees and kist. At which I could not contein my selfe from laughing.
>
> Their saw we also a great number of relicts of one St. Martin. They had his scull enclosed (give his scull and not of some theife it may be) in a bowl of beaten silver.[111]

Clenche relates with heavy irony the pious legends told him in this monastery:

> Marmoustier. A Large Abby, wherein is kept the *St.Ampoule*, that anointed Henry the Fourth; it ebbs and flows with the Moon, and was sent from heaven to cure St. Martins legg, which the Devil made him break, by stealing away the Stair-case from his Chamber (now a pretty Marble Chappel on the side of the Church); they also show a vast Tunn wherein he kept his Wine, which probably was the Fiend that stole away the Stairs.[112]

During his stay at Poitiers Lauder visited a great many churches, including that of St. Radegund. He went there to see that saint's tomb on 14 August, her day, but, he writes, 'we had a difficulty of accez, such multitude was their dronning over their prayers, *Sainte Radegonde, Radegonde, priez pour nous et nos ames*, and this 100 tymes over, at each tyme kissing the sepulchre stone which standes reasonably hy. From this, we went to hir Chappell that stands besydes the Church of St.Croix, to sy the impression that Christ left with his foot (so sottish is their delusion) on a hard great stone when he appeared to Ste. Radegonde as she was praying at that stone'. Continuing his tour of churches, Lauder moved on to the Église Ste.Croix where, as he and his companion were entering, they met '2 women leading a young lass about the Age of 18 who appeared evidently to be distracted or possessed by some Dewill, by hir horrid looks, hir antick gestures, and hir strange gapes: hir they had had in the Church and had caused hir kneel, they praying before the Altar for hir to Ste.Radegonde, whom they believed had the power to cure her'. Here the Scottish youth clashed with a devout Catholic woman:

> Having entred the Church, standing and looking earnestly about to al the corners of the church, and particularly to the Altar, which was wery fine, with as great gravity as at any tyme, a woman of faschion on hir knees (for indeed all that ware in the Church ware on their knees but my selfe) fixing hir eyes upon me and observing that I nether had gone to the font for water, nether kneelled, in a great heat of zeal she told me, *ne venez icy pour prophaner ce sainct lieu.* I suddenly replied, *Vous estez bien devotieuse, Madame; mais peut estre Votre ignorance prophane ce sainct lieu d'avantage que ma presence.* This being spoken in the audience of severals, and amongs others of a preist, I conceived it would not be my worst to retire, which I did.[113]

No doubt, given the attitude of the mass of French Catholics towards Protestants in the 1660s, he was wise to beat a retreat.

Awkward incidents of this kind could arise when relics were shown as Locke recounts when he visited Tarascon where, according to his guide book, the head of St.Martha was preserved in the principal church:

> All the other Saints we had made visits to, received us very civily & allowed time to our curiosity to survey them, but St. Martha allowd us but a short apparition. For the priest that shewd us these sacred things, first producing the arme in silver guilt, the fingers whereof were loaden with rings with stones of value on them, & holding it out to us, & discoursing upon it, but findeing we paid not that reverence was expected, he approachd it very neare the mouth of one of the company & told him again

that the bones that appeared through the cristal were the bones of St.Martha, which not prevailing with the hardened heretick for a kisse, he turned about in fury, put it up in the cubbard, drew the curtain before all the other things, & with the same quicknesse he that had refused to kisse, turnd about, went his way, & the rest followd him.

On both his visits to Toulouse Locke comments sarcastically on the relics in one of the churches. On the first occasion he wrote: 'At the Church of St. Sernin they tell us they have the bodies entire of 6 of the Apostles and the head of a 7th. This is much, considering what need there is of such reliques in other places, but yet notwithstanding they promise you 7 of the 12 Apostles . . .We saw not these Apostles, but being told by a spiritual guide of the infalible church, we believed, which was enough for us'. Eighteen months later he mentions that he had seen the relics, adding: 'We were told of the wonders these & other reliques have donne, being caried in procession, & espetially the head of St.Edward, one of our Kings of England, which caried in procession, deliverd the town from a plague some years since'.[114]

Visitors to Marseilles mention the relics which they saw there. Mortoft, for instance, visited the old cathedral, now disused: 'There is a very fine Church in this City, of which they say Lazarus was Bishop, where they have his Image all of silver and many Reliquez, as two of the stones that put to death St.Stephen, and a piece of linen that was wound about the dead Body of Christ, and twenty such things which they keepe with much ceremony and respect'. He also visited the Abbaye St.Victor: 'Over against the Port, on the other side of the water, is the Church of St.Victor, where his head is kept, And made of silver and gilded over, weighing six hundred pound weight, with many other Reliques and curiosityes which are there to be seen'.[115]

In contrast to this fairly objective account of what he saw we have a somewhat more sceptical description by Veryard: 'In a subterranean Vault, they shew'd us the entire Cross of St.Andrew, the Tomb of Four of the Seven Sleepers, and a Chappel where Women are prohibited to enter, which is shut up, for the most part, since a Queen of France, presuming to go in, was, as they say, immediately struck dead'.[116] Buxton adopts an even more sceptical tone:

In the church, they showed us a grot wherein lay a figure representing Mary Magdalen as if alive, that we could plainly see it from the entrance; it was about the height of a baker's oven: they say it is 500 paces long and she lived in this very grot seven years; here were likewise opened to us two cabinets or cupboards where were shown us several relics, the head of St.Vittoire, the titular Saint of the church, in a chased head of silver gilt weighing 600 libs., several heads of Bishops that were

Saints, and children that were martyrs; a thumb of Mary
Magdalen; a silver case in which is the box that did hold the
ointment shed on the head of our Saviour; a cross wherein is a
piece of the true cross; two that were martyred among the nuns
with St. Urselin, one of them being her companion. They shewd
us a stone four fingers thick which we could see the light
through; also the tomb of Pope Urbin, the saint that died at
Avignon, and by a well in the cloister they showed us some
marks in a stone pillar which they told us were the marks or
gripes of the Devil's claw.

Buxton's companion made this scepticism perfectly clear when he
insisted on cross-examining the monk who showed them the lady
chapel: 'Mr.Mole asked the priest or father if this Notre Dame did
any miracles; he answers we must believe she did, being the fourth
person in heaven and our Intercessor; M. he said that there were
several Notre Dames in several places, he therefore asked if some did
not more than other some. The father replied that some did more
then other some, but at length he began to seem a little angry'.[117]
When in Marseilles our travellers often went to visit the famous
place of pilgrimages at Ste.Baume. Mortoft is, as usual, fairly neutral
in his account of what he saw: 'There are many Religious people
belonging to this Convent, which shew to those strangers that come
many Reliques which they keepe with much ceremony; as the stones
that put St. Stephen to death, and the Markes of the Lying In of the
Virgin Mary, and the Reliques of Mary Magdaline so that it is
esteemed by all Catholickes to be one of the most famousest places
for Devotion in all France, which drawes multitudes of People on
Festival dayes to this place'.[118] When Skippon visited it a few years
later, he was obviously less impressed: 'Their church is a great cave,
where they say, S. Mary Magdalen did 33 years penance. Behind the
high alter lies a fair marble statue of that saint in a sleeping leaning
posture; for they have a tradition, that in that very place she used to
sleep, and that part of the rock was miraculously raised to serve her as
a pillow, which is constantly observed to be dry, whereas all other
parts of the cave, they say, is moist, water always distilling from the
roof'.[119] And with these observations on Ste.Baume, which is only a
few miles from St.Maximin where we started, we may conclude our
tour of the churches and monasteries visited by our travellers.
    Almost to a man Protestants, our travellers noted on their journeys
through France all sorts of features of Catholicism which were
repugnant to them. The cult of the Virgin is several times noted with
obvious disfavour by Locke, in particular during his visit to Amiens
cathedral on his journey back to England:

In Nostre Dame, the great church, over the holy water basen the left hand as one enters the west dore is this inscription:

Aqua benedicta sit nobis solus et vita
Hujus aquae factus propulset demonis actus.
Alhoneur de dieu et de la vierge mere NN. ont offert ce benistier. 1656.
Just the same on the other side.

At the next pillar the Virgin treading on a serpent & death's head with these words: Conteret caput tuum. A table hanging by with this notice: Cest image de Nostre dame de victoire a été bénite par Monsr. levesque d'Amiens 23 Sept. 1634 Lequel a concedé 40 jours de pardon a ceux et celles qui diront trois fois ave Maria devant cette image.

At the next pillar an image of the Virgin & God the Father crowning her, with these words: Trahe nos post te ...[120] suos, & a table promise 40 days' indulgence to any one who shall say before this image on their knees thrice this prayer: Mater misericordiae ora pro nobis.[121]

It was obviously from the same viewpoint that at the other end of the country, while visiting Notre Dame de la Garde at Marseilles, Buxton noted that the chapel had 'in great letters upon it, *"Virgo maria ora pro nobis"'*.[122]

The saying of masses for the dead was again a practice which did not appeal to Protestant travellers. A striking example of the repugnance this inspired is furnished by Locke:

At Angers in the Minims' church hang up several tables in brasse with the pictures buy [*sic*] of the devout women (for I saw noe men soe pious) who made the donations. On these tables of brasse are mentioned certaine masses, some to be sung, some a base voix, to be celebrated on certain days to perpetuity pour le repos de leurs ames, for the founding of which masses have been given by some £400, by others £600 & by others almost £1000, & in some 'tis pour le repos de leurs ames et de leurs parents deja decedes, and in one of them is purchased also the exposeing of the Host on certaine days. Soe that if there be any benefit to be had from these things, it is, it seems, for those who have faith & mony enough to pay for them.[123]

Clearly Locke regarded this practice simply as one of the ways in which the Catholic clergy enriched themselves.

To the majority of our travellers most French Catholics appeared extremely superstitious. Lauder is very scornful of what he saw of their attitude to thunder:

I cannot forget the effect I have sein the thunder produce in the papists. When they hear a clap coming they all wery religiously signe theyr forfronts and their breast with the signe of the cross, in the wertue of which they are confident that clap can do them no scaith. Some we have sein run to their beads and their knees and mumble over their prayers, others away to the church and doune before the Altar and blaither anything that comes in their cheek.[124]

He was not the only traveller to be interrogated about his religion.[125] Skippon says of the French: 'They will ask whether you are of the religion, i.e. Protestant; or of the *Église*, i.e. Roman Catholick religion, the first time you fall into their company'.[126] When Kennet visited a Carmelite house, he records, 'Addressed myself to one of the Seniors. His first question whither I was a Roman catholick, his next compliment that I was certainly damned'.[127] 'The first Complement many Frenchmen make a Stranger', Northleigh complained, 'is an enquiry of what Religion he is? a question so rude, I use to answer as abruptly, by telling him I was a Christian'.[128]

Yet several travellers detected signs that many Catholics were lukewarm or even less attached to their religion. At the beginning of our period Dallington observes that it was 'naturall to the French, to be a great scoffer; for men of light and unsteadie braines, have commonly sudden and sharpe conceites', and he then relates the example of the death-bed behaviour of two men to show 'how little esteeme they hold of the Romane Religion in heart, though they make profession thereof in shew':

> The one of these being very sicke, &, as was thought, in danger of death, his ghostly father comes to him with his *Corpus domini*, and tels him, that hearing of the extremitie wherein he was, he had brought him his Saviour, to comfort him before his departure. The sicke Gentleman withdrawing the Curtaine, and seeing there the fat lubberly Frier with the Oast in his hand, answereth, I know it is our Saviour; he comes to me as he went to Jerusalem, *C'est un ane qui le porte*: He is carried by an Asse.
>
> The other Gentleman upon like danger of sicknesse, having the Frier come to him to instruct him in the Faith, and after, to give him the Oast, and then the extreme unction (it was on a Friday) tolde him that hee must beleeve, that this *Corpus domini* which he brought, was the very reall flesh, blood and bone of our Saviour. Which after the sicke man had freely confessed, the Frier offered it him to receyve for his comfort. Nay, quoth the other, *Vous m'excuseré, car je ne mange point de chair le vendredi*: You shall excuse me, for I eate no flesh on Fridayes. So that yee see the French will rather lose his god, then his good jest.[129]

Heylyn was shocked by what seemed to him the irreverent and

blasphemous behaviour of the average Frenchman in church:

> Follow him to Church, and there he will shew himself most irreverent and irreligious; I speak not this of all, but of the generall. At a Masse in the Cordeliers Church in Paris, I saw two French Papists, even when the most sacred mystery of their faith was celebrating, break out into such a blasphemous and Atheisticall laughter, that even an Ethnick would have hated it. It was well they were known to be Catholicks; otherwise some French hot-head or other, would have sent them laughing to Pluto.[130]

For his part Evelyn found French Catholics somewhat lukewarm Christians:

> The Roman Catholicks of France are nothing so precise, secret, and bigotish as are either the Recusants of England, Spain, or Italy; but are for the most part an indifferent sort of Christians, naturally not so superstitious and devout, nor in such Vassallage to his Holinesse. as in other parts of Europe, where the same opinions are professed; which indifferency, whether I may approve of, or condemn, I need not declare here.[131]

Both Skippon and Locke have some comments to make on the observance of Lent in Paris. During this period of the year the Hôtel-Dieu had a monopoly of the sale of meat which was only to be purchased by people having a certificate from the Church authorities. Skippon noted: 'In Lent time no butchers can sell flesh, the hospital having the gain of all the flesh that is eaten at Paris in this season, which must be a considerable profit, if they always, as they did this Lent, sell flesh at eight sols per lb'.[132] While Skippon implies that a fair amount of meat was eaten there during Lent, Locke goes much further: 'The observation of Lent at Paris is come almost to noe thing. Meat is openly to be had in the shambles & a dispensation commonly to be had from the Curat without any more adoe, & people of sense laugh at it'.[133] On the other hand in 1714 the author of *A New Journey* got into serious trouble when he endeavoured to eat meat on a fast day while on the long journey down the Seine to Rouen:

> We came to a small dirty Village call'd Bonier, we cou'd get nothing to eat but Eggs, it being a Fast Day; but I had brought some cold Meat with me from Poissy, (as I would advise any Person to do, who Travel that Way) neither did I forget a Bottle of good Brandy, which is very useful upon the Water; the People were very much offended to see me eat Flesh upon such a Day; especially the Watermen, who swore that they wou'd not take me into their Boat, least they should all Perish thro' my Impiety; so that I was forc'd to desist, tho' I had a very good Stomach to my Victual.[134]

Travellers in the second half of the century were well aware of the existence of the very austere, indeed puritanical trend in French Catholicism represented by Jansenism. Locke himself gives a brief, though within its limits accurate account of the history of the movement from its origins down to the so-called 'Paix de l'Église' in 1668:

> Jansenius in some of his books says that Bellarmin, Suarez & Vasquese, 3 Jesuits, were Pelagiani aut Semipelagiani. This soe much provoked that order that they were resolved to ruin Jansenius & all his adherents, & they got the Popes Alexander 7 & Innocent 10 to condemne 5 propositions in Jansenius, which the Jansenists say are noe where in his works, & there upon have undertaken to mainteine that the Pope is infallible, not only in matter of doctrine, but also in matter of fact; & the Pope & King of France ordeind here in France about the year '55 that all the ecclesiastiques of France, even to the nuns, should subscribe (je reconnois), that these 5 propositions were in Jansenius in the sense condemned by the Pope, the execution whereof was rigorously observed for many years till the King some years since mitigated it by an edict.[135]

In 1652, the year before the five propositions were condemned by a papal bull, Finch made the following note about the conflict between Jesuits and Jansenists: 'There's a difference between the Jesuits and the Sorbonists concerning some points of predestination which gives them the name of Jansenists because they defend the doctrine of Jansenius a Bishop, which points differ little from Calvinisme. The Sorbonists about September, 1651, sent three of the doctors of Sorbon to Rome to know whether to assent to St. Austen was erroneous but could nor yet cannot gett audience'.[136] This note is not altogether accurate although at that stage — several years before Antoine Arnauld's expulsion from the Sorbonne — Jansenism undoubtedly had many supporters in the Faculty of Theology.

In the following decade there are echoes of this controversy in Lauder's journal. In addition to stating, not without some exaggeration, that the members of the Oratoire 'are usually all Jansenists', he records an argument which he had with a *curé* in which the first subject discussed was 'the Jansenists opinion about Praedestination, which by a bull from the present Pope, Alexander the 7,[137] had bein a little before condemned at Paris'. There is also a curious entry which reflects the attempt of the enemies of Jansenism to equate it with the heresy of Calvinism: 'We can not forget a Anagram that one hes found in Cornelius Jansenius, to wit, *Calvini sensus in ore*.'[138]

In a letter of Sir Philip Perceval's tutor, written from Angers in 1677, there is an interesting reference to events leading up to Innocent XI's bull condemning Jesuit moral teaching: 'Lately, passes being asked for, these doctors of Louvain, who intend for Rome, were denied by this King, so that they since are resolved to go through Germany. They go, as I am informed, to complain against the morals of Jesuits, whereof one of the articles is this: A man having loved God though but for one woman in his life [*sic*] is sure to go to Heaven'. The writer was in touch with Henri Arnauld, the Jansenist Bishop of Angers, and was allowed to see his correspondence with Innocent XI who was sympathetic to his theological views and who refers specifically to the example he set other bishops by never leaving his diocese:

> The Bishop of Angers has done me the favour to show me a copy of his letter to the Pope and the answer to it, but is resolved to give no copy of it; therefore I cannot send it verbatim, but the substance is this: The bishop declared how joyful he was when at Rome to see him promoted to the cardinalship, that his joy would be perfect if the care of his flock would have given him leave to have now gone to Rome to have kissed his feet. The Pope answers, he very well remembers the merits, piety, and learning of the Abbot of St. Nicolas (for at that time the bishop had no higher title), but he commends the care he takes of his people, wishing other bishops to be such as he, and offers whatsoever depends upon him for the good and benefit of his bishopric. Now the bishop is past eighty years, brother to Mr. Arneud, and uncle to Mons. de Pomgrone.[139]

Covel, writing at roughly the same time as Locke penned his entry on the subject, also noted the lull in the Jansenist controversy[140], but this was not to last. However, none of our travellers comment on the events which were to lead to the destruction of Port Royal des Champs and the bull *Unigenitus*.

Evelyn was not the only traveller to point out that French Catholics were not 'in such Vassallage to his Holinesse as in other parts of Europe, where the same opinions are professed'.[141] Overbury observes that, though the Catholic Church in France was very wealthy, it was 'otherwise nothing as potent as else-where, partly because the Inquisition is not admitted in France, but principally because the Popes ordinary power is much restrayned there, by the Liberties which the French Church claymeth'. He points out that what the Pope loses, the King gains, since he has in his hands the conferment of most high posts in the Church and receives some revenue from his clergy in the form of the *don gratuit*.[142]

Heylyn has a great deal more to say on this subject. 'The French

Church', he declares, 'is the freest of any in Christendome, that have not yet quitted their subjection to the Pope, as alwayes protesting against the Inquisitions, not submitting themselves to the Councell of Trent, and paying very little to his Holinesse, of the plentifull revenue, wherewith God and good men have blessed it'. Of the Pope he writes elsewhere: 'His wings are shrewdly clipped in this Countrey, neither can he fly at all, but as far as they please to suffer him'. He goes on: 'For his temporall power they never could be induced to acknowledge it, as we see in their stories, *anno* 1610. the Divines of Paris in a Declaration of theirs tendred to the Queen Mother, affirmed the suprematie of the Pope, to be an *Erroneous Doctrine*, and the ground of that *hellish position of deposing and killing of Kings*'.

The refusal of the French clergy to receive the Council of Trent, Heylyn explains, was due to it being 'an especiall authorizer of the Popes spirituall supremacy. By this means the Bishops keep in their hands, their own full authority: whereof an obedience to the decrees of that Councell would deprive them'. He refers once again to the stand taken in these matters by the Sorbonne: 'The University of Paris in their Declaration, *anno* 1610 above mentioned, plainly affirme, that it is directly opposite to the Doctrine of the Church which the University of Paris alwayes maintained, that the Pope hath the power of a Monarch in the spirituall government of the Church'. He adds that the Crown stood on the same side as the French clergy: 'The Kings themselves also befriend their Clergy in this cause; and therefore not only protested against the Councell of Trent, wherein this spirituall tyranny was generally consented to by the Catholic faction. But Henry II also would not acknowledge them to be a Councell, calling them another name then *Conventus Tridentinus*. An indignity which the Fathers took very offensively'.[143]

The clash between Louis XIV and Rome which in 1682 led the Asemblée du Clergé to define in the famous Four Articles the 'libertés de l'Égluse gallicane' is reflected in the writings of two of our travellers — Burnet and Northleigh. When Burnet visited France in the following year, he found that in the tense atmosphere of the time when a complete break with Rome seemed possible, his *History of the Reformation in England* was surprisingly popular. He met the Prince de Condé who, he says, 'had read my history of the Reformation, that was then translated into French, and seemed pleased with it. So were many of the great lawyers; in particular Harlay, then Attorney General, and now first President of the Court of Parliament of Paris. The contests with Rome were then very high; for the Assembly of the Clergy had past some articles very derogatory to the Papal authority:

So many fancied, that matter might go to a rupture: and Harlay said very publickly, that, if that should happen, I had laid before them a good plan to copy from'. The doctors of the Sorbonne whom he met, 'seemed to think that almost every thing among them was out of order; and wished for a regular Reformation; But their notion of the unity of the Church kept them still in a communion that they seemed uneasy in: And they said very freely, they wondered how any one that was once out of their communion should desire to come back into it ... They declared themselves for abolishing the Papal authority, and for reducing the Pope to the old Primacy again'.

However, he found them very pessimistic about this being achieved as, despite the Four Articles of 1682, they foresaw that the King would sooner or later patch up matters with Rome. This was indeed to happen within the next ten years. The French bishops, the theologians told Burnet, 'seemed now to be against the Pope: But it was only because he was in the interests of the House of Austria: For they would declare him infallible the next day after he should turn to the interest of France'.[144]

Northleigh offers a great deal of interesting detail about this clash between France and the Papacy. Amongst the medals he found available in Paris he was 'surpris'd to see two they had made, upon their Pope Innocent XI. which in Revenge to his averseness to France they had caus'd to be stamp'd: One was our Sir Edmundbury Godfrey strangling;[145] with this Motto: *Jussu Pontificis*: Another, His Holiness's Head or Bust on one side; on the other, the Altar, Pix, and Chalice all overturn'd: with this inscription: *Pontificis, qui credat? opus*'. In a long passage he describes how laymen were increasingly opposed to all forms of clerical encroachment in secular matters, and not only that of the Papacy:

> The Laity have of late been jealous, and look'd with an evil Eye on the Increase of the Clergy, both in their personal Number, and Ecclesiastical Usurpations, who under the countenance of the Pope, and the Precedent he sets them in this Practice, would take in the temporal Power under the Notion of *in ordine ad spiritualia*; pretending to be Judges of all matrimonial Contracts, from its being with them a Sacrament: (i.e.) for sacred Ends, usurping upon Secularity, and the Administration of Oaths, and judging of them too to be their own, because they concern'd the Souls of Men: Their Frauds in Beneficiary Affairs: the Dangers of alienating their Allegiance by Appeals to the Pope, a foreign Power: That drawing in the Wealth of the Kingdom into their Churches, then sending the Substance of France over the Alps to the See of Rome. These pragmatical Pranks of the Priests since, has put their People

almost upon the Projects of our Henry the VIII. There has risen
in a Country always the most part Catholicks, and now totally
so, an Averseness to the Priests Encroachments at home, and
the Pretensions of the Pope's Power from abroad.

Writing after Innocent XI had been succeeded in 1689 by
Alexander VIII and by Innocent XII in 1691, he describes how the
clash between Louis XIV and the first of these popes 'was like to have
lost him the most Christian King, and made Schismaticks; or (as they
make us) Hereticks of the whole Gallican Church'. However, by now
the breach between Versailles and Rome was being healed: 'The
Pliantry of the late and present Pope, and their unexpected
Preconization of so many Bishops,[146] shows that they are at last come
to a little better understanding'.

Louis XIV's relations with these three popes are described at some
length by Northleigh:

> They have always mightily bestir'd them selves for a pope of
> their own party ... Innocent XI's stiffness for the Austrian
> Family, made Louis XIVth. very stubborn; and his disputing
> with him his Regale[147] in France, made him so bold as to set up
> his Franchises at Rome.[148] Alexander Xth. they so much
> labour'd for, and for whom the Cardinals d'Estree, Fustenburgh
> and Bouillon did sufficiently bestir themselves for, at my being
> there, deceived them; and having but some little relicks and
> remains left of an exhausted life, left the Peace too at large, and
> quietly provided for the Family of the Ottoboni, and his good
> Friends at Venice, and so made way for Pignatelli, a Man more
> for their purposes, who a Bishop of Naples, and Subject to
> Spain, has made a shift to shake off that Relation, and to side
> with France, perhaps in hopes to have that Kingdom by their
> Arms to be put into his more absolute possession as well as right,
> and to have the Revenue of the whole, instead of being packt off
> with a Spanish Gennet, and a few Feudatory peices of Eight.

Finally he offers some ironical comments on the title of 'le roi très
chrétien' given to Louis XIV as to other kings of France: 'I think this
Title, with that of the Eldest Son of the Church, the Popes of late have
with some Regret allow'd him; especially since the two great Contests
of the Franchises and the Regale; and what he would with more
difficulty obtain, were it now again to be granted'.[149]

VI LA RELIGION PRÉTENDUE RÉFORMÉE

Though not uncritical of certain features of Calvinism, especially of the subversive behaviour of many of its adherents in the early part of the century when they formed a state within the state, our travellers generally give it much more sympathetic treatment than they give to Roman Catholicism. The persecution to which the Huguenots were subjected during the personal reign of Louis XIV drew stronger and stronger condemnation as it intensified; the Revocation of the Edict of Nantes and its consequences for the Calvinist population were spoken of with horror by travellers of that period, irrespective of their political or religious views.

It is impossible to speak with any precision either of the total population of France in the seventeenth century or of the total number of Huguenots, but as an approximation it is generally accepted that out of a total population of some twenty million roughly five per cent. were Calvinists. Though Locke does not attempt to give an estimate for the total population, he suggests that they formed a rather higher proportion, noting a figure which was no doubt derived from Huguenot sources: 'The Protestants of France are thought to be $^1/_{16}$ part', adding: 'In Languedoc they are thought to be 200,000'.[1] Languedoc was, of course, one of the main Protestant strongholds, but Heylyn rightly observes that for the most part the Protestants were thinly spread over a great part of the country, 'having ... no Province which they can call theirs; but living dispersed and scattered over the Countrey'.[2] As our travellers visited the different parts of France, they put down very frequently the numbers of Protestants in the different towns they passed through, giving figures ranging from several thousand to nil.

They quite often made contact with Protestant pastors in different parts of the country. They were not always as unfortunate as Kennet who found the pastor he wanted to converse with could not do so in Latin. After denouncing the ignorance of the Catholic clergy, Heylyn goes on to give a very flattering opinion of the Protestant pastors. What he calls the 'blockishness' of the Catholic clergy should, he argues, be 'an excellent advantage to the Protestant Ministers, could they but well humour it, and likely to be a fair enlargement of their party, if well husbanded'. He suggests, however, that they ought to change their tactics in seeking to win over Catholics: 'To deal with them by main force of argument, and in the fervent spirit of zeal, as the Protestants too often do, is not the way; men uncapable of opposition, as this people generally are, and furious if once thwarted; must be tamed as Alexander did his horse Bucephalus'. Later he speaks very highly of the learning and diligence of the pastors: 'As for their Ministery, it is indeed very learned in their studies, and exceeding painful in their calling. By the first they confute the ignorance of the Roman Clergy; by the second their lazinesse. And questionlesse it behoveth them so to be, for living in a Countrey full of opposition, they are enforced to a necessity of book-learning, to maintain the cause, and being continually as it were beset with spies, they do the oftner frequent the Pulpits, to hold up their credits'. He then proceeds to speak of the education they received: 'For the education of them being children, they have private Schools; when they are better grown, they may have free recourse unto any of the French Academies; besides the new University of Saumur, which is wholly theirs, and is the chiefe place of their study'.[3]

None of our travellers visited the academy at Sedan, but several, starting with Thomas Wentworth, offer some information about the one at the Huguenot stronghold of Saumur. He writes: 'Hear is an university whear ther is a philosophy divinity lectour; they have every weeke disputations, and propositions, whear thear are many Scots men; and many townes in France send tow or three young men to study, which when they are approved by the university, are mad ministers of the towne by whome [they] are maintained, after the death of him that was possessor, and in the interim spend their time in study att the charge of the towne'.[4] Later in the century both Reresby and Lauder gave some account of this academy. In considering what Reresby has to say about it, one has to bear in mind that, like other travellers, he thought in terms of Oxford and Cambridge colleges when writing of any French university, including Paris: 'It is since an university, where those of the reformed churches send their children to be educated and instructed in all sorts of sciences, but especially in divinity, this and Montauban being the only two nurseries of learning they have in all France,[5] and these but mean ones for two reasons: — first, the want of accommodation for scholars, there being no colleges in either, except the schools: secondly, the little encouragement given to professors and readers, who have no reward but the benevolence of their scholars'.[6] While in Saumur Lauder stayed with a Scotsman from whom he sought information about the academy:

I, amongs other things, enquired of Mr. Doull what was their manner in graduating their students their. He told me it was wholly the same with that in other places. They gave out Theses which the students defended, only they had a pretty ceremony about the close: each of these to be graduated got a laurell branch, on the leaves wheirof was every mans name engraven in golden letters. Item, he said that when he reflected on the attendance that the Regents in Scotland gave to their classes, he thought he saw another Egyptiacall bondage, for with them they attended only 4 dayes of the weeke, and in these no longer than they took account of their former lesson, and gave them out a new one, which they send them home to gett.[6a]

Wentworth was obviously very interested in the academy at Montauban as he goes into quite a lot of detail about it:

Hear is an university for them of the religion . . . I sawe the ceremony for taking the degree of Master of arte the principal whearof is that after the be met in a place appointed and one of them which have taken the degree have made an oration, all thear gownes being bownd about them with a string, they being untide and have laurel branches put into their hands in signe of freedome. Hear be many Scotsmen and many of the professors are of that nation.

He went back the next day for more: 'In the Morning I heard thear disputations which was betwixt the Masters of arts that whear made the day before and the Bachelers of arts which weare very cold'. When he returned later in the day, he was better satisfied: 'In the afternoone I heard the continuance of their disputations, which was good, the Professors them selfes disputing'. Like Reresby later in Saumur, he was not impressed by the buildings or financial arrangements: 'Thear is one colledge; itt is properly but a scoole for thear be no fellows, only a colledge to read in and not so much as loging for the professors'. Finally he noted the length of the studies required for degrees: 'The Bachelors takes thear degree after a yeare study and they [are] Masters after tow'.[6b]

Heylyn provides a certain amount of detail about the stipends received by Protestant pastors, In describing his journey from Dieppe, he mentions the Protestant church at Arques, and adds: 'Their preachers Mr. Corteau and Mr. Mondenis, who have each of them an yearly stipend of 40 1. or thereabouts; a poor pay, if the faithfull discharge of that duty were not a reward unto it self, above the value of gold and silver'. Later in his general remarks on Protestant pastors he writes: 'The maintenance which is allotted to them, scarce amounteth to a competency, though by that name, they please to call it . . . This competence may come unto 40 or 50 1. yearly, or a little more'.[7]

While at Montpellier, Skippon recorded among other matters concerning the Huguenot population there the names of the pastors: 'The ministers that preach here, are, 1.Burdeaü, formerly an Augustine monk, he preaches after the puritanical way in England. 2. Bertau. 3. Eustace. 4. Chouin. 5. Carsenac'.[8] A decade later Locke mentions two conversations with René Bertheau who was to leave Montpellier and seek refuge in England after the Revocation. In the second of these he was told that 'there was very little piety or religion among their people and that the lives of the Reformed was no better than that of the Papists'.[9] The same view had earlier been expressed by the well-known Huguenot physician, Charles Barbeyrac, who told Locke: 'The Protestants live not better then the Papists'. Later in Blois he met the pastor, Michel Janiçon, whom he describes as 'a very ingenious & civil man'.[10]

While in Montpellier, in 1676, Locke made several entries about the Calvinist system of church government for some of which René Bertheau is mentioned as his informant. After 1659 the Huguenots were not allowed to hold another national synod, but Locke gives a good deal of detail about the provincial synod of Languedoc, noting first: 'This year the Synod of this province meet here at Montpellier. They meet some times at other places. They consist of about 50 Pastors and as many Elders, each church sending one of each sort'. Locke noted that the provincial synod met every year 'but not without leave from the King' and that it made 'ecclesiasticall laws for this province, but suitable still to the laws made by the Nationall Synod'.

The part played by the provincial synod in the ordination, appointment and removal of pastors Locke describes thus:

These have power to reprehend or wholy displace any scandalous pastor. They also admit people to ordination and to be pastors in certain churches, noe body being by them put into orders that hath not a place. The manner is this. When any church wants a pastor, as for example at Montpellier any one of their 4 pastors is dead or gon, the candidates apply themselves to the Consistory of that Church. Whom they like best, they appoint to preach before the congregation. If they approve of that, at the next Synod he presents himself. They appoint 4 pastors to examin him in the tongues, university learning & divinity. Espetially he is to produce the testimonials of the university where he studied, of his life & learning. He preaches before them a French & Latin sermon &, if all these are passable, they appoint 2 pastors to ordein him, but before his ordination he 3 successive Sundays preaches in his congregation. This being donne, the 2 appointed come. The senior makes a sermon teaching the duty of a minister, after which, coming out of the pulpit, he & the other come to him that is to be ordeind, read severall chapters to him in the Epistles wherein the minister's duty is conteind, & then, after a prayer, they lay their hands upon him & make a declaration to this purpose: that, by authority & licence of the provinciall synond, he has power to preach, forgive sins, to bless marriages & to administer the sacraments, & thereupon he is pastor of that place. The allowance that he shall have depends on the consistory. After this upon removall to an other church he is not to be ordeind, but he cannot remove without the leave and approbation of the synod.[11]

Locke also carefully describes the composition and functions of the consistory of every Protestant church:

All the power of church discipline is in the Consistory of every particular church. The consistory of this of Montpellier consists of their 4 Pastors & 24 Diacones which they call Anciens. These, by majority of votes, order all their church affairs as their publique stock, censures, etc. The majority of votes determin the matter, though there be noe one of the Pastors of that side. If there be any disagreement or controversy of law amongst them, they refer it to some of the sober Gentry of the towne, & lawyers that are Protestants, for they have here still 6 Councellors[12] of the Religion, & the Advocates may be of what religion they please.

The Consistory manage their Church censures thus. If any one live scandalously, they first reprouv him in private. If he mends not, he is called before the Consistory & admonished there. If that works not, the same is donne in the publique congregation, & if after he stands incorrigible, he is excluded from the Eucarist. This is the utmost of their power. All things are proved in the Consistory by witnesses which were formerly sworne, but the King hath taken from them the power of giveing oaths.

The consistory here at Montpellier are chosen every 6 years, at other places in other circuits of time, as at Nismes every yeare. The present consistory choos the next Anciens & commonly severall of the former are reteind. The names of the new chosen Anciens or Elders are reported to the congregation, & if any one of them be after ward excepted against in the consistory with sufficient reason & proof, he is laid by & an other chosen.

Two days later Locke adds to this account of the functions of the consistory:

Publique admonitions of their consistory happen seldom. The

last two instances were, one for strikeing a cuff on the eare in the church on a communion day, for which he was hinderd from receiving. The other for marrying his daughter to a Papist, for which he stood excommunicate six months, but their excommunication reaches noe farther then exclusion from the Eucharist, not from the church & sermons.

Locke completes this sentence in a later entry to which he gives a cross-reference: 'but here is now noe feare of excommunication upon that account, the King haveing made a law that persons of different religions shall not marry, which often causes the change of religion, especially sequioris sexus'.[13]

Writing some ten years earlier, the Calvinist, Lauder, has some interesting comments to make on the use made of excommunication in the French Church compared with the practice of the Church of Scotland:

> Its not leasum for a man or woman of the Religion to marry with a Papist; which if they do, they most come and make a publick confession of the fault and of the scandal they have given by such a marriage before the whole church. Experience has learned them to use it wery sparingly and meekly, for when they would have put it in execution on som they have lost them, they choosing rather to turn papists then do it. We are not so strick in this point as they are; for with us *licet sed non expedit cum non omne quod liceat honestum est.*.
>
> Out of the same fear of loosing them they use wery sparingly the dart of excommunication except against such as lives al the more scandalously.[14]

If Lauder took for granted the role played by laymen in the government of the French Church while Locke treats the matter with complete objectivity, Heylyn who had recently been ordained an Anglican priest was scandalized by the French Calvinists' rejection of bishops and by the position held by lay elders. He pens on this subject a passage which exhibits all his powers of vituperation:

> As are their Churches, such is their Discipline, naked of all Antiquity, and almost as modern as the men which imbrace it. The power and calling of Bishops, they abrogated with the Masse, upon no other cause then that Geneva had done it. As if that excellent man Mr. Calvin had been the Pythagoras of our age . . . The Hierarchie of Bishops thus cast out, they have brought in their places the Lay-Elders, a kind of Monster never heard of in the Scriptures, or first times of the Gospell. These men leap from the stall to the bench, and there partly sleeping, and partly stroaking of their beards; enact laws of Government for the Church, so that we may justly take up the complaint of

the Satyrist, saying, *Surgunt nobis e sterquilinio Magistratus, nec dum lotis manibus publica tractant negotia*: yet to these very men composed equally of ignorance and a trade, are the most weighty matters of the Church committed. In them is the power of ordaining Priests, of conferring places of charge, and even of the severest censure of the Church, Excommunication. When any businesse which concerneth the good of the Congregation is befallen, they must be called to councell, and you shall finde them there as soon as ever they can put off their Aprons; having blurted out there a little Classical non-sense, and passed their contents rather by nodding of their heads, then any other sensible articulation, they hasten to their shops, as Quintilian the Dictator in Florus did to his plough.

Locke is obviously a much more reliable guide, as Heylyn mixes up the powers of the provincial synod and the consistory, and in the process somewhat exaggerates the powers of the elders. It is, however, clear that he has conditions in England very much in mind in writing this diatribe since it concludes:

Such a plat-form, though it be, that needeth no further confutation then to know it, yet had it been tolerable if the contrivers of it had not endeavoured to impose it on all the Reformation. By which means what great troubles have been raised by the great zelots here in England, there is none so young, but hath heard some Tragicall relations. God be magnified, and our late King praised, by whom this weed hath been snatched up out of the garden of this our Israel.[15]

In view of later events in England this last sentence reads rather oddly today.

Almost all our travellers not only visited various *temples*, but they also attended services in them. Several offer interesting descriptions both of the buildings and of what went on inside them. Although Heylyn's Anglican prejudices somewhat detract from what he writes on the subject, he does describe things vividly:

Let us now look upon them in their Churches, which we shall finde as empty of magnificence as ceremony. To talke amongst them of Common-prayers, were to fright them with the second coming of the Masse; and to mention Prayers at the buriall of the-dead, were to perswade them of a Purgatory. Painted glasse in a Church window, is accounted for the flag and ensigne of Antichrist: and for Organs, no question but they are deemed to be the Devils bagpipes. Shew them a Surplice, and they cry out, a rag of the Whore of Babylon; yet a sheet on a woman, when she is in child-bed, is a greater abomination then the other. A strange people, that could never think the Masse-book sufficiently reformed, til they had taken away Prayers; nor that their Churches could ever be handsome, until they were ragged.[16]

Naturally the *temple* most frequented by our travellers was the one which served the Huguenots of Paris; it had to be outside the capital, at Charenton. Skippon attended a service there and, some twenty years before the Revocation, saw amongst the congregation two of its aristocratic members: 'Their temple is a long square building of stone, tall roof'd and lightsome, double galleries round. Here we saw marshal de Turenne, and monsieur Rouvigny, who is delegate from the French Protestants to the court, where they say he is a favourite'.[17] The number of people attending services at Charenton could be very large; Coryate writes at the beginning of the century: 'Peter Molinus[18] a most famous and learned Protestant preacheth usually every second Sunday at a place called Charenton about four miles from Paris, where he hath a very great Audience, sometimes at the least five thousand people'.[19]

Evelyn offers an interesting account of a visit to Charenton in 1644 (he was obviously much more favourably impressed by what he saw and heard than Heylyn):

> March 6, being Sunday, I went to Charenton 2 leagues from Paris, to heare & see the manner of the French-Protestant Churches service: The place of meeting they call the Temple, being a very faire & spacious roome built of Free-stone, and very decently adorn'd within with payntings of the Tables of the Law, the Lords Prayer & Creede: The Pulpit stands at the upper end in the middle, having a Parque or Enclosure of seates about it, where the Elders, & persons of greatest quality & strangers sit: The rest of the Congregation on formes & low stooles, but none in Pewes, as in our Churches, to their great disgrace and nothing so orderly as here, where the stoles & other comber are removed when the Assembly rises: I was greately pleased with their harmonious singing the Psalmes, which they all learne perfectly well from the tablature, which, I heard, their children are as duely taught, as their Catechisme.[20]

Edward Browne who mentions several occasions on which he attended services at Charenton adds further information about the *temple*, including a description of the way in which many members of the congregation reached it from Paris, by water:

> It is a large Church with two Galleries, handsome Pillers, and well ordered windowes. There may a great number of people hear. The Minister according to their custome preaches with his hat on. Hee was in a black Canvas doublet & such a gowne as our undergraduats wear in Cambridge. In the afternoon I returned by water by abundance of Islands down the pleasant river of

Seine to Paris. They sing Psalmes as wee row along.

On another occasion he writes: 'The boats being gone before, I walked to Charenton with two Englishmen more. I begin to understand the Minister. In the afternoon he asketh a little boy some questions and onely expounds upon them. They sing Psalmes often, & take a text to preach on in the forenoon'.[21]

Only seven years before the *temple* at Charenton was demolished after the Revocation, Covel went to a service at which he reckoned that at least 6,000 people were present. Among various things which he noted about the service was that 'in the prayer after sermon they mention the King of France'. He also writes: 'I saw one turne protestant in Consistory he standing, the minister asked him if he renounced 1st. the Pope not head of the church. 2. transsubstantiation. 3. the sacrifice of the masse. 4. invocation of saints. 5. worship of images. 6. praying for the dead. Though there is no prescribed forme for this the minister speakes what he please to this purpose'.[22]

During his short trip to the Calais region only three years before the Revocation, Kennet attended a service at the *temple* at Guines. He noted that the building was 'in the form of a Trapeze with double galleries round' and that to it were attached, as well as a reader, two pastors, one of whom resided in Guines and the other in Calais. It was a communion service at which he was present:

> The Reader at some distance from the pulpit, reads the lessons & sets the psalms. Their sermons sett off with eager repetitions, very vehement expressions & variety of actions. The Sacrament administred after Sermon, the table placed under the pulpit, fenced off with seats enclosed for persons of better rank. The bread divided in a dish, and the wine poured out into 2 large cups. The 2 ministers assisting, the one consecrates the bread & administers to himself, then to the other, the 2d the same with the wine. Then the communicants are admitted singly by order & at the entrance of each the minister distributes to each a peice of bread. When the table is filld round, at the pronouncing of a praescribed benediction, they all eat; and soon after the minister that consecrated the wine takes the 2 cups & delivers them to 2 persons in the middle, so they pass round without any genuflexion. After which with another short benediction they depart & give room to new successive sets till all have received.[23]

During his tour of France in 1658 Mortoft was greatly impressed by the size of the congregations in the *temples* which he visited. At Rouen, for instance, he writes: 'The Protestants, of which the Towne is pretty full, have their Church some 3 mile out of the Citty, which is very large and full of people, so that sometymes there are esteemed to be above 1,400 communicants'. At both Tours and La Rochelle he found the *temple* 'very full', while in the Protestant stronghold of Montauban he noted that 'they are almost all Protestants that inhabit in this Citty, having two Temples within the Citty to resort too, wherein in one of them is preaching or praying every day of the yeare'.[24]

Reresby was not at all impressed by the *temple* at Blois: 'I know not what to resemble it to better, as to shape, than a barn, nor is it much better adorned; all that is allowed to be painted or written within being only the ten commandments; they have neither steeples nor bells; the women sit separate from the men, and the ministers preach covered'.[25] Lauder, as a Scottish Presbyterian, felt quite at home at the services he attended in Poitiers:

> The forme of the protestant churches differs not much from ours. On the Sabath morning during the gathering of the congregation they sing a psalme; the minister coming up by a short sett forme of exhortation, stirring them up to join with him in prayers, he reads a sett forme confession of sines out of their priers ecclesiastiques or Liturgie; which being ended they singes a psalme, which the minister nominates, reading the first 2 or 3 lines of that to be sung, after which they read no more the line, as we do, but the people follows it out as we do in Glory to the Father. The psalms being ended, the minister has a conceaved prayer of himselfe adapted for the most part to what hees to discourse on. This being ended he reads his text. Having preached, then reads a prayer out of their Liturgy, then sings a psalme, and then the blissing.[26]

Skippon gives a somewhat livelier account of services which he attended at Montpellier where he noted that there were seven thousand Huguenots,[27]

> who have two temples where they have sermons every morning: Lord's days after dinner little boys answer'd their catechisms with much confidence. The elders sit about the pulpit, the women in the middle of the church, and the men round about in galleries and other seats. There are very great congregations, that give good attention at sermon-time; but when the chapters are reading before sermon, not a word can be heard by reason of loud talking, and many were so irreverent as to have their hats on while they sung psalms. Before any reading of chapters, if they stay any time, some or other in the congregation will begin and set a psalm, which the rest join in. After sermon the collectors receive peoples charity at the door, the third part whereof belongs to the ministers.[28]

Locke noted a curious incident at one of the many Protestant services which he attended in Montpellier: 'Elders of the church sent the clerk to remove some women that were in the Galery among the men, but they kept their seats'.[29] Skippon also provides a curious account of a Protestant fast day in Montpellier: 'The second of November a fast was kept very strictly here, all the hugonots shutting their shops, and, without refreshing themselves at dinner-time, remain'd the whole day in the temples: The people whisperingly repeat the minister's prayers, not omitting the blessing'.[30]

Kennet observed with interest a multiple baptism: '4 children baptized. The water in a bason set in an iron standard at the right hand of the pulpit, the children held up and sprinkled, the minister continuing in the pulpit'. He also witnessed a wedding and the feasting which followed: 'Sunday. Severall waggons prepared with tilts and 4 horses in coach order to carry the wedding guests to Guine. The Bridegroom cloathed in black the 1st day. 3 couple married without any repetition of the office, a ticket of their severall names being read, the minister officiating in the pulpit'. What followed seems very far removed from the fast day at Montpellier: 'At our return to Ardre a very solemn bride supper praepared: after which they danced with music until bed time'. Nor was that the end of the festivities: 'Monday. The wedding entertainment continued. The custom for the vulgar people at such solemnities to set at table from 8 in the morning till 4 in the afternoon with supplies of fresh dishes without any rising up & with very small intermissions from eating & drinking'.[31] Evelyn attended the funeral of an Englishman at Charenton, but was not impressed by the churchyard, as he speaks of the burial having taken place 'in a Cabbage-Garden'.[32]

The various stages in the history of Protestantism in seventeenth-century France are clearly mirrored in the writings of our travellers. The first period, down to the collapse of Protestant military power in 1629 under Richelieu and the withdrawal of the privileges enjoyed by the Huguenots which made of them a state within a state, was followed by a period in which they enjoyed a fair degree of religious freedom. This came to an end with the personal reign of Louis XIV who gradually intensified persecution until in 1685 the Edict of Nantes was revoked. The forced conversion of the great majority of Protestants and the exodus of the remainder to other countries are commented on very unfavourably by the travellers who visited France during this part of the reign.

Henry IV's attitude to the Protestants towards the end of his reign is summed up briefly by Carew:

> The body of those of the reformed religion is a great thorn in his foot, being not only constrained to tolerate them as a

different regiment from the rest of his realm, but to give fortresses into their hands also, and to pay them for keeping them against himself ... This king, by alluring those that are most eminent among the Protestants, either for learning, or military, or civil ableness, by pensions; but debarring all of that profession from employments, which he may bestow upon others; and by labouring an union, or at least a common liturgy, which might serve both sides, to content the generality, seeketh gently to supplant them.[32a]

Writing at the same date Overbury goes into far more detail. He stresses the military strength of the Huguenots and the protection which they enjoyed under the Edict of Nantes:

Concerning the state of the Protestants in France, during Peace they are protected by their Edict: For their two Agents at Court defend the Generall from wrong, and their *Chambres mipartyes* every particular person; And if troubles should arise, some scatter'd particulars might be in danger, but the maine body is safe, safe to defend themselves, though all France joyne against them, and if it breake out into Factions, the safest, because they are both ready and united.

According to Overbury the Huguenots had several strong points — their *places de sûreté*, 'two of which command the River of Loyre', their concentration in a number of provinces such as Poitou, Saintonge, Gascony, Languedoc and Dauphiné which he describes as 'neere the Sea, so consequently fit to receive succors from abroad, and remote from Paris, so that the qualitie of an Army is much wasted before it can approach them'. Another advantage lay in their aristocratic leaders, Bouillon and Lesdiguières, and finally the aid which they could count on from abroad of which he writes:

The Protestant partie being growne stronger of late, as the Low Countries, and more united, as England and Scotland, part of that strengthe reflects upon them; and even the King of Spaine himselfe, which is Enemie to France in generall, would rather give them succour, then see them utterly extirpated: And yet no Forraine Prince can ever make further use of them, then to disturbe France, not to invade it himselfe. For as soone as they get an Edict with better Conditions, they turne head against him that now succoured them, as they did against us, at New-Haven.[33]

Overbury estimates the number of Huguenots as 'not above the seventeene or eighteenth part of the people', but he adds that 'of the Gentlemen there are 6000. of the Religion'. He does, however, note certain weaknesses in their position since the Edict of Nantes. Although their numbers had increased, particularly in Paris,

Normandy and Dauphiné, there had been a falling off in their support among the gentry, 'which losse commeth to passe', he declares, 'by reason that the King when he findes any Gent. that will but hearken, tempts him with preferment, and those he findes utterly obstinate, suppresseth. And by such meanes hee hath done them more harm in Peace, then both his Predecessors in Warre'. Other measures taken by Henry IV which had weakened the position of the Protestants he describes as follows:

> In all their assemblies hee corrupts some of their Ministers to betray their Counsell in hand; and of the 100 & 6000. Crownes a yeare, which he paies the Protestants to entertaine their Ministers, and pay their Garrisons, hee hath gotten the bestowing of 16000. of them upon what Gentleman of the Religion he pleaseth, when by that meanes he moderates, if not gaines: and besides, they were wont to impose upon him their two Deputies which are to stay at Court, but now he makes them propose sixe, out of which he chuseth the two, and by that obligeth those.[34]

Even by this date important safeguards won by the Huguenots in the Edict of Nantes were being whittled away.

When Thomas Wentworth made his tour of France in 1612, early in the reign of Louis XIII, he was particularly struck by what he saw at La Rochelle, the strongest of the Huguenot *places de sûreté*. He describes in considerable detail the towers and other defences of the harbour and then those of the town which, he declares, 'is on the land side marvellous strongly defended with new fortifications that I thinke, when itt is finished, may for strenthe compare with most townes in Europe, having still the strenth of the old wall which alone was accounted one of the strongest in France'. The towne was defended by its own citizens: 'The city is garded by the towns men them selfe whear every man keeps his turne without exception, noe not the Maior himself. The Catholicks are likewise to garde thear turne but not themselfs, but are to hier sum of the religion in ther roomes'. The townsmen were determined not to be taken by surprise: 'Upon the Sunday the gates are shut till after dinner and 200 men in armes to walke up an downe the towne and to garde itt for feare of a surprise, they being at the sermon'. After relating an attempt by the Regent, Marie de Médicis, to encroach upon the town's semi-autonomy, he describes the system of municipal government, concluding: 'The towne stands chefly upon merchandize and is well frequented by English, French and Flemans. The chef commodities that they English bring is lead and cloth'.

He was also impressed by the fortifications of Montauban which, in

1621, was to successfully resist a siege by Louis XIII at the head of the royal army. He describes it as 'one of the Principal towns in France that holds for them of the religion and one of the strongest'. Once again he carefully examined both the existing and the new fortifications which were being built: 'I sawe the same morning the new fortifications which be all of bricke, but not yeat finished. They be esperons answearing one an other whearof some have casimats, some not. They are a la moderne, and not much unlike them of Rochelle, but nothing so strong'.[34a]

After the assassination of Concini, power was in the hands of the Duc de Luynes who was very hostile to the Protestants. Lord Herbert, the British ambassador, describes in his *Life* how Luynes urged the young Louis XIII to make war on his Protestant subjects, 'saying, he would neither be a great Prince as long as he suffered so Puissant a Party to remaine within his Dominions, nor could justly stile himself the most Christian King, as long as he permitted such Hereticks to be in that great number they were, or to hold those strong Places which by publick Edict were assigned to them; and therefore that he should extirpate them as the Spaniards Had done the Moors, who are all banished into other Countreys as we may find in their Histories'.[35] When war broke out between the King and his Protestant subjects, Herbert was instructed by James I to proceed to the royal army in the South and to offer to mediate; he became involved in a violent argument with Luynes which led to his temporary recall to England. Herbert was obviously far more sympathetic towards the Huguenots than Heylyn.

The latter who was in France in 1625, after the arrival in power of Richelieu, but before his destruction of the political and military power of the Huguenots, was critical of their behaviour since the end of the Wars of Religion. Indeed he goes further back than that and denounces the Huguenots' destruction of Orleans cathedral in 1568 as 'an action little savouring of humanity, and lesse of Religion: the very Heathens themselves never demolishing any of the Churches, of those Towns which they had taken. But in this action, the Hugonots consulted only with rashnesse, and a zealous fury, thinking no title so glorious as to be called the Scourge of Papists, and the overthrowers of Popish Churches'. Similarly he disapproved of their aversion to crucifixes as revealed in their destruction of the crosses placed between Paris and St. Denis:

> It could not but call to mind the hate of that Nation unto that harmlesse monument of Christs sufferings, the Crosse; which is grown it seemeth, so exorbitant, that the Papists make use of it to discover an Hugonot. I remember as I passed by water from

Amiens to Abbeville, we met in the boat with a levie of French Gentlewomen; to one of them, with that French as I had, I applyed myself, and she perceiving me to be English, questioned my Religion. I answered (as I safely might) that I was a Catholick; and she for her better satisfaction proffered me the little crosse which was on the top of her beads to kisse, (and rather should I desire to kisse it then many of their lips) whereupon the rest of the company gave of me this verdict, that I was *Un vrai Christien, & ne point un Hugonot.*[36]

Summing up the position of the Christian religion in France, Heylyn writes: 'Of the two parts of the body, we see the Papists flourishing and in triumph; whilest that of the Protestant is in misery and affliction'.[37] In a long passage he describes the position of the Huguenots before their revolts from 1620 onwards as an extremely happy one, guaranteed as it was by the Edict of Nantes:

Before the year 1620 when they fell first into the Kings disfavour, they were possessed of almost 100 good Towns, well fortified for their safety; besides beautifull houses and ample possessions in the Villages, they slept every man under his own Vine and his own Fig-tree; neither fearing, nor needing to fear the least disturbance: with those of the Catholick party, they were grown so intimate and entire, by reason of their inter-marriages, that a very few years would have them incorporated, if not into one faith, yet into one family. For their better satisfaction in matters of Justice, it pleased King Henry the fourth, to erect a Chamber in the Court of the Parliament of Paris purposely for them. It consisteth of one President and 16 Counsellours; their office to take knowledge of all the Causes and Suits of them of the reformed Religion, as well within the jurisdiction of the Parliament of Paris, as also in Normandy and Britain, till there should be a Chamber in the Parliaments of Burdeaux and Grenoble, and one at the Chastres for the Parliament of Tholoza. These Chambers were called *Les Chambres de l'Édit.*[38]

The Huguenots, he declares, had brought their recent misfortunes on their own heads, given the natural determination of Louis XIII to be master in his own kingdom:

They had made themselves masters of 99 Towns, well fortifyed and enabled for a siege: a strength too great for any one faction to keep together, under a King which desires to be himself, and rule his people. In the opinion of this their potency, they call Assemblies, Parliaments as it were, when and as often as they pleased. There they consulted of the common affairs of Religion, made new Laws of government, removed and rechanged their general officers; the Kings leave all this while

never as much as formally demanded. Had they only been guilty
of too much power, that crime alone had been sufficient to have
raised a war against them, it not standing with the safety and
honour of a King, not to be the absolute commander of his own
Subjects. But in this their licentious calling of Assemblies, they
abused their power into a neglect, and not dissolving them at his
Majesties commandment, they increased their neglect into a
disobedience.

Heylyn is particularly severe on the summoning of a General
Assembly at La Rochelle at the end of 1620 despite this being
forbidden by the King:

In their Assemblie, therefore they make Lawes and Orders to
regulate their disobedience, as, That no peace should be made
without the consent of the general Convocation, about paying of
Souldiers wages, for the detaining of the Revenues of the King
and Clergy, and the like. They also there divided France into
seven circles or parts, assigning over every circle severall
Generals and Lieutenants, and prescribed Orders how those
Generals should proceed in the wars.

Thus we see the Kings Army leavied upon no slight ground,
his Regall authority was neglected, his especiall Edicts violated,
his gracious profers slighted, and his Revenues forbidden him,
and his Realm divided before his face, and allotted unto officers
not of his own electing.

It is true that Heylyn devotes a whole page to a violent attack on the
way in which in 1622 the Protestant inhabitants of Négrepelisse (near
Montauban) were put to the sword by the royal army in the civil war.
'Though the Protestants deserved affliction for their disobedience',
he declares, 'yet this was an execution above the nature of a
punishment, a misery beyond the condition of the crime'.[39]

None of our travellers was in France during the period between
1625 and 1629 in which Richelieu smashed the political and military
power of the Huguenot minority, but later writers, particularly
Evelyn, were well aware of the weakened position in which the
French Protestants now found themselves. In 1652 he writes of what
he calls 'the poor Protestants':

They are now so inconsiderable. since the late successes of
Cardinal Richlieu, and especially our Nations reproach, and
their misfortune at La Rochelle; that for the present they
possess no one place of strength, or any other singular immunity
above others, as being defeated of all Eminent Persons, either of
Birth or Charge, who might be able to defend or counsel them at
need; the Court having now rendered most of them Proselytes,
by Preferments or Interests, or other effectual means: Howbeit,
such as remain (and of which too there are likewise a very

considerable body) are permitted peaceably to enjoy their Consciences, upon renovation of the late Edict of Pacification; and are undoubtedly, in case of any considerable Rebellion, capable to form a very ballancing and pondrous party; but with nothing that front and confidence which within these twenty years past, they might have done, when they durst even beard the King, and protect such as retired to them, from his displeasure, in most of his now strongest Towns and places of Importance; but the Scean is now much altered, and they shrewdly contracted especially since the stir under that late and incomparable Duke of Rohan: the folly of their own private Interests, having evidently proved their fatal destruction; as it is most frequently seen to fall out (first or last) amongst all contrivers of Civil and Popular Dissentions.

In view of the theological controversies which raged among the French Protestants in this period Evelyn's final remarks on them are somewhat surprising: 'Thus far I must needs vindicate the Protestants of France, That we finde not amongst them those frequent Schismatiques and broachers of ridiculous Enthusiasms as abound amongst us; every particular so unamimously concurring with their Pastor, That, in truth, they are herein not unworthy to be commended'.[40] Such a view of the situation was obviously inspired by Evelyn's aversion to the Puritan sects in England.

Though Reresby does not offer any general survey of the position of either Catholicism or Protestantism in the 1650s when he was in France, in his account of the Paris Parlement he does make one remark which shows the weakened position of the Huguenots. In a sentence describing the *Chambre de l'Édit* he inserts a significant parenthesis when he writes that it was 'erected in favour of the reformed . . .to determine differences between them and the Romanists, and to give redress (though of late they seldom do) as to matters of encroachments made upon their liberties established by law, whether spiritual or temporal'.[41]

The persecution of the Huguenots which began with the personal reign of Louis XIV and led finally to the Revocation of the Edict of Nantes is very well documented in the accounts of visits to France left by our travellers as these happen to be particularly numerous in this period. It was also a subject which interested them because of the sympathy which they generally felt for the plight of the Huguenots, especially as the persecution intensified.

At the beginning of 1679, before that persecution reached its height, Covel who was on his way back from Constantinople could write: 'The French acts much the Grand Signiors policy in many things, suppressing the Hugenots, taking their children'.[42] Looking back on his visit to France in 1683, Burnet comments thus on the position of the Protestants:

> The method that carried over the men of the finest parts among them to Popery was this: They brought themselves to doubt of the whole Christian Religion: When that was once done, it seemed a more indifferent thing of what side or form they continued to be outwardly. The base practice of buying many over with pensions, and of driving others over with perpetual ill usage and the acts of the highest injustice and violence, and the vile artifices in bringing on and carrying so many processes against most of their Churches, as not comprehended within the edict of Nantes, were a reproach both to the greatness of their King and to the justice of their Courts. Many new edicts were coming out every day against them, which contradicted the edict of Nantes in the most express words possible: And yet to all these a strange clause was added, That the King did not intend by them to recal, nor to go against any article of the edict of Nantes, which he would maintain inviolable.[43]

Northleigh was also reflecting on earlier events when he wrote of the differing attitudes of French Catholics to the Huguenots before the Revocation:

> The Profession of the Protestant Religion, tho' they differ so much among themselves, they of late all agreed should be rooted out, tho' some by more milder Methods than others; the former, the King and his Bonner the Archbishop of Paris,[44] thought best to follow at first; till having got the Ascendant by Artifice, they found Fire and Sword to make Converts faster, or drive the unconverted out of the Kingdom sooner: This is variously resented among them, as a Politick Act or Unchristan, according as they are more or less biggotted.[45]

Already by the middle of the 1660s Lauder and Skippon were recording the destruction of Huguenot *temples* by governmental action on all sorts of pretexts. In 1665 Lauder writes in his somewhat naïve style:

> The Protestant Churches throw Poictou keip a solemne fast 28 of Octobre, with the Papists St.Simons day. The occasion was to deprecate Gods wrath which he showed he had conceived by reason he threathned them in sewerall places with Scarcity of his word and removing of his candlestick, since sewerall temples ware throwen doune, as that at Partenay, etc. For that effect they sent 4 of the Religion, the eminentest amongs them in the Province to the King with a supplication. We had 3 preachings. We eated no flech that day for fear of giving occasion to the Papists to mock: we suped on a soup, fried eggs, roosted chaistains, and apples with peirs.[46]

In the same year at Nîmes Skippon recorded: 'The protestants of this city are three parts of four, and they had two temples, but one is lately pull'd down'. He adds another grievance: 'They had a college and professors, but now the Jesuits are masters'.[47]

Much later, in 1681, John Buxton observed of Grenoble — 'many people, about the tenth part of protestants, being about 2,000', adding: 'They were at first half protestants; we saw their temple, a neat building a little without the town. But the Romanists threaten to have it down and make them go a league further to build another'.[48] As so often, it is Locke who furnishes most detail on the persecution of the Protestants. In February 1676, shortly after his arrival in Montpellier, he noted: 'They have within these 10 years at least 160 churches pulled down'; three years later, just before his return to England, he gives a still higher figure and observes that the process was being speeded up: 'The Protestants within these 20 years have had above 300 churches demolished, & within these 2 months 15 more condemned'.[49] The sort of pretext on which these demolitions were ordered is shown by Locke in describing what happened at Uzès in Languedoc: 'Their Temple is orderd to be puld down, the only one they had left them, though 3/4 of the town be Protestants. The pretence given is that their Temple being too near the papish church, their singing of psalms disturbed the service'. At Aix he noted: 'In this towne are 4 familys of Protestants, as there are 8 at Touloun. They goe 3 leagues to church. They had formerly 13 churches in Provence, but 9 of them have been puld down within these 5 or 6 yeares'.[50]

In the course of his travels Locke observed how all sorts of restrictions were imposed on the activities of Protestants. After recording, like Skippon, that at Nîmes the Protestants had lost one of their two *temples*, he adds: '2 of their Consuls are Protestants, two Papists, but are not permitted to receive the sacrament in their robes as formerly. The Protestants had built them here too an hospitall for their sick, but never used, because the preists trouble them when there'. Shortly after his arrival at Montpellier he observed how the right which the Edict of Nantes conferred on the Protestant nobility and gentry to have pastors, known as *ministres de fief*, to conduct services in the private chapels on their estates, was being eroded: 'This yeare they have refused the King's allowance of the meeting of their Synod of this province of Languedoc because by it the ministers that live in Noblemen's & gentlemen's houses are excluded. They have their agents at Court solliciting to have it with its due freedome'.[51] For once the Protestants won their case; this *arrêt du Conseil* was eventually withdrawn.

In examining the tax of 6 deniers a pound on meat entering

Montpellier which was levied by the municipal authorities Locke
noted how the Protestant pastors were deprived of the greater part of
the revenue which was due to them: '$\frac{1}{2}$ ought to goe to the
maintenance of the Protestant ministers by the agreement of the
peace, & they had it formerly paid them, but now they allow them but
1 d per lb., nor doe they indeed pay them that, for 1 d. per lb. amounts
in a year to between 5 & 6,000 livres & they pay them but 1,400 livres
par annum'. More serious because of the effect on Protestant
education was the decree mentioned by Locke in August 1676: 'This
fortnight Protestant ministers forbid to teach above 2 scholars at
once'.[52]

Skippon had earlier noted at Nîmes the restrictions placed on
Protestant burials: 'The protestants have a burying-place without the
city, and bury their dead either betimes in the morning or after
sun-set, the king of late years not suffering them to accompany the
corpse at any other time; 30 persons is the greatest number that can
go along with it; the women are troublesome when they go, because
they howl and cry in a strange manner'. Protestants faced dangers
even in public places. In describing his visit to the Palais de Justice in
Paris, Skippon notes a curious point: 'In the hall are many shops and
galleries. One Varennes is the only Protestant bookseller here, who,
to signify whether mass is said or not, hangs out a pastboard having on
one side the letter *N*. and on the other the letter *O*. for *No* and *Ouy*,
i.e. *Yes*. This is taken notice of by the Protestants that come to the
hall, that they may avoid the elevation of the host'.[53] At Orleans
Lauder, who was obviously not prepared to recognize such a popish
proceeding as taking off his hat to the sacrament as it passed through
the streets, found himself in a difficult position: 'One day as I was ...
entring in a lane ... I meit in the teeth the priests carrieing the
Sacrament (as they call it) with a crosse to some sick person: my
conscience not suffering me to lift of my hat to it, I turned back as fast
as I could and betook me selfe to another street wheir I thought I
might be safe: it followed me to that same very street, only
fortunately I got a trumpket[54] wheir I sheltered myselfe til it passed
by'.[55] One of the things which Kennet noted when he went from
Calais to nearby Guines to attend a service at the Protestant *temple*
was that it was 'a custom for the protestants formerly at 1 miles
distance from Calais to sing psalms in the severall boats till they came
to Guine, but of late forbidden by authority'.[56]

While in the South Locke noticed various ways in which the
position of the Protestants was being systematically weakened. The
Chambre mi-partie established at Castres in Languedoc to enable
them to receive fair treatment had been removed from this

predominantly Protestant town to the Catholic stronghold of Castelnaudary. Locke commented on this somewhat ironically: 'Since the removal of the Chamber to Castlenaudary they have found a way at Castres to imploy them selves in making Crapon, so that the Bishop who caused the removal of the Chamber, would now get it back again'. Locke also noted that the Protestant barons who were entitled to a seat in the Estates of the province were not allowed to attend its sessions: 'Barons that are of the Religion in this Province are not permitted to come themselves into the States, but may depute any one of the papists and send him in their room'. Protestants were gradually excluded from municipal office. Of the *Consuls* of Montpellier Locke noted:'They were formerly 3 Protestants & 3 Papists, but the Protestants have been excluded'. Just after his arrival in the South he wrote of Uzès, a town with a large majority of Protestants: 'This week the Protestants there have an order from the King to choose noe more consuls of the town of the Religion'.[57]

One method used by Louis XIV to secure conversions was to refuse to bestow posts within his gift on Protestants. Noblemen who were army or naval officers found all promotion blocked. Locke cites the example of the most important Protestant nobleman in Languedoc:

> The Marquis de Mealeauze whose grandmother was sister to Turenne, lives about Castres in Languedoc. The young man hath between 40 or 50,000 livres per annum. Served 2 or 3 campaigns and was buying of a regiment lately, but the King refused to confirm the bargain unlesse he would change his religion; but if he would do that, he promised him great matters. He refused to change and was retired to his estate. He is the most considerable man of the Religion in these parts.[58]

The policy succeeded with this nobleman as it had done with his more famous great-uncle; two years later Bossuet received his abjuration. Posts in the army and navy were not the only ones affected. Covel made the following entry in his journal in 1678: 'The King is ill affected to the protestants. The duke of Orleans beg'd an office (which ever belong'd to a protestant) of councellor of finances for a protestant his freind; the King chekt him & told him he thought you had understood my mind well enough, is to disadvantage that party what I can rather then advance them.'[59] While at La Rochelle, Locke noted various consequences for the Protestants of their defeat fifty years earlier; fairly recently they had suffered serious disabilities: 'Noe Protestants are sufferd to set up trades (c'est a dire estre metrisé) in Rochell, nor noe Protestants to live there that were not borne in the town.' Earlier in Languedoc he had noted the considerable restrictions on the number of Protestants who could be admitted to the guilds: 'But 1/3 of any trade in any town suffered to pass masters, i.e. to set up, of those of the Religion'.[60]

After what would seem an ironical marginal note 'Toleration' Locke penned a paragraph on the position of those Protestants who dissented from the articles of faith of their church:

> If any one hold tenets contrary to their articles of faith, the King punishes him, soe that you must be here either of the Romish or their church; for not long since it happend to one here, who was inclineing to and vented some Arrian doctrines, the Governor complained to the King. He sent order he should be tried, & soe was sent to Tholose where upon triall, he denying it utterly, was permitted to scape out of prison; but had he owned it, he had been burnt as an Heretick.[61]

A somewhat strange situation . . .

From the time of his arrival in the South at the end of 1675 Locke collected information about the morale of the Huguenots in the face of the growing persecution. At Nîmes on the way to Montpellier he observed: 'Notwithstanding their discouragement, I doe not finde that many of them goe over. One of them told me, when I asked him the question, that the Papists did noe thing except by force or money'. At Montpellier he questioned Dr. Barbeyrac about their position:

> The Protestants have here common justice generally, unlesse it be against a new convert, whom they will favour. They pay noe more taxes then their neighbours, are only incapable of publique charges & offices . . . They & the papist laity live together friendly enough in these parts. They sometimes get & sometimes loose proselytes. There is noe thing don against those that come over to the reformed religion, unless they be such as have before turned papist & relaps: these sometimes they prosecute. The number of Protestants in these latter years neither increases nor decreases much. Those that go over to the Church of Rome are usually drawn away by fair promises that most commonly faile them, or else mony if they be pore.

Shortly afterwards he entered a somewhat different account of the matter: 'They tell me that the number of Protestants within these twenty or thirty last years are manifestly increased, & doe dayly, notwithstanding their losse every day of something, some priviledg or other'. A final note on the subject is somewhat less subjective: 'The Christenings of the Religion at Montpellier are about 300 & the Funerals about 260'.[62]

If relations between Protestants and Catholics could, as at Montpellier, be fairly good, our travellers did note occasions when this was obviously not the case. At Marseilles in 1612 Thomas Wentworth penned this extraordinary sentence: 'Hear be a 100 of the

Religion whearof tow be captains of 2 galleys, but dare not be knowne, for the would be kild, the people not suffering any of the religion to gouverne'.[62a] Some fifty years later Downes, after recording his presence at the *temple* outside Rouen, tells the story of the danger run by its pastor, De Langle, from a Catholic mob:

> M[r] de Langres, the sonne of the best preacher escaped narrowly being Massacred about 10 days since. A protestant maid raving in a feaver, her freinds called Mons[r] de Langres. In the Intrim a romanist desird to call a preist, she consenting, and the preist arriving before Mons. de Langres, hee demanding why the preist was there, was answerd the maid would turn Catholick. Hee going to take his leave, the rabble of the people hearing of a conversion of a Huguanot, flock'd to the dore & if Mons[r] de Langres had not bin securd in Mons[r] Bonders house and afterwards conveighed away in a president's coach, he had bin murdered by the rabble.[62b]

The persecutions suffered by the Huguenots down to 1679 are so well summarized by the author of *Popery and Tyranny* that his account of the matter is worth reproducing:

> As to what concerns Protestants, they are diminished in their number, and weakened by these means.
>
> 1. By making them incapable of all Offices and Charges of Judicature, the Court of Parliament, and other high Charges in State or Army; and in truth, by making their Profession an obstacle to all Preferments.
>
> 2. Forbidding all Marriages between them and Catholicks.
>
> 3. Whensoever they are turned, to make it highly Penal to Return.
>
> The Names of the Nobility turned Roman Catholicks of late years, Marshall Turin, Le Duc de Duras: and the Counte de Lorge his Brother: the Count de Lorge Mountgomery, Messieurs de Pons, two Brothers: Monsieur de St. Miscua in Xaintoign: Mounsieur de la Roachel: Mounsieur de Pellisson: Mounsieur the Prince de Tarrant Son to the Duke of Tours.
>
> 4. Under Pretence that their Temples have been erected since the Edict of Nantes without Licence, or upon holy Ground belonging to the Catholick Church, as they call themselves, demolishing Multitudes of them thereby, forcing them to the Inconveniency of four or five Leagues if not more, out of their respective City and Towns, and suppressing all private Chappels belonging to the Protestant Gentry, upon Pretence of Non-residence.
>
> 5. Demolishing all Places of Strength where they abode in Numbers, and erecting Cittadels to awe these Towns where they are numerous.

6. By taking away Hospitals and all other Provisions for their Poor, given by the Protestants, not allowing them to make any Gifts for Perpetuity, nor admitting them the Privilege of other Hospitals provided for the rest of his Subjects.

7. By Conniving at the Clergy, when contrary to Law, they force their Children from them, and concealing them from their Parents, bred them up in their own Religion.

8. By restraining Catholicks from taking Protestants Children their Apprentices, and prohibiting Catholicks from placing their Children with Protestants.[62c]

Serious as these disabilities were, much worse was to follow.

Men like Locke and Covel whose stay in France did not extend beyond 1679, left before the intensified persecution which led to the Revocation of the Edict of Nantes. They were not there during the *dragonnades,* a means of procuring conversions by letting unruly troops loose on Protestant communities. Even so, on his travels through Western France in 1678 Locke picked up at Niort complaints about this kind of treatment:

> Here a pore bookseller's wife, which by the largenesse & furniture of her shop seemed not to have either much stock or trade, told me that, there being last winter 1,200 soldiers quarterd in the towne, two were apointed for their share (for they were Protestants), which, considering that they were to have 3 meales a day of flesh, breakfast, dinner & supper, besides a collation in the afternoon, all which was better to give them, & a 5th meale too if they desired it, rather then displease them, these 2 soldiers, for the 3 months they were there, cost them at least 40 ecus.[63]

The *dragonnades* proper are described in vivid language by Burnet, who was in France five years later. After Louis XIV had made up his mind to revoke the edict, he declares:

> Mr. de Louvoy, seeing the King so set on the matter, proposed to him a method, which he believed would shorten the work, and do it effectually: Which was, to let loose some bodies of Dragoons to live upon the Protestants on discretion. They were put under no restraint, but only to avoid rapes, and the killing them. This was begun in Bearn. And the people were so struck with it, that, seeing they were to be eat up first, and, if that prevailed not, to be cast in prison, when all was taken from them, till they should change, and being required only to promise to reunite themselves to the Church, they, overcome with fear, and having no time for consulting together, did universally comply. This did so animate the Court, that, upon it the same methods were taken in most places of Guienne,

Languedoc, and Dauphinè, where the greatest numbers of the Protestants were. A dismal consternation and feebleness ran thro' most of them so that great numbers yielded.

Burnet spent part of the summer of 1685 in France which he left just before the Revocation. He continues:

Upon which the King, now resolved to go thro with what had been long projected, published the edict repealing the edict of Nantes, in which (tho' that edict was declared to be a perpetual and irrevocable law) he set forth, that it was only intended to quiet matters by it, till more effectual ways should be taken for the conversion of Hereticks. He also promised in it, that, tho' all the public exercises of that religion were now suppressed, yet those of that persuasion who lived quietly should not be disturbed on that account, while at the same time not only the Dragoons, but all the Clergy, and the bigots of France, broke out into all the instances of rage and fury against such as did not change upon their being required in the King's name to be of his religion, for that was the stile everywhere.

Burnet's account of the treatment meted out to the Huguenots after the Revocation is not secondhand, since at the beginning of 1686 he returned from Italy to Marseilles and travelled through the South of France on his way to Geneva. In the volume of *Letters* addressed to Robert Boyle which he published in Rotterdam in that year he describes his horror at the treatment meted out to the Huguenot minority.[64] Here we may continue with the account which he later gave in the *History of His Own Time*; though just as indignant, it is more concise:

Men and women of all ages, who would not yield, were not only stript of all they had, but kept long from sleep, driven about from place to place, and hunted out of their retirements. The women were carried in to Nunneries, in many of which they were almost starved, whipt, and barbarously treated. Some few of the Bishops, and of the secular Clergy, to make the matter easier, drew formularies, importing that they were resolved to reunite themselves to the Catholick Church, and that they renounced the errors of Luther and Calvin. People in such extremities are easy to put a stretched sense on any words, that they may give them present relief. So it was said, what harm was it to promise to be united to the Catholick Church: And the renouncing those men's errors did not renounce their good and sound doctrine. But it was very visible, with what intent those subscriptions or promises were asked of them: So their compliance in the matter was a pure equivocation. But, how weak and faulty soever they might be in this, it must be acknowledged, here was one of the most violent persecutions

that is to be found in history. In many respects it exceeded them
all, both in the several inventions of cruelty, and in its long
continuance.

At this point he draws on his experiences during his journey through
the parts of Southern France where most of the Huguenots were to be
found:

> I went over the greatest part of France while it was in its
> hottest rage, from Marseilles to Montpelier and from thence to
> Lions, and so to Geneva. I saw and knew so many instances of
> their injustice and violence, that it exceeded even what could
> have been well imagined; for all men set their thoughts on work
> to invent new methods of cruelty. In all the Towns thro' which I
> past, I heard the most dismal accounts of those things possible;
> but chiefly at Valence, where one Dherapine seemed to exceed
> even the furies of Inquisitors. One in the streets could have
> known the new converts, as they were passing by them, by a
> cloudy dejection that appeared in their looks and deportment.
> Such as endeavoured to make their escape, and were seized, (for
> guards and secret agents were spread along the whole roads and
> frontier of France) were, if men, condemned to the gallies, and,
> if women, to monasteries. To compleat their cruelty, orders
> were given that such of the new converts, as did not at their
> death receive the Sacrament, should be denied burial, and that
> their bodies should be left where other dead carcases were cast
> out, to be devoured by wolves or dogs. This was executed in
> several places with the utmost barbarity: And it gave all people
> so much horror, that, finding the ill effect of it, it was let fall. This
> hurt none, but struck all that saw it even with more horror than
> those sufferings that were more felt. The fury that appeared on
> this occasion did spread it self with a sort of contagion: For the
> Intendants and other officers, that had been mild and gentle in
> the former parts of their life, seemed now to have laid aside the
> compassion of Christians, the breeding of Gentlemen, and the
> common impressions of humanity. The greatest part of the
> Clergy, the Regulars especially, were so transported with the
> zeal that their King shewed on this occasion, that their sermons
> were full of the most inflamed eloquence that they could invent,
> magnifying their King in strains too indecent and blasphemous
> to be mentioned by me.[65]

Other travellers have something to say about the Revocation and
the persecution which preceded and followed it. Bromley mentions
that Nîmes was 'before the late Persecution eminent for the great
Resort of the Protestants' and adds: 'The King is building a strong
Fort on an Eminence a little above the City, to subject that, and to be
a defence against the Hugonots, that were very numerous in these
parts, and that now are New Converts'.[66] In 1687 Ferrier observed

that Angers was 'since this last persecution very much depopulated', but a more striking passage on this subject occurs in his account of a visit to the Hôpital Général in Lyons: 'We saw there severall protestant women who are coop't up into a little yard & are fed with nothing but bread & water. We would fain have gone into their yard to have talk't with them, but demanding leave were answered that it was not permitted to any to goe to them'.[67]

In the course of his travels in the South Veryard passed through Castelnaudary which he describes as 'a small City, the Inhabitants whereof were lately almost all Protestants, but, having been reconcil'd by Dragoon Missioners, stile themselves at present *Catholiques par force*'. After visiting the Grande Chartreuse, he and his companions made their way on foot through the mountains to Savoy, and found themselves in danger of being arrested as fugitive Protestants:

> We lodg'd that Night at a Village call'd S.Pierre, where they kept Watch at that time to apprehend Protestants that endeavoured to make their escape out of the Kingdom, contrary to the King's Edict. These arm'd Mountaineers began to handle us somewhat roughly, 'till I appeas'd, by telling the Captain that we had the King's Pass, as indeed we had, but durst not produce it, fearing least they might take it away and plunder us, as they had serv'd several Gentlemen not long before. Wherefore thinking to put them off with a Billet of Health we had from the Townhouse at Lions, I drew a Paper out of my Pocket, and without opening it, gave it the Captain, imagining it had been that; but it prov'd by a mistake to be a printed Bill given out by the English Rope-dancers whilst we were at Avignon. He had no sooner open'd it but I perceiv'd my Errour; however imagining, as it prov'd, that their Wits might be as barren and uncultivated as their Mountains, I let them hand it round from one to another, and could not but smile to see them view and admire the King's Arms at the top of the Paper, mumbling it over to themselves to pass for Book-learn'd, and at length to return it, telling us withal, 'twas enough to carry us thro' the whole World.[68]

Northleigh has some strong comments to make on the Revocation. He speaks scathingly of a medal which he saw in Paris 'of their King with his Bustum on one side, and on the reverse a Column broken in the middle: on the upper part of which hung a label or a Scroll of Parchment, with this written: *Edictum Nancii reversum*; a Glory that some of his Subjects have Reason to turn into a great Reproach'. Later he returns to this subject: 'The famous reversing of the Edict of Nantes, which as I have observ'd before, was made so monumental an Act of Arbitrariness, as to merit to be immortaliz'd on a Medal;

shows that their equitable Laws, are never like to be very lasting; and the hard Usage of his Protestant Subjects, which I have known even under his Nose, Papists in Paris condemn, makes it manifest, That he does not govern always for the Good of all his Kingdom'. He has another severe observation to make on the treatment meted out to the Huguenot minority as well as on absolute monarchy: ''Tis with an ill Grace too the French oft reflect upon the Tyranny of Spain, and the Severities of their Inquisition, when their own Subjects in general sufficiently feel the first, and the poor fetter'd or fugitive Hugenots have woful experience of the latter'.

Travelling by boat up the Seine from Paris to Fontainebleau, he passed by Charenton which he describes as 'a pretty little Place seated on the Banks of the Marn and Sein; and remarkable once for the number of Protestants that by particular Edict were permitted to enjoy more eminent Privileges, all now in the common Calamity, subverted and infring'd'. In his account of Rouen he points to the economic consequences of the persecution: 'This was a Place that suffer'd severely, and was the Scene of much Confusion during all their Civil Wars; and upon this last Persecution, the Hugenots here have been as much troubled, being a Trading Place of Business; which by any Severities, especially in Matters of Religion, will soon be obstructed'.

The most striking passage on this subject is the one in which Northleigh relates how on the Normandy coast he and his companions were taken for Huguenots fleeing the country. Less fortunate than Northleigh and his party, these were often not only arrested but also sent to the galleys:

> Passing on through a little Village call'd Franchenville, whose name was only worth noting for the Disturbance it gave us, for it being in the hottest Time of their prosecuting of the Hugenots, an idle drunken Fellow had rais'd all the Countrey upon some of us for fugitive Protestants; where as soon as we arriv'd, all the Mob Militia of the Place came out against us, arm'd with old rusty Guns and Fowling-pieces, Pikes, Staves, and Flails, and all the Rustic Magazine of the Village, and seiz'd us for Fugitives; and tho' with Peter our Speech might have bewrayed and discover'd us, yet it was with much ado after all our Passes produc'd, and an whole Night under a strict Guard and an harder Lodging, that we were permitted to go on our Journey.

The passage ends with this comment on the fate of fugitive Huguenots: 'And yet was it more criminal for them to fly from it; for several of them about that very time, were seiz'd skulking about the Coast; and were then sending to the Galleys of Thoulon and Marseilles'.[69]

Nearly thirty years later, in 1714, strict watch was being kept at French ports for returning Huguenots, if we are to believe the amusing account of his arrival at Calais provided by the author of *A New Journey*:

When we went before the Governour, he examin'd us whence we came, whither we were bound, of what Religion? Being answer'd that we were Protestant Subjects of the Queen of Great Britain, that the Curiosity of Travelling made us come from England, we were dismiss'd; but there were two French Men that came over with us, the one a Papist and the other a Huguenot, as they had own'd to us on Board, they being, during the Voyage, at Daggers drawn about Religion, and always disputing. Before we went to the Governour, the Huguenot was mightily afraid that the other would inform against him; but I prevail'd with the Papist, in urging how mild the English Government was to suffer him (who was establish'd there) to have the free Exercise of his Religion, how dangerous it wou'd be for him after his return, were it known that he had been the Cause of any Trouble to a Person that was under her Majesty's Protection, so that he promised he would say nothing against the other; however, the Governour guessing by their Countenance that they were French, singled them out from the rest, and sent for a Clergyman to examine them. I staid after the rest of the Company to know the fate of the poor Huguenot; the Papist was first examin'd, and order'd to say his *Pater Noster, Ave Maria, Credo,* &c. after which the Huguenot was asked how many Sacraments there were, to which he boldly answered Seven, which he nam'd; then being ask'd what was the Eucharist, he with the same Impudence answer'd, That it was the real Body and Blood of Christ, hidden under the species of the Bread and Wine, whereupon he was dismiss'd as a bon Catholick.

Like other refugees before and since, the Huguenots who came to England were not necessarily popular as the author's comments on this episode show:

I smil'd to see what a Tool Religion is made of; when people profess one on this side, and another on the other side of the Water, as many of these Huguenots do, tho' here they profess so great a Zeal for the Protestant Religion, and pretend that they forsook all for the sake thereof; whereas a Multitude of them took that pretence to come over, tho' the real cause was Poverty or Debts, and that they live in much more Plenty than ever they did in their own Country, to the great detriment of the English Tradesmen, whom they daily undermine in their dealing.[70]

VII EDUCATION

It is only very rarely that our travellers' accounts offer glimpses of the illiteracy of the great mass of the population in seventeenth-century France. There is the occasion when Veryard found that frontier guards could take a publicity bill for a passport.[1] Or again there is Evelyn's account of what he saw in the Cimetière des Saints Innocents in Paris where scriveners found clients among the illiterate, especially women; 'Here I observed that divers clearks got their livelyhod by inditing letters for poore mayds & other ignorant people, who come to them for advise, and write for them into the Country, both to their Sweete-hearts, Parents & friends, every large grave stone a little Elevated serving them for Table'.[2] Nothing whatever is said about such schools as existed to offer an elementary education to the masses.

In contrast they have a good deal to say about secondary and higher education. Although religious orders such as the Jesuits and more recently the Oratorians offered stiff competition, the universities — particularly that of Paris — provided a great deal of the equivalent of secondary education in their faculties of arts which fed the higher faculties of theology, law and medicine. The existence of a considerable number of provincial universities is noted by our travellers, but unless they possessed a well-known faculty such as medicine at Montpellier or law at Orleans they seldom say anything of note about them. Such comments as they offer are generally far from complimentary. Toulouse earns some particularly unflattering remarks. 'Heere is a famous university', wrote an anonymous diarist in 1648, 'but the scholars are extreamely insolent, and for the most part demand mony from all passengers, which, if they refuse, they way lay them and kill them'.[2a] In 1662 Bertie visited various colleges in Toulouse which, he declared, were 'not to be compared to ours in England, being pitiful holes and in them nothing remarkable'. A few days later he wrote: 'We viewed afterward the schools of Divinity, Physic and Civil Law, which are very poor. A good barn would make a better show'.[2b] Although less rude, Shaw was certainly not impressed by what he saw at Douai at the end of the century:

> Douay glories most in its University, which yet is much inferior to that of Louvain. Its Publick Schools make a wretched

appearance; and it has but Ten Colleges, though more frequented by our English Catholicks than Louvain, or evern than
St. Omer's; for there is a Convent of English Cordeliers and
another of about Thirty English Benedictines; a great College of
Secular Priests and Students of one Hundred and Fifty, a Seminary of about Sixty English Youths, another of so many Scots,
and a Convent of Scots Jesuits.[2c]

Although the author of *A New Journey* claims to have spent seven
years as a student at the University of Orleans, when he later returned
there, all he could find to say about this period in his life was that
every summer several students were drowned while swimming in the
extremely cold river.[3]

However, the University of Paris receives a good deal of attention.
Heylyn, for instance, delves into its history as well as dealing with its
present condition. Like other travellers he was far from impressed
with the buildings and endowments of its colleges which he inevitably
compares with those of the two English universities: 'These Colleges
for their buildings are very inelegant, and generally little beholding to
the curiousity of the artificers. So confused and so proportioned in
respect of our Colledges in England, as Exeter in Oxford was some 12
years since, in comparison of the rest: or as the two Temples in
London now are, in reference to Lincolns Inne. The revenues of them
are sutable to the Fabricks, as mean and curtailed. I could not learn of
any Colledge, that hath greater allowances then that of Sorbonne:
and how small a trifle that is, we shall tell you presently'.[4] Heylyn
enters into some detail on the administration of the university,
though his account is not very accurate.

In speaking of the Latin Quarter Evelyn puts forward the same
view of its colleges: 'They reckon no lesse than 65 Colleges, but they
in nothing approach ours at Oxford for state and order'.[5] Reresby
devotes only a few lines to the university and is, of course, wrong in
maintaining that no students were lodged in the colleges: 'The
university . . . contains fifty-five colleges, but few of them endowed,
except one called *la Sorbonne*, and that of late by Cardinal Richelieu;
so that they are only places of publick lecture, the scholars having
both their lodging and other accommodation in the town'.[6]

Among later travellers Veryard offers merely brief and vague
comments on the university, but Northleigh devotes several pages to
the Latin Quarter since he declares that it is 'what will chiefly come
under an Inquisitive Traveller's, or Studious Scholar's Consider-
ation'. After noting the tradition that the university was founded by
Charlemagne, he adds: 'The University celebrates a Feast in Honour
of Charlemagne their Founder, at which time their publick Exercises

cease in their Colleges, and all the Regents meet at the College of Navarre, where there are Speeches and Panegyricks made on their Royal Founder'. More important, he correctly notes that the university was now in a state of decline: 'It was formerly well fill'd with Students, and abounded in more Colleges; but the number of both is diminisht now, and not above 8 or 9, in which any publick Exercise is perform'd, of which the Sorbonne, the College du Plessis, which is a sort of Nursery to that, the College of Navarr, and D'Harcourt are the chiefest'. In contrast to Heylyn's lurid account of the criminal activities of certain students,[7] Northleigh points out that by this date such immunities as members of the university formerly enjoyed had more or less vanished: 'They had the Priviledge of being free from Arrests, and the Civil and Criminal Jurisdiction of the Town; but those Franchises are not so much allow'd or insisted on now'. His account of the constitution of the university is at times somewhat confused, but what he has to say about the 'four nations' of the Faculty of Arts is correct and it also gives rise to an amusing comment:

> And for their Faculty of Arts, they have compos'd it of what they call their *Quatre Nations*, 1. Of one *Nation de France*. 2. *De Picardy*. 3. *De Normandy*. 4. *De Allemagne*. Anciently instead of the last, they had that *D'Angleterre*, but some of their Authors think that our English Nation was left out for the Germans, from the frequent Wars we formerly had with that Crown, and the Animosities the *Belle* [sic] *Esprits* or Ingenious of both Nations had against one another, and for the same Reason, I think they get now a new Nation for that of the Germans, with whom in the last Age they have been at as much Enmity, and where I am sure the French Nation is as much hated.[8]

At the very end of the century Joseph Shaw speaks slightingly of the university, taken as a whole, describing it as 'being dwindled into nothing, its Fifty five Colledges all ruinous, but about Eight or Nine, and none of these considerable, except that of the Four Nations'.[8a]

Much more interesting than the general remarks on the University of Paris are the observations on what was going on in the different faculties and colleges. Not all of our travellers made as thorough a study of these as Richard Symonds who in 1649 went on foot round the Latin Quarter, making copious notes on what he saw and was able to pick up in conversation; but other travellers contribute their quota of information though on a more modest scale.

The most impressive of all the colleges, the Sorbonne, may be left till we come to the faculty of theology. The remaining colleges had a great variety of functions. Some merely lodged and fed their students who went elsewhere for their instruction. Although others had a great many of their students in lodgings in the city, they lodged and fed a certain proportion of them. Some provided teaching in a narrow range of subjects, others taught everything from the rudiments of Latin right through to theology. For instance, of the Collège des Bons Enfants Symonds writes: 'Some call it the College des Petits Enfans. But no boyes there now, for there are 5 or 6 Preists there which are called Les Peres de La Mission. They enterteyne some Pensioners. Only one Classe here pour Le Theologie ... They eat together in their Refectorie'. The Collège des Chollets he describes thus: 'Faire buildings. It may be reckond the 4th or 5th College. About 36 Students in it Which are all Students in Theology. It has no Classes'. 'No classes in this Colledge', he writes of the Collège de Séez, 'They are all de Prestres par tout, as the Worshipfull Cobler within the gate told me'. The position of the Collège des Écossais is described with mild irony: 'One of that Renowned Nation told me there that there was 8 now there. 12 afore the late War. They onely 1y & eat here, & go to the Colleges neare for discipline'.[9]

The subjects pursued by the students were by no means limited to theology. Of the Collège de Justice Symonds writes: 'In the Chappel, which is antient, & having old painted glasse, is one of their Classes, for there are but 2 Classes in this College. The Chapel is the Classe for Philosophy .... All the Schollars lye not in the College, but in Pensions neare'. Similarly he notes of the Collège de Narbonne: 'This is a poore, small College. One of the students told me it has but 2 Classes, Phisick & Philosophy. Afore the Warr, & at best times but 12 Schollars in it'.[10]

The college which most impressed our travellers was the Collège de Navarre, which Heylyn, writing before Richelieu's rebuilding of the Sorbonne, describes as 'the fairest and largest of all the rest'.[11] Evelyn visited this college which, he declares, 'is a well-built spacious Quadrangle, having a very noble Library'.[12] Symond's notes take us far beyond these generalities:

> As you go up the hill, on the left hand are small, low buildings, which are small Schooles for Boyes, every Schollar having a Gowne of severall colors as at Cambridge, and a Velvet hatt, many. The bigger have Caps, black. The Masters in Black Gownes & Caps like the Jesuites. These Schooles have Secunda Classis, 3tia Classis &c. written over the Dore. Within 5 or 6 low plankes for the children to sit on. But in each Corner is a stately kind of a Throne, with a Deske afore it. Over the chiefe is written in faire letters painted IMPERATOR PRIMUS. CONSUL is written over a seate next it, better then the low

forme & not so good as the Emperors. IMPERATOR SECUNDUS, CONSUL the other Corner. A Rare incouragement to Learning, making the Lads dispute for these places. Upon the beame in this Schoole is painted *Tendit ad alta per ardua Virtus*. Another Classis or Schoole Had 3 Thrones or desks at the Upper end And Imp. 1 & 2^{dus} & a Crowne painted over each. Next the wall on each side 2 high formes & these Words painted upon the Wall: Censor, Senator, Tribunus, Proctor, Consul. The formes in the middle which stand close are lower. There the Master has a faire kind of pulpit deske for himselfe. Upon the beame this: Immensum Gloria calcar habet. They give here large & faire guilt books to him that has acquird the Seat of Emperor for his incouragement ... Many little Courts, Great halls & Schooles for Rhetorique, Logick, &c in this College. Here is no general eating in the Hall, but the Lads are in several pensions with several persons in the College & neare abouts. 300l a yeare for Lads Dyet & 5l a month to their preceptiur. Here most of the Nobility's sons are borded.[13]

When Bertie arrived in Paris in the summer of 1660, he too made a tour of the Latin Quarter; he was particularly impressed by this college which he describes as 'one of the ancientist in Paris':

Here is within an ancient cloister which I saw in no other college. Here I saw an act of the scholars or masque, which they performed in Latin, being very well dressed, and at the end of every part there were dancing that acted the furies and many other antique postures. The music played till they had ended their act. All this time the Masters and Presidents of the college were present to see who performed his part best, and to them that did well not only then but in the school they presented books, which custom they have not only in one particular college but throughout the whole university, as a reward for their industry in their studies all the year before.[14]

Later in the century Northleigh goes into a certain amount of detail on this college and makes one significant observation: 'This College formerly was one of the most famous in their University; and only the Sons of the Nobility resided here as Pensioners, now all sorts are promiscuously admitted'.[15]

Another college about which Symonds furnished some details is the Collège du Plessis: 'It has 2 Courts, first old, poore & narrow, & has divers Classes, 2.3.4.5. Classis Rhetorica, Logica, Where a younge Batchelor in his black stuff gowne with an [epaulette]^{16} on his left shoulder & Cap, a little different from the Jesuites, in a kind of a pulpit deske reads to his auditors, they sitting with hatts on, he reading 3 times distinctly for them to write'.[17] Northleigh describes this college as 'a Nursery to the famous Sorbonne, and who have the Government of it' and as being 'well built with all convenient Lodgings for the Students'.[18]

The Collège d'Harcourt is fairly rapidly disposed of by Symonds: 'Within is two Courts, pretty large, an old low Chappel. A Very Scurvy Hall; within are many little tables which stand promiscuously. Seaven Classes or Schooles in this College. Every Classe has a Master, and there is about 100 Schollars, all in gownes like our youngsters at Cambridge'. This entry ends with a curious note which scarcely indicates that the foundation was in a prosperous state: 'Over the way, right against this great gate, is a little gate over which are the last 2 above mentioned Coates, & is a Court belonging to this foundation. But now over the gate is: L'on prend Pensionaires ici'.[19]

For more detail about what went on in this college we must look to Northleigh who furnishes an interesting account of the disputations in which the pupils took part when they had reached the stage of philosophy:

> Their College D'Harcour is a spacious Building, not far from the Sorbonne, where there are exercises held for what they call Basses Classes; or inferior Forms of Students; who sometimes in Logick or Philosophy have perform'd very good Exercises, Their Disputants generally print a large sheet of their Theses, dedicated to some Saint above, or Patron below; in which all the Subjects and Questions are rehears'd and recited on which they are to dispute; all the Schools and all present have the Privilege to oppose the Respondents; and their manner of Argument is not confin'd to the formality of Mode and Figure, as our Syllogistical Rules oblige us to in Oxford, and to which our Disputants in Cambridge do not so strictly adhere; but what is propos'd is commonly Categorically and not Hypothetically put; so that the whole Proposition is generally granted or deny'd, and so the Dispute more Liberal and unconfin'd.

Northleigh was apparently present at several disputations in this college, although he describes only one of them, that in which a young English Catholic distinguished himself:

> I remember at one of the times I was present there, that one of our English Roman Catholick Sir J.W. a Person of great Note and as great Estate, had his eldest Son, that had been for some time educated there, that perform'd a very good piece of Exercise; or as we may call it in Cambridge (kept a good Act) and with a pretty fluentness of Elocution, and readiness in the Latin tongue; and a strenuousness and dexterity in his Replications and Answers, defended his Part very handsomely against all his Opponents; and tho' our own Country affords us

v

Colleges with which no foreign ones can compare; yet I could not be but pleas'd to see a Countryman of our own in so distant a place come off with that Credit and Applause; and a Person in view of so fair a Fortune and Estate, which generally makes them more neglectful, especially of the Learning of the Schools.[20]

Edward Browne offers a laconic note on a logic disputation which he attended at another college, the Collège Montaigu: 'I heard a dispute in logick in Collegio Montis acuti'.[21] Symonds gives quite a detailed description of the college in the course of which he stresses its reputation for harsh discipline:

Hugh Capet gave certaine lands for the breeding of poore boyes here. That is the reason they call it the College of Capet. This has a long square court & pretty large. Over sundry doors is written in fair letter

1ᵃ Classis		Rhetorica
2ᵃ Classis	for formes of	Phisica &c
3ᵃ Classis	boyes	
4ᵃ Classis		

The Chappel is small & low. In this College they were wont to putt incorrigible sturdy boyes that were not ruld by their parents to give them meat with blowes, sometimes fast them. But now this discipline is rather used at St.Lazarr.[22] Tis a threatening saying in the Country schools of France to uncontrolable boyes. Weele send you to the College of Capet.

Here in one of the Schooles which lookes like a Prison is Imperator as at the College Navar. A Schollar that lay in the towne told me he paid 10 Crownes a yeare to the Lectures of Philosophy in this College. A little boy at my landladyes payed 5l a moneth in one of these Classes, In the Phisick Classe a young Gent. that lay in the towne paid 20 Crownes for 2 yeare. They read 3 howres morning & the students write, & after dispute & after questions with their hatts on. 10 Crownes for Rhetorique & as much for Phisick a yeare in each. They call the cheife that Reades Monsʳ le Regent.

Other colleges about which Symonds has something significant to say include the Collège de Lisieux: 'This is a large Court within, an old little Chappel which stands entire, & lookes somewhat like a College Chappel. It has 7 Classes in it. Many Schollars ly in the College & are in Pension with the Master of the howse called Le Principal. More schollars ly in the Towne & come to the severall Classes'. Of the Collège de Beauvais he writes: 'It is a faire lofty Court within & the Classes large. 100 persons, as an old schoolmaster or precepteur told me. 6 Classes de humanité & one of Philosophie'. The Collège des Grassins also receives a brief note from which the following may be extracted: 'Within is a pretty faire Court. Those boyes that are in pension in the College dyne togeather in the hall. 5 or 6 severall Classes as appears by the writing over severall dores'.[23]

One college which did not yet exist during Symonds's time in Paris was later to attract a good deal of attention — the Collège des Quatre Nations which was founded under Mazarin's will when he died in 1661, though it was not actually opened until 1688. It now houses the Institut de France and the Bibliothèque Mazarine. In 1664 Downes noted: 'The college de Quatre Nations a stately fabrick now building against the Louvre'.[24] In the following year Edward Browne wrote to his father about the progress being made on the Louvre: 'The colledg for the four nations over against it, ordered to be built by Cardinal Mazarine's will, may be perfected in three yeares more'[24a] — a very optimistic forecast. In the same year Wren offered a more professional verdict on the building: 'The College of The four Nations is usually admir'd, but the Artist hath purposely set it ill-favouredly, that he might shew his Wit in struggling with an inconvenient Situation'.[24b] In 1666 Skippon provided a little more detail about the foundation: 'Cardinal Mazarin left a great legacy to build the college of four nations: Italian, French, Spanish and German: a good part of it was now finished, the front is stately made like a theatre, and it fronts towards the Louvre, being placed on the opposite side of the River Seine'.[25]

In 1675 Clenche writes in his usual denigrating style as if the building had been completed: 'Quatre Nations, A Church and Schools built by Cardinal Mazarin; the Building pretty good, but the Cupola most remarkable, having much gilding about it; and like other French things, finer without than within'.[26] Of the travellers who were in Paris in the following decade Veryard manages to get a completely wrong idea of the founder's intentions since he declares that his purpose was 'to instruct young Gentlemen in the French, High-Dutch, Italian and Spanish Languages'.[27] Northleigh whose second visit seems to have taken place after the opening of the college states correctly that Mazarin's aim was to provide for 'the Education of the Youth of four several Nations, ... those Countries where the Arms of France have extended their Conquest' — that is. Pinerolo (in Piedmont), Alsace, the Spanish Netherlands and Roussillon. He was much impressed by the library, the first to be opened to the public in Paris. He describes it in some detail after making the following general observations on the college: 'The College within has two Courts for Schools and Apartments to lodge Scholars; the Library is a very good Collection of Books made by the Cardinal; Persons are permitted to come and study there at certain hours, which was not allow'd heretofore: There are good Annual Revenues, set apart for the Maintenance and Reparation of the College'.[28]

At secondary level the University of Paris encountered considerable competition from religious orders which went in for teaching. The Oratory, founded in 1611, established a number of colleges up and down the country, though not in Paris itself. Reresby noted the order's presence in Saumur alongside the Protestant academy: 'The Romanists have here also a college or school, under the care of the Fathers of the Oratory, a fraternity lately established to lessen the interest of the Jesuits, which the other orders suspected to grow too considerable, by having so wholly under their care the instruction of youth'.[29]

The important part in education played by the Jesuits since they established their first college in the provinces in 1558 is underlined by many of our travellers. In describing his visit to Orleans in 1625 Heylyn mentions their newly founded college which, he says, is 'not yet fully finished'; he then embarks on a long and generally eulogistic account of the education which the society offered, though otherwise he regards it as a somewhat sinister organization.

He begins by praising the attention which its members give to learning compared with those in other religious orders:

> That time which the other spent at high Masses, and at their Canonicall hours, these men bestowed upon their books: they being exempted from these duties by their order. Upon this ground they trouble not their heads with the crotchets of Musick, nor spend their moneths upon the chanting out of their services. They have other matters to imploy their brains upon, such as are the ruin of Kingdoms, and desolation of Countries.

After this somewhat discordant note comes praise of their educational methods:

> To this advantage of leasure is added the exact method of their teaching, which is indeed so excellent, that the Protestants themselves in some places send their sons to their Schools; upon desire to have them prove exquisite in those arts they teach. To them resort the children of the rich as well as of the poor, and that in such abundance, that wheresoever they settle, other houses become in a manner desolate, or frequented only by those of the more heavie and phlegmatick constitutions. Into their Schooles when they have received them, they place them in that forum or Classis into which they are best fitted to enter. Of these Classes, the lowest is for Grammar: the second for Composition, or the making of Theames as we call it; the third for Poetry: the fourth for Oratory: the fifth for Greek Grammar and compositions: the sixt for the Poesie and Rhetorick of that language: the seventh for

Logick: and the eight and last for Philosophy. In each of these Schooles there is a severall Reader or Institutor, who only mindeth that art, and the perfection of it, which for that year he teacheth. That year ended, he removeth both himself and Scholars with him, into the Classis or Schooles next beyond him, till he hath brought them through the whole studies of humanity. In this last forme, which is that of Philosophy, he continueth two years, which once expired, his Scholars are made perfect in the University of learning, and themselves manumitted from their labours and permitted private studies.

Heylyn notes one striking effect which the Jesuits' training had on their pupils:

> Nor do they only teach their Scholars an exactnesse in those several parts of Learning which they handle, but they also endeavour to breed in them an obstinacy of mind, and a sturdy eagernesse of spirit to make them thereby hot prosecutors of their own opinions, and impatient of any contrary consideration. This is it which maketh all those of their education, to affect victory in all the controversies of wit or knowledge, with such a violence, that even in their verry Grammaticall disputations, you shall find little boyes maintain arguments with such a fierie impatience, that you would think it above the nature of their years.

Heylyn next points to the strength which the Society draws both from attracting pupils of noble birth and at the same time taking in boys from modest homes through offering them a free education:

> All this they performe freely and for nothing; the poor Paisants son being by them equally instructed, with that of the Noblest. By this means they get into their Society, great honour, and great strength; honour in furnishing their Schooles with so many persons of excellent quality or Nobility, of whom afterwards they make their best advantages for their strength also. As for those of the poorer sort, they have also their ends upon them; for by this free and liberall education of their children, the common people do infinitely affect them; besides that, out of that ranke of their Scholars they assume such into their fraternity, whom they finde to be of a rare wit and excellent spirit, or any other way fitted for their profession. Thus do they make their own purposes out of all conditions, and refuse no fish which either they can draw into their nets, or which will offer it self unto them.

Heylyn concludes these general observations with some remarks about the role of the Jesuits in the Counter-Reformation: 'It is thought by men of wisdome and judgement, that the planting of a College of Jesuits in any place, is the only sure way to reestablish that

Religion which they professe, and in time to eate out the contrary'.

He provides a brief account of the struggles which the Jesuits had to establish a college in Paris in face of opposition from the University. He relates (with some wrong dates, here corrected) how they were expelled from France in 1593 and, though recalled in 1603, until 1618 they were not allowed to teach everything from the humanities to theology in their Paris college.

Of this college — the Collège de Clermont, renamed in 1682 the Collège Louis-le-Grand — he has relatively little to say, though he does relate a curious anecdote to illustrate the Jesuits' strict obedience to the rules of their order: 'This I am witnesse to, that whereas the Divinity Lecture is to end at the tilling of a Bell; one of the Society in the College of Clermont, reading about the fall of the Angels, ended his Lecture with these words, *Denique in quibuscumque*; for then was the warning given, and he durst not se far trespasse upon his rule, as to speak out his sentence'.[30]

Evelyn has a curiously confused account of his contact with the Jesuits in Paris in the company of an Irishman who had been a friar in Spain and whom he describes as 'an excellent disputant'. At one moment he speaks of going with him 'to the Jesuites Colledge to be witnesse of his polemical talent' and at the next he gives a description of the Jesuits' church in the Rue St. Antoine which is a long way from the Rue St. Jacques where their college was situated. However, he relates how the ex-friar and the Jesuits who showed him their library, 'began a very hot dispute upon some poynts of divinity, which our Cavalier contested onely to shew his excessive pride, and to that indiscrete height, as the Jesuits would hardly bring us to our Coach, being put beside all patience'.[31]

Fortunately Symond's visits to educational establishments in Paris included one to the Collège de Clermont which gave rise to a detailed account of what he saw there: From this the following is extracted:

COLLEGE DES JESUITES DICT DE CLAIRMONT

This is scituate in Rue S. Jacques below the Jacobins over the way. A lofty building with faire Courts. Over the Gate in golden Letters let into black Marble

COLLEGIUM CLAROMANTANUM
SOCIETATIS IHESU
I H S

In this Court over severall dores in gold letters cutt into black Marble Tertia Quarta Phisica Metaphysica Logica Theologia. Next to the Chappel over the dore

+
S.   IGNATIO
SACRUM

Here the Schollers eat generally in the Hall. Most are pensioners. A vast multitude of little lads come every day to Schoole to this College out of the Towne which have their teaching for nothing, but perhaps not much regarded without guifts. 400 lads in the 6 Classe. All are taught to read afore admitted here. About 3000 Schollars are taught in this College . . . .

Le Vacance is one time onely in the year for a Moneths time; all Schooles & Classes are broke up during the time of Vendange. And then in the Court is erected a Theatre covered with cloth all over the Court. Here is a Comedy acted by the Schollars & students. No women act. No man suffered to enter with a sword & none admitted without a Ticket or billet.

There is a Correcteur General who whips the boyes when he is calld, the lad kneeling.[32]

A decade or so later, on a similar tour of the Latin Quarter, Bertie also came across the Collège de Clermont:

This is the Jesuits' College in which there are several schools, some for philosophy, some for humanity, others for arithmetic. Here was the first place I observed the scholars in their gowns, those which learn humanity, or rather those which are like our English school boys, wear velvet ringled hats and serge gowns, and the philosophers wear a little square cap resembling the Jesuits their masters, only that it is a great deal less. Every school hath a door into the court, whereupon there are written the titles of the seven liberal sciences resembling the schools at Oxford, so every school hath its several classes.[32a]

Towards the end of his first stay in Paris Edward Browne was given the chance to see one of the plays performed at the Collège de Clermont. He introduces the topic with the following entry: 'Pere Macbree, a Jesuit, came to invite us to a tragedy at the Jesuit's College. I had a Thesis given mee, dedicated to the King of England, which was susteined by Fitz Patrick the Sunday following the Embassadeur of England being there present at the disporte'. When the great day arrived, he met at first with a disappointment:

About nine in the morning I went to Collegium Claromantanum to get a place to hear the Comedy that was to bee acted there, but seeing the difficulty to get in by reason of the rudeness of the Swisses and the great croude of People, I came home again, dispairing to get a place, till Mr. Dicas about noon call'd mee and by the help of his friend plac'd mee just by the Stage, where I saw and heard very well. It was the tragedy of Herminigilde in latine.[33] The whole Court of the College was covered at the top with Sayles, at the bottom built with Scaffalds behinde and set with Chairs and formes nigher to the Stage.

The Stage was large and nobly Guilt, all the windowes were taken down and in every Chamber quantité des spectateurs. Betwixt every act were 4 or 5 dances. After the tragedy was ended they did donner la priz, by sound of trompet pronounce such a Scoller, of such a Classis, to have excelled in oratory, verses for which such a book was to be given him more particularly thus, the trunkes of bookes to be bestowed on the Jesuists Schollars were brought on to the Stage. There was a throne on the middle of the Stage, the Actors set upon the steps, one of them only standing on the top named aloude in order those which had made good Exercises; the trumpets blowing for every one, hee that was Calld, was hoisd up the Stage, at the table presented with a book and a laurel croune put on his head.[34]

Though at moments a little incoherent, this account of the end of the school year is a useful expansion of what Symonds has to say on this same subject.

Shortly after this Skippon visited the college; he adds something to these two accounts of it:

Clermont college is a fair, square and tall building that belongs to the Jesuits, who teach here in several schools about 2000 boys, many of which are gentlemens sons pension'd here, having several halls to dine in, and long chambers to lodge in; they say about 400 boys live here in this manner, and are not suffered to go out of the gate without leave. Many of the scholars wear colour'd gowns, fashion'd like the sophisters in Cambridge, and they have large velvet (round) caps when they learn logick, and square caps when they read philosophy. At a dispute we saw the duke of Guise, a young lad. One father . . ., a Scotsman, procured us the sight of the machines describing excellently well the motions of the planets, according to the systems of Ptolomy, Tycho Brahe, Copernicus, and the Semi Copernicans. Several sorts of clock-dials for a day, month, year, and one for the platonick year, which were all moved by one and the same machine that moves the foremention'd spheres of Ptolomy, &c. invented by father d'Arrouis.[35]

Veryard who visited Paris shortly after the college had changed its name to Louis-le-Grand, comments fairly briefly on it in his review of the Quartier Latin: 'Clermont is at present possessed by the Jesuites, where they teach Humanity, Philosophy, and Divinity; but such as Study under them can take no Degrees in the University, unless they begin, prosecute, and finish a second Course in some other College'.[36] He ends by quoting the same satirical couplet as Northleigh. In addition to quoting these satirical Latin verses on the Collège Louis-le-Grand and the provincial Collège de La Flèche,[37]

Northleigh offers one or two remarks on the Paris college and on the role of the Jesuits in education:

> This Society has here as they have in all Places where they nest, the Guidance and Government of all the Youth, and of the best rank, of which they make no small advantage; The Sieur Fouquet their last high and mighty Minister of State, that fell into as deep Disgrace, had been a good Benefactor to them; and probably tutor'd under them; the Library which he built them here is indeed the best thing they have to boast of, for number of Books and Manuscripts; among which they have heap'd up many whom they call Heretical of Protestants, and of Socinians whom both sides call so . . . In August they have a publick Play and Ball perform'd generally with great applause by their Youth, where the best Performers without distinction are encouraged by the King, with a Royal Prize.[38]

At the end of the century Shaw bears grudging testimony to the college's success when he writes of the Jesuits: 'They every where Engross the Education of Youth, insomuch, that sometimes they have Fourteen or Fifteen Hundred in this Colledge'.[39]

In their journeys through the provinces other travellers besides Heylyn encountered various Jesuit colleges and on a number of them they offer remarks of some interest. The College at La Flèche, founded by Henry IV, attracted a good deal of attention from those who happened to pass through the region between Angers or Saumur and Le Mans. In 1612, when Thomas Wentworth visited it, the buildings were still far from finished although the college was already functioning (Descartes was then one of its pupils). He was obviously much impressed with what he saw of this 'very faire colledg':

> The plot, if itt be finished, must be 3 square courts. One which is now finished for the pensioners, the second which is begune for ther scooles and church, the third for the fathers which is not begun excepting the kings house which is on one side, which is finished; but they intend upon the makinge of their colledge into an university to turne the kings house to be the loging for the Master. Thear are but as yeat within the colledg 160 pensioners, 40 Novaties, and 30 fathers and as many Scollers that logeth in the towne that makes upe the number of 1300; for the better understanding whearof . . . the pensioners are gentlemens sones that are ther placed by ther fathers to study and do loge in the Colledge 10 or 12 togeather in severall beds in one chamber, and to every chamber a father to Looke that the younge boys study, most of which after turne Novitiats when they have time for itt. Thes have thear diett in the house, butt the scollers are thos that are att bord in the towne, and comes only to ther lectors.[40]

The anonymous traveller who visited the college in 1648 found it 'about the bignesse of St. Johns College in Oxford', but added that 'the building is not so beautifull, nor the library so bigge as the college library'.[41] For Robert Montagu who visited La Flèche in the following year, it was 'the statelyest colledge in all France'; one feature which particularly struck him was 'a very fine play house with a theatre of 3 stories high where the scholars play twice a yeare in Latin'.[41a] Thomas Browne was much impressed with what he saw at La Flèche — 'a town which was given by the king unto the Jesuits for an university, which is now the most famous one in France'. He adds: 'The Jesuits church is a very brave structure, and richly adorned'.[42]

Reresby does not add a great deal to these descriptions of the college, but he does make some general observations on the Jesuits as educators and he also tells the sad story of one noble family being extinguished by their wiles:

> It is not the least of those many policies practised by this order, to admit of none into their society, but either the noble, the rich or the ingenuous, which their having so much of the youth under their instruction and care, gives them opportunity sufficient to cull out. But to show more plainly their industry in this kind, where there is any thing to be acquired; it will not be impertinent to mention what I had from the mouth of a sad father, a count, of good estate and family in Dauphiny, concerning his children.
>
> He told me he had three sons, all sent to perform their studies with the Jesuits: the first being melancholy, gave them better opportunity to work into him to leave the world, and lead a religious life; the second (by the example of his brother, and the insinuation of his masters) did the same, notwithstanding all the dissuasions of his friends; the third, being about twelve years old, was then taken away, lest he might be prevailed upon by the same arts, and sent to an academy at Paris, not so much to study exercises as diversions. When he came out, his father allowed him an extraordinary equipage, coach and horses, a numerous retinue, and, indeed whatever he desired to enamour him the more of the world; all which was not sufficient to efface his first impressions, renewed by a visit he made to his brothers, so that no endeavours could oppose his entering into the same cloister, leaving his father without a son, though not without many heirs, the greatest part of his estate by this means going to the college.[43]

Lauder never actually went to La Flèche, but he too picked up and inserted in his journal the same Latin distich on the Jesuits' college as Northleigh was to set down a couple of decades later.[44] He did, however, have contacts with other Jesuit colleges, first at Orleans:

Just the Sabath before my parting from Orleans began the
Jesuits Logick and Ethick theses to be disputed: the Master of
Ogilvy and I went to hear, who bleetly stayed at behind all
almost; I as give I had been a person interested thrust into the
wery first rank wheir at the distributor I demanded a pair of
Theses, who civilly gave me a pair, against which tho I had not
sein them till then, I durst have ventured an extemporary
argument, give I had known their ceremonies they used in their
disputing and proponing, which I fand litle differing from our
oune mode. The most part of the impugners ware of the
religious orders; some of them very sharply, some tolerably and
some pittifully. The first that began was a Minim against a
Logicall Thesis that was thus, *Relatio et Terminus non
distinguuntur*. The fellows argument was that usual one, *quae
separantur distinguuntur et haec* etc., the Lad answered by a
distinction, *quae separantur per se verum: per accidens, falsum*;
and so they went on. The lad chanced to transmit a proposition
one tyme: the fellow in a drollery replied, *si tu transmittas ego —
revocabo*.

While at Poitiers, he records an anecdote about a disputation in the
Jesuits' college there: 'Tuo boyes studieing the grammar in the Jesuits
Colledge at Poictiers, disputing before the regent on their Lesson, the
on demanded, *Mater cuius generis est*: the other, knowing that the
mother of the proponer had the very ill name of a whore, replied
wittily, *distinguo*: *da distinctionem* then; replied, *si intelligas de mea
est foeminini*; *de tua, est communis*'. Lauder has one more entry on
the subject, on a point for which the Jesuit colleges had a bad
reputation: 'The Jesuites whipes their scollers very cruelly, yea they
whipt on to death at Poictiers: yet the father could obtaine nothing
against them'.[45]

Because of the city's geographical situation the Jesuit college at
Lyons drew more comments from our travellers than any of those
outside Paris. Coryate gives a particularly long account of this college
which had been taken over by the Jesuits some forty years before his
travels, and he depicts it as being in a very flourishing state:

I was at the Colledge of the Jesuites, wherein are to be
observed many goodly things: The severall Schooles wherein
the seven liberall sciences are professed and lectures thereof
publiquely read. In their Grammar schoole I saw a great
multitude of yong Gentlemen and other Schollers of meaner
fortunes at their exercises. It is a very faire Schoole adorned with
many things which doe much beautifie it, especially the curious
pictures ... One of the Jesuits that used me very kindly, shewed
me their library, which is an exceeding sumptuous thing, and
passing wel furnished with books. He shewed me the King of

Spaines Bible, which was bestowed on them by the French King
Henry the fourth. Of all faculties they have great store of bookes
in that library, but especially of Divinity . . . Besides, they have
workes of all the learned men of their order that have written,
and the pictures of all those of that order that have suffered
death for preaching their doctrine. Amongst the rest the picture
of Edmund Campion, with an Elogium subscribed in golden
letters, signifying why, how, and where he dyed . . .[46] Of the
Society of them there are threescore and no more. But of those
punies, those tyrones that are brought up under those
threescore, there are no lesse then a thousand and five
hundred.[47]

For a man who was later to write a famous treatise on education
Locke showed strangely little interest in the Jesuit colleges. The only
one on which he comments is that of Lyons, and even then he has
nothing to say about the education offered there.

We saw the Jesuits' Colledg. At the first entrance there is a
pretty large quadrangle, all the sides of which are high buildings,
having the walls coverd with various pretty well painted figures,
representing some of the 4 parts of the world, others other
things which, for want of time & a instructer, we could not soe
particularly observe. Only there was represented, in one row of
them continued quite round the square, in certain squares put at
a distance, the most considerable accidents that had happened
to this citty. Within we saw noe thing but the library which is the
best that ever I saw except Oxford.[48]

Another visitor to Lyons in the second half of the century,
Northleigh, was also impressed by the college, though he found the
library in a state of some disorder after a recent fire:

The Jesuites College you find here, as in most other Places the
finest; seated on the side of the Rhosne; the Quadrangle
regular, and neatly painted in Fresco, too fine to be expos'd to
Wind and Weather, which on the East side begins to decay from
the western Winds beating stiff upon it, and bearing the Storms
down from the Mountains. I was present at some of their
Exercises for their Degrees; for which they dispute in one of
their Schools as they did in Paris. In their Chappel is a pretty
Altar-piece of Lapis lazuli, with a good piece of Painting of
Blanchard's who was then their best Hand, and dy'ed at our
being there.[49] They have a good Room for a Library, but the
Books are not so extraordinary; and even those then in
Disorder, occasion'd as one of the Fathers told me, by the Fire
they had not long before.[50]

Bromley and Ferrier also made entries on this subject, but they add
nothing to what other travellers have to say about this college.

On his way out of France Ferrier did, however, visit another of the Society's colleges, though he found it in rather a bad state. The college at Saint-Omer was of special interest to English travellers (it is the ancestor of Stonyhurst College): 'The first thing we visited was the English Jesuits Colledge, which is now rebuilding, the greatest part of it being about 3 years since burnt to the ground, it will be very fine when finished but as yet can see little of it'.[51] A similar curiosity had driven Kennet in 1682 (two years before the fire) to borrow a horse and ride over from Calais. The result is an interesting description of the college as it then was:

Visited the English Covent. The inscription over the gate: *Dieu convert les Anglois*. After admittance conducted by a seniour Jesuite through the whole Colledge. A very capacious Theatre with an open Area, severall covered galleries & a convenient stage whereon upon solemn occasions, they have publick Actings. Their School divided into several apartments for each science with a distinct master. Their dormitory in long, large galleries with single beds & each schollers name wrot over. Their stare case so contriv'd that by a lamp placed at the bottom the whole ascent is enlightened. Billiard tables & bowling allys & other conveniences for recreation allowed without liberty of going out of their gates.

After set hours of school a publick, long study for retirement, each scholler his appropriated place with a desk, an inkstandard, crucifix & some picture; the seats so placed as 1 candle serves 4; at the upper end a repository of manuscripts & some other rareties raild off. An infirmitory separate from the other buildings with an apothecaries shop at the end & all other conveniences.

Lads admitted of any age with an allowance of 25 1. per annum by their parents. Diet, washing, &c. praepared within their own walls by respective officers clad in the same apparel & called brethren. Their Refectory set round with severall tables for the respective classes, adorned with severall pictures; 2 balconies raised on each side about the middle where some scholastick exercises are performed every meal.

The next section concerns English rather than French history, because of its connection with Titus Oates and the recent Popish Plot:

Entertained with a gentile breakfast & placed at the same table where Oats sate at the same time he swore to have been in England. Oats branded with many bitter epithets. His degree at Salamanca a notorious sham. He was such an unteachable dunce that to get rid of him from St. Omers, they sent him of some message to Valladolid in Spain where he continued not long before he was expelled, at which time he run back to England.

Kennet then continues his account of his visit to the college:

> The chappell bedecked with very glittering ornaments. Yet it was disowned that they paid any religious worship to any of their pictures; my objection of their occasionall, if not intentionall idolatry replied to by an acknowledgement that the common people were to be kept in a devout kind of ignorance, & that the neglect of this peice of policy must needs be repented of by the Church of England.
>
> Many wheedling invitations & winning proposals to tarry & be adopted into their Society, being complimentally dismisst.[52]

Shaw visited St.Omer at the end of the century and reported rather sourly on what he found there:

> There is a Convent of about Thirty English Jesuits, and a Seminary or School, where I counted One hundred sixty three English Youths that were bred up in a Religion inconsistent with, and destructive to that publickly profess'd in their Native Country: and tho' they knew me a Protestant, yet they received me with all the Civility and Address that insinuates into the Heart, and captivates the Souls of Men. A League off St. Omers at Watte is another English Jesuit's *Noviciat* or Seminary, where lies buried Father Peters, the late King James's Confessor.[52a]

Before passing on to our travellers' impressions of the three higher faculties in French universities, we may pause to have a look at what they have to say about a special form of education provided for young noblemen in the numerous *académies* to be found both in Paris and the provinces. The meaning of the term is admirably explained by Howell in his *Instructions for forreine travell*: 'For private Gentlemen and Cadets, there be diverse Academies in Paris, Colledge-like, where for 150 pistoles a yeare, which come to about 100 l. sterling per annum of our money, one may be very well accommodated, with lodging and diet for himself and a man, and to be taught to Ride, to Fence, to manage Armes, to Dance, Vault, and ply the Mathematiques'.[53] Lord Willoughby, according to Pridgeon, 'went into Mons. Devaux Academy in the fauxbourgs of St.Jermins at Paris' in November 1647 and left it in the following July, and in January 1649 he 'entered to ride esterne in Mons. de Loche his Academie at Angers', a town in which he remained until March.[54]

When Evelyn was in Paris in 1644, he made the following entry in his diary:

> Here I also frequently went to see them ride & exercise the Greate-horse; especially at the Academy of Monsieur du Plessis, and de Veaus; which are particular Scholes of that Art frequented by the Nobility; and besides the riding of the Great

Horse Young-Gentlemen are taught to Fence, daunce, play on musique & some skill in Fortification & the Mathematics: and truely the designe is admirable & very worthy; some of them being at the Charge of keeping neere a hundred brave horse, all of them manag'd to the great saddle.

He also noted the presence of such an *académie* at Richelieu: 'To this Towne belongs the Academy, where besides the exercise of the Horse, Armes, Dauncing &c. All Siences are read in the Vulgar French; Professors stipendiated by the greate Cardinal, who by this, the Cheape living there, & divers Priviledges, not onely designd the improvement of the vulgar Language, but to draw People & strangers to the Towne'.[55] He does point out, however, that since Richelieu's death two years earlier the town was only thinly inhabited, partly because of its remote position. In his *State of France* he stresses the importance of the *académies* in the military training of French noblemen who formed a great part of the cavalry: 'The Horse is an exercise unto which they have so naturall a disposition and addresse, that the whole earth doth not contain so many Academies dedicated chiefly to this Discipline, and other martiall Gymnastiques, wherein they handsomely attain to competent perfection in whatsoever is active and proper for their youth and inclinations'.[56]

Later Edward Browne was to satisfy his curiosity by a visit to 'Dr. Veaux's Academy' where he 'saw a great many ride the great horse';[57] while Locke informed his pupil's father, Sir John Banks, that the youth had decided not to 'put himself into an Academy', but that 'he rides in one of them'.[58]

Returning now to universities, the first higher faculty to be considered is that of theology. Here the Sorbonne received inevitably a great deal of attention. Heylyn who was in Paris before the buildings were reconstructed at Richelieu's expense, furnishes some interesting information about the way of living of the fellows of the Maison et Société de Sorbonne who resided there:

It consisteth meerly of Doctors of Divinity: neither can any of another profession, nor any of the same profession not so graduated, be admitted into it. At this time their number is about 70; their allowance, a pint of wine (their pinte is but a thought lesse then our quart) and a certain quantity of bread daily. Meat they have none allowed them, unless they pay for it: but the pay is not much: for five Sols (which amounteth to sixpence English) a day, they may challenge a competency of flesh or fish, to be served to them at their chambers.

On the more academic side of the lives of the doctors of theology he adds:

These Doctors have the sole power and authority of conferring degrees in Divinity: the Rector and other officers of the University, having nothing to do in it. To them alone belongeth the examination of the students in the faculty, the approbation, and the bestowing of the honour: and to their Lectures do all such assiduously repair, as are that way minded. All of them in their turnes discharge this office of reading, and that by sixes in a day: three of them making good the Pulpit in the forenoon, and as many in the afternoon.[59]

Evelyn among others was much impressed by the new Sorbonne created by Richelieu: 'The restauration which the late Cardinal de Richlieu has made to it of most excellent moderne building, together with the sumptuous Church of admirable Architecture is far superior to the rest: The Cupola, Portico and whole Designe of the Church is very magnificent'.[60] Symonds has for once very little of interest to say about this particular college as he merely describes the buildings, but he makes one pungent remark which reflects on all the other Paris colleges: 'Nothing in all the University like a College but this'.[61] On the other hand Finch compares the college unfavourably with what could be found in Oxford or Cambridge: 'The Sorbonne is the best built College in Paris but not so well built as many in our University'.[62]

Evelyn did go inside the building, accompanying the Irish ex-friar who had earlier disconcerted the Jesuits:

We enter'd into some of the Scholes, and in that of Divinity we found a grave Doctor in his chaire with a multitude of Auditors, who all are Writers after his dictats, this they call a Course: After we had sate a little, up starts our Cavalier and rudely enough begins to dispute with the Doctor, at which (and especially to see a fellow clad in the Spanish habit which is in Paris the greatest bugbare imaginable) both the Scholars & Doctor fell into such a fit of laughter, as no body could be heard speake for a while; but silence being obtained, he began to speake Latine, and make his Apology in so good a style, that their derision was turn'd to admiration, & beginning to argue, he so baffled the Professor that with universal applause they all rose up and did him very great honors, waiting on us to the very streete and Coach, & testifying a greate deale of satisfaction.[63]

There is a very brief passage on the University of Paris in Evelyn's *State of France*: 'Amongst the Faculties of Paris, there are some good and dextrous Divines; but their School Exercises are dull and perfunctory things, in competition with what was wont to be performed here in our Universities'.[64] What this comparison was based on is not made clear.

Locke maintained a masterly silence on the subject of the Faculty of Theology, but in the same period Covel does offer some information on the members of the Sorbonne: 'They have 200 of that society, but there is room onely for 37. According to their seniority they take place, which is reckon'd in yeares, not standing. They have no profits, onely their chamber. Every one a key to the Library'.[65] Burnet appears to have been the only traveller to have had any sort of real discussion with members of the Sorbonne. In his account of his visit to France in 1683, when a breach with Rome seemed imminent, he mentions three men — Faur, Pique and Brayer — with whom he talked. He drew the conclusion that 'they were generally learned only in one point: Faur was the best read in ecclesiastical history of any man I saw among them: And I never knew any of that Church that understood the Scriptures so well as Pique did'.[66]

Of the travellers in this period of the century Northleigh is the one who devotes most attention to the Sorbonne which he describes as 'a Seminary sufficiently stock'd with studious and learned Men; as well as a Structure and Foundation nobly built and endowed; and for both, one of the best Ornaments of Paris: as it presents itself at present to the Strangers View, it has all the Meen and Magnitude of a modern piece of Architecture: The old Foundation was but plain and ordinary'. After a brief account of the great court and a long description of the library he explains how a doctorate was obtained: 'Their manner here of Commencing or taking their Degrees, is only first to be oblig'd for three years to hear Lectures in publick; then they may be admitted to the Batchelors, and then two years after to proceed as Licentiates; who are generally the Opponents of those that afterward come to take upon them the *Doctoratus*.'

There follow some rather sarcastic comments on the Sorbonne's subservience to Louis XIV in his recent clash with the Papacy:

> These Gentlemen, at first a sort of Royal Foundation, have very gratefully since adher'd to the Crown, their first Founder, and seldom stuck to let their Principles run parallel in everything that related to the Regale, insomuch that this Latitude of their Principles or narrowness of their Souls is condemn'd by several of their own Religion, as an obsequious piece of Impiety, and the serving of their King before their God; and an ingenious Person of their own Persuasion discoursing with me upon this Subject, said to me very seriously, That at any time upon His Majesty's Request, the Sorbonne and the Parliament wou'd be for setting up a new Church, and modelling a new State.

Northleigh also offers some interesting comments on the disputations at which he was present, though he expresses some surprise at the way in which ticklish questions were handled:

I was some time at some of their Exercises and Disputations, which they managed with much Order and Decency; their Batchelors of Divinity wear their Lambskins and Tippets like our Batchelors of Arts in Oxford, and their Subjects on which they exercise them selves, are commonly, the Sacrament, and Transubstantiation; the Trinity, and Incarnation, which being in that Church with them so much the sole Object of their Faith, even to the subjecting of all Sense and Reason; made me admire they would admit of any Reasoning or Dispute among them about it; especially concerning their Sacramental or miraculous Conversion; upon which the Opponent cannot but urge if he will argue strenuously, all the stout Arguments of those Authors they make so Heretical; and so publickly not only doubt but disprove, what they so implicitly are bound to believe.

He goes on to explain that he is against any 'scholastick Disputes in publick on the Subjects of Divinity' since in England too 'many that come with itching Ears may go away with perplex'd Hearts'.[67] When he was in Paris in 1713, Berkeley satisfied his curiosity about this institution: 'I was present at a disputation in the Sorbonne, which indeed had much of the French fire in it'.[67a]

In contrast the Paris Faculty of Law receives little attention. It has to be remembered that until 1679 an ordinance of Charles IX prevented it from teaching civil law. It was only then that the teaching of both Roman and French civil law was authorized. That explains why, writing thirty years earlier, Symonds should call the Faculty building in the Rue St.Jean de Beauvais 'le College de Droit canon'. His description of it has some interest:

Tis not so properly a College as Les Escoles publiques de Droict Canon, for onely the 4 Professors which are Doctors lye in this place. There is an Upper Roome being a little Hall which is cald La Sale de Reception des Bachelers or Aula Examinandorum Baccalauriorum. In the window of that Hall is the picture of St. Ambrose in a Miter, crosier & Cope, and a Doctor in a Red gowne kneeling & praying to him.

This Howse is properly a place of Reading or professing the Canon Law. They have Termes & Vacacons & have Lectiones par totum Annum Accademicum every Munday, Tuesday, Wednesday & friday. Tis our Vacacon from August to November. Below is a large, old, Low Roome, having a Pew of old pillars of stone in the middle & deskes and seates for the Professors & the rest. This is the Schooles. In one Window 6 Professors in Red Gownes as above, kneelinge to the Virgin. It seemes formerly there were 6 & now reduct to 4. Three of these professors are maried & may live in the Towne.[68]

This is all that our travellers have to offer on the Paris Law Faculty, though there are frequent references to others in the accounts of their travels in the provinces. Some of these are too insignificant to be worth quoting — those to Caen and Cahors. The Law Faculty at Valence earns several mentions. Evelyn, for instance, writes: 'The Towne having an University famous for the Civil Law is much frequented',[69] and Clenche offers his usual sneer: 'Valence, another Wall'd City not worth notice, unless the breeding Lawyers can make it valuable'.[70] On his way down the Rhone valley Locke stopped at Valence of which he noted: 'The Cathedral the plainest I had any where seen. The Schola Juris et Medicinae here very meane'.[71] Bromley who also visited this Faculty of Law is rather non-committal in his remarks: 'I saw the Colledge, consisting of one small Court, in which are the Schools, where the Lectures are read by the Professors, and the Library'.[72]

The provincial law faculty which attracted the most attention was Orleans. Heylyn indeed devotes several pages to it, pointing out first of all that the University was really simply a Law School. If one allows for some exaggeration in his observations, they will be seen to convey a certain number of interesting facts:

> The place in which they read their Lectures, is called *les grand escoles*, and part of the City, *La Universite*; neither of which attributes it can any way remit. Colledge they have none, either to lodge the students, or entertain the Professors, the former sojourning in divers places of the Town, these last in their severall houses. As for their place of reading which they call *Les grans escoles*, it is only an old barn converted into a School, by the addition of five ranks of formes, and a pew in the middle, you never saw a thing so mock its own name.

From this he passes to the officers of the University:

> The present professors are Mr. Furner, the Rector at my being there; Mr. Tuillerie, and Mr. Grand. The fourth of them named Mr. Augrand, was newly dead, and his place like a dead pay among the Souldiers not supplyed; in which estate was the function of Mr. Brodee, whose office it was to read the Book of Institutions, unto such as come newly to the Town. They read each of them an hour, in their turns, every morning in the week, unlesse Holydayes and Thursdayes, their hearers taking their Lectures in their tables. Their principall office is that of the Rector, which every three months descends down unto the next, so that once in a year, every one of the professors hath his turn of being Rector. The next in dignity unto him is the Chancellour, whose office is during life, and in whose name all degrees are given, and the Letters Authenticall, as they term them, granted.

The present Chancellour is named Mr. Bouchier, Dr. of Divinity, and of both the laws, and Prebend also of St.Croix; his place is in the gift of the Bishop of Orleans, and so are the Chancellors Places in all France at the bestowing of the Diocesan.

After pointing out that this had at first been the position at Oxford, Heylyn goes on to deal in his usual boisterous style with a point which is amply documented in contemporary French sources — that to secure a law degree in Orleans the essential thing was to pay the necessary fees:

In the bestowing of their degrees here, they are very liberall, and deny no man that is able to pay his fees. *Legem ponere* is with them more powerful then *legem dicere*, and he that hath but his gold ready, shall have a sooner dispatch, then the best Scholar upon ticket . . . It is the money which disputeth best with them . . . The exercise which is to be performed, before the degree taken, is very little, and as trivially performed. When you have chosen the Law which you mean to defend, they conduct you into an old ruinous chamber. They call it their Library; for my part, I should have thought it to have been the warehouse of some second hand Bookseller. Those few books which were there, were as old as Printing; and could hardly make amongst them one cover, to resist the violence of a rat. They stood not up endlong, but lay one upon the other, and were joyned together with cobwebs in stead of strings. He that would ever guesse them to have been looked into since the long reign of ignorance, might justly have condemned his own charity; for my part, I was prone to believe that the three last centuries of years had never seen the inside of them; or that the poor paper had been troubled with the disease called *Noli me tangere*. In this unluckie roome do they hold their disputations, unlesse they be solemn and full of expectation, and after two or three arguments urged, commend the sufficiency of the Respondent, and pronounce him worthy of his degree. That done, they cause his Authenticall Letters to be sealed; and in them they tell the Reader with what diligence and pains they sifted the Candidati; that it is necessary to the Commonwealth of learning, that industry should be honoured; and that on that ground they have thought it fitting *post angustias solamen, post vigilias requietem, post dolorem gaudia,* (for so as I remember goeth the form) *to recompense the labours of* N.N. *with the degree of Doctor or Licentiate*; with a great deal of the like formall foolery, *Et ad hunc modum fiunt Doctores.*[73]

Orleans attracted many foreigners, especially Germans, who, Heylyn observed, 'have here a corporation, and indeed do make among themselves a better University, then the University'. He is full of praise for the way in which the German students conducted their affairs:

> This Corporation consisteth of a Procurator, a Questor, an Assessor, two Bibliothecarii, & 12 Counsellors. They have all of them their distinct jurisdiction, and are solemnly elected by the rest of the company every third month. The Consulship of Rome was never so welcome to Cicero, as the office of Procurator is to a Dutch Gentleman; he for the time of his command ordering the affaires of all his Nation; and to say truth, being much respected by those of the Town. It is his office to admit of the young comers, to receive the moneys due at their admission, and to receive an account of the dispensing of it of the Questor at the expiring of his charge. The office of Assessor is like that of a Clerk of the Councels, and the Secretary mixt. For he registreth the Acts of their Councels, writeth Letters in the name of the House to each of the French Kings, at their new coming to the Crown; and if any prime or extraordinary Ambassador cometh to the Town, he entertaineth him with a speech. The Bibliothecarii looke to the Library, in which they are bound to remain three hours in a day of their severall turns. A pretty room it is, very plentifully furnished with choise books, and that at small charge; for it is here the custome, that every one of the Nation at his departure, must leave with them one book, of what kind or price it best pleaseth him. Besides, each of the officers at the resigning up of his charge, giveth unto the new Questor a piece of gold about the value of a Pistolet, to be expended according as the necessitie of the state requires; which most an end is bestowed upon the Increase of their Library.

The only criticism which Heylyn allows himself of what he calls 'a hearty and a loving Nation' is that when they speak Latin, they should really learn to speak it 'more congruously'.[74]

Some twenty years later when Evelyn visited Orleans, he has some comments to make on the university. He was obviously less favourably disposed towards the Germans he found there when he wrote: 'The Language for being here spoken in greate purity, as well for divers other Priveleges, & the University, makes the Towne to be much frequented by strangers, especially Germans; which causes the English to make no long sojourne here; but such as can drinke & debauch'. He gives a fuller account than Heylyn of the division of the students (as in the Paris Faculty of Arts) into 'nations' and speaks more favourably of the library facilities: 'The University is very antient: divided now by the students into that of 4 Nations French, High-Dutch, Normans and Picardins who have each their respective protectors, severall Officers, Treasurers, Consuls, Seales, &c. There are in it two reasonable faire Libraries publique: whenc one may borrow a booke to ones Chamber, giving but a note under hand, which is a custome extraordinary, & a confidence that has cost many Liberarys deare'.[75] Some forty years later on his way back from Italy Bromley also passed through Orleans, but he was not greatly impressed by its university which, he notes, is 'most famous for the study of the Law'. He adds: 'The Publick Schools, where the Professors and Exercises be performed [*sic*], are mean'.[76]

When Lauder arrived in Paris towards the end of April 1665 with the intention of proceeding straight to Poitiers where his father was sending him to improve his French and study some law, 'since the Colledge was just upon the point of rising', he was advised to stay for a time at Orleans where he could not only brush up his French, but also find a law tutor to give him lessons on Justinian's *Institutes*. He remained at Orleans, taking lessons on law, until the middle of July and then moved on to Poitiers. It was not, however, until the middle of November that a new session of the Faculty of Law began: 'On the 17 of November opened the Law University at Poictiers, at present the most famous and renouned in France, usually consisting of above tuo 100 scholers, some coming to it from Navarre in the very skirts of Spain, sewerals from Tholouse, Bordeaux, Angiers, Orleans, Paris, Rouan, yea from Berry it selfe, tho formerly Bourges was more renouned — their's almost nothing to be had their now — and tho in all these places their be Universities'. The local dignitaries were present on this occasion: 'The Rector of the University was their, the Mair, the Eschewines, the President of the Palais, the University of the Physicians, with a great heap of all orders, especially Jesuits'.

To mark the occasion four of the five professors delivered Latin orations:

> On its opening Mr. Umeau . . . who that year explained of the *Digest* belonging *ad nuptias*, made a harangue of wery neit Latin, which is the property of the University. His text was out of the 4th book of the *Code*, Title 5, *de condictio Indeb. 1.*, *penultima*, whence he took occasion to discourse of the Discord among the Jurisconsults raising 2 quaestiones. 1°, *utrum recentiores sunt praeferendi antiquoribus*: 2ᵈᵒ, *utrum juniores natu maioribus*, wheir he ran out on the advantage of youth: *Quot video Juvenes candidatos tot mihl videor videre aequissimus Servios, sublimissimus Papinianos gravissimos Ulpianos et disertissimos Cicerones: quod plura stellae indubio sunt jae magnitudines in Sphaera nostra Literariâ . . .*
>
> Mr. Filleau . . . gives a paratitle on the title *pro socio*: he is one of the merriest carles that can be, but assuredly the learnest man in that part of France, for the Law. *Pro socio, pro socio*, quoth

he, whats that to say *pro socio*, Tribonian speaks false Latin or non-sense, always with sick familiar expressions.

Mr Roy,[77] whose father was Doctor before him, explained that year Title of the Code *de rescindenda vendit*. Mr. Gaultier, who left Angiers and came to be a Doctor their, explained the title of the canon Law, *de simoniâ et ne quid pro spiritualibus exigatur*.

That is all that Lauder has to say about the professors of law at Poitiers except for an entry in which he mentions the odd pronunciation of Greek of one of them[78] and except for his contacts with another Scotsman who also taught in the law faculty.

Although he always refers to him as 'Mr. Alexander', this must have been Alexander Strachan. Lauder took private lessons from him, but, partly no doubt owing to the difference of religion, relations between them seem to have been cool:

> For Mr. Alex[r] its some 17 years since he came to France: he had nothing imaginable. Seing he could make no fortune unless he turned his coat, he turned Papist; and tho he had passed his course of Philosophy at Aberdeen,[79] yet he began his grammar with the Jesuits; then studied his philosophy, then married his wife (who was a bookbinders wife in the toune and had been a woman of very il report) 50 year old and mor, only for hir gear, and she took him because he was bony. Studied hard the Law (Pacius, as he told me, giving him the first insight) and about some 5 year ago having given his trials was choosen *institutaire*.[80] He is nothing without his books, and if ye chap him on that he hath not lately meditate on, he is very confused. He is not wery much thought of by the French, he affectats to rigorous a gravity like a Spaniards, for which sewerall (as my host) cannot indure him. Also his pensioners are not the best treated . . .
>
> He began his lessons 23 of November. A Frenchman casting up the Rubrics of the Digest, he found *de edendo*. He showed himself very offended whey Tribonius had forgot Titulus *de Bibendo* also . . .
>
> Mr. Alex[r] in salaire hath only 600 livres, the other 4 each 1000, also sewerall obventions and casualities divided amongs them, of which he gets no scare, as when any buyes the Doctorat.[81]

Our travellers had among them several doctors and two medical students so that there is far more information about the last of the higher university faculties to be considered. In his tour of the University of Paris Symonds offers an interesting account of the building occupied by the Faculty of Medicine in the Rue de la Bûcherie:

Escholes de Medecine is a low Roome square with pillars in
the middle betwene the Place Maubert & the Hospital de Hostel
Dieu. Here every Sunday after Vespers one of the Physick
Professors which are to the number of 26 have lectures, the
young Students sitting round about, every one after another
asking the Professor who is a Doctor what question he thinkes
fitt, & the doctor resolves him. The question is put in Latine, &
he answers in French, but much mingled with Latine & storyes
& merry Tales. That Cardinales were *voraces omnium
beneficiorum*. Their Readings are printed & a woman sitting at
the dore sells them to the Students at a reasonable price. That
the most common medicines were best to be used. Exclaymed
against the rare drugs of Judyes[82] & of quacks curealls.

Other dayes in the forenoone I have seene one in the Chaire
which is a large deske, high, reading to young Students that sitt
below. He reades twice till they write every word. His habit is
like that of Abbots or lawyers, such a Cap &c.[83]

The medical student, Edward Browne, on his arrival in Paris
towards the end of April 1664 began to attend lectures given in the
Faculty of Medicine:

This afternoon I heard Dr. Moureau, Dr. of Physick, read in
the Physick schools at 4 of the clock & after him Dr. Pattin at 5
of the Clock. This latter is the maddest fellow for a professor
that ever I heard speake, but I was much disappointed in my
expectation of understanding all hee said by reason hee used the
French tongue so much. I was taken with one custome here,
which is the freeness of their manner of instructing, where any
auditour objects what hee lists or asks any question of the
Professor even in the middle of his discourse.[84]

A few weeks later he told his father what lectures he was attending: 'I
heare four physick lectures, Dr. Maureau reads *de hernia*; Dr.
Dyneau, *de febribus*; Dr. Pattin answers all doubts and questions
proposed; Dr. Le Bell reads of chirurgicall operations'.[85] During his
stay in Paris he occasionally records his impressions of the different
professors. Of one lecture of Alexandre Denyau he writes, for
instance: 'His lecture was about one of Gallen's Definitions of a
Feavor, upon which hee discoursed very rationally as to the logicall
proofs of this Definition'.[86] Guy Pattin (1602-72) certainly comes in
for most mentions. 'It is the old Guido Patin that reads here, to whom
Praevolius dedicates his books'. he told his father. 'Hee is very old,
yet very pleasant in his discourse, and hearty; hee is much followed, is
a Gallenist, and doth often laugh at the chymists'.[87] Shortly before he
left Paris for Italy he had an accidental encounter with Patin: 'As I
was standing in Bouillet's shop, in comes Dr. Patin. Bouillet told him

whose son I was; he saluted mee very kindly, asked mee many things concerning my father, whom hee knew onely as Author of Religio Medici, discoursed with mee very lovingly, and told mee he would write to my father'.[88] His references to the other professors are generally limited to recording his presence at their lectures, though occasionally he gives a little more detail, as here: 'At ten of the Clock in the morning, I went to the Schoole and heard Le Bel read a lecture de Hernia so longe as I lost my dinner'. He also mentions attending in August an anatomy lecture given by Dyneau's son: 'After dinner I went with Dr. Napper, my Chamber fellow, to Juillet's, a Chirurgien's house right over against us, who with Dr. Dyneau Junior, son to Dyneau one of the Professors, begins this day to read an anatomy lecture. There was a sceleton laid on the table. His discourse this day was much the same with the first Chapter of Galen de Ossibus'.[89]

The lectures at the Faculty of Medicine were not the only ones in Paris available to anyone interested in the subject. Earlier Evelyn had attended lectures on chemistry at the Jardin Royal des Plantes given by Nicolas Lefèvre who in 1660 was to come to England at the invitation of Charles II: 'I frequented a Course of Chymistrie, the famous Monsieur le Febvre operating upon most of the Nobler processes'. This was in 1647. Four years later he began to attend another course given by the same lecturer: 'I went to see Monsieur Feburs course of Chymistrie, where I found Sir K. Digby, and divers curious Persons of Learning & quality: It was at his first opening his Course and praeliminarys in order to operation'.[90] During his first stay in Paris in 1644 he had taken care to visit the Jardin des Plantes which had its part to play in medical education:

> I tooke Coach and went to see the famous Garden Royale which is an enclosure wall'd in, consisting of all sorts of varietys of grounds, for the planting & culture of Medical simples. It is certainly for all advantages very well chosen, having within it both hills, meadows, growne Wood, & Upland, both artificial and naturall: nor is the furniture inferiour, being very richly stord with exotic plants: has a fayre fountaine in the middle of the Parterre, a very noble house, Chapel, Laboratory, Orangerie & other accommodations for the Praesident, who is allwayes one of the Kings chiefe Physitians.

Five years later he went there to hear a botany lecture given by the Scotsman, William Davison, who was keeper of the garden from 1647 to 1651: 'I went to heare Dr. D'Avinson's Lecture in the Physick Garden, & see his Laboratorie: he being *Prefect* of that excellent Garden & professor *Botanicus*'.[91]

When Edward Browne arrived in Paris in 1664, he tried to take private lessons in chemistry, but he seems to have given up the idea as he told his father that the chemist, a certain Barlet who lived in the Collège de Cambrai, 'askes three pistoles, and speakes French when hee showes it'. However, he adds, 'in the physick garden there will, in a short time, be showne all the operations in chymistry publickly, thrice in a week'.[92] The lectures at the Jardin des Plantes did not begin until well into June. On Tuesday, 8 June, on his return from a church service at Charenton, he writes: 'As I came home I found the Bills set up which gave notice that the Physick Garden opened on Tuesday next, and that the Chymistry Lectures begun then too'. Both courses in fact began on that day, first that on botany, given by Professor Jonquet:

> Wee went betimes to the Physick Garden, where Joncquet Shewed the Plants. After hee had made a peece, hee shewd us but two Plantes this day, onely the first bed, Alsine and Anagallis, with their many differences: Alsine Hederacea, Alsine foliis Chamaedrios, Alsine Montana maxima, Als. Media, Als. Minima, Al. Petraea, Al. muscosa, and divers other differences. Anagallis aquatica, Anag. rotundifolia, Anag, flore rubra, flora ceruleo, and many others.

At this point he breaks off with the observation: 'I shall quickly fill up my book if I should write all the names of plants I see, and there will come out a Catalogue after this lecture is ended'. The chemistry lectures began later in the day: 'I went in the afternoon to the Chymick lecture, which is also in Jardin royall. At three of the Clock Glaser, L'Apotheacaire du roy, shows the Chymicall operations. I came somewhat late to day. They shewd all their Vessels and told the names of them'.

On Friday, 13 June, he again attended both lectures:

> I went betimes to the Physick Garden, where were shown Many sorts of Violets, of Hesperis or Viola Matronalis, of Scabiosa, Jacea. The Jacca Pinea I gat a head of, but I have seen that of Mountpelier ten times bigger Jacea cui in squammis fibrae negra. Jacea Lustanica sempervivens is a pretty plant. Many sorts of Lucoium or stock Gillyflowre, of Roses many differences, & of Verbena . . . In the Afternoon I came to the Chymick lecture, but could not enter till the house was full. Hee set Acetum to distill, he Calcined Tartar, hee shewd us filtration per manicam Hippocratis, hee drew off some of the Spirit of [wine] Rectifiing through an instrument of his like this, the Phlegme not being able to ascend so well as the nimble spirit through so many turnings and windings.

The next day he wrote the following account of the lectures which he had attended:

I went to the Garden where was shown Stoebe, Cyanus, Tragopogon, Scornzonira, Verbaseum, Aconitum lycocthonon, & Doronicum, Digitalis, Ephemeron, and all their Sorts. It raining very fast I kept my selfe dry under a Firre at the Corner of the Physick Garden and then went home. In the afternoon to the Chymick Lecture. The Vinegar continues distilling in arena. The spirit of wine, hee shewd us an experiment to know if it were fully rectified. Putting gunpowder into a spoon and powring the spirit upon it, Light it; if it bee very pure it will set fire on the Gunpowder. Hee mixed Vitriol and Saltpeter pulveris, an. q.v. and put it in an earthen Cornüe, luting it to a large Glasse recipient to draw of Aqua Fortis. Hee took his Tartarum Calcinatum, which being not well done was black, pouderd it, mixed water with it, bouled it, and then let the ly filtrate through a Paper and a Linnen Cloath under, handsomely Contrived as ever I saw. Then evaporated the water and there remained a gray salt.

Hee tooke Antimony and Salt Petre, pulveris'd them and put them in a pot together, whose Cover was bored through. Then put in a light cole and after a whissing and whiting the Pot the Businesse was done.

On the following Monday when he was again present morning and afternoon, he found out how to have a good seat at the chemistry lecture:

I went to the Physick Garden, where these plants were shown, Blattaria, Verbasculum seu Primula veris, Sanicula, Horminum, Æthiops, Salvia, with the innumerable sorts of Ranuculi. In the afternoon I went to the Chymick lecture, where, I having [given] the Fellow Trente Sols beforehande, I entred very soon and stood very nigh. Hee tooke sal Tartari and set over the fire, continually stirring it lest it should fundere. Then boyling on it again the Lixivium, hee evaporated, and there remained a white Salt. Hee mixt dried poudred Clay and Poudred purified Nitre and put them into a retort and set them into the furnise for to distil Spiritus nitri in the same manner as aqua fortis. The Vinegre continues distilling. Hee made a Sal Antifebrile as hee calls it, in this manner, to ii ozs. of Salt petre et ii ozs, Flor. Sulph. Pulveris he pour'd vi ozs, of distilled urine, put them in a cornüe, put them upon a furnace de sable, then put to it a very large recipient not luted. The operation is delightfull to see, afterward mix the Distilled water with the Salt that remaines in the Cornüs (casting away the floures of Sulphur that rise), dissolve them upon the Sand Philtrate and Evapor. Next the Purification of Gold with Antimony and Salt petre, as is described in his book. Then the making of Aqua regis, by adding a forth part of Sal Armoniac to Aqua fortis, then set them on the sand till the Aqua fortis dissolves the Sal Armoniac.

The next day's lectures are described in much less detail, no doubt because he was beginning to feel unwell: 'These following plants and their different species ware shown: Pulsatilla, Anemone, Fumaria, Chelidonium, Nigella, Aquilegia, Consolida regalis, Millefolium . . . In the afternoon to the Chymick lecture. Hee separated Gold from Silver with Aqua regis and Silver from Gold with aqua fortis. I began to bee ill and came but late, so as I had an ill place'. The next morning he just managed to drag himself to the botany lecture: 'I still found myselfe ill, yet the desire I had of Seeing the Garden made mee Get up betimes. The weather was so bad as the Professor was forc'd to set under a great Acacia tree and name all the plants hee did intende to teach and to showe them afterward'.

That was on 18 June; it was not until Wednesday, 2 July, that he was able to return to the Jardin des Plantes to attend a lecture:

> In the afternoon I went to the Physick Garden to hear the Chymick Lecture. Hee tooke Butyrum Antimony, Spiritus Nitri ana, mixt them togeather, and destilld them to siccity, poure on the sp. nitri twice more, and destill as before. Your Bezor miner [all] you have at the bottome of the Cucurlite. He poured on spirit of wine divers times, burning it, to moderate the force of his Turbith Minerall which hee had made before. Hee continued his distillation of Butyrum antimony. Hee having dissolved Coral, of halfe the liquor hee made Sala Corlli, of the other half magisterium.

The next day he was well enough to attend both lectures:

> In the morning I rose betimes and saw the plants. Branca Ursina, Spina tomentosa, spinosissima, ramosa, Natonensis, Cinara, Vulg. Hisp. Cretica, Eryngium, Dypsacus, 3 Tragi Spina Solstitialis, flo. flavo (it is somewhat like Cardus Stellatus), Tragacantha poterion Matthioli, like to Tragacanth Anonis seu resta bovis. In the afternoon to the Chymists. Hee shewd us the Asphaltum seu olei Carabis. Hee tooke dryed wormwood in flower & put it into the Caldron to ferment with water & salt. Hee broke his glasse in [which] hee had sublimed Mercury and sublimat for Mercurius dulcis, threw it away which was at the Bottome and at the Top, Poudred that in the middle and set it to sublime again. To prepare his Panchimagogum, hee tooke of Agarick, Scammony an. i oz. upon which he pourd his best Sp. Vini., put in a bolts head and set on the sand.

The entry concludes in amusing fashion: 'Hee gave us notice that the weather being hott hee must repose himselfe next day'.

Two days later he was again feeling unwell and missed the botany lecture, though he managed to attend the chemistry lecture in the afternoon:

Hee Seperated his Ol.Chy. absynthy thus: hee took a piece of Cotton wool, twisted it about, tied a little glasse with his mouth to the mouth of the Great glasse which contained the Aq. Absor., dipped the Cotton in the Oyle, bent it, put the lower end into the little glasse, Hee kept his great Glasse full by pouring a little as the Oyle ran through the Cotton. Hee tooke a great Quantity of wormwood, dryed well, and burnt it towards his making Sal. Absinthii. His Panchimagogue infuseth still upon the ashes.

This appears to have been the last lecture which Edward Browne attended at the Jardin des Plantes during his first stay in Paris; on the following Monday (7 July) he wrote in his journal: 'This day Glaser made an end of showing his operations. I was somewhat indisposed and so was forced to repose my selfe'.[93]

When he returned from Italy a year later, he wrote to his father in somewhat unflattering terms of the lectures on botany given at the Jardin des Plantes: 'The lecture of plants heere is only the naming of them, their degrees in heat and cold, and sometimes their use in physick, scarce a word more then may be seen in every herball'. In this letter, dated 11 July, he adds: 'The next weeke will putt an end to the course of chymisterie and the plants; but I will begin a private course'. Two days later he wrote: 'Barlet's course of chymistry is not yet begun, so as I shall not see that, but goe the oftner to Glaser's, and to his partner which is now parted from him, and workes in another place of the towne'. In his last letter from Paris, sent at the end of September, he writes somewhat enigmatically, after describing the amputation of an arm which he had witnessed at the Hôtel-Dieu: 'I have not the least thoughts of staying here this winter. The anatomies beginning already, there will be nothing that can keep mee here much longer, unlesse it bee the chymick lecture; if it begins within these ten days I will hear it, so as I may set out the first of your November, if not, I believe I shall come sooner'.[94]

Several of the doctors who visited Paris later in the century have comments to offer on the Jardin des Plantes. Northleigh. for instance, writes:

Among the many memorable places I often visited their *Jardin Royal*, a Plat set aside for Botanism. Mr. Du Verney, a good Physician, excellent Anatomist, and as civil a Person inhabited here, and gave me access; and here they have a good anatomy School also, fill'd with the Skeletons of several Animals, especially one of a very large Elephant, with other Curiositys of Nature and Art. The Garden is furnish'd and kept at the King's Cost; when the Season best fits, they hold several Lectures here on the Plants. The place seem'd to me longer, though not larger than ours in Oxford. The King has also his Laboratory here supply'd with good Operators, where there is publick Admittance to their Operations, and the Poor have the benefit of the Medicines and Compositions.

Altogether Northleigh was much impressed with Paris as a centre for medical education, though he makes one important reservation:

> So that, with the help of these Hospitals, some of which I visited for to see their cutting of the Stone, where they have certainly the best Lythotomists or Chyrurgions in that Art, and where were whole Iron Chests full of Stones cut out, and what with the help of their many Liberal good Professors in Anatomy, their Chymick Lectures, Botanic Garden, &c., I look upon Paris, if it would allow Liberty of Religion to all Students, to be preferable for the Study of Physick to Leyden, Padua, Montpellier, Oxford, Cambridge, or any of the Universities I have seen or heard of, notwithstanding the renowned preference some of them have got for the benefitting those that profess themselves Students in the Faculty.

In contrast he has relatively little to say about the Faculty of Medicine, perpetrating in the process an absurd confusion between 'Bûcherie' and 'Boucherie': 'For the study of Physick, (besides the Conveniences that are in and about the Jardin Royal) in the Rue de Boucherie they have an Anatomical Theatre for the dissecting of Human Bodies, a little improperly plac'd where those of Beasts are Butcher'd and cut up'.[95]

Both Veryard and Lister stress rather the scientific work which went on in the Jardin des Plantes. The former writes: 'The Physick Garden, in the Suburbs of S.Marcel, is well stor'd with all sorts of Plants, and its Management committed to one of the King's Physicians. Here we saw the ingenuous Mons. Tournefort, who has wonderfully enrich'd the Garden with Plants, and, indeed, the Science with divers new Discoveries'.[96] Lister goes into rather more detail in his account of the garden:

> As to the King's Physick Garden, it is a very great Piece of Ground, well furnisht with Plants, and open also to walk in, to all People of Note. There is great variety of Ground in it, as Woods, Ponds, Meadows, Mounts, besides a vast Level, by which it is fitted for the Reception and Growth of most sorts of Plants.
> I first saw it in March with Dr.Turnefort, and Mr. Breman, a very Understanding and Painful Gardner. The Green Houses well stored with tender Exoticks, and the Parterrs with Simples; though but a few of them then to be seen; yet by the Trees and Shrubs, and some Plants which did not lose their Heads, I could well judge of the Furniture.

> Dr.Turnfort told me, that he shewed 100 Plants every Lesson, and he had in the Summer 30 Lessons, which made 3000 Plants; Besides the very early and late Plants, which he reckoned could not be less than a 1000 more.

After noting down the names of various rare plants which he had seen in the greenhouses, Lister offers some details about the finances of the establishment: 'This Garden is endowed by the King and the Duke of Orleans, and has 2000 l. a year Sterling Rents belonging to it, whereof 500 l. is given to the chief Physician who over-looks all, and the rest to the Botanic Reader, Dr. Turnfort, and Under-Gardners, with Lodgings for all'.[97]

There were medical faculties in a number of provincial universities, though some of these existed only on paper, as we see from Lauder's account of the one at Poitiers:

> About the 12 of December 1665 at Poictiers ware programmes affixed thorow the toune intimating that the Physitians Colledge would sit doune shortly, and that their Doyen Deacon, on Renatus Cothereau, a very learned man in his lessons, *Podagram hominum terrorem artuum que flagellum medicinali bellio acriter prosequeretur*; hence it hath this exclamation, *accurite itaque cives festinate arthici.*
>
> The same Renatus had a harangue at the beginning wherein he descryved very pedantically the lamentable effects it produces on the body of man: amongs his salutations I observed this, *Themidis nostra Argonaut a sacratissime, fidelissime, aequissime.* They get no auditors to their lessons, whence its only but for faschions sake that they begin their colledge, of which they have nothing but the name.[98]

There was, however, one outstanding provincial faculty, that of Montpellier, which attracted the attention of quite a number of our travellers, though not, it must be said, in a way to reflect adequately its reputation in the medical world. On his tour in 1612 Thomas Wentworth visited both the Faculty and the famous botanical garden:

> We saw the university scole for Phisike whear they take three degres. First they be bachelur, Licentiats and docteurs. The bachelers, when they take this degree, put on a rede old gowne with which they walke thourowe the towne, which they say was the gowne of Rablais who, going up the stares to the seat (whear the professor sitts to fulfill that sum[?] ceremony necessary for the taking of his degree), voluntary fell downe with his nose upon the stare, arising kepte a snorting; the reason asked, saide he felt the smel of many an asse that had gone thear before him. The licentiats may practise in all places except in the towne, the doctors in all places without exception. This university for

Phisike is composed of 6 professors and 8 Docteurs . . . After dinner we saw the kings garden, which is very lardge and famouse for the number of simples that are thear gathered togaither from most places in the world.[98a]

Fifty years later Bertie also devoted considerable attention to the medical faculty, not forgetting Rabelais:

The next thing most remarkable is the Schools of Physic, where you see all the professors' pictures in a scarlet and black robe, with a black square cap having on top a tuft of red silk. Among the rest of the pictures is shewn that of François Rabelais, as also his robe and capuchon conserved in great veneration. Behind the schools are many little gardens, among the rest one in which the Theatrum Anatomicum stands which is well contrived. In the middle is a table that turns round, that when any member is dissected, all the spectators may view it distinctly. Here is an ancient chair of white marble where the Professor himself sits. When any person goes out batchelor, the Professors say to him, *Vade et occide Cain.*[98b]

When Skippon visited Montpellier in 1665, he was present at the graduation ceremony for a new doctor:

The building of the schools is very meane. In one we saw the creation of a doctor of physick; the professor first made a speech, then musick play'd, after that the new doctor was adorn'd with a chain, and the girdle, and kissed, &c., then musick again, and the new doctor made his speech, then musick again; then he gave the professors, &c. thanks, and musick play'd once more: Clapping of hands was the students applause: The new-created doctor had a black gown and purple cap, and the professor had a purple gown & cap: The new doctor went up and down the town with the musick before him, and a beadle with the mace, a professor on each side of him, and a troop of scholars at his heels: In the school or room where he was created hang the picture of many Montpellier physicians; 17 publick exercises must be perform'd before you attain the degree of a doctor. There were several women present while the solemnity was of creating this doctor.

Skippon also gives some information about the teaching of anatomy in this faculty: 'Every stranger gives 20 sols to see an anatomy. Dr. Chiqueneau is the present reader, The anatomy theatre is a building that stands alone in a garden; it hath stone seats, and over the door are stones carv'd with a lyon devouring a woman'. He also noted the existence of a memento of an illustrious graduate of this faculty: 'They shew here Rablais's robe, which is now an old piece of scarlet'.[99]

Although during his long stay in Montpellier Locke was on friendly terms with a number of doctors (chiefly Protestants), he does not appear to have been favourably impressed by its medical faculty. He gives a laconic account of a disputation at which he was present: 'Disputation at the Physick Schoole. Much French, hard Latin, little Logic and little Reason. Vitulo tu dignus et hic'. A few days later he penned an even more pungent entry on the same subject: 'At the Physick Schoole a Scholler answering the first time, a Professor moderating. 6 other professors oppose with great violence of Latin & French, Grimasse & hand'.

Locke's other entries concerning the faculty of medicine describe a graduation ceremony. Not only is his account longer and livelier than Skippon's, but he also works in some criticisms of the speeches delivered on this occasion:

> The manner of making a doctor in physic was this. First came in an officer with a mace on his shoulder, very much like the one of the squire bedles' staves in Oxford. On the end of it hung a square, black cap such as the Doctors usually weare, but coverd upon the top with Sleasie silk, red, which was like a buff rampant, for it spread on each side as far as the edges of the cap. After him followed one of the professors in his scarlet robes which were of damask, & a black cap on, coverd with sleasy silk as the other. After him followed the inceptor, bare in a black gown like a batchelor of arts. The Doctor ascended into the chair & sat him downe. The inceptor followed him & stood just at the entrance. The chaire is a large, stone pulpit much like that in the Divinity Schoole at Oxford. As soon as they were got into that station, a company of fidlers that were placed behind the company in a corner of the room, strooke up. When they had plaid a litle while, the professor made signs to them to hold that he might have opportunity to entertaine the company, which he did with a speech against innovation as long as an ordinary declamation. When he had don, the musick took their turne, & then the inceptor began his speech, wherein I found litle for edification, it being, I believe, chiefly designed to complement the Chancellor[100] & other professors who were present. In the midle of his speech he made a pause, & then we had an interlude of musick, & soe went on till he came to thank us all for our company & soe concluded. Then the Doctor put on his head the cap that had marchd in on the Bedle's staff in signe of his Doctorship, put a ring on his finger, girt him about the loins with a gold chain, made him sit downe by him that haveing taken pains he might now take ease, kissd & imbraced him in token of the friendship ought to be amongst them & afterwards deliverd a booke into his hands, & soe the ceremony ended with the

inceptor making legs to each of the professors when he was come down into the midle of the roome, they sitting on both sides, & turning at every leg to salute them in their order. The professors are the Chancellor & 6 others.

Two days later Locke decided to correct and amplify his description of this occasion with the following entry:

When the Doctor had don his speech, he put on the cap & ring & used the other ceremonys to the inceptor, & then after that it was the inceptor made his speech. When all was don, they retired, professors & inceptor, into another room & there the Chancellor, takeing the cap coverd with Slesy crimson silke & in his crimson damaske robes, goes along with the inceptor through the great streets to his lodging, the musick playing al the way before, the other professors accompanying him & the scholars following, where the dore was all hung round with bays. The Chancellor enterd, where he & the rest of the professors dine with the inceptor. Of the rest he took leave at the dore.[101]

Though these entries do not furnish Locke's considered opinion of this famous medical faculty, they indicate clearly enough that he was not very favourably impressed by what he saw of it.

Veryard, another doctor, had a rather higher opinion of the Montpellier faculty:

The City is neither very large, nor well-built, but considerable for its University, chiefly frequented by Students in Physick, and serv'd by Professors of very eminent Learning. They could hardly have chosen a more agreeable and commodious Seat in all France; for the Climate is extreemly serene and temperate, and the whole Country abounds with such variety of Vegitables (above any other part of the Kingdom) that it may well serve for a Physick Garden, and Nature seems to have design'd it for that very purpose. The Degrees conferr'd in Physick are those of Bachelour, Licentiate, and Doctor ... The Physick Garden joyns to the Town, and is well stor'd with Plants methodically digested into several partitions, each having an Inscription over the Door, shewing what sorts it contains.[102]

Curiously enough, the most detailed and objective account of this medical faculty comes not from a doctor, but from a man who was later to play a certain role in English politics. In his account of Montpellier Bromley notes that 'the Study of the Law flourishes less here than in other Universities' and concentrates his attention on the faculty of medicine:

Here is the most famous University of France for the Study of Physick. The Publick Schools where the Lectures are read, and Exercises for Degrees, performed, are meanly built; no one has lodgings in them but the Chancellor; And near to them is the Anatomy-School; it is round with a Table in the middle, and several Rows of Benches, one above another, like a Theatre, for the Spectators more conveniently to behold the Operations.

He then goes on to describe the constitution of the faculty:

The Bishop of Montpellier is always Protector of the University. The Chancellor is of the King's appointment, and generally a professed Physician, he having a Duty incumbent on him, to read Lectures in Anatomy and Botanism. Besides him, there are seven Professors that read publickly in the Schools, presiding in Disputations and other Exercises, and divide the whole body of Physick among them to explain. The Chancellor has one thousand Crowns allowed him by the King, the other Professors not above two hundred each, and the whole of their Gains exceeds not four hundred.

He next describes how the professors were elected, first the theory, then the actual practice:

These Professors are elected in a very solemn manner: When there happens to be a Vacancy, Notice is given into all the provinces of the Kingdom, and any one that has been created Doctor in this University, has Liberty to appear as a Candidate. The Competitors go through a long course of Disputations; at which are present the Bishop of Montpellier, and divers Persons of Quality: After these are over, (which last at several times near a Year), the Professors vote for the worthiest. This formerly was, and indeed ought still to be their Method; but of late, though the Formalities of this Election are continued, yet Bribes to the Professors, or a Recommendation from the King's chief Physician, are surest to succeed; so mercenary are they grown, to the disparagement of the University, as well as scandal of Learning.

Finally Bromley has this to say of the students and the course of study which they had to follow:

There are ordinarily two hundred Students belonging to this University, none whereof are admitted without the Votes of the Professors, and an Examination of their Manners and Learning; but the Professors receive such advantage from them, that it is rarely known any are rejected. They live in the Town, and are not obliged to any particular Habits; but from their Matriculation must duly attend the Lectures for a Year and a half; after which they begin to do Exercises, which lasts about six Months longer; so that in two Years they commence Doctors. Their Exercises are said to be strict; but a Learned and Eminent Doctor among them, frankly confessed to me, that he never knew more than one e'er denied his Degree for Insufficiency, or

Immorality. They are first Batchelors, then Licentiates, by a License signed by the Bishop, and afterwards Doctors. When they are made Doctors, they swear themselves not to be Bastards, nor ever to have exercised any Mechanick Trade, as if a Bastard or Mechanick would be a Disgrace to that honourable Profession. About Twenty, one year with another, go out Doctors.[103]

It is unfortunately rare to find in our travellers' observations on the France of their day such a clear and detailed account of a given topic.

It remains to say something about another Paris institution of higher education, one which was outside the University — the Collège Royal, the ancestor of the Collège de France which can trace its history back to its foundation by Francis I in 1530. Northleigh is the only traveller to give a useful account of this institution:

They have another sort of College call'd their College Royal; which was begun to be founded by Francis the first, but the Wars diverted him from finishing it, intended for Law, Physick, Mathematics, and the Oriental Languages. Henry the 4 attempted to go on with it. But the Assassin took him off and prevented it; but Mary de Medicis with this King's Father, then her young Son, went with it as far as we now find it. The Professors here are paid by the King, and separated from the Body of the University.[104]

It was not until eighty years after its birth that the college acquired even the foundation stone of a building. This was laid in 1610 by the young Louis XIII shortly after his father's death; even then it was not until 1634 that the first wing of the building was completed, and all that was provided was two lecture rooms with a gallery for the library. The college had to wait for the second wing until the next reign but one.[105]

Although Edward Browne never mentions the Collège Royal, he certainly went to lectures by three of its professors. Besides those of Guy Patin on medicine (presumably given in the building of the Faculty of Medicine), he also attended lectures by two mathematicians, Gilles Personier Roberval (1602-75) and François Blondel (1618-86). Early during his first stay in Paris in 1664 he wrote: 'I heard Dr. Pattin and after Ægidius Personerius Roberval, Ramei professor, for the Mathematicks. Hee read in French upon the 47 proposition of the first book of Euclid'. Who gave the 'Mathematick lecture' which he attended four days later he does not say, but in the following week he wrote: 'I heard Roberval at six a clock at night read a mathematick lecture, di librâ'. On two occasions he attended lectures given both by Roberval and Blondel. The two entries read: 'I heard Blondel read a Mathematick lecture at 5 of the Clock. At 6 I heard Roberval', and 'I heard Blondel & Roberval read Mathematick lectures'. Later he recorded his attendance at two more lectures given by Roberval. The second reference is insignificant but of the first lecture he wrote: 'I heard Roberval read. Hee Gave two Good reasons why the Sun was not as hot when it was low as when twas high. 1. because the same Quantity of rayes lightned or struck upon a Greater part of the earth towards night or Morning then at Noon. 2. That the beams of Sun passed through more vapours'.[106]

Although the modern reader cannot help feeling that, since they were there, our travellers might well have provided even more information about secondary and higher education, what both students and more mature men offer on this subject is undoubtedly of interest.

VIII LITERARY AND INTELLECTUAL LIFE

This chapter is bound to appear somewhat scrappy. It contains contributions from a relatively small number of travellers, and it is clearly impossible to arrange their scattered observations in a completely logical fashion. Yet hidden away in their writings there are interesting scraps of information and a variety of comments on things which they saw and heard which deserve to be brought to light.

Although Lauder's observations on French life are occasionally somewhat puerile, he can often be quite shrewd in his comments, as in the following generalization on one trait of the French national character:

> Yet we discovered a beastly proud principle that we have observed the French from the hiest to the lowest (let him be never so base or so ignorant) to carry about with them, to wit, that they are born to teach all the rest of the world knowledge and manners. What may be the mater and nutrix of this proud thought is not difficult to ghess; since without doubt its occasioned by the great confluence of strangers of all sorts (excepting only the Italian and Spaniard, who think they have to good breeding at home to come and seik it of the French) who are drawn with the sweitness of the country, and the common civility of the inhabitants.

He also has an extremely interesting comment to make on the universal appeal of the French language and on the extraordinary change which had come over it since the latter part of the sixteenth century:

> To abstract from the Antiquitie of tongues, the most eloquent language at present is the French, which gets such acceptance every wheir and relishes so weill in eaches pallat that its almost universal. This it ounes to its *beauxs esprits*, who hath reformed it in such a faschion that it miskeens the garbe it had 50 or 60 years ago, witnesse l'*Historie du Serre,*[1], Montaign'es Essayes and Du Barta'es Weeks,[2] who with others have written marvelously weill in the language of their tyme, but at present is found no ways smooth nor agriable.[3]

Though this transformation of the language can scarcely have been observed by Lauder completely unaided, it is none the less correctly noted.

The universality of the French language which Lauder accepted without comment appeared to Northleigh, writing at the end of the century, to present a grave threat to the rest of Europe:

> The French Tongue spreads it self mightily, and becomes almost universal, which is more ominous than some may imagin, and makes way for the Monarchy to be so too. 'Tis not above an hundred years ago, their public Acts ran all in Latin, but since for the promoting their own language, they have abolish'd that, tho always used among Civil Lawyers, and have ordered all Process to run in French,[4] whereas we retain yet, tho' their old Enemies, our old French Law their Norman introduc'd. The Universality of the French Tongue, which some little Pedantick Grammarians may recommend to us as requisite for all Princes of Europe, that they may agree in a General Language as well as General Consanguinity, is indeed a particular good way of arguing which some Monsieurs may use, who set up a French School or Academy; but indeed a Melancholy Argument of an Universal Empire approaching, of Necks fitted for the Foreign Yoak, when their Tongues are fitted for the Foreign Language, and making what their Fathers never knew, to be their Mother-Tongue; all Flanders, and its Capital Brussels, has been long since so instructed, and which in time we may find may fit them the better for a French Government instead of a Spanish one, who when he has forgot his own language may well stand for a Cypher. The old Emperour is wiser, who perhaps upon these Considerations does discourage, if not prohibit the French to be spoken in the German Court.[5]

The primitive methods by which news was then diffused inside France are occasionally touched on by our travellers. France's first newspaper, the weekly *Gazette*, had been founded in 1631 by Théophraste Renaudot; this was very much an official organ and it was supplemented by news sheets published in French in Holland and also by manuscript *nouvelles à la main* produced in Paris. There were other unauthorized publications which commented on the affairs of the moment, as Howell points out in 1642 in his *Instructions for forreine travel*:

> There are in Paris every week commonly some Odde, Pamphlets and Pasquils dispersed, and drop'd up and down; for there is no where else that monstrous liberty (yet London hath exceeded her farre now of late, the more I am sorry) which with the Gazets and Courants hee should do well to reade weekly, and raise Discours thereon, for though there be many triviall passages in them, yet are they couched in very good Language,

and one shall feel the generall pulse of Christendome in them, and know the names of the most famous men that are up and down the World in action.[6]

Both Edward Browne and Locke mention the *Gazette*. Soon after his arrival in Paris the former bought a copy to try to improve his French, and later he read a copy in the rooms of an English friend.[7] Locke summarizes an item from the *Gazette* concerning the reduction in taxes at the end of the war in 1678.[8] Lister points out that the Gazette appeared only weekly and that its circulation was very small. 'The Gazettes come out but once a week, and but few people buy them'.[9]

Lauder has a curious entry on the way in which, while at Poitiers, he obtained news of what was happening back home in Scotland: 'In the gazetts or news books (which every friday we get from the Fullions [Feuillants] or Bernardines at their Convent, such correspondence does the orders of the country keip with thess at Paris), we heard newes passing at home. The place they bring it from they terme it Barwick, on the borders of Scotland'.[10] An interesting example of French government propaganda abroad is furnished by a letter of Sir Philip Perceval who was in Rome in May 1678 at a moment when England and France were on the brink of war:

> There is a certain kind of news-book which comes from Paris every week; it is not printed, but fairly written on a sheet of paper, and is from top to bottom nothing but a satirical pamphlet which exclaims against the English and their government, saying that the parliament makes no more of their king than if he were but a doge of Venice, that they have permitted Arianism, Anabaptists, Quakers, and I know not how many other sorts of religions, but that the good Roman Catholics are still oppressed.[11]

On his arrival in Paris in 1666 Skippon duly noted the existence of the first scientific and literary periodical to be published in Europe (it had begun to appear in January of the previous year): 'Every Monday comes out *journal des Sçavans*, a pamphlet written by one Galloyer a Parisian, and but a young man'.[12]

The interest taken by Louis XIV and his court in literature and particularly literary parlour games is noted by Locke: 'That which the French recommended, people at court here were composing sonnets or epigrams etc., and at present a good quality in esteem is to sing'.[13] Almost at the same time Covel noted the same phenomenon and even brings the king himself into his entry on the subject: 'They were much given to riddles and oenigma's in the court here. The king made this on himself and the D.ˢ Montespan ᵢ.ᵉ which signifyes in french il est couché sur elle, for they call e turned so, *e couché*, and L they pronounce, elle, est, è'.[14]

While in Paris, a fair number of our travellers seem to have attended the different theatres of the capital, yet for the most part their comments on what they saw going on inside them are very disappointing. Locke, for instance, went at least a dozen times to the theatre with his pupil, Caleb Banks; but except that we know that on one of these occasions they went to the Opéra, we learn nothing about the expedition except what it cost. Those who actually get as far as expressing an opinion of what they saw in one of the great ages of French drama are generally very critical. Clenche sneers at most things French, so that it is not surprising that he should have a low opinion of the plays and operas which he saw in Paris: 'Theatres much worse than ours, so are their Plays: in their Opera's their Scenes are infinitely inferior to those of Venice, as well as their Voices and manner of singing, being as unlike as Froggs and Nightingals'.[15] Even Veryard, who is generally much less difficult to please, was obviously unenthusiastic: 'Play Houses are in vogue at Paris, though all Players are excommunicate. In my Opinion they come far short of ours in England'[16] On the other hand Lauder was very much struck by what he saw of the theatre on a visit to the Louvre even if he had to hand over good Scots money for the privilege:

> All we saw of it was the extrinsecks, excepting only the king's comedy house which the force of money unlocked and cost open; which truly was a very pleasant sight, nothing to be sein their but that which by reason of gilding glittered like gold. But the thing that most commended it was its rare, curious, and most conceity machines: their they had the skies, boats, dragons, vildernesses, the sune itselfe so artificially represented that under night with candle light nothing could appear liker them.[17]

While in Paris in 1676 Sir Philip Perceval went to see the Italian actors perform, but this raises a curious point as it is generally accepted that by this date there was in force a royal ordinance banning servants in livery from entering the Paris theatres 'même en payant'. However, Perceval's tutor lists among the expenses which they incurred in Paris: 'to go to an Italian play for us and the servants, 3l. 15s'.[18] This was the price of 5 tickets to the *parterre*.

That was the part of the theatre to which Edward Browne went when in 1664 he saw Molière and his company perform in their theatre at the Palais Royal; believe it or not, he was far from impressed by what he saw: 'In the afternoon I heard a Comedy at Palais royall. They were Monseir's Comedians; they had a farce after it. I gave Quinze Solz to stand upon the grounde. The name of it was Coeur de mari [*L'École des maris*]. They are not to bee compar'd to the Londoners'.[19] Two years later Skippon, accompanied no doubt by

Ray, went to the same theatre where he saw the Italian actors as well
as Molière's company. The Italians seem to have made more of an
impression judging by the condescending remark which he makes
about the performance of the Troupe de Monsieur:

> Palais Cardinal is a fair palace with handsome walks. Here
> madame Henrietta the dutchess of Orleans lives. At one side of
> this house is a publick stage where the Italian and French
> comedians act by turns. I saw here *Il maritaggio d'una Statua*, a
> merry play, where the famous buffoon Scaramuccio acted.
> Three antick dances pleased the spectators. The *Quattre
> Scaramuccie* was another pleasant Italian comedy. We stood in
> the *parterre*, or pit, and paid 30 sols apiece for seeing the first,[20]
> and but 15 sols for the last.
>
> We saw a French comedy entitled, *L'estourdie*, which was
> better acted than we expected. We paid for seeing this, and
> standing in the pit, 15 sols a man.[21]

Neither Skippon nor Browne, it will be noticed, as much as mentions
the name of Molière.

No doubt one reason for their coolness towards the French
comedies which they saw was their scanty knowledge of the language.
At the end of the century Lister attended both the Opéra and the
Comédie Française (the latter now had a monopoly of stage plays
since the expulsion of the Italian actors in the previous year), and in
speaking of both theatres he freely admits the handicap presented by
his poor French. On his visits to the Opéra he writes:

> I did not see many Opera's, not being so good a French-Man
> as to understand them, when Sung: The Opera, called *l'Europe
> Gallante*, I was at several times, and it is lookt upon as one of the
> very best. It is extreamly fine, and the Musick and Singing
> admirable: The Stage large and magnificent, and well filled with
> Actors: The Scenes well suited to the thing, and as quick in the
> removal of them, as can be thought. The Dancing exquisite, as
> being performd by the best Masters of that Profession in Town:
> The Cloathing rich, proper, and with great variety.

Lister expresses some surprise at the popularity of the Opéra and
particularly at its vogue among the aristocracy: 'There are great
numbers of the Nobility that come daily to them, and some that can
Sing them all: And it was one thing that was troublesome to us
Strangers, to disturb the Box by these voluntary Songs of some parts
of the Opera or other; That the Spectators may be said to be here as
much Actors as those imployed upon the very Stage'.

In addition to attending the Opéra in the Palais Royal theatre in
which it had been installed since Molière's death Lister also paid visits
to the Comédie Française in its theatre in the Rue des Fossés

Saint-Germain on the Left Bank which had been opened in 1689. He is less fulsome in his praise of what he saw there: 'The Disposition of the Theatre is much the same; but something less: And here the Stage it self is to be let; where for Strangers, the Places are most commodious, to hear and see'. He was thus far from disapproving of the presence of spectators on the stage despite its obvious disadvantages. Once again he freely admits that his enjoyment of the plays he saw there was limited by his inadequate French: 'I heard many Tragedies, but without gust for want of Language: But after them, the Little Plays were very Diverting to me, particularly those of Moliere, *Vendange de Suresne, Pourcegnac, Crispin Medecin, le Medecin malgre luy, le Malade Imaginaire*'.[22] Lister concludes his remarks on the theatre with an observation which implies a contrast with Restoration drama: 'This I must needs say, That Obscenity and Immorality are not at all upon the French Stage, no more than in the Civil Conversation of People of Fashion and good Breeding'.[23]

Very little is known of the theatrical activity which went on in the provinces of seventeenth-century France. The existence of numerous companies of strolling players is well attested, but information about where they performed and especially what plays were in their repertoire is not easy to come by. Locke encountered one of these companies, the Troupe de Monsieur le Prince, which toured the provinces when it was not performing for Condé at Chantilly. Locke saw it perform there, but instead of telling us what play or plays it performed, he enters into the most futile detail about the visit to Chantilly of one of Henry IV's illegitimate sons, Henri de Bourbon, Duc de Verneuil, and his duchess: 'The Duke & Dutchesse of Vernuele came in the evening from Verneule to Chantilly to visit the Prince, & at the play which they were at (the Prince's players being in the house & playing every night) had this of particular to entertaine them that severall pots of African marigolds [were] set before the scenes which were two screens, as a particular marke of their reception'.[24]

It is, however, possible to scrape together from Lauder's journal some information about plays performed by strolling players in Orleans and Poitiers in the middle of the 1660s. In his accounts for his stay in Orleans in the summer of 1665 one finds 'for seeing a comedy 10 souse'. What the play in question was he does not say, but during his stay at Poitiers, yet before he mentions the arrival of a company of actors there, he suddenly refers to two plays, *Le Baron de la Crasse*, a very popular play by Raymond Poisson, first performed in 1660, and an older comedy which was to live on the stage until nearly the end of the century, *Les Visionnaires* by Desmaretz de Saint Sorlin, first performed in 1637.[25] It is possible that he had seen both plays in Orleans.

What he has to tell us about his visits to the theatre in Poitiers is rather more precise. 'About the beginning of February 1666 came Comoedians to Poictiers. I went and saw them severall times', he tells us in his journal, and in his accounts he lists three visits to the theatre: '15 sous at the comoedy: ... 18 souse at another comoedy: ... 20 souse at a comoedy, called les Intrigues des Carosses a Cinq Sols, the farce was la Femme Ruse ou Industrieuse'. *La Femme rusée*, otherwise known as *La Femme industrieuse*, was a one-act play by the actor, Dorimond, published in 1661. *Les Intrigues des carrosses à cinq sols*, first performed in 1662, was a fairly ephemeral comedy by another actor, Chevalier, inspired by Paris's first attempt at a public transport system.[26] Information about the plays which he saw at the other two performances can be gleaned from the journal. At the first he saw Pierre Corneille's tragedy, *Oedipe*, with which in 1659 he inaugurated the second and less successful part of his career, and *Le Mariage de Rien*, a one-act farce by Antoine de Montfleury, published in 1660. Another of these performances he describes in the following terms: 'We was at comoedy, the farce of which was called *Le cocus imaginaire*'.[27] He fails to tell us what the main play of the performance was. The farce was, of course, Molière's one-act verse play, *Sganarelle ou Le Cocu imaginaire*, first performed in 1660.[28] Given the penury of information about the plays performed by the strolling players of the time, even these meagre details have been gratefully received by French historians of the theatre.[29]

Lauder also provides some interesting information on another topic. Several of our travellers — in particular Locke and, later in the century, Lister — made a point of visiting the libraries of Paris, from the Bibliothèque du Roi to those of the religious houses whose rich collections of books and manuscripts were to be taken over by the State during the Revolution. In the nature of things these were learned libraries, and our travellers' comments on what they saw there are inevitably somewhat technical for a book of this kind. They do not throw any light on the question of how the literate minority of the population could get hold of such relatively expensive items as books. One tends to think of circulating libraries run by booksellers as an eighteenth-century phenomenon in France as in England, but there are scraps of evidence to show that these already existed both in Paris and the provinces from about the middle of the previous century. During his stay in Poitiers Lauder twice noted in his accounts payments for the hire of romances from a bookseller: 'I have payed 18 souse for the lean of Romances from Mr. Courtois, as Celie and the sundry parts of Almahide, penned by Scuderie' and '15 souse for Romances'.[30] Such evidence is important as it throws light on the diffusion of books in seventeenth-century France; it shows that they could be obtained and read more cheaply than by buying them.

By a coincidence the only French writer whom any of our travellers claims to have met in the flesh was Madeleine de Scudéry, though because of her great age Lister's encounter with her in 1698 was a sad disappointment:

Amongst the Persons of Distinction and Fame, I was desirous to see Madameoiselle de Scuderie, now 91 years of Age. Her Mind is yet vigorous, tho' her Body is in Ruins. I confess, this Visit was a perfect Mortification, to see the sad Decay of Nature in a Woman once so famous. To hear her Talk, with her lips hanging about a toothless Mouth, and not to be able to Command her Words from flying abroad at Random, puts me in mind of the Sybil's uttering Oracles . . .

She shewed me the Skeletons of two Chameleons, which she had kept near four years alive: In Winter she lodged them in Cotton; and in the fiercest Weather, she put them under a Ball of Copper, full of hot water.

In her Closet she shewed me an Original of Madame Maintenon, her old Friend and Acquaintance, which she affirmed was very like her: and, indeed, she was then very beautiful.[31]

There is not a single reference to Racine in any of our travellers' writings, but during his long stay in the South of France in the 1660s Lister picked up some anecdotes about Pierre Corneille:

Memoires de la conversation ëue par
fois avec Mr de la Mothe. 1665 à Montpelier
sur le sujet de Mr de Corneille.

M'a dit qu'estant à table avec M^r l'Abbé de Cerisy[32] M. de Corneille et avec d'autres honnestes gens à Rouen, Mr Corneille qui estoit assis aupres de luy à mi-repas, luy donna un coup de poing sur l'espaule avec un cry, qui fut suvy de paroles, qui le temoignoient assez qu'il songeoit allieurs. ah! que j'ay de la peine à faire mourir cette fille! come il avoit surpris la companie, il fut obligé à dire la verité et en demandant pardon, il les assuroit, qu'il n'estoit propre pour la conversation, et qu'il ne scauroit s'empescher resver sur quelque une de ses comedies qu'il avoit sur les mains, et qui fut l'occasion de ses paroles.

Une autre fois m'a dit qu'ayant l'honneur de connoistre M. de Corneille particulierement il m'asseuroit sur son sujet, que quand il travailloit sur le Cid, il ne sçavoit ce que ce est que les Regles de la Poesie & que apres il ne fut pas seulement persuadé

par les instances de M. de la Mothe de les estudier, mais qu'il
contribuoit encor à sa Lecture et qu'il lui presta le Poetique de
Scaliger.

Que Mr de Corneille l'aisné fut né 1606 par le quel conte il
avoit 6 ans moins que luy.

Que ce fut de façon de M. de Corneille quand il pensoit a
travailler à quelque une de ses Pieces de Teatre, de se mettre au
lit et de se faire couvrir avec plusieurs grosses Couvertures afin
de s'eschauffer et se faire suer, Apres qu'il eut demeuré
quelques momens en cet estat la en sortant de lit, il demanda à
escrire.[33]

When he returned to Paris in 1698, twenty-five years after
Molière's death, Lister wrote a long eulogy of him:

In this all agree, that tho' Moliere's Plays have less of Intrigue
in them; yet his Characters of Persons are incomparable, so true
and just, that nothing can be more: And for this Reason, so
many of them are only of two or three Acts; for without an
Intrigue well laid, the Characters would have failed him, in
which was his Excellency. However, this is now so much become
a Custom on the French Stage; that you ever have one of these
little Pieces tack'd to the Tragedy, that you may please your self
according to your Appetite.

'Tis said, Moliere Died suddenly in Acting the *Malade
Imaginaire*: Which is a good instance of his well Personating the
Play he made, and how he could really put himself into any
Passion he had in his Head. Also of the great danger strong and
vehement Passions may cause in weak Constitutions, such as Joy
and Fear; which History tells us, have killed very many
suddenly. He is reported to have said, going off the Stage,
*Messieurs J ay joue le Malade Imaginaire; Mais je suis
veritablement fort Malade*; and he died within two hours after.
This Account of Moliere is not in his life by Perrault,[34] but it is
true: And he yet has blamed him for his Folly, in persecuting the
Art of Physick, not the Men, in divers of his Plays.

Moliere sent for Dr. M---, a Physitian in Paris of great
Esteeme and Worth, and now in London, a Refugee. Dr. M---
sent him word, he would come to him, upon two Conditions; the
one, that he should Answer him only to such Questions as he
should ask him, and not otherwise Discourse him; the other,
that he should oblige himself to take the Medecines he should
prescribe for him. But Moliere finding the Doctor too hard for
him, and not easily to be Dupt, refused them. His Business, it
seems, was to make a Comical Scene in exposing one of the
Learnedest Men of the Profession, as he had done the Quacks. If
this was his intention, as in all probability it was, Moliere had as
much Malice, as Wit; which is only to be used to correct the

Vitiousness and Folly of Men pretending to Knowledge, and not the Arts themselves.[35]

Despite these reservations, natural enough in a practising physician, Lister's comments reflect the high prestige which Molière now enjoyed after the struggles of his somewhat turbulent career in Paris.

Occasionally one of our travellers would jot down scraps of information which throw light on problems of literary history. The contemporary French poet in whom Locke was most interested appears to have been Boileau. Among the books which he acquired during his stay in the South of France was 'Boiloes Satyrs', and in a list made in the following year a set of his *Oeuvres* is mentioned. In the notebook which he kept in Paris between 30 June 1677 and 30 June 1678 we find the following entry on 'Boyloe' communicated by a 'Mr Duncom':

Les Satyrs
Epistres
Art Poetique d' Horace
Lutrin
Sublime de Longine
2 Additional Chants of his Lutrin, his satyr of mariage and 2 or 3 other new ones are now in presse.[36]

The last sentence was a little premature as Satire X, directed against women, did not appear until 1694, but this note does prove that a version of it already existed long before that date.

Several of our travellers appreciated French epigrams, including those which concerned literature. Locke took the trouble to copy into his journal in 1679 one directed against the latest tragedy of Nicolas Pradon, Racine's rival over *Phèdre*:

Sur la Troade de Pradon
Quand jay veu de Pradon la piece miserable
    Admirant du destin le Caprice fatal,
Pour ta pert ay-je-dit Illion deplorable
    Auras-tu toujours un cheval?[37]

An epigram on Boileau which relates to the 'Querelle de *Phèdre*' two years earlier in the course of which the poet had been threatened with a beating and was even (as here) alleged to have received one, was copied down in Paris by Sir Philip Perceval, by a strange coincidence on the previous day:

Monsieur Boylo, who is a very remarkable man, has given occasion to an abbé[38] in this town to say of him what follows:
    Boylo cet autheur satirique
    Grace a la vertu du Baston

> A change de note et de ton
> Ce remede quand on l'applique
> Mille fois mieux qu'une replique
> Range la rime à la raison.[39]

If we pass now to our travellers' contacts with French scholars we find another coincidence — that two men as different as Lord Herbert and Coryate encountered in Paris in the same year, 1608, the great classical scholar, Isaac Casaubon (1559–1614). This was only two years before he left France for England at the invitation of James I. Herbert writes briefly, but enthusiastically of his debt to Casaubon: 'Coming now to Paris through the Recommendation of the Lord Ambassador I was lodged in the house of that Incomparable scholler Isaak Cawsabon by whose learned Conversation I much benefited my selfe'.[40] Coryate for his part devotes a couple of enthusiastic pages to his meetings with Casaubon:

> I enjoyed one thing in Paris, which I most desired above all other things, and oftentimes wished for before I saw the citie, even the sight and company of that rare ornament of learning Isaac Casaubonus, with whom I had much familiar conversation at his house, neare unto St.Germans gate within the citie. I found him very affable and courteous, and learned in his discourses, and by so much the more willing to give me entertainment, by how much the more I made relation to him of his learned workes, whereof some I have read. For many excellent bookes hath this man (who is the very glory of the French Protestants) set forth to the great benefite and utility of the Common-weale of learning . . . Surely I beleeve he is a man as famous in France for his admirable knowledge in the polite learning and liberall sciences, as ever was Guilielmus Budeus in his time.

Coryate goes on to speak of what he calls 'two most memorable notes' which he derived from this scholar. The first was that some Englishman should write an account of the great achievements of Elizabeth I; the second reveals all the fiery bigotry of a devout Huguenot of the time:

> The other was, that I might see the next morning (if I would be abroad in the streetes) a certaine prophane and superstitious ceremony of the Papists, which might be very fitly compared to a ceremony of the Pagans in Greece, called $\pi\alpha\sigma\tau o\phi\acute{o}\rho\iota\alpha$, which signified the carrying of a bedde. For even as they carried a bedde abroad in solemne procession upon certaine dayes, with the Images of some of their gods upon it: so may you to morrow morning being Corpus Christi day (sayed he) see in the streets of this City a bedde carried after a very Ethnicall manner, or rather

a Cannopy in the forme of a bedde, under which the Bishop of the city with certaine Priests that carry the Sacrament do walke; which indeed I saw performed with great company of strange ceremonies, as I have before written.[41]

At the other end of the century Lister visited a famous pair of classical scholars, André Dacier (1651–1722) and his wife, Anne (c.1654–1720), the daughter of the famous Tanneguy Lefebvre:

I Visited Monsieur Dacier and his Lady, two very obliging Persons, and both of great Worth, and very Learned.

I think our Profession is much beholden to him, for his late elegant Translation of Hippocrates into French, with Learned Notes upon him. I wish he may live to finish what he hath so happily begun. I read over the Two Volumes which he has Printed with great delight.

After expressing dissent from Dacier's opinion that Hippocrates knew of the circulation of the blood, Lister continues:

He told me he had two more Volumes ready for the Press, and did intend not to give it over till he had gone through all the Works of Hippocrates . . .[42]

I must needs say this for Madam Dacier, his Wife, though I knew her by her Writings, before I saw her, the Learnedest Woman in Europe, and the true Daughter and Disciple of Tanaquil Faber; yet her great Learning did not alter her genteel Air in Conversation, or in the least appear in her Discourse; which was easie, modest, and nothing affected.[43]

Another great scholar whom Lister visited in Paris was the Benedictine, Jean Mabillon (1632–1707), whose *De Re diplomatica* had appeared in 1681. Lister saw him several times in the Abbey of St.Germain:

I visited in this Convent, at his Chamber, Pere Mabillon, who has so well deserved of the Commonwealth of Learning by his Writings, and particularly that Excellent Book *De re Diplomaticâ*; he seemed to me to be a very good Natured and Free-hearted Man; and was very well pleased to hear, that our Catalogue of English Manuscripts was so forward in the Press at Oxford. He thankfully owned the favour of the Cotton Library; and was very sorry to hear of Dr. Bernard's Death, of whom he spoke very kindly; but he expressed a wonderful Esteem for Dr. Gale, the Dean of York.

Lister's account of another conversation with Mabillon throws interesting light on the decline of Latin as an international language in the learned world:

In another Conversation I had with P. Mabillon (for he was my neighbour, and I was often with him) telling him the Account

x

we had brought us of Palmyra, and the Tracts that were writ of it, and that more was intended to be publisht about it, he was much concerned, that those Accounts, which were pure Matters of Learning in general, were written in English; and he told me, he was afraid it might be with us, as it was with them, since they cultivated their own Language so much, they began to neglect the Ancient Tongues, the Greek and the Latin.[44]

Mabillon's reaction also illustrates the well-known fact that in seventeenth-century France English was known only by a handful of people.

None of our travellers in the first half of the century recorded any encounter with the greatest philosopher of the age, Descartes. Locke did, however, note that in 1676 his philosophy was disapproved of by the authorities. The marginal note 'Cartesiana Philosophia' introduces the entry: 'The New philosophie prohibited to be taught in universities, schooles & Academies'. The information about the ban on the teaching of Descartes's philosophy came presumably from one of his disciples, Pierre Régis (1632–1707), as the entry follows directly on one relating a conversation with him. He had acquired a considerable reputation in the South of France as a popularizer of Cartesianism which, despite the official ban on its teaching, was in process of becoming the fashionable philosophy. Locke undoubtedly met him again later in Paris, but the conversations with him which he recorded have nothing to do with philosophy.[45] A much more illustrious disciple of Descartes, Nicolas Malebranche, does not make an appearance in Locke's travel papers except that while in France he acquired a copy of his most famous work, *La Recherche de la vérité*. Once more the indefatigable Lister must be called upon to give a personal view of the philosopher whom he sought out at the Oratoire in Paris: 'He is a very tall, lean man, of a ready Wit and chearful conversation. After an hours discourse, he carried me into the Publick Library of the House'.[46]

Some uncertainty surrounds the precise nature of the contacts between Berkeley and Malebranche. Berkeley is known to have spent a month in Paris towards the end of 1713, and he again passed through France on his way to Italy three years later. According to Joseph Stock, his first biographer, on his second visit

> Mr. Berkeley took care to pay his respects to his rival in metaphysical sagacity, the illustrious Pere Malebranche. He found this ingenious father in his cell, cooking in a small pipkin a medicine for a disorder with which he was then troubled, an inflammation of the lungs. The conversation naturally turned on our author's system, of which the other had received some

knowledge from a translation just published. But the issue of this debate proved tragical to poor Malebranche. In the heat of disputation he raised his voice so high, and gave way so freely to the natural impetuosity of a man of parts and a Frenchman, that he brought on himself a violent encrease of his disorder, which carried him off a few days after. [46a]

While the story of the demise of this occasionalist philosopher has given rise to a rather weak joke, that Berkeley did not kill Malebranche, but that he was the occasional cause of his death, there is no evidence that Berkeley was in Paris in October 1715 when Malebranche died. On the other hand there are two references to Malebranche in Berkeley's letters some two years earlier. In a letter of 24 November 1713 he wrote of a certain abbé d'Aubigne: 'Today he is to introduce me to Father Malebranche, a famous philosopher in this city'. The next day he wrote to another correspondent: 'To-morrow I intend to visit Father Malebranche, and discourse him on certain points'.[46b] This *could* mean that he made two visits — the first to make Malebranche's acquaintance, and the second to discuss some specific questions with him; but the exact nature of their relations remains obscure.

During the period which Locke spent in Paris, although he was already in his mid-forties, he was still virtually unknown; the writings which were to bring him fame did not begin to appear until a decade later. He was, however, received in the circles which met at the houses of two learned men, Henri Justel (1620–93) and Nicolas Thoynard (1629–1706). Justel was a wealthy Huguenot who took refuge in England in 1681; he was naturalized, elected to the Royal Society and appointed Librarian of St.James's Palace; Locke shared his interest in what he called 'les Commodités de la vie', those inventions which contributed to making life easier and pleasanter, and several of their conversations which he records deal with such matters. Thus he made the following entry with the marginal note 'Ederdons': 'There is a sort of down to be got in Norway a pound whereof put between two Sarcenets is enough to make a coverlet, which is very light & very warme & may be caried in a very little roome. It costs 12 or 15 £ Tournoys per lb. They call it Ederdons.Mr. Justell'.[47] Nicolas Thoynard with whom Locke was to keep up a long correspondence after his return to England, came to Paris from Orleans in 1652 to pursue his scholarly interests. He combined biblical researches which led to his posthumous *Evangeliorum harmonia graeco-latina*, with a strong interest in scientific and technical problems, especially ballistics. There are several references in Locke's journal to the *Harmonia*: parts of this had already been

printed and he was given a copy. From Thoynard Locke also derived
various notes on the customs and products of countries which he had
visited, and he copied down without comment descriptions of the
guns which Thoynard had invented. Covel who was also present on
one of these occasions describes those which he saw in some detail,
but ends his account by calling them 'but dangerous bables at the
best'.[48]

The various academies established in France in the seventeenth
century attracted a certain amount of attention. The first of these, the
Académie Française, is briefly mentioned by Northleigh in describing
visits to the Louvre: 'Their Academy for the French Tongue founded
by this King's Father, at the Request and Sollicitation of Richlieu was
since kept here, compos'd of the King as head and Protector, and
about forty or fifty of their most famous Wits and Vertuoso's, their
Businesse being to cultivate their Language, and bring it to the
greatest purity and Perfection'.[49] In addition to leaving vague the
number of its members (forty), this account also lays rather excessive
stress on language.

The Académie de Peinture et de Sculpture, founded in 1648, and
reorganized by Colbert in 1664, undoubtedly impressed Locke who
devotes quite a long entry to a visit which he paid to it:

> At the Academy for Painting & Sculpture one sees in the
> great roome severall peices done by the cheif masters of that
> Academy, & here it is they meet once a month. They are about
> 80 in all. Out of them are chosen 2 every two months to teach,
> each one his month, those young lads who are admitted. They
> pay here for their being taught but 10s. per week, which is meant
> not for a reward, but as a meanes to excite emulation for those
> that doe very well pay noe thing at all. Every yeare they trye for
> the prize which the King gives by the hands of Mr. Colbert, who
> is a Protector of this Academie. The prize is worth about £400 &
> is 3 or 4 medalls of gold. Those usually who get it are also sent
> into Italy & mainteind there at the King's cost to perfect them.
> Thus this Kingdome is like to be furnished with excellent
> masters in painting and sculpture.[50]

Northleigh combines his account of this academy with that of the
Académie d'Architecture created by Colbert in 1671; he too thought
that in this respect Paris was better provided for than London. After
describing the Palais Royal, he goes on:

> They have a Palace near that of the Royal one, and which part
> the Cardinal design'd for his Library, call'd le Palais Brion,
> where are kept the two famous Academies of Architecture and
> Paintings; this Encouragement is wanting in London,
> Conferences and Consultation, with Observation of Nature and

the Life, are indeed the Life of all Mechanical Arts, as well as Liberal Sciences. The first of these was founded by Monsieur Colbert, of which the fam'd Architects, Mansard and Perault who translated Vetruvius were Members: Mr. Blondel who made the Mathematicks for the Dauphin, and the Sieur Felibien the Secretary fam'd for several works. They meet two or three times a Week, and have a Room in which they keep several curious Models to descant on, and to imitate. In that of the Painters, erected by Noyers Secretary of State, who brought their famous Poussin out of Italy; it lay neglected for a while, till Monsieur Colbert setled some Pensions and recovered it. Monsieur Le Brun their chief Painter was of late the chief President and Rector, and consists of a number of Virtuoso's of several Professions.[51]

Contacts with artists seem to have been few. Evelyn records a visit to the famous engraver, Abraham Bosse, who had recently produced a book on perspective: 'I went to that excellent Ingraver Du Bosse for his instruction about some difficulties in Perspective deliverd in his booke'. He had more dealings with another well-known engraver, Robert Nanteuil. In 1650 he wrote: 'I sate to the famous Sculptor Nanteuil (afterwards made a knight by the French King for his Art) who engraved my Picture in Coper'. There seems no foundation for the statement about Louis XIV's ennoblement of Nanteuil, but he also executed engravings of Evelyn's wife and her parents. Moreover at the end of the year Evelyn added: 'Monsieur Nanteuils presented me with my owne Picture, don all with a pen, an extraordinary curiosity,[52] — this was apparently the drawing in black-lead for the engraved portrait. The only other mention of an actual encounter with an artist is in Lister's description of a visit to the sculptor, François Girardon. Although most of the account which he gives of his visit is devoted to the ancient statues which Girardon possessed, he has this to say about his studio: 'But, indeed, that which most surprised me in the Louvre was the *Artellier* or Work-house of Monsieur Gerardon; he that made Cardinal Richelieu's Tomb, and the *Statua Equestris* designed for the Place de Vendosme; he told me he had been almost 10 years in making the Model with assiduity and daily application'.[53]

Lister also visited the famous landscape architect, André Le Nôtre (1613-1700), by now a very old man, though not quite as old as he is here said to be:

Monsieur le Nostre's Cabinet, or Rooms wherein he keeps his fine things, the Controller of the Kings Gardens, at the side of the Tuilleries, was worth seeing. He is a very ingenious old Gentleman, and the Ordinance and Design of most of the Royal and great Gardens in and about Paris are of his invention, and he has lived to see them in perfection. This Gentleman is 89 years old, and quick and lively. He entertained me very Civilly. There were in the 3 Appartments, into which it is divided, (the uppermost of which is an Octogon Room with a Dome) a great Collection of choice Pictures, Porcelains, some of which were Jars of a most extraordinary size; some old Roman Heads and Busto's, and intire Statues; a great Collection of Stamps very richly bound up in Books; but he had lately made a Draught of his best Pictures, to the value of 50000 Crowns, and had presented them to the King at Versailles. There was not any thing of Natural History in all his Cabinet.

On one of the occasions on which Lister went to see Le Nôtre he was shown his collection of medals; this leads on to an account of his relations with Louis XIV whom he, naturally enough, praises:

The French King has a particular Kindness for him, and has greatly enricht him, and no Man talks with more freedom to him; he is much delighted with his Humour, and will sit and see his Medals, and when he comes to any Medal that makes against him, he will say, *Sire, voyla une, qu est bien contre vous*! as though the Matter pleased him, and he was glad to find it to shew it the King. Monsieur le Nostre spoke much of the good Humour of his Master; he affirmed to me he was never seen in Passion, and gave me many instances of Occasions, that would have caused most Men to have raged; which yet he put by with all the Temper imaginable.[54]

The Académie des Sciences attracted relatively little attention. This is not altogether surprising; although it was founded in 1666, only four years after the Royal Society received its charter, it operated on a fairly modest scale until it was reorganized in 1699. It was, as usual, one of Colbert's creations, but although Louis XIV became its patron and paid it an official visit in 1681, it had only modest quarters in the Bibliothèque du Roi and by the time of its reorganization had produced only two volumes of the *Mémoires* which it published in imitation of the *Philosophical Transactions*. Its membership was relatively small; in 1666 it had 21 members, a mere handful of whom survived until 1699, and by that date only 41 more had entered the academy, some of these dying before its reorganization.

Only Northleigh and Lister comment in any sort of detail on this academy and neither was greatly impressed. Northleigh writes in rather vague terms, though he makes it clear that he thought the French academy inferior to the Royal Society:

The Academy of Sciences was Establish'd by the late

Monsieur Colbert, a friendly Promoter of Learning and Arts; the true Muses' Maecenas of this Age, where the Mathematicks, Physick and Natural Philosophy, meet with all Advantages for their Promotion, tho' our Royal Society far exceeds it both in the number of its Fellows, the form of its Constitution, and the Advances it has made, (so to use our great Verulam's Words and Work) in the *Augmentation of Sciences*; for theirs is only made up of a few, of fourteen or fifteen Fellows or Members, Monsieur Du Verney one of our Faculty, a good Anatomist and Physician being one.[55]

Lister also stresses the small number of members of the academy to the point of exaggeration unless, like Northleigh, he really means those who regularly attended its meetings. In general, while mentioning various weaknesses, he tends to speak more highly of it:

I cannot say much of the meeting of these Gentlemen of the Académie Royale de Sciences, there are but few of them, about 12 or 16 Members; all Pensioned by the King in some manner or other.

They endeavoured in the War time to have printed *Monthly Transactions* or Memoirs after the manner of ours in London; but could not carry them on above two Volumes or Years, for without great Correspondence this can hardly be done. And ours is certainly one of the best Registers that ever was thought on, to preserve a vast number of scattered Observations in Natural History, which otherwise would run the hazard to be lost, besides the Account of Learning in Printed Books...

The Abbot Bignon is President, Nephew to Monsieur Pontchartrain. I was informed by some of them, that they have this great advantage to incourage them in the pursuit of Natural Philosophy, that if any of the Members shall give in a Bill of Charges of any Experiments which he shall have made; or shall desire the Impression of any Book, and bring in the Charges of Graving required for such Book, the President allowing it and signing it, the Money is forthwith reimbursed by the King. As it was done in Dr. Turnfort's *Elements de Botanique*, the Cuts of that Book cost the King 12000 Livres. And the Cuts intended, and now Graving for another Book of new Plants found in his Voyages into Portugal and Spain, will cost 100 1. Sterling.

Also, if Monsieur Merrie, for Example, shall require live Tortoises for the making good the Experiments about the heart, they shall be brought him, as many as he pleases, at the King's Charges.

Lister has to concede that this happy state of affairs had been somewhat affected by the Nine Years War which had just ended, for he adds: 'These, besides their Pensions, I say, were some of the

Advantages they have enjoyed; but the War, for this reason, has lain heavy upon the Philosophers too.'

Lister adds a few more details about the Academy in his account of a conversation with the mathematician, the Marquis de l'Hôpital:

> He told me, it was not possible for them to continue the Monthly Memoirs, as they had done for two years only, because they were but very few in number of that Society, and had very little Correspondence. Indeed, I did inquire once of some of that Body, why they did not take in more since there were very many deserving Men in the City, as I instanc'd in Father Plumier: They owned he would be an Honour to the Body, but they avoided to make a President for the Admission of any Regulars whatsoever.[56]

In contrast no fewer than eight of our travellers produced accounts, long or short, of a visit to the Observatoire, an offshoot of the Académie des Sciences which occasionally met there. The building was erected between 1667 and 1672. It was used not only for astronomical observations, but also, as we shall see, for various scientific experiments; the staircase, for instance was made to extend from roof to cellar for astronomical observations and use in the study of falling bodies. Even Clenche, who saw it in 1675 when work on it was apparently not absolutely complete, was for once impressed:

> Observatoire, a Building not quite finish'd for the King's Chymists and Mathematical experiments, which besides the sinking it has below the Surface of the ground, there is a descent of 171 large steps, which go so low into the rock, that at one side you meet the river Seine; from the bottom of this, by a hole quite through the Building, the Stars may be seen at Noon-day; round about it are Labratories in two degrees of Stories; the Building is Stone, without any Timber; the Chambers Arch'd as well as the rest; the Quaries just by it, which yield a Stone so soft, that at first Digging they work almost as easie as Wood.[57]

Unlike most of the other travellers Locke does not attempt to provide an overall picture of the building; he contents himself with calculating its height from top to bottom: 'The building at the Observatoire is 131 stairs up & the descent underground 160 stairs. Down each stair being 6 inches or something better, makes from the bottom to the top 186 foot'.[58] However, as we shall see in a moment, he makes up for this with some interesting comments on his conversations with the astronomers working there. Covel enters into some technical detail (the two men do not agree about the number of steps down from the ground level):

> The observatoir, Two admirable Telescopes. I saw the

satellites of Jupiter and the rings of Saturn. Mr. Cassin[59], an Italian learned & very civil, describing now the moon. The puteus is deep 171 staires, each stair high 8½ of my palm's division. There are several vaults cut in the mines of Paris stone. In the end of one good water soak through from a loft . . . The vaults warme, but the puteus very extreamely hot, and a great steame constantly coming out and reverberating into water, it being a great snow without.[60]

A letter written in 1681 by a cousin of John Buxton makes the inevitable comparison with the even newer Observatory at Greenwich, but it also shows that the writer picked up from the inhabitants of Paris their suspicions of the purposes for which the building might be used:

> The Observatory — a house for the same use and of the same nature (though much finer) than Flamstead's at Greenwich — is worth seeing. This is also very strong, so that most people think it to be well designed to curb the city if they ever prove stubborn. It stands upon a hill and with great guns possibly might command the town. The bottom of the cellar is nearly two hundred stairs from the even ground. When we were at the bottom we walked very far; we might [*sic*] but they would not suffer us to go any further, what their reason was I cannot tell.[61]

Veryard's account of his visit again contains a tribute to Cassini:

> The Observatoire is a stately square Structure, erected by the present King at the further end of the Suburbs of S.Jacques, with an high wooden Tower adjoyning for the use of Astronomers. Here we had the honour of being very kindly receiv'd by the ingenuous Signor Cassini, a Man naturally inclin'd to the contemplation of the Heavens, and famous thro' the whole World for divers Discoveries and useful Observations he has enrich'd that Science withal. He gave us a sight of all his Instruments, and other Curiosities, amongst which were divers extraordinary Telescopes and Metallick Specula.[62]

Ferrier and his companions who visited the Observatoire after the Gobelins apparently did not make very much of their visit.

> We being so near would not neglect seeing the observatoir where lives the chief Astrologer[63] of the city; it is a square house built of stone of an indifferent height standing on a hill. He has made severall engines which we saw but could understand none of them; there is a burning glass of so strange a force that it would melt a copper farthing in a moment & burne all things that comes near it if set in the sun. And also in the side of the hill he has built a small room; it is square, and if you put your mouth into any of the corners & another put his into any of the others &

whispers never so easily you shall understand him very plain,
when standing at his back you shall not hear the least noise.[64]

Northleigh who was first in Paris round about the same time offers
a more detailed and comprehensible account, and one which is at
times critical:

> Another observable Place, is their Place made for
> Observation, and that in all astronomical Matters, call'd their
> Observatoire; built by this King for the Encouragement of that
> Science in 1667; a strong Pile without Wood or Iron, supported
> by Vaults, in which the Stairs are remarkable that lead you up to
> the Terras, three vaulted Stories high; after the manner that
> they build their Floors and Rooms at Genoa . . . The learn'd
> Cassini keeps his Apartment below, and their famed La Hyre,[65]
> both renown'd Astronomers, above: Below you descend also
> into a deep Cave, with little Alleys about near two hundred
> Steps down, contriv'd for the same Design that some
> Astronomers use to descend into some Wells, to discover the
> Motion of the Stars at Noon-day; there being here from this
> deep Abyss a thorough Prospect up thro' the whole Building to
> the Sky. But the Design did not answer the End it was design'd
> for; for none of the Constellations or Stars are visible; and
> nothing but the Light appears, which they impute to the not
> passing of any Stars thro' the Zenith of Paris; a thing one would
> think, their Artists might have foreseen, without the help of
> Telescopes, when they first undertook the Design, so as not to
> have proceeded upon an useless and unpracticable Experiment:
> They call this Perspect *le Puits*, perhaps from *Puteus* or *Puits*, an
> old obsolete word for a Well: They keep here all their
> Mathematical Instruments; a Building (tho' better contriv'd) of
> the same Nature and Design than ours at Greenwich: They built
> up by it their *Tour de Charpente*, or Timber-Tower, all
> Carpenter's Work, for the carrying up their Tubes and
> Telescopes: This Monsieur Cassini, that carries on all the Study
> here as chief Supervisor, is the same that was Professor of
> Bolognia; and made the memorable Meridian Line that bears
> his Name in one of the Churches of that Place: He is caress'd
> here much by the King, and has a considerable annual Pension
> allow'd him.[66]

Perhaps the clearest account of the Observatoire is that furnished
by Lister of his visit in 1698:

> I was by invitation from Monsieur Cassini at the Observatoire
> Royal, built on a rising Ground just without the City Walls; This
> Building is very fine, and great Art is used in the Vaulted Cut
> Roofs and Winding Staircases. The Stones are laid inside,
> outside, with the most regularity I ever saw in any Modern

Building; In all this Building there is neither Iron nor Wood, but all firmly covered with Stone, Vault upon Vault. The Platform a-top is very spacious, and gives a large and fair view of all Paris, and the Countrey about it; it is Paved with Black Flint in small squares, which I make no doubt are set in Cement or Tarras, that is, the *Pulvis Puteolanus.*

We were shewed a Room well furnisht with Models of all sorts of Machines; and a very large Burning Glass, about 3 foot diameter, which at that time of the year, viz. in the beginning of February, did fire Wood into a flame, in the very moment it came into and past through the Focus.

I was indisposed, and so could not accept of the Favour that was offered me of seeing the Moon in their Telescopes; and to go down into the Vault, which was contrived for seeing the Stars at Noon-tide, but without success. I was told by Monsieur Roman afterwards that there was a Rock formed in the Cave by the dropping of a Spring of Petrifying Water; of which Nature are all the Wells in Paris.

In the Flore of one of the Octogone Towers they have designed with great accurateness and neatness with Ink an Universal Map in a vast Circle. The North-Pole is in the Center. This is a Correction of other Maps upon the latest and best Observations.

His Nephew Moraldi was with him; as for his only Son,[67] he was in London at that time: I afterwards was with him at his Fathers, a very hopeful young Gentleman; and well instructed by his Father in the Mathematicks, and all other useful Learning.[68]

The traveller who seems to have had the closest relations with the astronomers at the Observatoire was Locke. He too describes a meeting with Cassini who in 1672 had discovered the second known satellite of Saturn and was at that time studying with the Danish astronomer, Olaf Römer (1644-1710), the eclipse of the satellites of Jupiter. In October 1677 Locke made the following entry:

At the Observatoire we saw the moone in 22 foot glasse & Jupiter with his 4 satellites in the same. The most remote was on the east & the other 3 on the west. We saw also Saturne & his ringe in a 32 glasse & one of his satelites on the west side, almost in the line of the longer axis of his ring as then appeard. Mr. Cassini told me that the declination of the needle at Paris is about $2\frac{1}{2}$ degrees to the westward. 'Twas between 8 & 9 at night that we saw these planets, but Saturne last of all & after 9.[69]

Locke also had dealings with the leading French astronomer of the time, Abbé Jean Picard (1620-82), who was one of the foundation members of the Académie des Sciences and held a chair at the

Collège Royal though he had only a modest lodging at the Observatoire. In March 1679 Locke relates the following technical conversation with the *abbé*:

> I examined my Universal foot[70] on which is the compas of proportion at Mr. L'Abbé Picar's & he found it just. He also told me that a Pendulum of seconds conteind of our English measure 39 1/8 inches, of the Paris measure 36 pouces 8½ lines or 36 $\frac{708}{1000}$ pouces.
>
> The foot of Paris being divided into 1440, i.e. tenths of a line, the English foot conteines of them 1351.
>
> The sun in its midle motion in 24 howers looses 3 minutes 56 seconds, by which any pendulum may be examined whether it goes well or noe, for 'tis but to observe any fixed star & the returne of the same star to the same meridian the next night, & if your watch wants then 3' 56", it is exact. Pendulum to go true must be fixed well to a firme wall, for set on the floore of a roome, it is shaken by treading & soe alters. Mr.l'Abbé Picar.[71]

Locke's main contact at the Observatoire was undoubtedly Römer who had come to France in 1672; three years later, as a result of his observation of the eclipses of Jupiter, he discovered the speed of light. When he visited England in 1679, he travelled with Locke. During the two days they spent in Calais Locke informed Thoynard about Römer's doings in this period, adding the usual joke about Channel crossings — 'et aujour'dhui je crois qu'il sacrifiera au Neptune du fond de son coeur ou estomack'.[72] Locke's first mention of a conversation with the astronomer occurs only a few weeks before they left Paris together. The references to this in the journal are at first sight somewhat obscure: 'At Mr. Romer's chamber in the Observatoire I saw his inclusum continet arcae Jovem. He also has a most admirable levell, but, being not there, I saw it not'. This is followed by a series of numbers headed by the words, 'Jupiter volvitur super axem suum horis 9-56'. Periodus revolutionum satellitum Jovis'.[73] The explanation of all this is to be found in another document in the Locke papers in the Bodleian Library.[74] This is endorsed by Locke 'Jupiter et Satellites, Mar.79' and is a rough sketch of a model of Jupiter and its satellites, on which Locke has inscribed Römer's name. As for the levelling instrument which he did not see on this occasion, this was one of Römer's numerous optical inventions, and Locke saw it in the following week: 'I was shewd by Mr. Romer an instrument to levell with which was very simple & of exceeding quick dispatch, it being a telescope of 4 glasses about a foot long or something more which shewd the levell when two threads, one where of was fixd & the other moved by a plummet, came to hide one an other'.[75] At the very end of his account of his journey home from France, when they had already reached the Thames estuary, Locke made two notes which were derived from Römer. Though the second of these — a note (complete with illustration) of 'Mr. Romer's steele' — is only of modest interest, the first obviously bears on his discovery of the speed of light: 'The motion of light is soe swift that it moves 1 diameter of the earth in 3''', & the distance of the sun from the earth being of 12,000 semidiameters of the earth, Light moves one semidiameter of the orbis magni in 10 minutes'.[76]

Locke was very interested in optics and he sought out two experts in this field. At Orleans he met Jean Hautefeuille (1647-1724), a well-known inventor of the time, from whom he derived a note on microscopes:

> The Microscopes that soe magnifie are noe thing but litle lens of glasse, made of the smallest threads of glasse melted, which run of them selves into that figure, but in melting them in the flame of a candle there mixes some grease with them, which [is] to be avoided, either by the flame of well burnt charcoals as I imagin, or the flame of spirit of wine. For Mr.Hautefeuille who tells me this, says he has in vain tried to melt them with a burning glasse . . .
> The manner of useing this litle microscope is to place it between a doubled plate of brasse or lead peirced with a very small hole & soe applying it to a thin peice of talke which holds the object to a peice of clear glasse, hold it as close as one can to the eye opposite to the light.[77]

We have already encountered Father Chérubin and the story of the persecutions he met with in the Capuchins' house in Paris.[78] Locke records a conversation with him about telescopes: 'I saw the P. Cherubin, the Capuchin soe famous in opticks, at least the practicall part, in telescopes. He there shewd me one made to looke in with both eyes at once. It was 3 foot & something more in length, & the glasses, both object & ocular glasses, soe placed at each end that by turneing a little key one appproached or separated the two object- or eye-glasses to that distance as may fit the eyes of the looker'.[79]

Thanks to his father's reputation, Edward Browne was not only introduced to Guy Patin some of whose lectures he had attended, but was also sought out by a well-known mathematician who wished to translate Sir Thomas's *Pseudodoxia Epidemica or Vulgar Errors*. This was Pierre Petit (1594-1677), appointed *commissaire provincial de l'artillerie* by Richelieu; his *Dissertation sur la nature des comètes* had just appeared when Edward Browne wrote to his father in September 1665:

> I was the last week with Mr. Peti, a mathematician, that hath been once or twice to see me when I was not within. Hee hath

got your Vulgar Errours translated, but tis halfe into English
and halfe into Latin, so that it cannot be printed so; hee doth not
understand English, but hath got this done for his owne
satisfaction. I beleeve he will present you with one of his books
de Cometis, which he hath lately written, upon an hypothesis of
his owne, different from Des Cartes. Hee hath divers fine
instruments, glasses, and other inventions in his chamber.[80]

Locke seems to have encountered quite frequently a well-known
mathematician of the time, Adrien Auzout (1622-91), a foundation
member of the Académie des Sciences, who also had a reputation as
an astronomer. Their conversations as recorded in Locke's journal
appear to have covered such diverse topics as a fever which Auzout
had once had, and comparisons of English and French measures and
of the bills of mortality in London and Paris.[81] Lister's conversations
with the Marquis de l'Hôpital (1661-1704) were chiefly concerned
with the break in Anglo-French intellectual relations caused by the
Nine Years War which had just ended:

The Marquis d'Hopital, one of the Académie des Sciences,
whom I found not at home, returned my Visit very obligingly. I
had a long Conversation with him about Philosophy and
Learning; and I perceived the Wars had made them altogether
Strangers to what had been doing in England. Nothing was more
pleasing to him, than to hear of Mr. Isaac Newton's
Preferment,[82] and that there were hopes, that they might expect
something more from him, he expressed a great desire to have
the whole Sett of the *Philosophic Transactions* brought over,
and many other Books, which he named, but had not yet
seen . . . .
I repaid the Marquis his Visit: He lives in a fine House, well
furnisht; the Garden pretty, with neat Trelliage, wrought with
Arches and other Ornaments.
He expressed a great Desire to see England, and Converse
with our Mathematicians, whose Works he coveted above all
things, and had ordered all to be brought him over.
His Lady also is very well Studied in the Mathematicks, and
makes one of the Learned Ladies in Paris.[83]

In 1678 Locke records an encounter at the Bibliothèque du Roi
where the Académie des Sciences then met, with one of its
foundation members, the physician and chemist, Samuel Cottereau
Du Clos. This entry is followed by a regular spate of medical notes
which Locke derived from him. Du Clos was an expert on mineral
waters (he published in 1675 his *Observations sur les eaux minérales*)
and another entry a few days later relates a conversation with him:
'Mr Duclos tels me that the best water about Paris is at Auteuil, a litle

towne upon the Sein below Paris neare the Bois de Bologne, & next to that is Luxembourg water. With that of Auteuil he hath cured diseases'. This is followed by a long list of the diseases in question and a bizarre story of how Du Clos claimed to have been an eye-witness of a father's love bringing life again to a son who had hanged himself. The story is rounded off in Locke's shorthand with a remark by another French acquaintance: 'Mr. Duclos great liar'.[84]

Another physician whom both Skippon and Lister encountered in Montpellier in 1665 was the Danish anatomist Niels Stensen, known as Steno (1638-86), who had arrived in that city in the course of his wanderings through Europe. Skippon attended one of his dissecting sessions:

> Monsieur Steno, a Dane, was at this time in Montpellier, and he is very happy in some anatomical discoveries, viz. the *Ductus Salivaris*, from the *Parotides* to the middle of the cheek: We were present at his dissection of an ox's head, and observ'd a blade of grass that was forc'd up that *Ductus*: In a Man the *Ductus* lies strait, but in a beast oblique.[85]

Lister was present not only at this dissection, but also at that of a dog, both of which he describes in considerable technical detail. After the first of these, he tells us, 'I visited Mr. Steno, whom I found infinitely taking & agreeable in conversation & I observed in him very much of the Galant & honest man as the French say, as well as the Scholler'.[86]

Among the learned men whom Veryard claimed to have been acquainted with in Paris was 'Mons. Verney, eminent for his dexterity in Dissecting, and Discoveries made in Anatomy'.[87] This was Joseph Guichard Duverney (1648-1730) who early acquired a reputation as an anatomist; he was elected to the Académie des Sciences in 1676 and appointed to the chair of anatomy at the Jardin des Plantes in the following year. There his lectures attracted large numbers of students, including many foreigners. Lister who undoubtedly had contacts with him is rather vague about their meetings beyond mentioning that on the first occasion his appointment to 'see Monsieur Verney at his Apartment at the upper-end of the Royal Physick Garden' came to nothing.[88] He seems to have had more to do with another anatomist, Jean Méry (1645-1722), with whom Duverney was not on good terms as they disagreed on the question of how the blood circulates in the body. Méry was admitted to the Académie des Sciences in 1684 and became *chirurgien en chef* at the Hôtel-Dieu in 1700.

Lister begins by describing his first visit to Méry:

> I saw Monsieur Merrie, a most painful and accurate

Anatomist, and free and communicative Person, at his House Rue de la Princesse. His Cabinet consisted of two Chambers: In the outward were great variety of Skeletons; also entire Preparations of the Nerves; in two of which he showed me the mistake of Willis,[89] and from thence gathered, that he was not much used to Dissect with his own Hand: The *Pia Mater* coating the Spinal Nerves but half way down the Back, where it ends: The *Dura Mater* coating the lowermost 20 pair; which, Willis, (as he said) has otherwise reported.

But that which much delighted my Curiosity, was the Demonstration of a blown and dried Heart of a Foetus; also the Heart of a Tortoise.

With these two objects Méry sought to demonstrate to Lister his views on how the blood circulated which can be summed up in his argument 'that the Blood in a Tortoise was in a manner Circulated like that in a Foetus, through the Body, the Lungs as it were or in good part slighted'. This was where he disagreed sharply with Duverney:

This Thought of Monsieur Merrie's has made a great Breach betwixt Monsieur Verney and himself; for which Reason I had not that freedom of Conversation as I could have wisht with both of them; but 'tis to be hoped that there may come good from an honest Emulation.

Two English Gentlemen came to Visit me, Mr. Bennis and Mr. Probie: They were lodged near the Royal Garden, where Monsieur Verney dwells, and makes his Anatomies, who in Three Months time shewed all the Parts of the Body to them. He had for this purpose at least Twenty Human Bodies, from the Gallows, the Chatelet, (where those are expos'd who are found Murthered in the Streets, which is a very common business at Paris) and from the Hospitals.

They told me, Monsieur Verney pretended to shew them a Valve, which did hinder Blood from falling back into the right Ventricle by the *Foramen Ovale*. This Valve they said he compared to the Papillae in the Kidneys, Musculous and Fleshy: That if Wind was blown into the *Vena Pulmonalis*, it did not pass through the *Foramen Ovale*, but stop there, by reason of the Valve. That he did believe contrary to Mr.Merrie, that no Blood did circulate through the Lungs in an Embrio.

Lister had several meetings with Méry in the course of which he received an account of an experiment carried out by Duverney at the Académie des Sciences:

I remember in Discourse that day with him, he told me, That Monsieur Verney had an old Cat, and a young Kitling just Born, put into the Air-Pump before the Académie Royalle des Sciences: That the Cat died after 16 Pumps, but the Kitling survived 500 Pumps; which favours in some measure the Command young Animals have of their Hearts.[90]

Another eminent physician whom Lister sought out in Paris was Joseph de Tournefort (1656-1708) who was appointed to the chair of botany at the Jardin des Plantes in 1683 and who in 1694 had published his *Éléments de botanique ou Méthode pour connaître les plantes* which involved him in controversy with Ray. In the course of their meeting Lister was shown Tournefort's large collection of shells, a subject in which he was particularly interested. After describing this he continues:

> I shall say nothing of his vast Collection of Seeds and Fruits, and dried Plants, which alone amount to 8000, and in this he equals, if not excells all the most curious Herborists in Europe. His Herborisations about Paris he gave me to carry for England, just then Printed off;[91] also he shewed me the Designs of about 100 European Non Descript Plants, in 8vo. which he intends next to publish.
>
> He also shewed me 10 or 12 single Sheets of Vellum, on each of which were Painted in Water Colours very lively, one single Plant, mostly in flower, by the best Artist in Paris,[92] at the King's Charge; Those are sent to Versailles, when the Doctor has put the names to them, and there kept: In this manner the King has above 2000 rare Plants, and they work daily upon others: The Limner has two Louis's for every Plant he Paints.[93]

He was also shown two rare plants, one of which had been brought by Father Plumier from Brazil.

This other botanist, Charles Plumier (1646-1704), seems to have made more of an impression on Lister, to judge by his account of their meeting:

> I was not better pleased with any Visit I made, than with that of Father Plumier, whom I found in his Cell in the Convent of the Minimes. He came home in the Sieur Ponti's Squadron and brought with him several Books in Folio of Designs and Paintings of Plants, Birds, Fishes, and Insects of the West-Indies; all done by himself very accurately. He is a very understanding Man in several parts of Natural History, but especially in Botanique. He had been formerly in America, at his return Printed, at the King's Charge, a Book of American Plants in Folio.[94] This Book was so well approved of, that he was sent again thither at the King's Charge, and returned after several years wandering about the Islands with this Cargo. He was more than once Shipwrackt, and lost his Specimens of all things, but preserved his Papers, as having fortunately lodged them in other Vessels; so that the Things themselves I did not see. He had designed and Dissected a Crocodile; one of the Sea

Tortoises; a Viper, and well described the Dissections.

The long description of the various things which Lister was shown concludes:

> He told me these Drawings would make 10 Books, as big as that he had publisht; and Two Books of Animals: He had been often at Versailles to get them into the King's *Imprimerie*, but as yet unsuccessfully; but hoped e're long to begin the Printing of them.[95] Note, That the Booksellers at Paris are very unwilling, or not able to Print Natural History; but all is done at the Kings Charge, and in his Presses.[96]

Lister was obviously impressed by the royal patronage of scientific research and particularly by the printing of very expensive works on natural history by the Imprimerie Royale.

Another scientist on whom Lister called was a mineralogist from Toulon, named Morin, who was elected to the Académie des Sciences in 1693:

> I visited Monsieur Morin, one of the Académie des Sciences, a Man very curious in Minerals; of which he shewed me some from Siam, as Jaspers, Onyxes, Agats, Loadstones, &c. He shewed me also excellent Tin Oar from Alsace. Also from France a great Block of a sort of Amethyst of 2 or 300 weight. Some parts of it (for he had several Plates sawed and polisht) were very fine, and had large Spots and Veins of a deep coloured Violet. It was designed for a Pavement in *Marchetterie*, of which he shewed me a *Carton* drawn in the Natural Colours.

> This put me in mind of a vast Amethyst I had seen at London, brought from New-Spain, and exposed to Sale; it weighed, as I remember, Eleven Pound odd Ounces; and was most perfectly figured both point and sides, after the manner of a Bristol Diamond, or common Rock Crystal; but this Block here was rude, and without any shape.[97]

Among Locke's acquaintances in Paris was the physician, Oriental traveller and philosopher, François Bernier (1620-88). Although Locke acquired during his stay in France Bernier's *Abrégé de la philosophie de Gassendi* which appeared in 1678, the journal does not furnish any evidence that he discussed philosophical matters with the author. The three entries all concern the East where Bernier had travelled for thirteen years (1656-69). Locke's library shows how interested he was in the accounts of Oriental travellers, and there is evidence to show that during his stays in Paris he also had contacts with two other famous travellers, Chardin and Tavernier.[98]

The first conversation with Bernier took place in October 1677:

> Mr. Bernier told me that the Heathens of Indostand pretend

to great antiquity; that they have books & historys in their language; that the nodus of their numbers is at 10 as ours & their circuit of days 7. That they are in number about 10 to 1 to the Mahumetans & that Aurang Zebe[99] had lately engaged himself very inconveniently in wars with them upon the account of religion, endeavouring to bring them by force to Mahumentanisme; & to discourage & bring over the Banians[100] or undoe them, he had given exemptions of Custome to the tradeing Mahumetans, by which meanes his revenue was very much lessened, the Banians makeing use of the names of Mahumetans to trade under & soe eluding his partiality.

The next recorded conversation was one between two doctors: 'Mr. Bernier told me that in the East Indies the gout & stone are diseases scarce known & a quartan very rarely. The endemial diseases of the country are burning feavers & dysentrys'. The third conversation reverted to a topic touched on in the first: 'Mr.Bernier told me that the Bramins Gentils, the old inhabitants of Indostan, count their time by weeks & give the dayes denominations as we doe by the seven planets & in the same order, their day denominated from the sun being the same with our Sunday, & soe of the rest, & in numbering make their nodus as we do at 10'.[101] With this meagre account of their meetings we have to content ourselves, though there is some evidence that relations between the two men were fairly close. Bernier was one of the three French acquaintances to whom Locke sent 'tortis shell knives & forks' on his return to England.

Another acquaintance which Locke made in Paris was that of Moïse Charas (1618-98). During his stay there most of Locke's letters were addressed to him 'chez Monsieur Charas Apothicaire rue de Boucherie Fauxbourg St. Germain'; indeed it seems that for at least part of his time in Paris Locke lodged with him as four letters written to him between November 1678 and January 1679 bear the extra words 'Logé chez lui'. Charas was a Huguenot who held the post of demonstrator in chemistry at the Jardin des Plantes. In 1680 he retired to England and was appointed apothecary to Charles II. After various travels he was converted to Catholicism, returned to Paris and in 1692 was admitted to the Académie des Sciences. From him Locke derived a number of medical notes,[102] but the other references in the journal do not tell us anything more about their intellectual relations.

Both Locke and Lister had contacts with a certain Hubin whom they describe as an eye-maker. He was presumably the author of *Machines nouvellement exécutées et en partie inventées par le sieur Hubin* (Paris, 1673), a copy of which Locke possessed. He relates how in February 1678 he carried out at Hubin's an experiment on water in a vacuum:

> Water sealed up in a glasse tube out of which the aire is drawn, being shaked, strikes against the end of the tube & gives a knock as if it were a solid body, but if it be let stand still a while, the first time you shake it, it makes noe more noise then that wherein the aire is included. This I tried at Mr. Hubin's in the Rue St. Martin over against the end of the Rue aux Ours, in glasses about 8 or 9 or so inches long & about an inch diameter. The cause he assigned was the parts of the liquor turnd into aire & upon shakeing returned into the liquor again. Q. whether this will do in all liquors & in longer tubes (they were above half full) & in all weathers alike? This was a moderate day for this time of year.[103]

Lister was more interested in what he saw of Hubin's products:

> At Hubins the Eye-maker, I saw Drawers full of all sorts of Eyes, admirable for the contrivance, to match with great exactness any Iris whatsoever: this being a case, where mis-matching is intolerable.
>
> He himself also formerly wrought in false pearl, and affirmed that the Glass Pearls were painted with a Paste made of the Scales of the Bleak[104] only; which he said was a good Trade here to the Fishermen, who sold the Scales for so much the Ounce. These Necklaces were formerly sold at great Prices, 2 or 3 Pistoles a-piece.[105]

The English instrument-maker, Michael Butterfield (?-1724), who was established in Paris, was also frequented by both Locke and Lister. He was several times employed by Colbert and published various books and papers, including two in the *Philosophical Transactions*. His first appearance in Locke's journal concerns a recently invented levelling instrument:

> At Mr. Butterfield's au Roy d'Angleterre, rue de Fosse, I saw a levelling instrument, made to hang & turne horizontally like a mariner's compasse. The sight was taken by a perspective glasse of four glasses, about a foot long, & between the first & 2nd glasse was placed one single filament of silk strech [sic] horizontally by which the levell was to be taken. This silke haire was soe ordered that it might be removed forwards or backwards soe as to fix it just in the focus of the eye glasse, & set higher or lower soe as to place it just in the levell. There was a heavy weight of lead hung down perpendicular about a foot long to keepe the telescope horizontall.

Locke appears to have got Butterfield to make him a rule showing as well as the universal foot which he had invented other measurements, for some time after this first mention we find the following entry in his journal:

Mr. Butterfield brought me home my rule.
V the universal foot.
P pes parisiensis.
D ... of Denmark.
L of Leyden.
E of England.
P.R. Palma Romana.

The only other mention of him occurs some six months later: 'Aune de Paris contient 3 pied 8 pous du Roi. This measure taken chez Mr. Butterfield upon a tradesman's aune'.[106] Lister was evidently much taken with Butterfield to whom he devotes over ten pages, mainly about his collection of loadstones. He begins with a magnificent eulogy of the instrument-maker: 'Mr. Butterfield is a right hearty honest Englishman, who has resided in France 35 years, is a very excellent Artist in making all sorts of Mathematical Instruments, and works for the King and all the Princes of the Blood, and his Work is sought after by all the Nations of Europe and Asia'.[107] However, after speaking of a two-hour session with Butterfield and the experiments with loadstones which he was shown, Lister devotes most of the remaining pages to his own views on magnetism.

In the provinces there was one famous private collection of mechanical gadgets which attracted the attention of many of our travellers. This was at Lyons in the house of Nicolas Grollier de Servières (1593-1686).[108] We have no fewer than nine descriptions of it by travellers who followed in the footsteps of Louis XIV who had been to see it in 1658. There is a full description of the contents by the owner's grandson in his *Recueil d'ouvrages curieux de mathématique et de mécanique ou description du cabinet de M. Grollier de Servières*, published in Lyons in 1719. Our travellers' opinions of both the owner and his collection tended to vary considerably.

Lassells has nothing but praise for both; he lists the collection at the end of his account of things to be seen in Lyons:

> Lastly the rare Cabinet of Monsieur Servier a most ingenious gentleman; where I saw most rare experiments in Mathematiks and Mechanicks; all made by his owne hand: as the sympatheticall balls, one springing up at the approach of the other held up a pretty distance off: the demonstration of a quick way how to passe an army over a river with one boat, and a wooden bridge easily to be foulded up upon one cart: the mouse dyall, where a little thing, like a mouse, by her insensible motion, markes the houres of the day. The Lizard Dyal is much like the former, onely the mouse moves upon a plain frame of wood which hath the houres marked on it; and the Lizard creeps

upward from houre to houre. The night dyall, shewing by a lighted lampe set behinde it, the houres of the night which are painted in colours upon oyled Paper, and turne about as the time goes. The Tortoise dyall, where a peice of cork cut like a Tortoise, being put into a puter dish of water, which hath the twelve houres of the day marked upon its brims, goeth up and downe the water a while, seeking out the houre of the day that is then; and there fixeing it self without stirring. The Rare engine teaching how to throw Grenados into beseiged townes, and into any precise place without fayling. The way how to set up a watch-tower with a man in it, to looke into a towne from without, and see how they are drawne up within the towne, a way how to change dineing Roomes three or four times, with their tables, the Seats and ghests being by the turning of a wheele transported sitting, out of one Roome into another; and so into three or four more Roomes variously hung with tables covered. The Desk dyall, which throwes up a little ball of yvory without rest, and thereby marketh the houre of the day, and sheweth what a clock it is: the Dyall of the Planets representing the dayes of the week by several figures in ivory of the planets: the Oval dyal in which the needle, that markes the houres, shrinketh in, or stretcheth out it self according as the oval goes: the dyall shewing to every one that toucheth it his predominant passion; with a world of other rare curiosityes, all made by this ingenious gentleman.[109]

Skippon who visited Lyons in 1665 gives a fairly detailed description of the collection. He begins by speaking of the good fortune which Ray and he had in being able to see it at all: 'We had good luck in seeing monsieur Servier's cabinet, his humour being very difficult. He was a soldier in his younger days; but about 22 years ago he retired hither, and invented many ingenious peices of clock-work, machines of water, &c which he hath described with his pen, and bound them up together in a thick folio, and made the models of them in wood with his own hand'.[110] Skippon then proceeds to list those things in his collection which they had not seen in Italy and Germany.

Locke who saw the collection ten years later was not impressed by the owner whom he describes as 'an old, morose, half-mad Gent.' and he encountered considerable difficulties when he started to ask his usual questions. He speaks of there being a great many models of pumps and other engines 'which, he haveing not latin nor I Fench, besides the particular temper of the man, I could not particularly enquire into'. He admired the examples of turning in ivory and wood, and although he speaks of 'some magneticall tricks rather then experiments', he does describe two things which he considered to be 'of use': 'A way he had there with 2 threads slideing upon a ruler to draw any plain figure into perspective, the place of view & distance being given. The other was the way of designeing any prospect by a mouving index & a pencill fastened to it mouving on paper, & a sight through which to govern the Index by your eyes'.[111]

Covel who came to Lyons three years later is pretty harsh in his judgement of both the man and his collections: 'With much adoe we got to see Monsieur Servier's knacks for they are no better though they make a foul noyse in the world . . . He is a very peevish, silly, doting old man. I found he spoke a little Italian, and then I wrought him like waxe; before he had us, if we would not have the patience to give him leave to discant on his own conceits, turne out, the door was open'. Most of the exhibits are dismissed with such comments as 'idle things' and 'common and ordinary'.[112] Ferrier, on the other hand, was very much taken with his visit in 1687. Indeed he declares that after the Charité in Lyons 'the next & greatest rarity & which was really worth the going from Paris thither to see, was Mr. Cerviere's Cabinet'. He concludes a detailed and admiring account of the exhibits with this description of their inventor: 'He is almost blind & yet he takes the greatest delight imaginable in shewing them not to every person but to those that look any way civill he makes no scruple at all'.[113] Veryard gives a much shorter account of his visit though he describes Servières as 'a very ingenious Gentleman of this Town, and a good Mechanick',[114] while Bromley who was shown round by him when he claimed to be eighty-four, gives a long and detailed account of his visit to 'the Closet of the ingenious Monsieur Serviers; which, to give it what is due, rather exceeded, than answered my Expectations'.[115]

That is all that can be gleaned from our travellers' accounts on the state of literature, scholarship, the arts, the newly founded academies, and the world of science and technology in seventeenth-century France. Yet scrappy as this chapter must appear, it no doubt brings together a number of points of interest to specialists in a variety of fields.

CONCLUSION

After all the material which is likely to be of interest to the modern reader has been extracted from our travellers' accounts of their journeys inside France and then arranged under appropriate headings, it is not difficult to think of a number of topics on which they remain completely silent. Again, there are subjects which they only just touch upon where today we would have welcomed a great deal more detail. There are also matters which they obviously misunderstood, partially or even completely.

Although a certain number wrote and published accounts of their travels and of what they had observed abroad with the object of enlightening their contemporaries about conditions in France, the great majority simply jotted down in their diaries or in their letters home their impressions of what they saw and heard there without any idea of providing material for the historians of later ages. Even with such help as they could derive from their knowledge of Latin, it is obvious that most of them were poorly equipped linguistically when it came to recording what they observed; they must sometimes have only half understood or even completely misunderstood what they saw and particularly what they heard on their travels. Inevitably they all saw the France of their day through the eyes of men and women of their own age with their national prejudices and also from the standpoint of their own particular political and religious convictions.

Yet, when all is said and done, they had one great advantage over the modern reader: they were *there* — on the roads, in the streets, the houses, the inns and the taverns as well as the palaces, the churches and the monasteries of seventeenth-century France. They encountered a great variety of men and women of all classes from peasants to great noblemen, both in Paris and in the endlessly varied provinces of France. However imperfect their contribution to an understanding of that country in their day, they do at least offer first hand impressions of life there three to four hundred years ago.

APPENDIX

The following accounts of travels in seventeenth-century France have not been made use of in the foregoing pages; though none is entirely devoid of interest, they did not offer anything that was not at least equally well expressed in other works:

Anonymous. British Library, Harleian MS. 6867, ff.36-40.

Starting at Florence on 3 March 1622, the author relates how he entered France from Savoy on 4 May and travelled to Paris via Lyons, Roanne and Orleans. He left Paris on 21 June and on the 27th sailed from Boulogne for Dover. He offers a very sketchy account of his travels through France.

Robert Boyle, *An Account of Philaretus during his Minority,* reproduced with ample annotation in R.W.E. Maddison, *The Life of the Honorable Robert Boyle, F.R.S.,* London, 1969 (see especially pp.24-53).

Robert Boyle and an elder brother, Francis (just married to Tom Killigrew's sister, Elizabeth) travelled with a tutor at the end of October 1640 via Rye, Dieppe, Paris and Lyons to Geneva. Except for an excursion through Savoy to Grenoble and the Grande Chartreuse, they remained there until September 1641. After travels in Italy they returned to France through Antibes and Marseilles in the spring of 1642, and Robert then travelled via Lyons to Geneva. He returned to England in the middle of 1644. *An Account of Philaretus* contains little of interest on France apart from a brief description of the galleys at Marseilles.

Sir Thomas Browne. Bodleian Library, Rawlinson MS. D. 108.11

Sir Thomas Browne (1605-1682) left a manuscript entitled 'A journey from Venice to Bourdeaux', five pages consisting mainly of jottings.

Thomas Denne. British Library, Add. MS. 28010, ff.55-58.

Thomas Denne (1623-1646) recorded a journey from Calais to Rouen which began at Dover on 26 January 1643/44 O.S. Though the account of his travels in France breaks off at that point, we know that he went further from three letters written from Paris on 20 May, 9 July and 1 August (Add. MS. 28000,

343

ff.330-331, 337, 339). From one of these we learn that between May and July he had travelled in the Loire valley, visiting Orleans, Blois and Angers, and had got as far as La Rochelle and the Ile de Ré. The fragment of a travel diary is printed almost *in extenso* in D. Gardiner, 'Some Travel Notes during the Thirty Years War', *History*, NS.xxv. (1941), pp.14-19.

William Edgeman. Bodleian Library, Clarendon MS. 137, ff. 12-17, 33-35

Edgeman accompanied Sir Edward Hyde (later first Earl of Clarendon) and Lord Cottington on their embassy to Spain. They entered France at Péronne, coming from the Spanish Netherlands, on 30 July 1649 and, after nearly two months in Paris, they crossed into Spain on 19 October. They returned to France on 22 March 1651 and, after spending a month in Paris, they arrived in Brussels on 30 May. The 1649 section of the diary contains some observations of interest.

Henry and Alexander Erskine and their tutor, John Shaw. Letters from France, 1616-1620. (Historical Manuscripts Commission, *Mar and Kellie MSS., Supplementary Report,* Vol.60.ii, pp.70-99).

Henry Erskine, third son of the Earl of Mar, succeeded to the barony of Cardcross; he died in 1628. He and his brother were in France from November 1616 to October 1618; they spent most of the time in the provinces, first in Bourges and then in Saumur. After travels in Italy, they came back to Paris in September 1619; they returned to London through the Low Countries by April 1620. There are some interesting passages in the letters, particularly about the Huguenots.

A.H. Mathew and A. Calthrop, *The Life of Sir Tobie Matthew, Bacon's alter ego,* London, 1907.

Tobie Matthew (1577-1655), a son of an archbishop of York, was ordained in Rome in 1614 and knighted by James I in 1623. He spent a good deal of time in France between 1604 and 1607, was there briefly in 1617, and in 1625, after playing some part in the negotiations for the marriage between Charles and Henrietta Maria, he was chosen to act as the queen's interpreter as she knew no English. Letters and extracts from his letters written in France are of some interest, particularly one written from Calais in June 1625 which gives a long description of Henrietta Maria.

Robert Moody. Bodleian Library, Rawlinson MS. D.84.

This account of the Continental travels of Banister Maynard (1642-1718) who succeeded in 1699 to the title of Baron

Maynard, was compiled by a servant who presented it to his master with a flowery dedication. It relates how, after taking part in the festivities for Louis XIV's marriage, Maynard left Paris with his tutor and servants on 7 September 1660 and after visiting Lyons, Grenoble and the Grande Chartreuse, he left France for Italy. He returned via the Spanish Netherlands and was back in Paris by the beginning of April 1662. In the autumn he made a journey down the Loire valley, also visiting La Flèche, Richelieu and Chartres. He remained in Paris until the spring of 1663, sailing from Dieppe from Dover on 9 April. The servant's account of these travels is almost entirely lacking in detail.

Sir Henry Slingsby, *The Diary*, ed. D. Parsons, London, 1836.

Sir Henry Slingsby (1601-1658) was executed for his part in a conspiracy against Oliver Cromwell. The only thing of interest in this volume is the instructions drawn up by Slingsby's father on 31 March 1610 O.S. for the tutor who was to accompany his elder son William to the Continent — 'Instructions for Mr Snell for the guiding of his pupil Willm Slingesbye' (pp.259-64). A letter from Henry to his brother (pp.265-6) shows that the latter was lodged in an *académie* in Paris.

BIBLIOGRAPHY

For a complete list of manuscripts and printed works on which this book is based see SOURCES AND ABBREVIATIONS (pp. 000). Other travellers' accounts of seventeenth-century France are listed in the appendix.

The following works are referred to in the notes:

Alembert, J.L. d', *Oeuvres philosophiques, historiques et littéraires*, ed. J.F. Bastien, 18 vols., Paris, 1805.

Berkeley, G., *Works*, London, 1784, 2 vols.

Black, J.B., *The Reign of Elizabeth 1558-1603*, Oxford, 1936.

Clarke, S., *A Generall Martyrologie, containing a collection of all the greatest persecutions which have befallen the Church of Christ from the Creation to our present time*, London, 1651.

Clarke, T.E.S. and Foxcroft, H.C. *A Life of Gilbert Burnet, Bishop of Salisbury*, Cambridge, 1907.

Hirst, V.M. 'The Authenticity of James Howell's Familiar Letters', *Modern Language Review*, 1959.

La Bruyère, J. de, *Les Caractères ou les moeurs de ce siècle,* ed. R. Garapon, Paris, 1962.

Lefranc, A., *Histoire du Collège de France depuis les origines jusqu'à la fin du premier empire*, Paris, 1893.

Magne, E., *Bibliographie générale des oeuvres de Nicolas Boileau-Despréaux*, 2 vols., Paris, 1929.

Parfaict, C. and F., *Histoire du théâtre français depuis son origine jusqu'à présent*, 15 vols., Amsterdam and Paris, 1735-49.

Patin, G., *Lettres*, ed. J.H. Reveillé-Parise, Paris, 1846, 3 vols.

Perrault, Ch., *Les Hommes illustres qui ont paru en France pendant ce siècle*, 2 vols., Paris, 1696.

Plattard, J. (ed.), *Un Étudiant écossais en France en 1665-1666. Journal de voyage de Sir John Lauder*, Paris, 1935.

Servières, N. Grollier de, *Recueil d'ouvrages curieux de mathématique et de mécanique, ou description du cabinet de M. Grollier de Servières*, Lyons, 1719.

Stoye, J.W., *English Travellers Abroad 1604-1667. Their influence on English Society and Politics*, London, 1952.

Tallemant des Réaux, G., *Historiettes*, ed. A. Adam, Paris, 1961, 2 vols.

NOTES

I THE TRAVELLERS AND HOW THEY TRAVELLED

1 Extracts from his diary and letters are quoted by permission of the Wentworth Woodhouse Trustees and the Director of Sheffield Public Libraries.
2 His *Epistolae Ho-elianae* raises an awkward problem. The first edition (1645) which is used here contains no dates, and those given in the 1650 edition are often obviously wrong. This has led to the suspicion that the letters were simply concocted while he was imprisoned in the Fleet. That there is a good case for accepting that the letters are authentic even if edited and sometimes run together, is shown by V.M.Hirst, 'The Authenticity of James Howell's Familiar Letters', *Modern Language Review*, Vol.LIV (1959), pp.558–61.
3 P.4.
4 Bodleian Library, Lister MSS.3, f.1.
5 Bodleian Library, Lister MSS.5, 19.
6 Pp.6, 25.
7 *An Account*, p.1.
8 Ibid., pp.50, 129, 34.
9 Pp.60–6.
10 *Crudities*, pp.10, 15, 64–5.
11 *Relation*, pp.227–8.
12 *Voyage*, pp.21–2.
13 *Travels*, p.6.
14 *Letters*, p.440.
15 *Remarks*, p.15.
16 *Journal*, pp.11, 4.
17 *An Account*, p.109.
18 *Journals*, pp.123–4.
19 *Relation*, p.183.
20 *Journey*, pp.170, 171, 174.
21 *An Account*, p.61.
22 *Diary*, Vol.II, pp.97, 146.
23 *Epistolae*, I.29, II.46.
24 *Memoirs and Travels*, pp.25, 30.
25 *Journal*, pp.4, 8, 11.
26 *Works*, p.70.
27 *Journals*, pp.3, 12, 16.
28 *Journal*, p.38.
29 *Travels*, p.17.
30 *Method for Travell*, [VI].
31 *Instructions*, pp.48–49.
32 *Letters*, pp.441, 444.
33 *Voyage*, p.20.

34 *Relation*, p.25.
35 Gilbert de Clérembault de Palluau.
36 Lauder is not consistent in spelling this expression which presumably corresponds to *quelque peu*.
37 'Stupid'.
37a 'Must be'.
38 *Journals*, pp.60–61.
39 P.56.
40 *Travels*, p.53.
41 *An Account*, p.716.
42 *Travels*, p.143.
43 *Memoirs*, p.131.
44 *An Account*, p.361.
45 *Diary*, Vol.III, p.16.
45a Gaillon, where the archbishop of Rouen had a palace.
46 *Itinerary*, p.196.
47 Pp.118–20.
48 *Observations*, p.196.
49 *Works*, pp.68–9.
50 *Travels*, pp.2–4.
51 *Diary*, Vol.II, pp.158–60, 532.
52 *An Account*, p.711.
53 *Travels*. pp.120–3.
54 *Diary*, Vol.II, p.533.
55 *Remarks*, p.366.
56 *Memoirs and Travels*, pp.21–2.
57 Pridgeon, *Diary*, p.240.
58 *Travels*, p.209.
59 *Journal*, p.35.
60 *Memoirs*, p.132.
61 *Works*, p.105.
62 *Travels*, pp.138, 143.
63 *Crudities*, pp.7, 9–10, 55.
64 *An Account*, p.81.
65 *Epistolae*, I.86.
66 *Itinerary*, p.184.
67 *Journal*, pp.67–8.
68 *Diary*, Vol.II, p.135.
69 *Remarks*, pp.370,4.
70 *Travels*, p.273.
71 *Memoirs and Travels*, p.5.
72 *Travels*, p.276.
73 *An Account*, p.724.
74 *Travels*, pp.16, 1.
75 *Diary*, Vol.II, pp.121–6.
76 *Travels*, pp.67–88.
77 *Journal*, p.60.
78 *Journal*, pp.17, 45.
79 *Journals*, p.24.
80 *Diary*, p.422.
81 *An Account*, pp.709, 713.
82 *Travels*, pp.148, 68.

83 *Memoirs*, p.131.
84 *Journal*, pp.66–7.
85 *Travels*, p.18.
86 P.119.
87 *Travels*, p.18.
88 *Crudities*, p.30.
89 *Diary*, Vol.II pp.162, 167.
90 *Diary*, pp.282, 279, 275.
91 *Travels*, pp.66, 227.
92 *Crudities*, pp.9, 18.
93 *Works*, p.69.
93a He appears to have been unaware that the French for 'chariot' is *char*, and that a *chariot* is a four-wheeled waggon.
94 *Relation*, pp.13, 26, 122, 158, 162.
95 *Memoirs*, p.139
96 *An Account*, pp.734, 733. The author of *A New Journey* writes of Dieppe (p.128): 'The chief Trade of this Town is in Fish, which the *Chasse-marees* (who are men that travel Night and Day with a drove of Horses all loaded with Fish, Oisters, &c. and each having a Bell as our Pack-horses have) carry to Paris.'
97 Pp.20, 108.
98 *Travels*, pp.2–4.
99 *An Account*, p.77.
100 *Observations*, p.83.
101 See above, pp.23–4 and Chap. IV, pp.166–8.
102 *Crudities*, p.10.
103 *An Account*, p.728.
104 *Journal*, p.36.
105 See Chap.II, pp.107–9
106 *Diary*, Vol.II, pp.135–6.
107 *Peregrination*, p.337.
108 *Diary*, f.11v.
109 Pp.26–8, 93.

II ECONOMIC AND SOCIAL CONDITIONS
(a) The Land and the Peasants
1 *Relation*, p.421. Thanks to their exports the French 'draw into their country greater store of silver and gold, then cometh into any region of Christendom, comparing quantity for quantity... At this present it is held, that there is far greater quantity (this King told me it was after the proportion of six to one) of the doublons and pistolets of Spain, in France, than in Spain itself.' (p.430).
2 *State of France*, p.91.
3. *An Account*, p.104.
4 *Relation*, pp.7–8.
5 *Remarks*, p.24.
6 *An Account*, p.86.
7 *Remarks*, p.35.
8 *An Account*, pp.95–6.
9 *Journey*, pp.210–11.
10 *Method for Travell*, T3v.
10a P.247.

11 *Observations*, p.16.
12 *Epistolae*, Section I, pp.25–6.
13 *Relation* pp.251, 256.
14 ibid. pp.258–61.
15 *Diary*, Vol.III, p.17.
16 *Travel Notes*, ff.31r, 32r, 78r.
17 *Memoirs and Travels*, pp.18, 4.
18 *Journals*, pp.16, 122.
19 Youths.
20 Handfuls.
21 Fellow.
22 Staff.
23 A smart blow.
24 *Journals*, pp.89–90.
25 *Location conduction*, the Roman contract of leasing and hiring.
26 Farmers.
27 *Journals*, pp.107, 82, 40.
28 *Crudities*, p.53.
29 *Peregrination*, p.419.
30 *Journal*, f.86v.
31 *An Account*, p.715.
32 *Observations*, pp.103–4.
33 *Travels*, p.278.
34 *Travels*, pp.88, 229, 236–7.
35 *Travels*, pp.236, 86.
36 *Voyage*, pp.20–1.
37 *Remarks*, p.12.
38 *Observations*, p.102.
39 *An Account*, pp.102, 69.
40 P.32.
41 *Travels*, pp.274, 89.
42 *Voyage*, p.20.
43 *Travel Notes*, f.31r.
44 *Travels*, pp.10, 45.
45 *Horse-hoing Husbandry*, pp.212, 18, 133, 94–7.
46 *Travels*, pp.103–5.
47 *Method for Travell*, p.03v.
48 *Relation*, p.463.
49 *Relation*, p.267.
50 Ibid., p.265.
51 Ibid., pp.271–2. The man who arrested Concini was the Marquis de Vitry
52 Pp.38, 39, 40, 37.
53 *Journals*, p.75.
54 *Memoirs*, Vol.I, pp.456–7.
55 *Memoirs and Travels*, pp.19–20.
56 *Journals*, p.92. By a *sous marky* is meant a *sou marqué* (1 1/4 *sous*).
57 *An Account*, p.733. See below, p.153.
57a Pp.1–2.
58 *An Account*, p.106.
59 *Observations*, pp.106–7, 121.
60 *Journey*, p.160.
61 *Travels*, p.110.
62 Ibid., p.147
63 Ibid., p.148.
64 Ibid., pp.207–8.
65 Ibid. p.208.
66 Ibid. p.237.
67 Ibid., pp.49, 137.
68 Ibid., p.116.

69 Ibid., p.232.
70 Ibid., p.64.
71 Ibid., p.222.
72 *Travels*, pp.225, 250–1, 221.
73 Ibid., p.49.

(b) The Towns, Trade and Industry
1 *State of France*, pp.109–10.
2 *Memoirs and Travels*, p.7.
3 *Journal*, p.61.
4 *Itinerary*, p.188.
5 *Relation*, p.69.
6 *Diary*, Vol.II. p.94.
7 *Epistolae*, Section I, pp.27–8.
8 *Method for Travell*, D2r.
9 *Crudities*, p.23.
10 *Relation*, p.102.
11 *Relation*, pp.70–1.
12 *Remarks*, p.8.
13 *State of France*, pp.76–7.
14 *Tour*, p.2.
15 *Journal*, pp.24–5.
16 *Relation*, p.66.
17 *An Account*, p.62.
18 *Description*, f.145v.
19 *Journal*, pp.7, 14.
20 The Palais du Luxembourg.
21 Ibid., p.21.
22 *An Account*, p.730.
23 Hired carriages.
24 *Journey*, pp.140–2.
24a *Letters to a Nobleman*, pp.108–9.
25 Ibid, pp.145–6.
26 *Tour*, p.5.
27 *Travels*, p.150.
28 *Journal*, pp.22–3.
29 *Observations*, p.22.
30 *An Account*, p.735.
31 *Remarks*, p.13.
32 *Tour*, p.2.
33 *Journal*, p.38.
34 Pp.118–19a (pp.113–20a are wrongly numbered).
35 *Works*, pp.20–1.
36 *Memoirs and Travels*, p.29.
37 *Journal*, p.35.
38 *Memoirs and Travels*, p.27.
39 *Book*, p.17.
40 *Travels*, pp.142, 237–8.
41 Ibid., p.75.
42 *Diary*, pp.131–3.
43 *Observations*, pp.463–4.
44 *Diary*, pp.281, 276.
45 *Letters*, pp.253–4.
46 *Remarks*, pp.36–8.
47 *Travels*, p.83.
48 *Remarks*, pp.38–9.
49 *Epistolae*, I.86.
50 *Observations*, p.445.
51 *An Account*, p.707.
52 *Voyage*, pp.32–3.
53 *Tour*, pp.19–20.
54 *Remarks*, p.13.
55 *An Account*, p.100.
55a *Works*, Vol.VIII, p.76.

56 *An Account*, p.707.
57 *Crudities*, p.56.
58 *Remarks*, p.13.
59 Yeast.
60 *Journals*, p.43.
61 *Journals*, p.58.
62 Ibid., p.76.
63 *State of France*, p.104.
64 Palm *(OED)*.
65 Ibid., p.40. While in Charenton to attend a Protestant service Edward Browne bought some bread and cherries 'and for a double drunk some water of a boy that carries it up and downe with a cup ready for you'. (*Journal*, p.21).
66 Frighten.
67 Ibid., p.120.
68 *Travels*, pp.48, 124, 18.
69 Skippon (*An Account*, p.714) gives a long list of those present there in August 1665.
70 *Observations*, p.454.
71 Ray, *Observations*, pp.454–5; Skippon, *An Account*, p.714; Locke, *Travels*, pp.24–7.
72 Ray, *Observations*, p.457; Locke, *Travels*, pp.43–4, 56, 94, 95, 99, 100, 101.
73 Ray, *Observations*, pp.458–9; Locke, *Travels*, pp.31–8, 90–1, 96.
74 *Travels*, pp.95–102.
75 *Travels*, pp.146, 147.
76 Ibid., pp.216–17.
77 *Diary*, Vol.II, pp.145–6.
78 *Travels*, pp.8, 245.
79 Ibid., pp.11, 15.
80 The *droit de marque*, a payment made for the placing on the cloth of a sign that it conformed with the regulations laid down by the government.
81 *Travels*, pp.131, 133.
82 *An Account*, p.727.
83 *Travels*. p.225.
84 Ibid., pp.189, 248.
85 *Remarks*, p.10.
86 *Observations*, p.86.
87 *Travels*, p.249.
88 *An Account*, pp.726–7, François de Vendôme, Duc de Beaufort (1616–69), commanded expeditions against Algerian pirates in these years, Olinda was a town in Brazil, famous for its sword blades.
89 Ibid., p.735.
90 *Observations*, p.80.
91 *Travels*. p.239.
92 See below, pp.173–9.
93 *Memoirs and Travels*, p.36.
93a Pp.11–15.
94 *An Account*, pp.108–9.
95 *Itinerary*, p.133.
96 *Memoirs and Travels*, p.36.
97 *An Account*, p.723.

98 *Journals*, p.40.
99 *An Account*, p.711.
100 *Works*, p.58.
101 *An Account*, p.61.
102 *Observations*, pp.1–2, 90.
103 *Crudities*, p.59.
104 *Journal*, p.68.
105 *Travel Notes*, f.78v.
106 *An Account*, p.727.
107 *Travels*, p.144.
108 *Diary*, pp.274–5.
109 *Travels*, pp.249–50. See also
   Bromley, *Remarks*, p.10; Lassels,
   Voyage, p.32; Northleigh,
   Observations, p.85; Skippon, *An
   Account* p.728; Symonds, *Travel
   Notes*, f.72r.
110 *Voyage*, pp.16–17.
111 *Tour*, p.17. Already in 1665 Downes
   had observed the beginning of work
   on the port and canal (*Notebook*,
   f.39).
112 See above, pp.22–3.
113 Louis de Froidour, *Lettre . . .
   concernant la relation et la
   description des travaux qui se font en
   Languedoc pour la communication
   des deux mers*, Toulouse, 1672.
114 *Travels*, pp.55, 133–4, 128–30.
115 *Diary*, p.281.
116 *An Account*, pp.84–5.
117 *Remarks*, p.32.
118 *Travels*, p.18.
119 *An Account*, p.732.
120 *Travel Notes*, f.48r.
121 *Observations*, pp.66, 83–4.
122 *Journey* p.20.
123 *Memoirs and Travels*, pp.11–12.
124 *An Account*, p.64.
125 *Observations*, p.18.
126 *Diary*, p.364.
127 *Diary*, Vol.II, pp.157–8, and *Voyage
   of Italy*, p.35.
128 *Travels*, pp.8, 245–6. An *ânée* was
   roughly 3½ cwts.
129 *Journal*, p.30.
130 *Travels*, p.8.
131 *Remarks*, pp.16–17.
132 *Travels*, p.195.
133 *Relation*, pp.98–9.
134 Exspute = 'Spit out' (*OED*).
135 *Descriptions*, f.14r-v.
136 *Journal*, p.65; *Diary*, p.280.
137 *Journal*, pp.5, 22–3; *Works*, p.113.
138 *An Account*, p.64.
139 *Observations*, p.19.
140 *Journal*, p.65; *Diary*, p.280.
141 *Observations*, pp.19–20.
142 *Travels*, pp.89, 146–7, 208.
143 *Relation*, p.435.
144 *Method for Travell*, 04v.
145 *State of France*, p.24.
146 *Epistolae*, II. pp.45–46.
147 *State of France*, p.65.
148 *Journey*, p.18.

149 *Travels*, p.104 (for another example
   see p.118.)
150 *Observations*, p.18.
150a *Relation*, pp.473–4.
151 *Relation*, p.134.
152 *State of France*, p.50.
153 Ibid. pp.77, 79.
154 *Travel Notes*, f.50v.
155 *Memoirs and Travels*, p.38.
156 *Journals*, p.145.
157 *Travels*, pp.94–5, 23.
158 Ibid., p.94.

III THE NOBILITY
1 *Life*, pp.42–9.
2 See Chap.V.
3 *Method for Travell*, S1r.
4 *State of France*, p.72.
5 *Memoirs and Travels*, p.3.
6 *Relation*, p.254.
7 *Memoirs and Travels*, pp.14, 37.
8 *Observations*, pp.102–3.
9 *Observations*, p.16.
10 A misprint for 'poverty'?
11 *State of France*, p.72.
12 *Travels*, pp.102, 209, 121.
13 *Method for Travell*, Tlr.
14 *State of France*, pp.77–8.
15 'A fresh supply of money' (*OED*).
16 *Memoirs and Travels*, p.37.
17 *State of France*, p.78.
18 *Travels*, pp.257–8, 268.
19 *Relation*, p.252.
20 *State of France*, p.74.
21 *Observations*, p.28.
22 *Memoirs and Travels*, p.37.
23 *State of France*, pp.78–9, 102–3.
24 *History*, Vol.I, p.565.
25 *Travels*, p.259.
26 *Relation*, pp.285–6.
27 *Travels*, p.62.
28 *An Account*, p.716.
29 MS.5, f.223r.
30 *Observations*, p.15.
31 *State of France*, p.73.
32 *Travels*, p.182.

IV JUSTICE
1 *Method for Travell*, Q3v.
2 *Relation*, p.7.
3 *State of France*, pp.74–5.
4 *Journals*, p.90.
5 *Observations*, pp.106, 49–50.
6 *Journals*, pp.90, 65, 87, 75.
7 *An Account*, p.733. The curious
   reader may consult on this case
   'Madame de Langey', in the
   Historiettes of G. Tallemant des
   Réaux, ed. A.Adam, Paris, 1961, 2
   vols., Vol.II., pp.887–96.
8 *Diary*, Vol.II, p.140.
9 Evelyn's father-in-law.
10 Ibid. Vol.III, p.4–8.
11 *Travels*, p.113.

12 The editor of this document prints 'friend', but this does not make sense.
13 *Letters*, p.64.
14 *Travels*, pp.30, 31, 58, 67.
15 *Relation*, pp.86–7.
16 'Without a coat'.
17 *Epistolae*, I, pp.30–1.
18 *Memoirs,* pp.20–1.
19 *Journey*, p.177.
20 Pp.52–3.
21 *Diary*, Vol.II, p.535.
22 *Journal*, pp.20–1.
23 *Crudities*, p.54.
24 Pp.67–8.
25 *Crudities*, p.18.
26 *An Account*, p.733.
27 *Journal*, p.32.
28 *Crudities*, pp.8, 48–9.
29 *Journals*, pp.118–19.
30 *Travels*, p.188.
31 *Journals*, p.77.
32 *Travels*, p.258.
33 *Crudities*, p.66.
34 *Journals*, p.70.
35 P.120.
36 *An Account*, p.93.
37 *Travels*, p.74.
38 *Diary*, Vol.II, pp.165–6.
39 *Diary*, p.275.
40 *Remarks*, pp.36–7.
41 *An Account*, p.93.
42 'Endow with a marriage portion'.
43 *Journals*, pp.60, 69–70, 110, 111.
44 Samuel Clarke, *A Generall Martyrologie, containing a collection of all the greatest persecutions which have befallen the Church of Christ from the Creation to our present times*, London, 1651.
45 'Palm'.
46 *Journals*, p.70.
47 *Diary*, Vol.III, pp.28–9.
48 *Les Caractères*, XIV.51.

V LEISURE
1 *Diary*, Vol.II, pp.130–1.
2 *Journey*, pp.178–9, 180–1.
3 *An Account*, p.732.
4 'Bargain' *(OED)*.
5 *Tour*, p.7.
6 Louis XIV's brother.
7 *Journey*, pp.174–6.
8 *Travel Notes*, ff.62r, 49r.
9 The Place de la Grève.
10 *Travels*, p.200.
11 *Observations*, p.67.
12 *Diary*, Vol.III, p.38.
13 *Method for Travell*, T4 v, VI r-v.
14 Ibid., T4. v.
15 *Relation*, p.135.
16 *Book*, pp.6, 11.
17 *An Account*, p.714.
18 *Travels*, p.17.
19 See above, p.102.

20 *Method for Travel*, T4 v- VI r.
21 *Journals*, p.11.
22 *Travels*, p.101.
23 *Method for Travell*, V2r-v.
24 *Relation*, pp.126–7.
25 *Travels*, pp.171, 68, 84, 113, 43.
26 *An Account*, pp.727, 718.
27 *Travels*, pp.18, 93, 95, 102.
28 Yards understood?
29 Cardinal Bonzi, Archbishop of Narbonne.
30 *Travels*, p.109.

III KING, COURT AND GOVERNMENT
1 *Itinerary*, p.194.
2 Ibid., p.185.
3 Ibid., pp.186–7.
4 *Method for Travell*, Tlv.
5 *Life*, p.49.
5a *Relation*, pp.478–81, 484, 486.
6 The Canal du Midi was not to be constructed until the time of Colbert.
7 *Observations*, pp.25–7.
8 *Epistolae*, I. pp.34–5.
9 *Observations*, p.28.
10 Ibid., pp.12–13.
11 *Crudities*, p.46.
11a *Relation*, p.493.
12 Pp.94–5.
13 *Relation*, p.205.
14 *Epistolae*, I. p.23.
15 Ibid., I. pp.38–9.
16 *Relation*, pp.167–8.
17 P.94.
18 Ibid., I. p.31, II. pp.4, 36.
19 Chap. VI.
20 *Relation*, pp.208–9.
21 *Book*, p.8.
22 *Relation*, pp.247–51. On pp.108–9 he tends to see the Parliament as a rather more forceful body because of such functions as appointing a regent.
23 Ibid., pp.214–15.
23a *Journal*, ff.69–70.
24 'The great shit-fire'.
25 *Epistolae*, VI. pp.33, 67–8.
26 *Life*, pp.104–5.
27 In the edition the word is followed by a question mark.
28 *Journal*, p.63.
29 Pp.12–16. Evelyn had noted this inscription on a visit to Le Havre in 1644 (*Diary*, Vol.II, p.125)
30 *Diary*, Vol.II, p.96.
31 *Diary*, p.419.
32 *Diary*, Vol.III, pp.32, 41–2, 43.
33 Pp.70–1.
34 Ff.36v, 52v–55v.
34a *Diary*, ff.37–38.
35 *Journal*, p.63.
36 *Calendar of State Papers, Domestic. Commonwealth 1651–4*, Vol.IV, pp.205–9.

37 In 1660.
38 Glandève de Niozelles.
39 *An Account*, p.719.
40 *Journals*, p.131.
41 See Veryard, *An Account*, p.69: Northleigh, *Observations*, p.67; and *A New Journey*, p.115.
42 *An Account*, p.70.
43 *Observations*, pp.67–8.
44 *Memoirs and Travels*, p.5.
45 Ibid., p.13.
46 Ibid., pp.18–19.
47 *State of France*, p.49.
48 *Journal*, pp.3–6.
49 *Works*, p.113.
50 Vol.I., p.207.
51 *An Account*, p.730.
52 *Travels*, pp.152, 171–3.
53 Left blank in MS.
54 *Travels*, pp.186–7, 252, 255.
55 She was his cousin.
56 Covel is fond of using Italian words. What is meant here is the old sense of *soucoupe*, defined by the 1694 *Dictionnaire de l'Académie française* as 'Espece d'assiette ayant un pied, sur laquelle on sert aux personnes de qualité le vase pour boire'.
57 Jeanne Pélagie de Rohan-Chabot (1651–98), wife of the Prince d'Épinoy.
58 *(OED):* '(of a hunted stag) to take to water or a marshy ground'.
59 *Journal*, f.89r-v.
60 *Journal*, p.26.
61 Marshal Armand Frédéric Schomberg (1619–90). A protestant, he left France in 1685 and was killed at the Battle of the Boyne.
62 *History*, Vol.I, p.565.
63 T.E.S. Clarke and H.C. Foxcroft, *A Life of Gilbert Burnet, Bishop of Salisbury*, Cambridge, 1907, pp.199–200.
64 *Observations*, pp.133–4.
65 *History*, pp.565–6.
66 *An Account*, p.70.
66a *Parentalia*, pp.261–2.
67 *Travels*, p.151 (see also pp.164–7, 175, 178, 180, 196).
68 *Observations*, p.71.
69 *An Account*, p.67.
70 *Journal*, p.27.
71 *Journey*, p.202.
72 Ibid., p.213. The frequency of these stays at Marly is somewhat exaggerated.
73 P.117.
74 Pp.89, 91.
75 *An Account*, p.107.
76 *Observations*, pp.7, 132, 134.
77 *An Account*, p.70.
78 *Journal*, f.91r.
79 *History*, Vol.I, p.565.
80 Ibid., Vol.I, p.207.

81 *An Account*, p.733
82 *Travels*, pp.157, 234.
83 *Tour*, p.14.
84 Left blank in MS.
85 *Travels*, p.237.
86 *An Account*, p.82.
87 *Observations*, pp.100–1.
88 *An Account*, pp.104–5.
89 *Description*, f.148r. While Bertie does mention the prisoners, he too tends to treat the Bastille as a tourist attraction: 'At the top of the building there is a very fine terrace walk from whence you may take a view of the whole town.' (*Diary*, p.285).
90 He was arrested on suspicion of being an English agent among the Huguenots of Languedoc. His imprisonment lasted from 1 April 1666 to 30 January 1667 when he was released on giving a written undertaking to obey 'la volonté de sa Majesté qui est de sortir de son royaume dans quinze jours'.
91 *An Account*, pp.733–4.
92 *Tour*, p.7.
93 *An Account*, p.65.
94 Pp.49, 51.
94a Pp.4–5.
95 *Travels*, pp.110, 115, 156.
96 Ibid., pp.132, 30.
97 *Letters to a Nobleman*, pp.135, xiii–xiv.
98 *Journey*, pp.196, 220.
99 Ibid., pp.213–14.
100 Ibid., pp.216–17.
101 *Works*, Vol.VIII, pp.80–2.

IV THE ARMED FORCES
1 *Observations*, pp.18–20.
2 *State of France*, pp.84–92.
3 *Observations*, pp.107–9.
4 *Travels*, pp.85, 106, 136.
4a P.8. The 'old Bodyes' = the *vieux corps*, the six oldest regiments.
5 Pp.19, 24–5.
6 *Travels*, pp.100, 23, 24.
7 See above, pp.37, 86.
8 *Observations*, pp.98–9.
9 *Travels*, p.59.
10 Vol.II, pp.83–4, 85, 561.
11 *Memoirs*, p.139.
12 *Journals*, pp.2–3.
13 *Letters*, p.56.
14 *Travels*, pp.185–6.
15 1 *double* out of each *livre* paid out by the *Trésoriers généraux des guerres*.
16 *Travels*, pp.1, 157, 159, 199.
17 A tear in the manuscript.
18 John Buxton, *Diary*, p.282.
19 *Journal*, p.24.
20 *An Account*, p.65.

21 *Observations*, pp.20–1.
22 *Travels*, pp.191, 192–4, 196–7, 200, 252, 285.
23 Ibid., pp.189, 9.
24 See above, pp.70–1.
25 In May 1684.
26 *Remarks*, pp.42–3.
27 *Observations*, pp.26, 19.
27a *Relation*, p.428.
28 *State of France*, pp.86–7.
29 *Observations*, pp.119–20.
30 *An Account*, p.106.
31 For the galleys as penal establishments see above, pp.109–11.
31a *Diary*, pp.131–2.
32 *Diary*, Vol.II, pp.164–5.
33 *Travels*, pp.73–4.
34 *Diary*, p.275.
35 *An Account*, p.93.
36 *An Account*, pp.720–1.
37 *Travels*, pp.77–9.
38 He gives the version: 'Je suis le plus grand sur l'onde/Comme mon Maitre sur le monde'.
39 *Remarks*, pp.41–3.
40 *Tour*, p.14.
41 *Travels*, pp.233–5.
42 *Observations*, pp.110–11.
43 *Diary*, Vol.I, p.88.

V THE ROMAN CATHOLIC CHURCH
1 *Journals*, p.2.
2 *Relation*, p.219.
3 *Observations*, p.14.
4 *State of France*, p.69.
5 *Journals*, p.86.
6 Skippon, *An Account*, p.734; *Popery and Tyranny*, p.17.
7 *Travels*, pp.46–7 and note.
8 The so-called *don gratuit*.
9 *Relation*, p.219.
10 *Memoirs and Travels*, p.3.
11 *Travels*, p.110.
12 See above, pp.50–1.
13 *Relation*, p.221.
14 *Memoirs and Travels*, p.37.
15 *An Account*, p.107.
16 *Journey*, pp.14–15.
17 *History*, Vol.I, pp.564–5, 566.
18 *Journal*, pp.31–2.
19 *Travels*, pp.29–30.
20 See above, pp.50–1.
21 *Relation*, pp.208, 218–20, 221.
22 *Journal*, p.64.
23 *Travels*, p.41. £3,000 was roughly equal to 40,000 livres. 40,000 écus was the equivalent of three times that sum.
24 *Travels*, p.258.
25 *Method for Travell*, R3v.
26 *Relation*, pp.220, 227–8.
27 *Travels*, p.284.
28 *Observations*, p.120.
29 *Journals*, pp.9–10.

30 *Journey*, pp.18–20. He returns to the same point on pp.133–5.
31 *Relation*, pp.226–7.
32 *Journals*, p.39.
33 *Journal*, p.64.
34 *An Account*, p.107.
35 Skippon, *An Account*, pp.362–3.
36 *Journal*, pp.13–14.
37 *Observations*, pp.32–3.
38 *Travels*, pp.121, 79.
39 *Diary*, pp.281–2.
40 *Memoirs*, p.11.
41 *Travels*, p.252.
42 Bodleian Library, Ashmole MS, 800, ff.21–27.
43 *Letter*, pp.89–91.
44 *Memoirs*, pp.106–9.
45 Pridgeon, *Diary*, pp.422, 444.
46 Bodleian Library, Rawlinson MS. D 76, f.29.
47 *Diary*, p.309.
47a *Travels*, pp.85–6.
48 *An Account*, p.710. See also Edward Browne, *Works*, p.71; Clenche, *Tour*, p.20; and Veryard, *An Account*, pp.101–2.
48a A Scottish form of *Chibol*, a kind of onion (*OED*).
48b *Journals*, pp.33–4, 62.
49 *Travels*, pp.260, 262.
50 Ibid., pp.38–9, 265–6.
51 *Journals*, pp.31–2.
52 *Travels*, pp.154–5, 266.
53 *Diary*, Vol.III, pp.27–8.
54 Skippon's comment is even more brutal — 'probably a cheat of monks and priests' (*An Account*, p.723).
55 *Travels*, p.70.
56 *Journals*, p.42.
57 *Journey*, pp.131, 133.
58 *Journals*, p.42.
59 Locke, *Travels*, p.98; Lauder, *Journals*, pp.9, 42.
60 *Travels*, p.274.
61 *Method for Travell*, p.[v].
62 *Relation*, p.157.
63 *Journals*, pp.42, 86.
64 *Travels*, p.257.
65 *An Account*, pp.76–7.
66 *Diary*, Vol.II, p.96.
67 *Diary*, Vol.III, p.23.
68 *Journal*, p.66.
69 The last five words should be ignored as the inscription in question was removed from the Paris Collège de Clermont; in 1649 Symonds (*Description*, f.78v) gave it as 'COLLEGIUM CLAROMANTANUM / SOCIETATIS IHESU / I H S'.
70 In the following century D'Alembert in his *De la Destruction des Jésuites* (*Oeuvres philosophiques, historiques et littéraires*, ed. J.F. Bastien, Paris, 1805, 18 vols., Vol.V, p.54) offers

this translation: 'Pour faire place au nom du Roi, / La croix de ces lieux est bannie; / Arrête, passant, et connois / Le Dieu de cette race impie.' This distich is also quoted by Veryard (*An Account*, p.66).

71 A marginal note adds: 'Alluding to La Flesche Mother of their Foundations'. This refers to their *collège* at La Flèche (Sarthe) which was founded by Henry IV in 1604 and which numbered Descartes among its pupils. The distich may be translated thus: 'Nola provided the fathers with the bow; bountiful France provided the arrow; who will provide the rope which they have deserved?' The meaning of 'Nola' is far from clear; Lauder who also quotes this satirical couplet (*Journals*, p.69) has 'dola'. However, the pun on *flèche* and *sagitta* and the concluding words are comprehensible enough.

72 *Observations*, pp.34–7.
73 *History*, Vol.I, pp.566–7.
74 See Chap.VII, pp.274–84.
75 *Journals*, p.12.
76 See Chap.VIII, pp.313–14.
76a 'Need'.
77 *Journals*, pp.30–1, 41–2, 52–3.
77a Daniel 11:38 'the god of forces'.
78 *Crudities*, pp.2–3.
79 *Voyage*, pp.23–4.
80 *Journal*, p.16. Symonds was a positive glutton for church services; he often enters into the most minute detail (*Travel Notes*, ff.59–70).
81 *Travels*, p.131.
82 *Journey*, p.174.
83 *Journals*, pp.126–7.
84 *Relation*, pp.124–5.
85 *Journey*, pp.227–8.
86 The diocese did not acquire an archbishop until 1622.
87 *Crudities*, pp.27–9.
88 *Diary*, Vol.III, p.35.
89 *Journal*, p.23.
90 *Diary*, Vol.II, p.146.
91 His Scottish landlord.
92 *Journals*, pp.11–12.
93 *Travels*, pp.98–9.
94 *Journal*, pp.32, 28.
95 The town proper as distinct from the Haute-Ville.
96 Heylyn later explains that these men 'are bound to visit all such as are infected with the Plague, to minister unto them all things necessary, and if they die, to shrowde them and carry them to their graves'.
97 *Relation*, p.194.
98 *Travels*, pp.82, 93.
99 *Journals*, p.92.
100 *Voyage*, p.44.

101 *Travels*. pp.81–2.
102 *Diary*, pp.277–8.
103 *Diary*, Vol.II, pp.90,87.
104 *Relation*, pp.58, 99–100, 102.
105 *An Account*, p.362.
106 *Works*, p.22.
107 *Travels*, p.223.
108 *Memoirs and Travels*, p.24.
109 *Journal*, p.35. See also Bertie, *Diary*, p.306.
110 i.e. 'la Religion', an abbreviated form of the official name for Calvinism, 'la Religion prétendue réformée'. Lauder writes elsewhere: 'The protestants in speaking of their religion before papists they dare not term it otherwise then *prétendue Réformée*' (*Journal*, p.79).
111 Ibid., pp.19–20.
112 *Tour*, p.11.
113 *Journals*, pp.34–5.
114 *Travels*, pp.87, 138, 242.
115 *Book*, p.34.
116 *An Account*, p.93.
117 *Diary*, pp.276–7.
118 *Book*, pp.34–5.
119 *An Account*, p.721.
120 One word illegible.
121 *Travels*, pp.273–4.
122 *Diary*, p.277.
123 *Travels*, pp.221–2.
124 *Journals*, p.51.
125 See above, p.211 and also p.251.
126 *An Account*, p.732
127 *Voyage*, p.17.
128 *Observations*, p.122.
129 *Method for Travell*, X2v–X3r.
130 *Relation*, p.38.
131 *State of France*, p.80.
132 *An Account*, p.730.
133 *Travels*, p.255.
134 P.119
135 *Travels*, p.262.
136 *Journal*, p.66.
137 The bull was issued by his predecessor, Innocent, X.
138 *Journals*, pp.44, 16, 75.
139 *Letters*, p.64. The last two names should obviously read Antoine Arnauld and Pomponne, secretary of state for foreign affairs.
140 *Journal*, f.88v.
141 *State of France*, p.80.
142 *Observation*, pp.14–15.
143 *Relation*, pp.219, 221–2.
144 *History*, Vol.I, pp.565–6.
145 The London magistrate to whom Titus Oates made his allegations of a popish plot; he was then found murdered.
146 Innocent XI had refused to institute the bishops appointed by Louis XIV and by 1689 thirty-five sees were vacant. Innocent XII reversed this policy by 'preconizing' or giving his

approval to those appointed to the vacant sees.

47 The *régale* took two forms: the *régale temporelle* which allowed the king to dispose of the revenue of vacant sees, and the *régale spirituelle* which gave him the right to appoint to all benefices to which the bishop normally appointed. Louis XIV extended the *régale* to all the dioceses in his kingdom.

48 In 1687 the Marquis de Lavardin (1643–1701) was sent as ambassador to Rome to maintain the right of sanctuary and other French diplomatic privileges. He was excommunicated by Innocent XI and Lous XIV retaliated by occupying the papal territory of Avignon.

49 *Observations*, pp.66–7, 104–5, 112–13, 132.

VI LA RELIGION PRÉTENDUE RÉFORMÉE

1 *Travels*, p.89.
2 *Relation*, p.217.
3 *Relation*, pp.228, 244–5.
4 *Diary*, p.53.
5 He leaves out Sedan.
6 *Memoirs and Travels*, pp.23–4.
6a *Journals*, p.23.
6b *Diary*, pp.78–9.
7 *Relation*, pp.14, 244.
8 *An Account*, p.716.
9 *Travels*, p.94.
10 Ibid., pp.28, 214.
11 Ibid, pp.45, 39–40.
12 Judges of the Cour des Comptes et des Aides.
13 Ibid., pp.42–3, 45, 47.
14 *Journals*, p.79.
15 *Relation*, pp.243–4.
16 *Relation*, p.242.
17 *An Account*, p.732.
18 Pierre Du Moulin (1568–1658).
19 *Crudities*, pp.36–7. Carew speaks of 'sometimes eight or ten thousand communicants', a number swollen by 'those, whom their business draweth to the court, or to Paris.' (*Relation*, p.444).
20 *Diary*, Vol.II, p.115.
21 *Journal*, pp.8, 11.
22 *Journal*, f.87v.
23 *Voyage*, p.14.
24 *Book*, pp.3, 11, 14, 20.
25 *Memoirs and Travels*, p.22.
26 *Journals*, pp.32–3.
27 Whereas Skippon gives the city's population as 25,000 or 21,000 Locke writes: 'They say there are 30,000 people in it, & that there are 8,000 communicants of the Protestant Church.'. (*Travels* p.40).
28 *An Account*, p.715.

29 *Travels*, p.101.
30 *An Account*, pp.715–16.
31 *Voyage*, p.21.
32 *Diary*, Vol.II, p.565.
32a *Relation*, p.441.
33 The reference is not to Newhaven, but to Le Havre. In September 1562 Condé and the other Huguenot leaders signed the secret treaty of Richmond whereby, in return for 3,000 English troops and a loan, England was to be allowed to garrison Le Havre until Calais (lost in 1558) was returned to her. Six months later Condé signed the peace of Amboise which gave the Huguenots toleration and other advantages, and by July the English troops in Le Havre had been compelled to surrender. (See J.B. Black, *The Reign of Elizabeth 1558–1603*, Oxford, 1936, pp.49–56.).
34 *Observations*, pp.23–5.
34a *Diary*, pp.55a–62, 78.
35 P.104.
36 *Relation*, pp.136, 163.
37 Ibid., p.247.
38 Ibid., pp.241–2. Evelyn's account of these courts is more accurate; after describing the *Chambre de l'Edit*, he gives those of Bordeaux, Grenoble and Castres their correct name of *chambres mi-partie* (*State of France*, pp.51–2, 55).
39 Ibid., pp.234–47.
40 *State of France*, pp.80–3.
41 *Memoirs and Travels*, pp.9–10.
42 *Journal*, f.92v.
43 *History*, Vol.I, p.567.
44 The archbishop was François de Harlay who died in 1695. Edward Bonner who was made Bishop of London in 1539 was zealous in persecuting Protestants during the reign of Henry VIII and especially that of Mary.
45 *Observations*, pp.105–6.
46 *Journals*, p.88.
47 *An Account*, p.714.
48 *Diary*, p.279.
49 *Travels*, pp.27–8, 271.
50 Ibid., pp.23, 83.
51 *Travels*, pp.15, 89.
52 Ibid., pp.58, 108.
53 *An Account*, pp.716, 731.
54 Spiral staircase.
55 *Journals*, p.14.
56 *Voyage*, p.13.
57 *Travels*, pp.128, 107, 48, 22–3.
58 Ibid., p.113.
59 *Journal*, f.87r.
60 *Travels*, pp.230, 113.
61 Ibid. p.40.
62 Ibid., pp.15, 27–8, 41, 66.

62a *Diary*, p.132.
62b *Notebook*, ff.6–7.
62c Pp.5–6.
63 *Travels*, pp.229–30.
64 Pp.254–8.
65 *History*, Vol.I., p.658–60.
66 *Remarks*, pp.25–6.
67 *Journal*, pp.35, 30.
68 *An Account*, pp.85, 102.
69 *Observations*, pp.67, 101–2, 113, 82, 77, 79–80.
70 Pp.13–15

VII EDUCATION
1 See above, p.263.
2 *Diary*, Vol.II, p.132.
2a *A breife description*, p.10.
2b *Diary*, pp.339, 341.
2c *Letters to a Nobleman*, p.94. Ushaw College is descended from the 'great College of Secular Priests'.
3 Pp.79–80.
4 *Relation*, pp.103–4
5 *Diary*, Vol.II, p.94.
6 *Memoirs and Travels*, p.7.
7 See above, pp.103–4.
8 *Observations*, pp.23–24.
8a *Letters to a Nobleman*, p.109.
9 *Description*, ff.50r, 56v, 67v, 80v.
10 *Ibid*., ff.66v, 67r.
11 *Relation*, p.81.
12 *Diary*, Vol.II, p.97.
13 *Description*, f.52r–53r.
14 *Diary*, p.289. He has briefer remarks to make about a number of other university colleges.
15 *Observations*, p.28.
16 Symonds offers a sketch instead of a word.
17 *Description*, f.65r.
18 *Observations*, p.29.
19 *Description*, f.66r.
20 *Observations*, pp.28–9.
21 *Journal*, p.11.
22 A house of correction for youths.
23 *Description*, ff.51v, 57r, 58r, 80r.
24 *Notebook*, f.8.
24a *Works*, pp.107–8.
24b *Parentalia*, p.261.
25 *An Account*, p.729.
26 *Tour*, p.6.
27 *An Account*, p.66.
28 *Observations*, pp.30–1. See also Shaw, *Letters to a Nobleman*, p.109.
29 *Memoirs and Travels*, p.24.
30 *Relation*, pp.153–7.
31 *Diary*, Vol.II, p.96.
32 *Description*, ff.78v–79v. He offers sketches of the back and side view of the Jesuit's dress including the hat.
32a *Diary*, p.284.

33 Presumably the *Hermenigildus* of Father Caussin.
34. *Journal*, pp.32–4.
35 *An Account*, p.731.
36 *An Account*, p.66.
37 *See above* p.210.
38 *Observations*, pp.35–6.
39 *Letters to a Nobleman*, p.110.
40 *Diary*, pp.58–9.
41 *A breife description*, p.5.
41a *Diary*, f.34. See also Bertie, *Diary*, p.319.
42 *Works*, p.21.
43 *Memoirs and Travels*, pp.30–1.
44 *Journals*, p.69. For the text of the distich, see above, p.210.
45 *Ibid*., pp.16–17, 77–8, 99.
46 He was hanged, drawn and quartered at Tyburn in 1581.
47 *Crudities*, pp.62–3.
48 *Travels*, p.5
49 Unknown to the usual reference works.
50 *Observations*, p.92.
51 *Journal*, p.39.
52 *Voyage*, pp.18–19.
52a *Letters to a Nobleman*, p.92.
53 P.27.
54 *Diary*, pp.419, 423.
55 *Diary*, Vol.II, pp.134, 150.
56 Pp.87–8.
57 *Journal*, p.25.
58 *Travels*, p.195.
59 *Relation*, pp.83–4.
60 *Diary*, Vol.II, p.97.
61 *A breife description*, f.43v.
62 *Journal*, p.66.
63 *Diary*, Vol.II, p.97.
64 P.100.
65 *Journal*, f.88v.
66 *History*, Vol.I, p.566.
67 *Observations*, pp.24, 26–7.
67a *Works*, Vol.VIII, p.75.
68 *Description*, f.57v.
69 *Diary*, Vol.II, p.160.
70 *Tour*, p.19.
71 *Travels*, p.9.
72 *Remarks*, p.23.
73 *Relation*, pp.146–8.
74 *Ibid*., pp.148–50.
75 *Diary*, Vol.II, p.138.
76 *Remarks*, p.368.
77 Leroy.
78 *Journals*, pp.4, 112–13, 124.
79 An Alexander Strachan received the degree of M.A. from the University of Aberdeen (King's College) in 1646.
80 A teacher of Justininian's *Institutes*.
81 *Journals*, pp.113–14.
82 The word is doubtful.
83 *Description*, f.61v.
84 *Journal*, pp.3–4.
85 *Works*, p.61.
86 *Journal*, p.4.

Notes

357

87 *Works,* p.63.
88 *Journal,* p.31. If Patin ever wrote
   this letter, it does not appear to have
   been preserved. He was, however, a
   great admirer of the *Religio Medici*
   (see his *Lettres,* ed. J.H.
   Reveillé-Parise, Paris, 1846, 3 vols.,
   Vol.I. pp.340, 354). When he
   returned from Italy to Paris, Edward
   Browne received a letter from his
   father which contained the request:
   'Present my services and thancks
   unto Dr. Patin' (*Works,* p.110).
89 *Journal,* pp.13, 33.
90 *Diary,* Vol.II, pp.534–5, Vol.III,
   p.49.
91 Ibid., Vol.II, pp.102, 565.
92 *Journal,* p.5; *Works,* p.61.
93 *Journal,* pp.21–8.
94 *Works,* pp.108, 109, 113.
95 *Observations,* pp.18, 21–2, 24.
96 *An Account,* p.67.
97 *Journey,* pp.182–4.
98 *Journals,* p.117.
98a *Diary,* pp.106–7. There is a short
   entry on the Montpellier faculty in
   A breife description, p.13.
98b *Diary,* p.346.
99 *An Account,* p.716.
100 Michel Chicoyneau who held the
   office from 1667 to 1701.
101 *Travels,* pp.50, 54, 57–8, 59.
102 *An Account,* pp.86–7.
103 *Remarks,* pp.27–30.
104 *Observations,* p.32. Symonds
   (*Description,* f.60v) has a curious
   note on this college: 'Is in the open
   place against the Fountayne in Rue
   S. Jacques. It has a lofty gate & an
   old rotten building within. Now
   converted to private uses. No
   Classes'.
105 A. Lefranc, *Histoire du Collège de
   France depuis ses origines jusqu'à la
   fin du premier empire,* Paris, 1893,
   pp.235–42.
106 *Journal,* pp.9, 11, 13, 14, 15, 31, 24.

VIII LITERARY AND
INTELLECTUAL LIFE

1 Presumably the *Inventaire général de
   l'histoire de France* of Jean de Serres
   (Paris, 1598).
2 The epic poem, *La Semaine, ou la
   Création du monde,* published in
   1578.
3 *Journals,* pp.49, 82.
4 By the Ordinance of
   Villers-Cotterêts, 1539.
5 *Observations,* pp.125–6.
6 P.27.
7 *Journal,* pp.4, 24.
8 *Travels,* p.199.
9 *Journey,* p.22.
10 *Journals,* p.47.

11 *Letters,* p.72.
12 *An Account,* p.730.
13 *Travels,* p.256.
14 *Journal,* f.87r.
15 *Tour,* p.7.
16 *An Account,* p.70.
17 *Journals,* p.5
18 *Letters,* p.52.
19 *Journal,* p.14.
20 Presumably because it was a new
   play; during a first run it was
   customary to double the prices for
   admission to the cheaper parts of the
   theatre.
21 *An Account,* p.731.
22 *Les Vendanges de Suresnes* was by
   Dancourt and *Crispin médecin* by
   Hauteroche.
23 *Journey,* pp.170–1, 173.
24 *Travels,* p.169.
25 *Journals,* pp.156, 109.
26 See above, p.57.
27 *Journals,* pp.124, 159, 127.
28 It will be noticed that except for *Les
   Visionnaires* all the plays he saw
   performed were fairly recent, though
   not new.
29 See J. Plattard (ed.), *Un Étudiant
   écossais en France en 1665–1666.
   Journal de voyage de Sir John
   Lauder,* Paris, 1935, pp.102–6.
30 *Journals,* pp.157, 159. *Clélie* was
   published in ten volumes in 1654–60
   and *Almahide ou l'esclave de la reine*
   in eight in 1660–3.
31 *Journey,* pp.93–4.
32 Germain Habert de Cerisy
   (1615–54), a foundation member of
   the Académie française.
33 Lister MS.5, ff.221v–222r. This
   passage was published in the *Revue
   d'Histoire du Théâtre,* Vol.IV
   (1950), pp.454–5 under the editor's
   title of 'Comment travaillait le grand
   Corneille'. It is by no means certain
   that this 'Mr de la Mothe' was a
   reliable witness.
34 Charles Perrault, *Les Hommes
   illustres qui ont paru en France
   pendant ce siècle,* Paris, 1696, 2
   vols., Vol.I, p.80.
35 *Journey,* pp.172–3.
36 *Travels,* p.xxxviii.
37 Ibid., p.265. This epigram is
   reproduced by C. and F. Parfaict,
   *Histoire du théâtre français depuis
   son origine jusqu'à présent,*
   Amsterdam and Paris, 1735–49, 15
   vols., Vol.XII, p.140.
38 According to E. Magne,
   *Bibliographie générale des oeuvres de
   Nicolas Boileau-Despréaux* (Paris,
   1929, 2 vols., Vol.II, p.213) it was
   the work of an *avocat* named Pierre
   Lemoyne.

39 *Letters*, p.80.
40 *Life*, p.49.
41 *Crudities*, pp.31–3. For Coryate's account of the Corpus Christi procession in Paris, see above, pp.216–17.
42 Only the two 1697 volumes of this translation were published.
43 *Journey*, pp.75–7.
44 Ibid., pp.119–20.
45 *Travels*, pp.60, 101, 107.
46 *Journey*, pp.131–2.
46a G. Berkeley. *Works*, London, 1784, 2 vols., Vol.I, p.viii.
46b *Works*, Vol.VIII, pp.74, 76.
47 *Travels*, pp.181–2.
48 *Journal*, f.88r.
49 *Observations*, p.8.
50 *Travels*, p.157.
51 *Observations*, pp.10–11.
52 *Diary*, Vol.II, p.568; Vol.III, pp.9–10, 22.
53 *Journey*, p.42.
54 *Journey*, pp.36–38.
55 *Observations*, pp.11–12.
56 *Journey*, pp.78–80, 95.
57 *Tour*, pp.5–6.
58 *Travels*, p.151.
59 Jean Dominique Cassini (1625–1712).
60 *Journal*, f.92v.
61 Buxton, *Diary*, p.282.
62 *An Account*, p.67.
63 In the now obsolete sense of 'astronomer'.
64 *Journal*, p.23.
65 Philippe de La Hire (1640–1718).
66 *Observations*, pp.51–2.
67 Jacques Cassini (1677–1756) who succeeded his father as director of the Observatoire.
68 *Journey*, pp.52–3.
69 *Travels*, p.176.
70 The universal or philosophical foot was a form of measurement invented by Locke (English foot =0.920 of his universal foot).
71 *Travels*, p.261.
72 Ibid., p.274n.
73 Ibid., p.263.
74 MS. Locke, c.31, fol.24.
75 *Travels*, p.282.
76 Ibid., pp.274–5.
77 Ibid, p.250.
78 See above, pp.203–4
79 *Travels*, p.260.
80 *Works*, pp.113–14.
81 *Travels*, pp.198, 251, 252, 253, 254, 256, 259, 272, 282.
82 Newton was appointed Warden of the Mint in 1696 and Master in 1699.
83 *Journey*, pp.94–6.
84 *Travels*, pp.200–2.
85 *An Account*, p.718.

86 Lister MS. 5, ff.224v–226r.
87 *An Account*, p.70.
88 *Journey*, p.63.
89 Thomas Willis (1621–75).
90 *Journey*, pp.64–9.
91 *Histoire des plantes qui naissent aux environs de Paris, avec leur usage dans la médecine* (Paris, 1698).
92 Claude Aubriet (1665–1742).
93 *Journey*, p.61.
94 *Description des plantes de l'Amérique* (Paris, 1693).
95 A large collection of his manuscripts remained unpublished.
96 *Journey*, pp.72–5.
97 Ibid., p.77.
98 *Travels*, p.xxxix.
99 The Mogul emperor of Hindustan (1619–1707)
100 Hindu traders.
101 *Travels*, pp.177, 200, 282.
102 Ibid., p.151n.
103 Ibid., pp.187–8.
104 A small river-fish.
105 *Journey*, p.144.
106 *Travels*, pp.161–2, 180, 195.
107 *Journey*, p.80.
108 These are the dates given by dictionaries of biography, but Ferrier who describes him as 'about four score years old' and 'almost blind' (*Journal*, pp.30–1), visited Lyons in May 1687.
109 *Voyage*, pp.35–8. There are earlier descriptions of the museum by Robert Montagu who visited it in the winter of 1650–1 (*Diary*, ff.42–3) and by Bertie who was in Lyons in 1662 (*Diary*, pp.364–5).
110 *An Account*, p.708.
111 *Travels*, pp.5–6.
112 *Journal*, f.86r.
113 *Journal*, pp.30–1.
114 *An Account*, p.101.
115 *Remarks*, p.20.

INDEX

BB

Index 361

Carcassonne, 69.
Carew, Sir George, xi, 2.
— wealth of France, 32, 348.
— peasant poverty, 34.
— burden of taxation, 44–5.
— *vénalité des charges*, 87.
— justice corrupt, 88–9.
— Henry IV, 125–6, 247–8.
— Sully, 126, 172.
— Louis XIII, 129.
— neglect of navy, 172.
— Protestantism, 247–8.
Carmelite friars, 109, 204–5, 230.
Carmelite nuns, 192.
carnival, 117, 122.
Carthusians, 26, 42, 189, 200–2.
Casaubon, Isaac, 318–19.
Cassini, Jean Dominique, 327–9.
Castelnaudary, 22, 77, 78, 257, 263.
Castres, 186, 251, 256–7.
Castries, Jean François, Marquis de, 66.
—, René Gaspard, Marquis de, 66.
—, Marquise de, 66–7.
Catherine de Médicis, 134.
Catholicism,
— clergy first order in state, 91, 182.
— — wealth, 162, 182–4.
— — tax exemptions, 47, 50–1, 128, 183–4.
— upper clergy, 16, 184–7.
— secular clergy, 187–8.
— — ignorance, 11, 237.
— regular clergy (male), 182–3, 188–91, 200–13.
— commendatory abbots, 191, 193.
— regular clergy (female), 182–3, 191–200.
— *confréries*, 220.
— lukewarm laymen, 230–1.
— Jansenism, 206, 232–3.
— Gallicanism, 231, 233–6, 287.
— relics, xvii, 219, 221–8.
— saints, 204, 205, 206, 209, 219, 220, 221–8.
— miracles, 206, 219, 221–8.
— Virgin Mary, 212–13, 220, 228–9.
— processions, 162, 216–21, 318–19.
— sermons, 205, 209, 211–13, 215.
— masses for the dead, 214, 229.
— holy water, 221.
— Lent 231.
Châlons-sur-Marne, 23, 27, 125.
Chalon-sur-Saône, 20, 29, 141.
Chambre de justice, 46.
Champagne, 124.
Chantilly, 91, 313.
Charas, Moïse, 337.
Chardin, Sir John, 336.
Charenton, 140.
— *temple*, 244–5, 247, 264, 296, 349, 355.
Charles I, 3, 151, 344.
Charles II, 3, 18, 101, 137, 138, 145, 148, 277, 295, 337.
Chartres, 224.
chasse-marée, 28, 348.

Châtel, Jean, 124.
Chaulnes, Duchesse de, 94.
chemistry, 295–9, 300, 332–3, 337.
Chérubin, Father, 203–4, 331.
Chesterfield, Lord, 102.
Chevalier, 314.
Chicoyneau, Michel, 302–4, 305.
circulating libraries, 314–15.
Clenche, John, xi, 6.
— Paris, 56, 58.
— Rouen, 60.
— Lyons, 64.
— Canal du Midi, 76–7.
— Foire St. Germain, 115.
— Bordeaux, 153.
— Bastille, 156–7.
— Rochefort, 178–9.
— Catholicism, 225.
— universities, 273, 289.
— theatres, 311.
— Observatoire, 326.
Clermont, 24, 107.
cloth industry, 68, 69.
coaches, 27–9.
coal, 70, 73–4.
— substitutes for, 73–4.
coffee houses, 57, 116.
Colbert, Jean Baptiste, 205, 338, 351.
— glass making, 57–8.
— Gobelins, 58.
— cloth industry, 69, 72.
— navy, 72, 173–4.
— trading companies, 72.
— Canal du Midi, 76.
— noblemen and trade, 90–1.
— *faux nobles*, 91.
— ducal sons-in-law, 94.
— Surintendant des Bâtiments, 149.
— academies, 322–5.
Collège Royal, 306–7.
Commines, Philippe de, 99–100.
Comtat Venaissin, 41.
Concini, Concino, Maréchal d'Ancre, 130–1, 250.
Condé, 123.
Condé, Henri de Bourbon, Prince de, 209.
Condé, Louis de Bourbon, Prince de, 96, 139–40, 141, 142, 234, 313.
Conflans, 117.
congrès, 100–1.
Conti, Armand de Bourbon, Prince de, 139, 191.
Conti, Louis Armand de Bourbon, Prince de, 96.
Conti, Marie Anne, Princesse de, 159.
Corneille, Pierre, 314, 315–16, 357.
Cornish, 15.
Coryate, Thomas, xi, 2, 23, 26, 27, 29.
— oral use of Latin, 11.
— *sabots*, 39.
— Paris, 54.
— Lyons, 65, 75.
— customs barriers, 75.
— executed criminals, 107.
— hanging in effigy, 107.